THE POLITICAL CHARACTER OF
ADOLESCENCE

M. KENT JENNINGS

AND

RICHARD G. NIEMI

The Political Character of Adolescence

THE INFLUENCE OF FAMILIES AND SCHOOLS

PRINCETON UNIVERSITY
PRESS

LCC: 73–16779

ISBN: 0–691–09362–8

Library of Congress Cataloging in Publication
data will be found on the last
printed page of this book

This book has been produced on VIP
Photo Composition in Caledonia

Printed in the United States of America
by Princeton University Press,
Princeton, New Jersey

To Our Children

Cynthia   Jennifer   Julie   Larkin
Nancy   Patricia   Steven

WHEN WE began the planning for this project in 1964 the field of political socialization was in its infancy. Since that time great strides have been taken, although the field is still perhaps in its childhood. Thanks to the early pioneers and the subsequent settlers our state of knowledge about how the political self is formed, what this self consists of, and the resultant individual and systemic consequences has expanded considerably. Not only has political socialization become a recognized part of the discipline of political science, it has also come to engage the interest of a wide range of social scientists, educators, and the lay public. Indeed, the question of political learning among the young has emerged, or reemerged, as a sensitive and important question of public policy during the past decade.

Most of the early systematic empirical research in this area focused on elementary schoolchildren. Much of it was informed by and inspired by the steadily growing awareness of the contours of adult political behavior. Our study was explicitly designed to bridge the gap between these studies about children on the one hand, and the adult populace on the other. The completion of high school is a watershed for most young adults. Many will be leaving the parental home, going on to further schooling, securing jobs, establishing families, and in general changing their mode of life in dramatic ways. Home, school, and the primary and secondary groups associated with them have to a great extent left what political imprint they are going to leave. Thus the focus of our study is on a national sample of high school seniors and the components of home and school which have had a bearing on their political development.

We have had the assistance of a great number of people at the University of Michigan's Institute for Social Research throughout the life of this project. Angus Campbell, Philip Converse, and Warren Miller established the basic parameters of the study and secured the initial funding. The latter two have continued to give advice and counsel at many points. The sample was drawn with care and ingenuity by Irene Hess and Jean Harter. During the execution of the field work Charles Cannell, William Eckerman, and especially Barbara Wagonfeld provided superb direction. Joan Scheffler helped construct the codes and showed great patience in supervising the coding operations.

A marvelous collection of former graduate students have aided us through the years. They include Paul Beck, Bruce Campbell, Steven Coombs, Michael Coveyou, Lee Ehman, Lawrence Fox, Roman Hedges, Sarah Barker Horack, George Levenson, George Moyser, Susan Koprince Sebert, and Michael Traugott. Printing their names here is an inadequate gesture of our gratitude and warm feelings. Maureen Kozumplik and Jane Willer were excellent project secretaries in every way. Peg Gross and Janice Brown, as usual, contributed their typing with skill and cheer. We also want to thank Sandy Thatcher of Princeton University Press for his warm encouragement and helpful advice.

It has been our good fortune to have had the benefit of contributions along the way from a variety of scholars and friends in other places. These include Jack Dennis, Fred Greenstein, Robert Hess, Robert E. Lane, Kenneth Langton, Bradbury Seasholes, and Harmon Zeigler.

In addition to the original funding from the Danforth Foundation, Jennings received subsequent support from the National Science Foundation and Niemi from the National Institute of Mental Health. Jennings also benefited from the indirect support given him during his visits to the Center for the Advanced Study of Educational Administration at the University of Oregon, and the Sociologisch Instituut at the Katholieke Hogeschool, The Netherlands.

It would be remiss not to thank in public fashion the respondents who supplied most of the materials on which this book is based. Special thanks go to the school administrators and teachers who facilitated the interviews in the high schools.

Most of Chapter 7 previously appeared in the *American Political Science Review* and is reprinted with permission. Chapter 10 is a considerably expanded version of an article originally appearing in the *Harvard Educational Review*. A portion of Chapter 2 also appears in Niemi's *How Family Members Perceive Each Other*, published by Yale University Press. A small part of Chapter 6 first appeared in the *Journal of Politics*.

I INTRODUCTION

CHAPTER ONE

Political Learning, Individual Behavior, and the Political System

THE SUMMER of 1971 witnessed a signal event in American political history. With the ratification of the twenty-sixth amendment, full-scale national suffrage became a reality for eighteen-year-olds. Just what the electoral consequences of that enfranchisement would be no one could be sure. Nor was there certainty about the form and magnitude of other political, legal, and social ramifications which would probably follow in the wake of the extension. If nothing else, however, the action had great symbolic importance for it indicated to both young and old that the age of political maturity had dropped and that the eighteen- to twenty-year-olds were now a legitimate part of the electoral process.

The events and discussions leading up to the constitutional change also brought into sharp focus questions of immense importance to the polity. What kind of preparation have young people had for political participation? Of what shape and intensity are their political values? What sorts of skills and pieces of information do they bring with them? Where and how do they acquire these values and skills? Do the youngsters embody a continuation of the previous generation's values and skills or are there vivid discontinuities? And what is the place of that mammoth training ground of American society—the educational system—in shaping these newly enfranchised voters?

Most such questions are, of course, not new to this period or to this society. Political philosophers and political rulers have been aware of them for centuries. But it is only within the last decade that much systematic thought and research have gone into this topic. To date this attention has led to numerous research proposals, an even greater number of suggested studies, varieties of hypotheses, an expanding bibliography, not a few arguments, and even several reliable findings. Our aim here is to contribute minimally to most of the listed categories, but at least to double or triple the last-named category. To do so we have gathered systematic information from not only a target population of high school seniors, but from parents, teachers, peers, and others. The resulting analysis is long, but we hope rewarding.

Any study of this magnitude must begin by indicating why such an investigation should be undertaken in the first place as well as some of the perspectives which guided the authors in the design, data collection, and

3

analysis stages. This we do in the rest of this chapter. The first two sections hinge on the question of why the political socialization process is important. Despite the widespread concern outlined above, the case for studying socialization at all is not open and shut. Moreover, precisely why political socialization is important is a matter of debate.

The second two sections convey some of our thoughts on how socialization should be studied, especially with an eye toward theoretical perspectives. The final pair of sections gives an overview of the remainder of the book as well as outlining the nature of the data base.

POLITICAL CHANGE AND STABILITY

In cultures where change occurs slowly the presumptive case for the power of socialization is strong. Value constellations and behavioral patterns would seem to emanate in large part from what one generation learns from the other. Similarly, when particular modes of behavior and feeling within a culture change only with glacial speed, the presumptive case is strong. If institutions, role definitions, and the larger environment remain relatively stable, succeeding generations can be successfully socialized into an existing, unchanging mold. This process is said to characterize the cultures of times past and those which are today in a pre-industrial state. Even in the past, however, periods of drastic change occurred. If one thinks only of Western societies, such movements as the introduction of Christianity, the rise of the nation-state, the Protestant Reformation, and the Industrial Revolution had profound effects on the social and political order. Since discontinuities of social and political behavior were thereby introduced, the traditional socialization techniques and outcomes were altered.

Still change came infrequently, and in most other non-Western societies it was even more infrequent. One may imagine a step movement in which the introduction of social, economic, or political structural changes set in motion certain socialization changes. These resultant modes of socialization then rested on a plateau lasting perhaps for several generations or more until another dramatic structural change came about. Physical isolation and the insulation of a culture from foreign practices historically helped preserve traditional ways of doing things. Barring outside influences, changes had to be self-generative.

In an era when transportation and communication devices have broken down virtually all barriers, culture enclaves are more difficult to maintain. Interdependencies and diffusion now abound. Given the rapid rates of technological change, complex social structures, and intercultural penetration, how is the socialization process to prepare people for living out their political lives?

Part of the answer to this question is strictly definitional. One of the most commonly accepted definitions of political socialization is that it deals with the acquisition of *prevailing* norms and modes of behavior. In this sense the "socialized" person is the one who has successfully internalized the prevailing norms of behavioral modes. Child development literature used socialization in this sense for decades. But this conceptualization is excessively narrow, especially when dealing with sociopolitical learning. In the first place virtually all societies have subcultural norms and behaviors. To this extent socialization has always been setting-specific and group-specific. Thus even if one were to accept the limited case of acquiring prevailing norms and behaviors this would still not necessarily mean that culture-wide uniformity was being passed on from generation to generation.

Let us concede, however, that some norms and behaviors are relatively pervasive in a society at a given point in time. A second problem with the argument that socialization processes are not compatible with change is that, as Greenstein says, " . . . some people grow up learning to reject, or simply depart from, existing norms. More generally, a person's behavior may be continuous or discontinuous with previous patterns of behavior whether his own or those of an earlier generation."[1] The question which socialization inquiries must ask is, why do these departures and innovations occur? It is reasonable to assume that different sets of socialization experiences play some part in this process. These differential patterns are most easily observed in marginal, *avant garde*, and laggardly elements in a society. If departures from and rejections of the status quo are more or less fixed for a period of time it seems fair to say that they have been "learned" in the same sense that the prevailing ones are. Within the past few years we have witnessed systematic studies pointing out differential socialization patterns and consequences within racial, regional, and student groups.[2]

Another argument may be raised against the assertion that political socialization inquiries inform us very little about political change. Some societies are more achieving than others, and McClelland[3] has argued

---

[1]Fred I. Greenstein, "A Note on the Ambiguity of 'Political Socialization': Definitions, Criticisms, and Strategies of Inquiry," *Journal of Politics*, 32 (November 1970), pp. 969–78, at 973.

[2]On race see, for example, Edward Greenberg, "Children and Government: A Comparison Across Racial Lines," *Midwest Journal of Political Science*, 14 (May 1970), pp. 249–75; on region see Dean Jaros, Herbert Hirsch, and Frederick J. Fleron, "The Malevolent Leader: Political Socialization in an American Subculture," *American Political Science Review*, 62 (June 1968), pp. 564–75; and within the voluminous literature on student groups one particularly relevant study in this connection is David L. Westby and Richard G. Braungart, "The Alienation of Generations and Status Politics: Alternative Explanations of Student Political Activism," in Roberta Sigel (ed.), *Learning About Politics* (New York: Random House, 1970), pp. 476–89.

[3]David C. McClelland, *The Achieving Society* (Princeton: Van Nostrand, 1961).

that levels of economic achievement are influenced by the levels of achievement motivation extant in the society. These motivations are primarily products of socialization practices. Some societies socialize their upcoming generations to have higher achievement motivations than others; this social-psychological attribute helps produce cross-country differences in rates of growth, according to McClelland's argument.

Although there is no comparable work on so monumental a scale in politics, it is not difficult to imagine similar processes at work. More to the point here, however, is that a willingness to accept and adapt to political change can be one of the messages of political socialization. Alternatively, rigid adherence and devotion to political forms can be emphasized. One thinks of theocratic, highly ritualistic societies in particular as ones which discourage the idea of change. Type of change is also a part of socialization. As Easton and Dennis point out, dispositions toward either peaceful or nonpeaceful means of political change can be passed on from one generation to the next.[4]

All of this is not to say, of course, that political change can be adequately or even primarily understood in terms of political socialization. Natural disasters, technological innovations, military conquest, and drastic alterations in the legal system are four of the most common sources of micro and macro level political changes. Even without socialization practices changing appreciably, these four sources can induce political change in relatively quick order. Thus the initial source of changes often lies outside changing socialization practices. It is important to note, however, that modifications in political socialization will probably follow in the wake of upheavals of this order.

A recent case in point is that of the People's Republic of China. Accompanying the victory of the Communists over the Nationalists came large-scale changes at both the micro and macro levels of society. These were accomplished largely by a change in regime and the goals of sanction agents. It is extremely significant, however, that intensive attempts to inculcate a new set of norms and behavioral roles also emerged. A more than temporary change in political regime seems almost inevitably to be followed by such efforts at resocialization of the old and new patterns of socialization for the young. While this stems in part from an effort to establish diffuse support for the regime, more specific beliefs and practices are also part of the content. Assuming the socialization efforts are successful, the perpetuation likelihood of the regime is enhanced.

We see, then, another connection between changes and socialization. Instead of thinking of socialization leading to change, we can visualize wide-scale institutional change leading to changing socialization practices

[4]David Easton and Jack Dennis, *Children in the Political System* (New York: McGraw-Hill, 1969), Chapter 2.

which are, in turn, designed to equip individuals for survival in that polity. Institutional changes need not be as drastic as regime change in order to bring about changes in socialization practices. The introduction of mass education is a type of political change which leads to profound differences in socialization content and processes.

Compliance Systems and Families as Agents of Change

Some sources of political change, such as natural disasters and technological innovations, are unpremeditated and their probable consequences largely unpredictable. Others consist of instruments more directly manipulable, and they are consciously employed for their expected impact. While both types are important, the latter are particularly salient to social and policy scientists because they represent societal efforts to encourage and discourage certain forms of behavior. We may think of most such sources as being embedded in compliance systems existing beyond the level of primary groups.

Compliance systems loom especially large in talking about political change, so much so that it has been argued that they make reliance on socialization processes unnecessary. A handy example, which illustrates the idea, concerns the public behavior of blacks in American society. Once legal sanctions were available and applied to the right of blacks to use public accommodations, to vote, and to engage in a variety of other public activities, sizeable elements of blacks took advantage of the sanction system and sizeable elements of whites acquiesced. There were and continue to be tests of the sanction system, but the important point is that major behavioral changes were induced with little or no alteration in socialization.

More generally the place of institutionally organized maintenance and sanction systems may be viewed as the prime determinant of ebbs and flows in modern societies. The place of pre-adult socialization agents, *especially the family*, is correspondingly reduced. Instead the various arms of the state—especially the law and its agents—and such institutions as educational and religious agencies become the prime purveyors both of stability and innovation. This argument was made especially forceful in an unpublished paper by Reiss.[5] He argues that these institutions hold the keys to transmitting and changing values and behaviors because of the positive and negative sanctions they wield. Thus the behavior of the same individual will vary depending upon the complex of sanctioning agents. The by-now classic example is that of twentieth century Germany. Within the space of a single lifetime the same individual could function success-

[5]Albert J. Reiss, "Social Organization and Socialization: Variations on a Theme about Generations" (Center for Research on Social Organization, University of Michigan, 1965).

fully under the Weimar Republic, the Nazi regime, and post-war Christian Democracy.

Reiss's argument is, therefore, especially compelling in times of rapid change. If change were simply a function of incremental alterations generated within the family, the societal change would be slow indeed and individual behavior would remain relatively constant. Thus if the major institutions demand and reinforce certain types of behavior, then that is the behavior which will, sooner or later, be observed. Nor is this necessarily a function of a police state and physical fear. Rather, behaviors and values will gravitate in the direction of the larger institutional incentives. And since these institutions are geared to overall societal needs and functions, they will vary their demands and sanctions as the situation dictates. Thus a different set of behaviors will be called for in times of political mobilization, economic stringency, external threat, inner turmoil, and so forth.

We will consider momentarily the implications of this theory for the family as socialization agent par excellence. First, however, let us consider the main arguments. One immediate response to the institutional supremacy view is that differential cross-culture and within-culture responses may be noted. If we take the case of the changing face of Germany, as an example, it could be argued that there is also an underlying thread of common socialization which enabled the German populace to perform successfully under the different regimes with their divergent requirements. Summarizing an assessment of Germany in their five nation study, Almond and Verba comment: "In Germany, then, the balance of the political culture is weighted in the direction of the subject role and of passive forms of participation. The government is viewed largely as an agency of administration. And the attachment to the political system is closely related to the ability of the government to satisfy pragmatic needs."[6] More recently the cross-cultural studies of pre-adults by Adelson and his colleagues, though limited in terms of their general significance, provide evidence of similar strains among contemporary German youth compared with Britishers and Americans.[7] Without wishing to push the argument too far, one might nevertheless introduce the competing explanation of socialization to compliance and pragmatism as a common theme throughout the past several decades of German experience. Both the acquiescence of the masses and the leadership of the elites

[6]Gabriel Almond and Sidney Verba, *The Civic Culture* (Princeton: Princeton University Press, 1963), p. 495.

[7]See, for example, Joseph Adelson, Bernard Green, and Robert P. O'Neill, "The Growth of the Idea of Law in Adolescence," *Developmental Psychology*, 1 (July 1969), pp. 327–32; and Judith Gallatin and Joseph Adelson, "Individual Rights and the Public Good," *Comparative Political Studies*, 3 (July 1970), pp. 226–42.

could in part be explained by the socialization emphasis on these two traits.

The introduction of the elite provides another caveat to the institutional supremacy argument. That is, why do leaders of institutions in some countries behave in one fashion in response to stimuli while leaders of institutions in other countries behave in different fashion to similar stimuli? One answer, of course, is that the stimuli are only similar and not the same. Granting that point, it still appears that the leaders of institutions in democratic nations tend to behave differently than those in autocratic countries. Since the leaders are not vulnerable to institutional demands and rewards in the same sense as the masses, that alone cannot account for behavioral differences across elites. It would not seem unreasonable that the socialization of leaders differs among countries, that the norms and expectations applied to leaders differ, and that the leaders are aware of these norms. Thus military coups are *de rigueur* in some polities and never occur in others.

In addition to cross-polity differences we may note that even within the same polity the response of different segments of society may be quite variant to the same set of institutional demands. Sometimes resistance is so great and reinforcement so ineffective that the demands are dropped. A supreme case in the United States was Prohibition. Although Prohibition was codified under more or less popular representation processes, it was enthusiastically resisted by sizeable segments of the populace. Ultimately the amendment was repealed.

A more current example rests in the United States' participation in the Vietnam war. It would be too much to credit differential socialization experiences with the checkered pattern of resistance to the war. Opportunity costs no doubt figured heavily in determining flagrant opposition. Yet it is not without importance that early opposition was most noticeable among certain segments of the population, namely, the intellectual community, college youth, and somewhat later, minority groups. The socialization of all these groups bears a different imprint than that of "middle America" either by timing, context, or content. And so, despite the authorization of the conflict by the major maintenance and sanctioning system in the society, noncompliant and nonsupportive behaviors eventually became rampant.

Let us return now to the question of pre-adult socialization in general and the family in particular. Even allowing that the foregoing reservations vitiate in part the institutional supremacy view, there is still no question that the impact of such institutions is great, especially in industrial societies. Where does this leave the family as a socialization agent? Most of the psychological theories of socialization have leaned heavily on the family as the crucible of learning. Social learning and psychoanalytic theories in particular predicate the formation of enduring basic value patterns and behavioral dispositions as occurring in the home. In a very strong sense the approach exemplified by Reiss is a direct challenge, one is tempted to say threat, to the long-established emphasis on the family.

Two thoughtful psychologists have responded to the issue. Both recognize the strength of the institutional argument, but both raise strong caveats to such a monistic interpretation. Although the discussions do not focus specifically on political orientations their application is straightforward. Maccoby, in the course of an essay on "Moral Values and Behavior in Childhood," makes several relevant points.[8] First, granting the fact that a passing over from one generation to the next would not generate the rate of change witnessed at various points in time, she notes that changes and shifts are not as great as the model of institutional control would hold. There are evidences of distinctive "cultural lag" or nonadherence (as suggested above). Moreover, certain dominant value structures such as the Judeo-Christian have had a long history, a persistence which, she contends, owes at least something to its inculcation in the child by the family.

She also postulates the family as a mediating mechanism:

> We could reasonably assume, then, that if there is a shift from one generation to another in a set of values, this shift has occurred partly because the socialization practices employed with the new generation, or the values being taught them, have changed by comparison with the teaching received by the previous generation in its childhood.[9]

Thus the family is by no means impervious to changing conditions and its socialization practices reflect these changes. At times this may mean withholding a value or behavioral norm which the parent holds dear but which simply no longer fits societal needs. Maccoby's example is that of the frugal, depression-reared parents who do not impose on their children the same moral values of thriftiness because the economic situation is vastly different; this despite the fact that the parents may themselves still bear the internalized norm. The parents are socializing the child into a more appropriate form of behavior in prosperous times. Intergenerational discontinuity there is, but the parents themselves are contributing to that by the fashion in which they socialize their children.[10] In sum, Maccoby argues there is nothing inconsistent between intergenerational changes in values and 1) social learning and developmental theories of

[8] Eleanor Maccoby, "Moral Values and Behavior in Childhood," in John A. Clausen (ed.), *Socialization and Society* (Boston: Little, Brown, 1968), Chapter 6, at pp. 263–67.

[9] *Ibid.*, pp. 264–65.

[10] An ingenious demonstration of this with respect to succeeding Russian generations in the twentieth century is provided in Alex Inkeles, "Social Change and Social Character: The Role of Parental Mediation," *Journal of Social Issues*, 11 (No. 2, 1955), pp. 12–23.

value transmission, or 2) the family as mediating agency between social conditions and progeny acquisition of values.

While making some of the same observations, Bandura strikes a somewhat different tone.[11] In the first place he notes, as we did above, that a system level model fails to account for the diverse patterns of socialization outcomes found even in subcultures. Second, Bandura responds to Reiss' proposition that under a conventional psychological theory of socialization change only occurs when the socialization process *fails* by noting that social learning is a continuous process and none but the most severe theories argue for complete introjection of parental values by children through time.

Finally, Bandura argues that assumed shortcomings of the family transmission model rest on faulty notions about modelling processes. Where multiple, diverse models exist for pre-adults they often reproduce some elements of more than one model. This can happen even within the family where, as shall be demonstrated in this book, the value constellations are by no means always congruent. When one adds to the family the variety of other models available to the growing child in a complex society, it is readily apparent that, as Bandura says, "much innovation of social behavior can occur entirely through identification."[12]

By substituting political for social and by thinking of political values as encompassing moral values (or vice versa depending upon one's prejudices), one can see what the argument is for the family's socialization role in political change as weighed against the primacy of institutional control. Not that these sources exhaust the source of values and behaviors, because there are other primary groups, to say nothing of impersonal sources such as the electronic and printed media, as well as experience itself as a teacher. But our concern for the moment is with the family vis-à-vis social institutions.

Socialization, Systems, And People

Because of their interest in the functioning of political systems, students of political socialization have been properly concerned with the systemic implications of political learning. Such concern is dramatic when compared with some other fields in socialization. One can read countless studies of childhood development, for example, without the slightest attention being paid to the macro level consequences of such development. More generally, the traditional psychological literature pays but

[11]Albert Bandura, "Social-Learning Theory of Identificatory Processes," in David A. Goslin (ed.), *Handbook of Socialization Theory Research* (Chicago: Rand McNally, 1969), Chapter 3, at pp. 250–52.

[12]*Ibid.*, p. 251.

scant attention to structural consequences. Hence the self-conscious attempt to link the study of political socialization to system level functioning, as exemplified by *Children in the Political System*,[13] is to be applauded.

Nevertheless, some reservations about the systemic approach need to be registered. Such a focus, which justifies the study of young people for what may be learned about system behavior, runs theoretical risks and carries a distinctive normative bias. From a theoretical-methodological viewpoint there are two crucial hedges involved. As with most approaches to the study of childhood socialization, a systemic approach assumes that later behavior will powerfully reflect what is observed at work among the children. This is a very plausible assumption, but the way in which these linkages manifest themselves is not at all understood, either in political or in other forms of socialization.

In addition to the assumption of an articulation between the present and the future, the systemic approach presumes that present socialization patterns explain the functioning of a system whose major manpower is supplied by people socialized in earlier times. This assumption, like the previous one, hinges on high rates of continuity and relatively slow rates of individual and system level change.

The riskiness of these assumptions is indicated by countless examples of political upheavals, coups, regime changes of other sorts, and redrawing of boundaries which are observable across a wide expanse of space and time. On a more limited but equally striking basis are rapid changes such as the unrest, growing distrust, and disaffection which struck the United States in the 1960's. Whereas the early studies of childhood socialization were interpreted partly in the reflection of more or less steady states, it became apparent that such an interpretation could not be rendered a few years later. Not that the early socialization studies should be faulted because they did not "predict" what would happen to those cohorts of youngsters when they reached college. As Greenstein has stressed, political behavior is a joint function of situational stimuli and psychological predispositions.[14] Rather, what we are saying is that attempts to explain functional aspects of an ongoing system in terms of current childhood socialization patterns are fraught with difficulty and prey to post factum constructions which have to be rebuilt to conform with manifest changes in the system.

Despite these caveats, it would be absurd not to undertake reasonable attempts to link micro level socialization processes with eventual outcomes. There is simply too much theoretical and practical importance in establishing and understanding as much of the linkage as possible.

[13]Easton and Dennis, *Children in the Political System.*
[14]Fred I. Greenstein, "The Impact of Personality on Politics: An Attempt to Clear Away the Underbrush," *American Political Science Review*, 61 (September 1967), pp. 629–41.

We would argue, however, that the justification for studying pre-adults should not rest solely on macro level consequences. Rather, we adopt the position that individual level effects *as well as* systemic implications constitute a reason for looking at pre-adult development. This contrast between systemic and individual effects is akin to the distinction between the structural versus the symbolic interactionist traditions in sociological theory. The former tradition holds that the matching up of the individual to structural statuses and roles is the measure of successful socialization and subsequent role performance. The latter, on the other hand, has been characterized as follows:

> Emphasis in this tradition is on interactional *process* in role relationships that are conceived primarily in interpersonal rather than social-structure terms. Socialization is viewed more as a process through which personality and selfhood emerge in the course of role-taking in progressively more sharply attuned communicative interaction than as one in which persons become equipped with beliefs, knowledge, skills, motives, and values that fit them to occupy a sequence of niches in the social structure.[15]

In terms of politics the former view looks at socialization for what it says about satisfying the requirements of political structures whereas the second asks what does socialization say about satisfying the requirements of individuals. Sears has captured the essence of the difference in the approaches. In contrast to the emphasis on how the individual meets systemic needs he observes:

> The other main alternative is to emphasize the individual's personal growth, his unfolding in his own way, his 'flowering,' his self-actualization, the opening of his experience to political life, and the development of his capacity to maximize his own idiosyncratic needs and values through the political system.[16]

Again, in contrasting the two approaches:

> . . . the political socialization literature often seems more interested in the good of the 'political system' than in the child's learning how most successfully to engage in his own idiosyncratic 'pursuit of happiness.'[17]

There are ways of weaving together these dual emphases; if one is used exclusive of the other the course of inquiry is profoundly different. Thus Easton and Dennis are interested in how diffuse support helps political systems persist, and, consequently, in how diffuse support develops

---

[15]M. Brewster Smith, "Competence and Socialization," in Clausen, *Socialization and Society*, p. 278.

[16]David Sears, "Book Review," *Midwest Journal of Political Science*, 15 (February 1971), p. 156.

[17]*Ibid.*, pp. 156–57

among pre-adults. A focus on how individuals attempt to achieve their values and needs through the political system would make quite different use of the concept of diffuse support. And perhaps the concept would not be central at all.

We favor an emphasis on both the systemic level and individual level consequences of political learning. To continue our reasoning it will be useful to borrow from currents now at work in psychology and social psychology. Two concepts receiving extraordinary and exciting attention in recent years have been social competence and moral judgments. Happily the applicability—some would say centrality—of these concepts to political behavior is transparent. Political competence or efficacy is a key component of political behavior and has figured predominantly in several major studies. Although moral judgment is just beginning to appear as a subject for political analysts, some essentials of the field, especially as developed by Kohlberg, are heavily laden with questions of lawful behavior and moral judgments within the parameters of the political system.[18]

Both of these topics have obvious relevance for how "societal needs" are met, but they also have obvious relevance for individuals and their needs. Smith makes these twin functions a major theme of his essay on "Competence and Socialization." As he says, "A comprehensive view of social competence should also keep in simultaneous view the two perspectives . . . that of society and its 'manpower' needs, and that of the person himself as the locus of humanistic values."[19] If it is important to know how competence affects the political system's responsiveness, allocative functions, and even persistence, it is no less consequential to know how it affects the individual's ability to be politically responsive, to receive a share of the allocations, and even to keep the political personality intact. Aside from the fact that political scientists have traditionally talked about the political development, maintenance, and pathologies of systems rather than of individuals, there is no particular reason why students of political socialization should not be concerned about both.

So too with the subject of moral judgment and behavior. It may be of great consequence for socio-political structures if the bulk of the population is at Kohlberg's lowest level of moral development, viz., punishment

---

[18]See, for example, Lawrence Kohlberg, *Stages in the Development of Moral Thought and Action* (New York: Holt, Rinehart, and Winston, 1969). Richard Merelman has made the most extensive attempt by a political scientist to utilize the moral development theorizing. See his "The Development of Political Ideology: A Framework for the Analysis of Political Socialization," *American Political Science Review*, 63 (September 1969), pp. 750–67; and "The Development of Policy Thinking in Adolescents," *American Political Science Review*, 65 (December 1971), pp. 1033–47.

[19]Smith, "Competence and Socialization," p. 276.

and obedience orientation (obey rules and avoid punishment). Likewise it is important to know the place of socialization in putting them there. But it is also of importance to know and understand the roots of these stages for what they tell us about the individual political personality. If, for example, we believe that moral-legal behavior is less pathological at stage 6 (morality of individual principle of conscience) than at stage 1, then we want to know how the stages come to be acquired, how they might be modified. In sum we are arguing for an approach to political learning which takes into consideration the needs of individuals as well as system structures.

SOME APPROACHES TO POLITICAL LEARNING

Given a rich historical tradition and everyday evidence about the importance of various sources of political learning, how are we to observe their consequences? Three leading formulations have been used by psychologists for the past several decades. A more recent psychological theory and another one growing out of sociological traditions have also been applied to political learning.

Observational Learning

The older psychological formulation which most reflects our thinking is what Bandura and his associates have come to call observational learning.[20] This is a term embracing a variety of other terms, principally modelling, but also matching, imitation, copying, contagion, cue-taking, and identification. There are conceptual differences between these terms, especially identification versus imitation, but for Bandura the overarching principles are the same. We shall mainly use the terms modelling, imitation, and observational learning.

The basic idea here is that the person, especially the young one, learns by observing the behavior of others. These others can be as intimate and close as members of the family, or as remote as heroes read about or viewed. The observer perceives a model's behavior and the perceptual response to that behavior establishes an association which forms the basis of the "learning." Especially under the force of sustained stimulations, imaginal and verbal representations of the modelling stimuli are formed. Once coded and stored " . . . they function as mediators for response retrieval and reproduction."[21]

Consistency of models, their status and power, and their provisions of

[20]Bandura, "Social-Learning Theory of Identificatory Processes."
[21]*Ibid.*, p. 220.

reinforcement are among several variables affecting in one way or another the adoption of the model's behaviors and values. It has, furthermore, been demonstrated that characteristics of the model may be learned but not necessarily performed. Both specific attributes of a model as well as common attributes abstracted from several models may be "matched."

Students of socialization have tended to focus on the family as a source of observational learning. It is here that most children spend virtually all of their pre-school years. Even after school starts the child returns to spend many more hours daily with family, to say nothing of the weekends. And whereas the network of models may be changing with great rapidity outside the home—teachers alternate every year or even daily, for example—the home remains relatively constant. Even when the home breaks up through divorce, death, or other changes in composition there are usually continuities involved.

Accompanying this continuity are two other forces. The power relationship, especially in the early years, is basically asymmetrical, so that the child typically reveres the parents and is also under their behavior control. The affective structure of the family also enhances the imitative process. While some children do grow up hating their parents, all the available evidence shows that even by late adolescence most children still feel warmly toward their parents.

The major way in which we will assess the impact of the family in shaping the child's political orientation is through comparing parent and offspring responses to the same stimuli in the interview situation. This is essentially a test for matching behavior, or observational learning. The greater the match or congruency, the greater the grounds for inferring that the students have learned through observation of their parents.[22] As experimental psychologists are quick to point out, such correlational evidence is not demonstrative. Without going into a full-scale exposition, we would argue that empirical plausibility, validation measures, and multivariate controls strengthen the case for an approach of this type. To which may be added the rejoinder that survey research dealing with naturalistic phenomena has the virtue of trying to capture a reflection of the "real" world rather than the "laboratory" world.

Observational learning is not, of course, restricted to the family. Peer groups and teachers are other prominent actors with whom the child interacts. We will have more to say about these latter two in Chapters 8 and 9. The important point here is that there are a variety of observational models, and that we will be able to match students with each of the three

[22]According to experimental evidence such matching behavior need not reflect the same stimuli to which the learner observed the model reacting. That is, generalized conceptual and behavioral propensities are adopted so that the learner would react to other stimuli in a fashion consistent with what the model would. For references see *ibid.*, pp. 252–53.

prime contenders as a means of detecting presumed observational learning.

There are a number of conditions which may facilitate or inhibit the modelling process. Some of them will be discussed when we talk about other theories of learning below. One of the major determinants employed in our own approach is that of homogeneity and heterogeneity of models. It stands to reason, and experimental evidence supports it, that children are more likely to learn (and probably perform) a given behavior if they have been surrounded by models who themselves behave in congruent fashion than if they are surrounded by models of varying behavior. The sheer availability of alternative responses is reduced where models are consistent, so that there is less to choose from. Consider, for example, a child growing up in a home where both parents roundly condemn the Democrats, applaud Republican speakers on television, always make a point of letting the child know they have voted Republican, and do precinct work for the GOP. The child has two revered models who behave in a similar fashion politically. Behavioral cues are, in essence, twice repeated. Incorporation of these cues, manifested later under appropriate environmental circumstances, seems most likely.

One may contrast this consistency with its opposite. To continue the example, imagine another child one of whose parents behaves as above on the Republican side, the other of whom does so on the Democratic side. Clearly the esteemed models present different images for the child to code. In the experimental situation, exposure to such heterogeneous models seems to result in innovative behaviors and diverse combinations representing amalgams of the models. Not necessarily at odds with this evidence is the wealth of material demonstrating that status differentials are involved in choosing between different models. So in the case of the child with inconsistent parents along partisan lines we would expect either a "novel" solution reflecting portions of both models or, if status and affect differ substantially, a solution more like that of the higher status and more warmly regarded model.

One may also approach this process from the point of view of the model rather than the learner-observer. If the model's behavior is more or less duplicated by other models, we would expect greater imitation of that model than when the behavior of other models is quite divergent. By the same token, we may say that the full effect of a given model is better understood if we know more about other models in the environment.

In this book we make use of the consistency approach primarily by looking at a subset of students for whom we have both mother and father interviews. But that does not exhaust the usage. A similar approach will be used by looking at consistency and inconsistency among parents and teachers and among parents and peer groups.

Reinforcement and Psychoanalytic Theory

Observational learning or imitation is a form of social learning theory. Another approach is basically a form of social learning also, leavened in part by psychoanalytic concepts. Reinforcement learning is the most common term and includes such processes as generalization and discrimination, habit strength, drive, mediation, and intrinsic and extrinsic reinforcement. To oversimplify grossly, the reinforcement approach says that behavior which is positively rewarded will be sustained and that which is negatively rewarded will be discontinued. In terms of the family, for example, if the parents praise the child for being kind, for getting good grades, or for wearing a "peace" symbol, then the child will be encouraged to persist in behavior of this and related sorts. Often observational learning and reinforcement work hand in glove so that the child is rewarded for imitating the parent. At other times discrepancies arise, as when parents beat their children in order to discourage aggressive behavior.

Valuable as this approach is, we have but slight occasion to use it in this book. This is largely because of our emphasis on imitation and observational learning throughout all stages of the study. Another, complementary reason is that reinforcement effects ordinarily require direct observations or experimental data to be systematically supported. Trying to capture reinforcement processes in a survey of the type we conducted would have been hazardous because it would have rested on child and parent recall of behaviors which they "think" were applied anywhere up to seventeen years ago. Rather than saying that reinforcement is not a viable approach to the study of political socialization we are simply saying that survey research does not lend itself at all well to its application.

A third approach comes from an older tradition and stems rather directly from psychoanalytic theory. Affective and power relationships involving parent and child are of prime concern here. The evolving conflicts and resolutions between parent and child are held to shape the general personality of the child and hence, at a further remove, the political personality. Such dimensions as "warmth-hostility," "restrictiveness-permissiveness," and "detachment-anxious emotional involvement" are employed.[23] Perhaps the most famous application to a politically relevant topic is *The Authoritarian Personality*.[24] And in general, relationships and dispositions toward authority figures continue to be the most common applications of psychoanalytic theory to politics.

[23]See Wesley C. Becker, "Consequences of Different Kinds of Parental Discipline," in Martin L. and Lois W. Hoffman (eds.), *Review of Child Development* (New York: Russell Sage Foundation, 1964), Vol. 1, pp. 169–208. It might be noted in passing that there is much controversy in the literature about the consequences of various child-rearing practices.

[24]T. W. Adorno, *et al.*, *The Authoritarian Personality* (New York: Harper, 1950).

Almost by definition this approach is clinical or experimental in nature although ingenious devices can be used to tap relevant dimensions for larger populations. Our own usage of concepts coming out of this tradition is restricted and even by the most generous definition does not satisfy the quality of data desired by the clinician or the experimenter. We did hypothesize, on the basis of theory and empirical research, that affective and power relationships would play a mediating role in the transmission of political orientations. That is, rather than look upon parental practices and the interactions between parent and child as determinative of certain political orientations, we chose to consider whether affective and power configurations affect the matching behavior of the students.

Cognitive Theory

Within recent years another theory of learning and socialization has gained increasing ascendency. In contrast to the other approaches mentioned so far, this one views the socializee as a very active rather than passive actor in the process. Usually referred to as a cognitive theory, the approach rejects the idea that the human is simply a *tabula rasa* being molded by forces in the environment.

Two leading exponents of the theory have been Brown and Kohlberg. For Brown the notion of generational discontinuities and active engagement of the individual in the socialization process are intertwined. He says:

> Socialization is sometimes understood to be simply the control of impulse, sometimes to be the acquisition of values; sometimes as conformity to norms and sometimes as internalization of the parental superego. All of these conceptions take insufficient account of the intellectual side of socialization and of the active creative role of the child.[25]

Values, for example, are not simply acquired positive and negative valences:

> For one thing values require to be conceptualized. In order to set a positive value on achievement and negative value on aggression, for instance, one must possess the two conceptions: achievement and aggression.[26]

Similarly, successful socialization is not necessarily the acting out of prevailing norms. Referring to moral development, for example, he observes:

> . . . the moral theory an individual forms by working over his moral experience can lead him to reject some part of the conventional moral-

[25]Roger Brown, *Social Psychology* (New York: Free Press, 1965), p. 194.
[26]*Ibid.*, p. 194.

ity. He is likely to argue, in support of his position, that the change he favors will make the total morality more consistent or that the substitution he offers will more truly realize the basic values of the culture than does the rejected part. . . . It does not seem correct to consider such persons to be negative outcomes, failures, of socialization. They have successfully internalized the norms but they have made a novel system of them and novel systems sometimes displace established ones.[27]

In the last sentence we see the linkage between the view of active participation in the socialization process and operational discontinuities. As noted earlier, discontinuities often occur as a result of larger structural changes in the society. However, they can also reflect more or less individually derived outcomes. Brown believes that children develop rule systems as they mature and that these systems can change the prevailing norms of society.

The passive versus active viewpoints of socialization need not be an "either-or" proposition, although people working in one vein are likely to make it sound that way. Zigler and Child make a strong case for holding fast to both approaches:

The active, mediational cognitive characteristics of the child are important in the socialization process at every stage of development; on the other hand, they do not determine every aspect of the socialized behavior which emerges.[28]

To paraphrase an example they give, we may take the case of obligation toward political participation. What constitutes the norm of obligation in one polity will have little to do with the active mediational structures of the developing child, but much to do with the particular character of that polity. In respect to conceptualizing the notion of obligation to participate, the child is an active agent; in respect to the particular content which defines that obligation in a given polity, the child is a relatively passive agent.

Two areas in which cognitive theory has been dramatically applied are in language development and in moral development. Of more relevance to us is moral development. Working in the tradition of Piaget, Kohlberg has revolutionized the study of moral development by emphasizing theoretically and attempting to test empirically the place of the

---

[27]*Ibid.*, p. 195. For an explicitly political application of the cognitive approach see R. W. Connell, *The Child's Construction of Politics* (Carlton, Victoria: Melbourne University Press, 1971).

[28]Edward Zigler and Irvin L. Child, "Socialization," in Gardiner Lindzey and Elliot Aronson (eds.), *Handbook of Social Psychology,* 2nd ed. (Reading: Addison-Wesley, 1969), Vol. 3, Chapter 24.

individual's own contribution to moral development.[29] Like Piaget, Kohlberg takes an invariant stage approach, but his stages are more elaborately described and they have somewhat different properties than Piaget's. We are not so much concerned with this as with the signal claim that movement through the stages of moral development is governed by cognitive growth. Certain levels of cognitive maturity seem to be a necessary condition for certain levels of moral judgments and are a necessary but not sufficient condition for moral behavior. Moreover, moral structures of thought result not from individuals simply receiving the moral structures bequeathed by society but from their interacting with and processing these structures.

This view stands in contrast to the two prominent social learning theories of identification (what we call observational learning) and reinforcement. Whereas social learning theorists would claim that progression is not necessarily stage wise and comes from social learning, the developmentalists would say they are bound to be stage wise and that cognitive growth accounts for them. There are, of course, several points of intersection between the stands. Our purpose here was to juxtapose them.[30]

Even very young children are not completely "empty slates," but let us assume that the initial formulation of political orientations, such as they are, mainly reflects outside forces impinging on them. As they grow older, however, children are surely no longer just mirrors that reflect, albeit in a distorted manner, only that which is currently around them. Rather their own attitudinal and cognitive structures serve to filter and process current ideas, suggestions, advice, and events that come to them from the outside.

It is true, of course, that we could theoretically trace individual political states at time t back to states at time t-1, through the states at t-2, . . . , back to the time at which all of the political orientations appear to be derived from outside sources. Even at that early state, however, cognitive differences make the handling of those first stimuli different across individuals; and even at that stage they are processing the materials. But the central point is that at time t, it is fully possible for them to look quite unlike any *or all* of the socialization agents then around them. In operational terms, the political character of high school seniors is far from completely determined by the political profiles of family, friends, peers, and "others" even if we could measure these sources in full detail.

---

[29]A recent exposition is Lawrence Kohlberg, "Stage and Sequence: The Cognitive Developmental Approach to Socialization," in Goslin, *Handbook of Socialization Theory and Research*, Chapter 6.

[30]For a lucid integration of the two approaches in the area of moral development see Maccoby, "Moral Values and Behavior in Childhood," pp. 251–62

These considerations lead us to expect that the articulation between values and behaviors of any given set of socializers and socializees will be far from uniform. In addition to the multiplicity of agents there is the factor of cognitive development itself which, while having broad uniformities in the sense of maturation, has vastly different properties in terms of how and with what results the individual "works over" the materials in the environment. Matching behavior on the basis of observational learning would ordinarily be expected to decrease under assumptions of the individual as an active agent in the socialization process. Our own efforts in this book make more indirect than direct use of the cognitive-developmental and activistic approach. But we do point out on occasion where and how adolescents seem to be carving out their own political personalities as intellectual and cognitive characteristics mediate external events.

Resource Availability

A final approach to the study of political learning takes its cue from sociology rather than psychology. For lack of a better term we shall call it resource availability. It proceeds from the premise that a social stratification system operates in the nation. This system bequeaths to people of different strata differential access to resources most useful in the political process. Children born into families of different social status have differential opportunities for acquiring certain predispositions and skills generally valued in society. This is not just a function of what they see their parents doing or of child-rearing practices, although this is part of the process. Rather, it also comes from the social space inhabited by their families. Thus children of middle class parents typically have better nutrition, live in safer neighborhoods, and have access to more varied learning experiences than do children from lower class families. These characteristics, in turn, may affect the formation of political orientations. In a more direct vein, the middle class child goes to "better" schools, interacts with children with greater social competence, has access to more varied learning encounters, and typically undergoes more apprenticeship experiences.

The major difficulty with the social stratification approach is that it deals with causes at a second or third remove. For example, since it is known that child-rearing practices vary by social class, the latter is used as a surrogate for child-rearing practices. The most serious consequence of this is that a great deal of noise enters the analysis because the relationship between class and child-rearing practices is extremely variable through time and space. Moreover, rearing practices include a multitude of specific practices, and these do not necessarily cohere together in a uniform pattern.[31] From another angle social class, however measured, covers a multitude of sins and virtues. Any relationship between class and political variables which is attributed to class-specific, child-rearing practices could be reflecting other aspects of social class. Still, there are times when the researcher needs a global variable such as class to serve as an indicator or best possible guess of some specific (unmeasured) attribute or to summarize a host of properties. It is in this sense that we will ordinarily use social class in our analysis.

Other global variables reflect the operation of the American stratification system and resource availability. The most common ones in our work are the variables of sex and race. In one sense these are very specific variables and everyone understands them in a physiological sense. But what do they stand for that makes them important in the socialization process? It is the accumulation and processing of a fantastic variety of events and treatments, expectations and performances into generally distinctive patternings which make them interesting and important in terms of political socialization outcomes. To enumerate all of these properties or to gather data on them in a single study is beyond imagination. Therefore, the surrogate designations of race and sex are employed with the understanding that some distinctive life history attributes are being grouped together and that some loss in information is thereby introduced.

AGENTS OF POLITICAL SOCIALIZATION

A major concern of much of the work in political socialization revolves around the sources of pre-adults' learning. This emphasis can be seen in most texts or readers in the field, in which one typically finds sections devoted to the various "agents" or "agencies" of socialization. Yet as one begins to theorize about the process of socialization and especially to study it empirically, the extraordinary complexity of this topic rapidly becomes apparent. A discussion of this complexity here will serve, first of all, to justify the devotion of major portions of Parts II and III—over two-thirds of the book—to this single concern. More importantly, it will help clarify both the contribution and the limitations of the present work in advancing our knowledge of this area.

It is by now a fairly standard procedure to divide up the pre-adult's environment into three or four broad classes. Family and school are at the top of the list, although there is considerable difference of opinion about which one is the more dominant. Peer groups are usually identified as another source of ideas, and while their exact contribution is debatable,

[31]See, for example, Becker, "Consequences of Different Kinds of Parental Discipline."

they are most often placed somewhere below family and school in the hierarchy of influence on pre-adults. Remaining sources are often clustered together as "other agents," which include such diverse factors as the mass media, secondary groups, political events, as well as idiosyncratic factors that affect groups or individuals. Sometimes a couple of these categories are combined, and occasionally one finds separate recognition of some component of the above categories, such as colleges as distinct from secondary schools.

This sort of classification is useful for conveying a quick overview of the major sources of observational learning for the developing child or youth. For research purposes, however, it needs to be explicated considerably. Consider the family for a moment. Not long ago one might have simply asked how well children reflect the political attitudes of their fathers, with the strong presumption of a high degree of similarity. Now we know that this is far too narrow a focus for an examination of family influence. Most obviously it is necessary to expand this view to include the mother's attitudes. Congruency of parental values cannot be automatically assumed, and there is considerable evidence throughout this volume that similarity of parental ideas has much to do with how well these ideas are transmitted to children. Similarly, our evidence clearly challenges the view of one-sided paternal dominance in the passage of political values.

Much further expansion of our view of the family is necessary however. For example, the procedure of correlating parent and student responses to identical questions is a useful approach and one which we will use often. It is highly likely, however, that this method underestimates the extent of parental influence on student values. In Chapters 2 and 3 we discuss and present evidence to support the contention that parents' actions and attitudes, broadly defined, have an impact on students' ideas beyond what is captured by the usual measures of congruency.

Recent research has also emphasized that numerous characteristics of the family unit play a part in the overall impact of the family. For one thing, family features may be part of an interaction effect (in the statistical sense) involving the transmission of political values. It has been suggested, for example, that children who get along well with their parents more readily adopt their political views.[32] As noted above, psychoanalytic theory has also suggested that family structure and the nature of interaction among family members can directly alter youth's political feelings. This is the thrust of Almond and Verba's inquiry into the participation of young people in family decisions.[33] Langton's work on maternal families

[32] See studies cited by Richard E. Dawson and Kenneth Prewitt, *Political Socialization* (Boston: Little, Brown, 1969), pp. 117 ff.

[33] Almond and Verba, *The Civic Culture*, Chapter 12.

in Jamaica is also based on this presumption.[34] Still other work cites parental forms of decision making, family discussion of politics, actual political participation, physical togetherness of the family, and parental punitiveness as possible determinants of children's political orientations. Also relevant is the dispute over the political and other effects of maternal dominance in American black families.

There are still other sorts of direct and indirect ways in which the family exerts its influence on young people's political views. Few studies have considered the role of siblings—particularly older brothers and sisters—in attitudinal development, and yet there are undoubtedly cases in which this is an important factor. Similarly, grandparents and in-laws are sometimes an important part of the child's environment.[35] The family's demographic characteristics also play a potentially powerful part in the socialization experience by partially determining where the child lives, exposure to varied experiences, the type of schooling obtained, and so on.

The kinds of complexities raised with respect to the family's influence could be repeated for the school, peer group, mass media, and other sources of political learning. Overall, then, the job of sorting out the differential and joint effects of socialization agents is a difficult task. But this is a problem that must be attacked if we are to understand how people come to be the way they are politically.

AN OVERVIEW OF OBJECTIVES

The complexities of theory, substance, and method make the study of political socialization particularly vexing, but at the same time exciting and challenging. In this book we try to make a contribution to sorting out the effects of various socialization agents in defining some processes of political learning, and in locating sources of change and continuity. Our goal has been to achieve considerable breadth of coverage at the inevitable expense of some depth. This decision was based on two major grounds. First, a narrow study of, say, expected political involvement or partisan attitudes or views on controversial issues would run the very considerable risk of lacking in significance to any wider circle of topics. Second, the array of categories and subcategories of socialization agents detailed above makes it imperative that we include as much of this variety

[34]Kenneth P. Langton, *Political Socialization* (New York: Oxford University Press, 1969), Chapter 2.

[35]Paul A. Beck and M. Kent Jennings, "Parents as 'Middlepersons' in Political Socialization," *Journal of Politics* (forthcoming).

as possible. Not to do so would severely limit any conclusions that we arrived at, since the chief influences might be the ones that we ignored.

To accomplish this broad coverage, a wide range of different orientations is introduced in Part II. A number of them, however, are taken up only in Chapter 6, where the need for an all-encompassing view is greatest. Prior to that an intensive investigation is made of four major orientations. We begin with partisanship because it is the measure where greatest intra family continuity is achieved. It will serve as a standard of sorts by which to judge the findings of subsequent chapters. Opinions on public policy issues, knowledge and images of political process, and perspectives on the citizenship role are then taken up in turn. The order is dictated by the approximate contribution of the family to the student profile in each area. Thus we will find that by Chapter 5 we are dealing with orientations on which continuity of familial views is of a relatively small order.

Although the format of Chapters 2-5 varies somewhat, we usually cover 1) the nature of the concept and its importance at the pre-adult and adult level; 2) the similarity of parents and students, both in an aggregate sense and at the level of student-parent pairs; 3) direct and indirect ways in which parents and the family affect the orientations of their children. In this manner we cover most aspects of the family that have been singled out as possibly important in the political socialization process. The two topics of homogeneous versus heterogeneous parents and mothers versus fathers are deemed sufficiently important that a separate chapter is devoted to them.

In Part III we turn to the school and peers as sources of students' political orientations. These chapters are directed toward the components of the school outlined above, especially curriculum and teachers, and to groups of friends. The rich array of substantive topics introduced in Part II is maintained insofar as possible and appropriate. Thus we achieve substantial breadth of coverage both in terms of the socialization agents considered and in terms of the range of orientations studied.

The design of the book, giving such a prominent place to the agents of socialization, could neglect a whole set of other important issues, especially those related to the role of socialization in promoting continuity or change at the individual, family, and system levels. That we have in fact not neglected other aspects of the socialization process should be indicated here.

Consider, for example, Greenstein's formulation, which is a paraphrase of a statement by Lasswell: "(1) Who (2) learns what (3) from whom (4) under what circumstances (5) with what effects."[36] Each of these topics is

---

[36]Fred I. Greenstein, *Children and Politics* (New Haven: Yale University Press, 1965), p. 12.

discussed throughout our chapters. The question of who learns is taken up both in the family and school setting, where we study the extent to which boys and girls, blacks and whites, politically interested and uninterested, absorb different political orientations. Our focus on what is learned winds its way through the various orientations mentioned above. The circumstances of socialization are considered in a number of ways. Frequent consideration is given, for example, to whether learning is direct and conscious or unintended and subconscious.

Specifying the effects of political learning is by far the most difficult part of Greenstein's scheme to accomplish, but we freely indicate what we feel are the effects of the patterns we find. In similar fashion, we could indicate our coverage of the three "processes" discussed by Dawson and Prewitt (age trends, methods of political learning, and discontinuities).[37]

More important than simply having covered these topics, however, is that in using the agent approach to organize much of the book, we have been very careful to consider both continuity and change. An expectation of a moderate degree of continuity obviously underlies the analysis of similarities between parents and students. But those who have seen our earlier work know that the seniors are far from mirror images of their parents. It is part of our task to account for the changes that occur as well as documenting whatever student-parent congruency exists. Similarly, we must account for those conditions that increase parent-student correspondence, as well as those in which students are very much unlike their parents. Both conditions are important elements in any theoretical formulation of the socialization process.

While data and commentary on the question of continuity versus change are thus found throughout the analysis, the major discussion of these topics occurs in Part IV. In Chapter 10 attention is given to continuity or change in political orientations across the life cycle. Particular attention is paid to the adult period (using SRC election study data), and in general the thesis of early "hardening" of orientations is challenged. Chapter 11 complements this by its analysis of aggregate change across the parent and student generations. The objective here is to show the degree to which the political orientations of students echo (in the aggregate) those found among parents when prominent socio-political indicators are used as controls. The emphasis is upon the variation in the "reproductive fidelity" of significant political strata.

By devoting these two chapters explicitly to questions of continuity and change, and by the frequent attention to these questions in the earlier parts, we hope that we have largely overcome the traditional imbalance in socialization research on the stability rather than the dynamics of political systems.

[37]Dawson and Prewitt, *Political Socialization*, Part II.

STUDY DESIGN AND EXECUTION

The data to be employed in this book were gathered by the Survey Research Center of the University of Michigan in the spring of 1965. The overall study was designed with an eye toward maximum flexibility in each of several ways. First and foremost, the students to be selected had to be a representative sample of a theoretically meaningful population. Secondly, samples of parents, teachers, and other agents had to be selected in such a way that they would be directly related to the core sample of students. Third, insofar as possible, the parent and teacher samples had to be useful by themselves, that is, apart from their connections with the student sample. Fourth, the interviews had to be structured to take maximum advantage of the sample design.

To accomplish these goals, interviews were held first with a national probability sample of 1,669 seniors distributed among 97 secondary schools, public and nonpublic.[38] The decision to have high school seniors as the central objects of inquiry rested on two major considerations. First, for the majority of young adults this is the last year in which they will be residing at home. It is important to capture their political world before they have come under the influence of forces encountered after leaving home. By so doing the socialization impact of parents and other family characteristics up to a crucial point in the life cycle can be more readily assessed. A corollary consideration is that this is the last year during which it would be relatively easy to carry out field operations for matching parents and their offspring.

A second major determining factor for the selection of high school seniors is that this is the last year in which they will be in schools where a special part of their education is devoted to civic education. Most of the direct efforts to build good citizens through the educational system end at this point. Regardless of whether they continue on to college the students will have now completed their exposure to organized education's political learning endeavors. It is propitious, then, to assess what the net impact of the schooling experience has been.

While these two considerations justify a focus on twelfth graders, they entail a specific loss. Obviously we do not include dropouts in the universe. By dropping our grade focus to tenth grade we would have retained a larger share of the cohort but at the sacrifice of the factors mentioned above. Since they comprised around one-fourth of the age cohort and since they are differentially distributed across social class, their exclusion affects our findings. Just how much is impossible to judge. Some of the possible sources of differential effects are reduced by the

[38]The central features of the study design are indicated in this section, and the details are spelled out in full in the Appendix.

presence of functional dropouts who nevertheless continue to show up physically at school. Different regulations and applications of the minimum age rules for school withdrawal also help even out the differences between dropouts and those who continue. Finally, these is some evidence that political differences between the two types are not great at that age. Having said all this we still feel the loss of that element of the cohort. Where we have reason to think their exclusion might have had particularly acute effects on our findings we draw attention to it and the probable consequences.

The students' parents provided the second crucial population to be sampled. In order to maximize analytic flexibility the parent sample was structured as follows. For a random third of the students the father was designated for interviewing, for another random third the mother was designated, and for the other third both parents were assigned. In the permanent absence of the designated parent, the other parent or parent surrogate was interviewed. Interviews were actually completed with at least one parent of 94 percent of the students and with both parents of 26 percent of the students, or 1,992 parents altogether. Due mainly to the fact that more mothers than fathers constitute the head of household in single-parent families, the sample of parents is composed of 56 percent mothers.

The teacher sample was composed of social studies teachers selected primarily on the basis of the number and variety of course-hours taught to the sample of students during grades 10-12. A selection scheme was prepared in which decisions were made about the relative value of "covering" more students with at least minimal depth (i.e., one teacher) versus covering fewer students with more depth (i.e., more than one teacher per student). This selection procedure proved to be satisfactory by a number of additional criteria as well, such as the variety of courses taught. It yielded a sample of 317 teachers. An attempt was also made to interview the principal in each of the sample schools. Interviews were successfully completed in 96 of the 97 cases.

A final source of data were paper-pencil, self-administered questionnaires given to all of the seniors in cooperating schools. This was an optional phase of the study which met with surprisingly widespread approval. The use of this material here is limited, but it is invaluable when studying peer group relationships and class-wide political orientations.

Each of the basic samples is sometimes used by itself. More often, however, our procedure is to match up students and parents or students and teachers to form a variety of pairs and triads. In the case of *student-parent pairs*, each student was matched with his/her own mother and/or father. Although the actual number of students for whom we have at least one parent respondent is 1,562, the base number of pairs used in the analysis is 1,992. In order to make maximum usage of the interviews gathered, the paired cases in which both the mother and father were interviewed (430) are each given half of their full value. That is, the student is counted twice—once with the mother and once with the father—but at half weight each time. The parent half of these "pairs" includes both the mother and father, each at half weight. The alternative to this procedure was to select randomly the mother or father when both had been interviewed. Half weighting reduces the sampling variability because it utilizes more cases.

Mother-father pairs were also constructed for the 430 families in which both parents were interviewed. Occasionally the focus is on mothers and fathers as pairs, although most such analysis appears elsewhere.[39] When students are also included in these 430 matches, we have *student-mother-father triads*. This combination proved highly useful and appears in nearly every chapter in which family socialization is discussed.

Student-teacher pairs were constructed by matching students with each social studies teacher whom they had and whom we interviewed. Since students had anywhere from zero to six different teachers, they are part of zero to six pairs. Teachers are paired as few as three times or as many as about 20 times. There turned out to be approximately 4000 of these pairs. In order to compensate for the fact that some students appeared much more often than others, each student-teacher pair was weighted by the reciprocal of the number of pairs of which the student was a member. Thus a student matched with four teachers was in four pairs, each weighted by a factor of 1/4. When parents are matched with students and added to these pairs, we have *student-parent-teacher triads*. This combination is used when we wish to compare students with their own parent(s) and teacher(s) simultaneously.

Interviewing instruments and procedures were designed and conducted according to the usual standards of the Survey Research Center. Details are found in the Appendix. We simply note here that the fourth goal mentioned above—structuring the interviews to take maximum advantage of the sample design—helped guide the design of the instruments. Specifically, many identical questions were used throughout interviews with all samples to facilitate comparison. Secondly, comparability was achieved with other studies whenever possible; later SRC studies in turn adopted questions from our study. This greatly facilitates comparison with data from adult cross-sections, as is done extensively in Chapter 10. Finally, each set of respondents was asked about other respondents even though in some cases data were obtained directly from those others.

[39]M. Kent Jennings and Richard G. Niemi, "The Division of Political Labor between Mothers and Fathers," *American Political Science Review,* 64 (March 1971), pp. 69-82.

This permitted an extensive analysis of the reliability and validity of the data.[40]

Weighting of Cases

Due to unavoidable problems in constructing the sampling frame, it proved necessary to weight cases in order to achieve a representative sample. The reasons for the weighting, and a more thorough description of it, are given in the Appendix. It is only necessary to make two essential points here. First, the weighted N always differs from the unweighted N, and it is the weighted figure that appears throughout the book. This is the most sensible procedure, especially for percentage tables in which readers may wish to have the number on which the percentages are based in order to make their own calculations.[41] However, it does mean that the numbers of cases cited in text and tables do not correspond to the numbers of interviews given above. To avoid confusion, Table A.3 in the Appendix lists the unweighted and weighted N's for each sample as well as for pairs and triads. We repeat, however, that all N's cited below in the text are weighted.

The second point that needs to be made is that the weights included nonintegers carried out to one decimal place. Hence, N's used throughout the analysis included a decimal number which has been rounded off for purposes of presentation (rounded up if over .5, down if less than .5 and to the even whole number if .5), Rounding after the calculations have been made results in very little error and enormously improves readability—as well as removing fractional persons.

This procedure entails only two minor problems. The first is that occasionally the stated N's and percentages seem incompatible. For example, a table may show a figure of 40 percent based on an N of 11, which is impossible with whole numbers. In fact, the fraction may have been 4.5/11.3, which is indeed 40 percent. The second problem is that some computer programs round off before printing the results while others print fractional results. This causes slight problems especially when the results are further manipulated by hand. For example, if two N's of 6.7 and 6.6 are added, the result, rounded off is 13; but if we round first and then add, the result is 14. In practice neither of these problems should cause difficulty.[42]

[40]See Richard G. Niemi, *How Family Members Perceive Each Other* (New Haven: Yale University Press, 1974).

[41]N's are especially useful for combining and otherwise reanalyzing tabular material. Thus N's are included except for some correlations, where they are less useful. Care has been taken to assure that the correlations are not based on exceedingly small numbers of cases.

[42]Partly due to this problem, there are occasionally minor discrepancies between results published here and in previously published papers. Similarly, reproduction of these results by other researchers may be very slightly different.

Methods of Analysis

Our methods in this book are rather eclectic, ranging from simple comparisons of student versus parent marginals, to rank-order correlations, to product-moment correlations and partials, to a form of regression analysis. For the most part this entails no particular problems, but we should perhaps comment on the use of two different kinds of correlations. Strictly speaking, virtually all of our data are ordinal rather than interval-level, so that rank-order but not product-moment correlations are appropriate. In the last few years, however, it has become fashionable to use the Pearson correlational machinery for data of this type as well as to calculate means and other statistics which assume interval-level properties. Justification for this usage has lately begun to appear in print.[43] Our use of the two kinds of techniques is a by-product of the changing practices in the profession. In Part II, where our chief purpose is to compare students' and parents' responses, we have taken the more conservative path by sticking to rank-order correlations. In Parts III and IV we have not hesitated to make interval-level assumptions where it facilitated the analysis.[44]

In any event, we should note that we have observed few instances in which the two kinds of correlations give widely divergent results. The rank-order correlation that we normally use—Kendall's tau-b—is a particularly conservative statistic,[45] usually resulting in lower figures than the Pearson correlation. The differences are very small in the lower ranges (on the order of .02 or so for correlations around .1 or .2), but get larger in the higher ranges (on the order of .10–15 for correlations of .6 and higher). But the point is that tau-b is rather consistently lower, rather than sometimes yielding higher and other times lower coefficients.[46]

[43]Robert P. Abelson and John W. Tukey, "Efficient Conversion of Non-metric Information into Metric Information," in Edward R. Tufte (ed.), *The Quantitative Analysis of Social Problems* (Reading: Addison-Wesley, 1970), pp. 407–17; Edward R. Tufte, "Improving Data Analysis in Political Science," *World Politics*, 21 (July 1969), pp. 641–54; Sanford Labovitz, "The Assignment of Numbers to Rank Order Categories," *American Sociological Review*, 35 (June 1970), pp. 515–24.

[44]Though the unbridled use of interval-level assumptions for rank-order data has sometimes been suggested, there is reason to take this step cautiously, especially when the variables have small numbers of categories. See Labovitz, "Assignment of Numbers to Rank Order Categories," pp. 521–23.

[45]This statistic is sometimes called tau-beta. See Richard G. Niemi, "A Note of Clarification of the Term 'Tau-Beta'," *Social Science Information*, 7 (December 1968), pp. 195–97. We have used τ_b even for nonsquare tables, having never observed more than a minor divergence between τ_b and τ_c.

[46]Using Monte Carlo methods Brent Rutherford shows the fluctuations of various nonparametric statistics under a variety of table configurations and marginal allocations. Tau-b tends to be more resistant than any other measure to such variations. Therefore, comparisons of tau-b's across a variety of ordinal relationships are relatively safe. See his "Non-Metric Correlational Methods: A Sensitivity Analysis Using Monte Carlo Simulation," paper presented at the 1971 Annual Meeting of the Pacific Sociological Association, Honolulu, Hawaii.

Whichever statistic(s) are used, if these differences are kept in mind by the reader, minimal confusion in interpreting the results should follow.

Comparisons are often presented both in terms of correlations and the corresponding contingency tables (percentage results). As has often been observed, the strength of the relationship as judged by the former often seems much weaker than when judged by the latter. Partly because of this, we often present both modes of comparison. In addition, the size of correlations is affected by the variance in the samples employed; in particular, we frequently find that relationships are especially striking (as judged by percentage differences) at the "tails" of distributions, but that the more extreme categories do not contain enough cases to heighten substantially the accompanying correlation. In instances such as these, both comparisons convey some of what needs to be said. Generally, our inclination is to rely most heavily on the correlations rather than percentage comparisons.[47]

[47]Our earlier comments on measuring student-parent agreement are apropos here, although the conclusions are not limited to measuring intergenerational agreement. While percentage comparisons "may have an intuitive appeal, [they have] several drawbacks. Percentage agreement is not based on the total configuration of a square matrix but only on the 'main diagonal.' Thus two tables which are similar in percentage agreement may represent widely differing amounts of agreement if deviations from perfect agreement are considered. Moreover, percentage agreement depends heavily on the number of categories used, so that the degree of parent-student similarity might vary for totally artificial reasons. Correlations are more resistant to changes in the definition of categories. Finally, correlations are based on relative rankings (and intervals in the case of product-moment correlations) rather than on absolute agreement as percentage agreement usually is. That is, if student scores tend to be higher (or lower) than parent scores on a particular variable, but the students are ranked similarly to their parents, a high correlation may be obtained with very little perfect agreement." M. Kent Jennings and Richard G. Niemi, "The Transmission of Political Values from Parent to Child," *American Political Science Review*, 62 (March 1968), pp. 169–84.

II   ADOLESCENTS AND THEIR PARENTS

CHAPTER TWO

Attachments to the Political Parties

T HE NATURE of parties and of the party system have come to be recognized as critical features of the adult political world. Attachments of the electorate to the parties have been related to events at the micro level of the individual voter and to events at the macro level of the functioning of political systems.[1] Comparative studies have shown that partisanship is an important phenomenon in many countries[2] and historical studies have begun to outline the impact of party affiliations in earlier years.[3] At the adult level, then, there is little doubt that partisanship is a singularly important political orientation.

At the pre-adult level partisanship is important, first of all, because it begins to develop early in life. By the age of ten or twelve most children recognize the terms Republican and Democrat, and they respond in a partisan or consciously Independent fashion to a question about voting preferences.[4] Party loyalties take shape before children acquire much knowledge about the parties themselves and before much is learned about political and social issues.[5] In fact, it is likely that partisanship itself affects the later acquisition of political knowledge and attitudes.

Party affiliations are also important because it has been shown that children often take on the partisan character of their parents. Especially when compared with other political orientations, the similarity of children's and parents' partisanship stands out as particularly strong.[6]

[1]See Angus Campbell, Philip E. Converse, Warren E. Milier and Donald E. Stokes, *The American Voter* (New York: Wiley, 1966), and *Elections and the Political Order* (New York: Wiley, 1966), and numerous other writings using this concept.

[2]Campbell, *et al.*, *Elections and the Political Order*; Gabriel Almond and Sidney Verba, *The Civic Culture* (Princeton: Princeton University Press, 1963).

[3]Walter Dean Burnham, "The Changing Shape of the American Political Universe," *American Political Science Review*, 59 (March 1965), pp. 7–28, especially pp. 22 ff; *Critical Elections and the Mainsprings of American Politics* (New York: Norton, 1970).

[4]Robert D. Hess and Judith V. Torney, *The Development of Political Attitudes in Children* (Chicago: Aldine, 1967), p. 90

[5]Fred I. Greenstein, *Children and Politics* (New Haven: Yale University Press, 1965), Chapter 4.

[6]M. Kent Jennings and Richard G. Niemi, "The Transmission of Political Values from Parent to Child," *American Political Science Review*, 62 (March 1968) pp. 169–84; Herbert H. Hyman, *Political Socialization* (Glencoe: Free Press, 1959), Chapter 4; Herbert McClosky and Harold E. Dahlgren, "Primary Group Influence on Party Loyalty," *American Political Science Review*, 53 (September 1959), pp. 757–76; Campbell, *et al.*, *The American Voter*, pp. 146–48.

Moreover, differentiation in the rate of parent-child transmission is associated with differences in the functioning of political systems.[7]

With high school seniors there are at least two added reasons for paying attention to party identification. At the end of their senior year, high school students are at or very close to voting age. Therefore, it is of interest to observe the relationship of partisan loyalties to the candidate preferences of youth. The aim is to see whether partisanship "works" for the student in the same way that it functions for the adult. At the same time, candidate preferences are important in their own right and can be viewed in relation to parents' preferences.

Second, with children at the age when many begin to leave the family, it seems relevant to get a parents'-eye view of the partisanship of their children. With younger children we might presume that most parents are unaware of their budding party feelings. For high school seniors, however, parents may well be cognizant of these developing orientations. By observing the extent to which this is true, insight may be gained into the nature of the transmission of party identification.

It should be pointed out that historical changes, such as the increase in the proportion of Independents after about 1966, mean that some of the parameters we cite would be different today. This is inevitable in any study made in a dynamic historical period. Nevertheless, the analysis should provide much needed insight into youthful partisanship, and especially its intergenerational sources, at a crucial juncture in our recent past.

STUDENT-PARENT PARTISANSHIP

Much needs to be said about student-parent partisanship at both the levels of aggregate distributions and individual student-parent pairs. As a beginning let us observe the overall similarity of students and parents. The substantial agreement between parent and student party affiliations is indicated by a correlation of .47,[8] a statistic nearly unaffected by the use of three, five, or all seven categories of the party identification spectrum generated by the question sequence.[9] The magnitude of this statistic reflects the twin facts of the presence of a large amount of exact agreement and the absence of many wide differences between students and

[7]Philip E. Converse and Georges Dupeux, "Politicization of the Electorate in France and the United States," *Public Opinion Quarterly*, 26 (Spring 1962), pp. 1–23.

[8]The figure is based on parent-student pairs in which both respondents have a party identification; eliminated are the two percent of the pairs in which one or both respondents are apolitical or undecided. The product-moment correlation for these data is .59.

[9]The standard SRC question was used: "Generally speaking, do you usually think of yourself as a Republican, a Democrat, an Independent, or what?" (If Republican or Democrat) "Would you call yourself a strong (R) (D) or not very strong (R) (D)?" (If Independent or other) "Do you think of yourself as closer to the Republican or Democratic party?"

parents. When the full 7x7 matrix of parent-student party loyalties is arranged as in Table 2.1, the cells in which parents and students are in unison account for a third of the cases. The cells representing maximum disagreement are very nearly empty. If we consider only the broad categories of Democrat, Independent, and Republican, 59 percent of the students fall under the same heading as their parents, and only seven percent bridge the wide gap between Republicans and Democrats.

TABLE 2.1
STUDENT-PARENT PARTY IDENTIFICATION

Students	Strong Dem.	Weak Dem.	Ind. Dem.	Parents Ind.	Ind. Rep.	Weak Rep.	Strong Rep.	Total
Strong Dem.	9.7%	5.8	1.6	1.1	.1	.3	.2	18.8%
Weak Dem.	8.0	9.0	2.1	1.6	.5	2.1	.9	24.2
	(32.6)[a]			(7.0)		(3.4)		(43.0)
Ind. Dem.	3.4	4.2	2.1	1.6	.8	1.6	.8	14.5
Ind.	1.8	2.6	1.7	2.7	.9	2.3	.8	12.8
Ind. Rep.	.5	.7	.8	1.2	.9	1.9	2.4	8.4
	(13.2)			(12.7)		(9.7)		(35.7)
Weak Rep.	.9	1.6	.7	.9	1.3	5.0	3.3	13.6
Strong Rep.	.5	.7	.2	.5	.5	1.9	3.5	7.7
	(3.6)			(4.1)		(13.6)		(21.3)
Total	24.7%	24.7	9.3	9.7	4.9	15.0	11.7	100.0%
	(49.4)			(23.9)		(26.7)		
$\tau_b = .47$								(1852)[b]

[a]The full 7×7 table is provided because of the considerable interest in party identification. However, for some purposes, reading ease among them, the 3×3 table is useful. It is given by the figures in parentheses; these figures are (within rounding error) the sum of the numbers just above them.
[b]In this and succeeding tables, N's are given in parentheses.

Surely this degree of student-parent similarity is significant, especially when compared with the correlations for other types of political orientations. Still, it is substantially less than perfect agreement, and one may wonder why it is not even higher. Part of the answer lies in the fact that we are dealing here with parental partisanship as reported by parents themselves. Intervening between this partisanship and the students' own orientations are the students' perceptions of their parents' position. Since these perceptions are sometimes inaccurate, students may adopt what they think are their parents' attitudes without really becoming like their parents. That misperceptions do affect the degree of student-parent similarity is indicated by the fact that the student-"parent" (i.e., the student's report of the parent) correlation is .58. This is .11 higher than the true student-parent correlation reported above. Thus part of the reason that students and parents are not even more like each other is that some students adopt what are in fact incorrect perceptions of parental attitudes.[10]

The similarity between parents and students suggests that transmission of party preferences from one generation to the next is carried out rather successfully in the American context. However, there are also indications that other factors have temporarily weakened the party affiliations of the younger generation. This is most obvious if we compare the marginal totals for parents and students in Table 2.1. The student sample contains almost 12 percent more Independents than the parent sample, drawing almost equally on the Republican and Democratic proportions of the sample. Similarly, among party identifiers a somewhat larger segment of the students is but weakly inclined toward their chosen party. Nor are these configurations simply an artifact of the restricted nature of the parent sample, since the distribution of party identification among the parents closely resembles that of the entire adult electorate as observed in November 1964 (SRC 1964 election study).[11]

This greater Independence of students is clearly a result of the development of partisanship over the life cycle. Data from the Chicago study show that the proportion of Independents grows steadily throughout the elementary years. By eighth grade, according to that study, about 37 percent of the students who have made any decision are Independents.[12] This coincides almost exactly with the 36 percent of the seniors claiming to be Independents. Since we know from adult studies that partisanship increases steadily over the adult years,[13] it appears that the maximum proportion of Independents is reached some time during the adolescent years. It is at this age of maximum Independence that we have captured our student respondents.

Turning to the party identifiers, we find that the ratio of Democrats to Republicans is almost the same in both the student (67 percent) and parent (65 percent) samples. In the transmission process some changes in party loyalties have occurred, but the net balance does not favor either party. The balance between new Republicans and new Democrats, however, is not a result of two equally attractive alternatives. The Democratic

[10]From a methodological point of view this finding is important because most studies rely on children's reports of parents' attitudes. In general this procedure overestimates the true student-parent correlation by about .10. See Richard G. Niemi, "Collecting Information about the Family: A Problem in Survey Methodology," in Jack Dennis (ed.), *Political Socialization: A Reader in Theory and Research* (New York: Wiley, 1973), Chapter 19.

[11]Obviously the differences in the distributions of students and parents lower the student-parent correlation. Since these distributions vary over the life cycle (see below in the text), the correlation itself may vary slightly with age of the respondents.

[12]Hess and Torney, *Development of Political Attitudes in Children*, p. 90. We have equated their "sometimes Democrat, sometimes Republican" category with Independents. The SRC question probably results in a slightly smaller number of Independents.

[13]Campbell, *et al.*, *The American Voter*, pp. 161–65.

TABLE 2.2
STUDENT PARTY IDENTIFICATION BY PARENT PARTY IDENTIFICATION

Students	Democrat	Parents Independent	Republican
Democrat	66%	29%	13%
Independent	27	53	36
Republican	7	17	51
Total	100%	99%	100%
	(914)	(442)	(495)

party has a visibly greater retaining and drawing power among the students. The data in Table 2.2 demonstrate this. Among students with a Democratic parent, almost two-thirds retain the parental party preference; the same is true of only half of the children of Republican parents. Among students who do not follow their parents' preference, a slightly larger percentage of the Republican offspring shift to the opposing party rather than to an Independent position. Similarly, children of Independent parents who adopt a party preference move disproportionately into the Democratic column. In short, the influences other than parental party identification acting on pre-adults in 1965—such as Democratic majorities in nation and states, and the aftermath of the Goldwater campaign (see below, p. 50—were significantly stronger in the direction of Democratism than of Republicanism.

The observation that defection rates from Democratic and Republican parents vary and yet the net balance of student Democrats and Republicans was virtually unchanged is noteworthy. The reason, of course, is not hard to find. A small *proportion* of students was attracted to the Republicans from a large *number* of Democratic parents (7 percent of 914 is 64 students). In contrast, a larger *proportion* of students was drawn off the smaller pool of Republican parents, resulting in an identical number of defectors (13 percent of 495 is 64 students). Similarly, if one analyzes defections from Independent parents, and from partisan parents to an Independent student position, the gains and losses to each party are nearly equal.[14]

These kinds of "transition probabilities" have been observed in other contexts, and the consequences of them (assuming they remain unchanged over a long period of time) have been worked out.[15] For present

[14]For the Democrats, -27% (914) $+ 29\%$ (442) $= -247 + 128$ for a net loss of 119 students. For the Republicans, -36% (495) $+ 17\%$ (442) $= -178 + 75$ or a net loss of 103 students.

[15]John G. Kemeny, Hazleton Mirkil, J. Laurie Snell, and Gerald L. Thompson, *Finite Mathematical Structures* (Englewood Cliffs: Prentice-Hall, 1959), Chapter 6.

purposes two main points stand out. The first point is simply to emphasize that one cannot facilely generalize from defection rates to subsequent states of affairs. The greater defection rates from Republican parents observed in Table 2.2 would not in the short run result in massive Republican losses in the new generation—even if these defection rates remained unchanged.

The second point follows closely from the first. Under different distributions of parents, similar defection rates could lead to short-run changes in the overall distribution of party identifiers. A case in point is the contemporary South. The defection rates in the South are much like those observed in Table 2.2. The Democratic party clearly has greater holding and pulling power among Southern youth. Yet the pool of Democratic parents is so much larger than the number of Republican parents, that the student distribution shifts in a Republican direction! Among party identifiers 78 percent of the parents are Democratic. This figure drops to 73 percent among the students.[16] This is a small change, but it is significant when the Democrats nationally and in the South have a greater attractiveness for young people. Put another way, the Democratic party is not sufficiently more attractive to Southern youth to maintain the enormous edge in popularity found among the older generation.

Owing to variations in the distribution of parental partisanship and to varying defection rates (although always with a Democratic advantage), a number of other distributional differences occur. The Northeast and Midwest, like the South, are areas in which parent and student partisanship are dissimilar. In both areas the advantage redounds to the Democrats. In the Northeast, 56 percent of parent identifiers and 61 percent of the student identifiers support the Democrats. The respective figures among Midwesterners are 58 percent and 68 percent. Only in the West are the proportions of Democrats and Republicans nearly identical in both generations (66 percent among parents and 64 percent among students).

Parent-student differences also occur along racial and religious lines, but the direction of the differences reveals the enormous pull of the post-Goldwater Democratic party on minority group members. Blacks[17] and Jews are among the most Democratic groups in the electorate. Ninety percent of the black parents and 89 percent of the Jewish parents

[16]Among Southern whites the change is even greater, from 75 percent Democratic among the parents to 66 percent among the students.

[17]Throughout the book the category "black" includes a small percentage of other non-whites—chiefly Puerto Rican—and Mexican Americans. This group makes up only about 6 percent of the "black" group. While every racial group or subgroup is to some extent distinctive, our judgment is that in many politically relevant circumstances, Puerto-Rican and Mexican Americans share many of the characteristics ordinarily associated with the black population. In the absence of a large enough number for separate analysis, the decision was made to include them with blacks.

who identified with a party chose the Democrats. Nonetheless the attraction of the party among the seniors was so great that even higher proportions of students called themselves Democrats. The exact figures are 96 percent among the black students and 91 percent among Jewish seniors. Catholics in 1965 were also heavily Democratic, gaining the support of 77 percent of the parental party identifiers. Among this group as well the lure of the Democrats was sufficient to raise their level of support among the younger generation. Of the Catholic seniors who identified with a party, 86 percent of them were Democrats. The Protestants, by far the largest religious group in the electorate, contain equal proportions of student and parent Democrats.

Turning to social strata, we still find the lure of the Democrats rather constant across all groups, but when this fact is combined with the distribution of party identifiers among the parents, an interesting result occurs. Among parents, as one would expect, there is a strong and nearly monotonic relationship between social class and the proportion of Democratic identifiers. If we take occupation of the head of the household as a measure of class (and using whites only, since blacks have already been discussed), some 75 percent of the partisans in the lowest stratum are Democrats; in the highest stratum this proportion falls to 51 percent.[18] However, due to the concentration of Democrats in the lowest stratum, the net shift in this segment of the student sample is in the *Republican* direction. At the same time, the nearly even division of partisans in the upper stratum allows the Democrats to take advantage of their attractiveness and manage a net gain. The proportion of Democrats in the lowest stratum thus drops to 69 percent, and in the highest stratum increases to 56 percent. Moreover, among the students the proportion of Democrats is more nearly curvilinear, with the highest figure in the middle status group. Hence a strong, nearly monotonic relationship between social class and party identification among the parents becomes a weaker, curvilinear pattern among the students. Remaining as a matter for speculation is whether the unusual pattern and relative lack of differentiation by class will be a permanent feature of the younger generation.

It should be noted that in all of these comparisons of regional, racial, religious and class differences, we have concentrated on the relative proportion of Democrats and Republicans in each sample. In every case a substantial number of students and parents are Independents. The proportion of Independents as well as the difference between students and parents remain fairly constant across these groups. The strongest exception to this statement is among blacks. For both black students and par-

[18]Both samples were divided into five strata according to the decile scale of the Duncan code. For the construction of this code, see the chapters by Otis Dudley Duncan in Albert J. Reiss, Jr., *Occupations and Social Values* (New York: Free Press, 1961).

ents the proportion of Independents is about ten percent below the figures for the entire samples. This also slightly lowers the proportion of Independents in the South.

Variations in Student-Parent Similarity

Widespread variations are observable in the degree of similarity between student and parent partisanship. We will take up these variations in several stages. First, differences along demographic lines will be noted. While such variations are certainly temporally bounded, they do reveal some of the reasons for deviations from familial attitudes. Secondly, family characteristics per se will be considered, where one of the chief considerations is the role of children's perceptions in the transmission process. Finally, we will observe the impact on student-parent similarity of two rather specific influences—the parents' voting behavior in 1964 and the partisanship of the students' friends.

The most noticeable feature of student-parent correspondence among demographic groups is the reduction in the correlations when one party has a special attraction. Blacks provide the most striking example. Offhand one would think that black students are very much like their parents, since there existed in 1965 such widespread agreement on which party better served their interests. Yet the student-parent correlation is an abysmal .12. The reason for this extraordinary low correspondence lies in the attractiveness of the Democrats to all young blacks regardless of parental preferences. Thus when the parent was a Democrat, as in most cases, the student followed suit more often than in the population as a whole (Table 2.2). In the few cases, however, in which the parent was an Independent or a Republican, the student remained just as likely to be a Democrat. Nor is this simply a matter of misperceptions by the students. Even when black seniors thought that their parents were Independents or Republicans, the same high proportion were themselves Democrats.

For Southern whites the same kind of attraction of one party kept the student-parent similarily slightly below that in other parts of the country: .43 versus .48 for the Northeast, .49 for the Midwest, and .52 for the West. In this case it was the Republicans who were *relatively* more attractive, even though the Democrats still had greater pulling power. Combined with the large number of blacks in the South, the overall transmission process is substantially weaker in this region (.39) than elsewhere.

Among religious groups we noted that the Democrats were particularly attractive to young Catholics. Correspondingly, the student-parent correlation among Catholic families (.41) is below the national norm. Jews may be an exception to our generalization, since the correlation is almost identical to the national figure despite the pull of the Democratic party. However, there are so few Jewish Independents or Republicans that the estimate of the correlation is unreliable. Among Protestants the student-parent correlation is a perfect match of the national figure.

Major variations in student-parent similarity are also found when the population is divided into a social status hierarchy. Using either the parents' occupation or education as a measure of status, there is a sizeable decrease in student-parent correspondence as one moves down the status ladder. Grouping the sample into five strata by occupation, the correlations fall monotonically from .53 in the highest status group to .33 in the lowest. Using parental education, the correlation is .53 among families where the parent had at least some college training; this figure drops to .49 among high school graduates and to .36 for those with some high school or with an education of eight grades or less. Of course one important implication of these findings is that the overall correlation reported at the beginning of this chapter (Table 2.1) probably overestimates slightly the true correlation for the entire cohort of seventeen and eighteen-year-olds. Similarly, studies relying on homogeneous populations, such as college students, are likely to discover considerable variation in the degree of student-parent correspondence.

One of the reasons for this relationship between social class and the amount of parent-student similarity is the heavy concentration of blacks in the lower strata. We have already seen that black students resemble their parents less closely than whites for reasons most likely unrelated to their family life. However, taking whites only, the relationship between social class and parent-student similarity still exists, although the differences are somewhat smaller. Among whites the explanation of variations by social class is probably found in the varying degrees of political interest in different social strata. Below it will be shown that students' knowledge of parents' partisanship varies directly with expressions of political interest, and that these more accurate perceptions of partisanship result in greater student-parent correspondence. Similarly, parental knowledge of students' feelings is more accurate where political interest is high, suggesting that parents in politically involved families are more likely to influence consciously the political ideas of their children. In any case, the findings reveal that the transmission of partisan loyalties from parent to child is affected significantly by the social status of the family.[19]

[19]Expected social mobility of the student was also considered as a possible concomitant of variations in student-parent similarity. The occupation the student expected to enter was compared with the occupation of the head of the household to generate a mobility measure. Neither the overall student-parent similarity nor the defection rate in one direction (Democratic or Republican) varied as one would predict. The absence of any effect of social mobility is consistent with recent findings on parent-student partisanship and on defection from partisanship in voting behavior. See Campbell, *et al.*, *The American Voter*, pp. 458–59; Arthur S. Goldberg, "Social Determinism and Rationality as Bases of Party Identification," *American Political Science Review*, 63 (March 1969), pp. 5–25; Richard W. Boyd, "Presidential Elections: An Explanation of Voting Defections," *American Political Science Review*, 63 (June 1969), pp. 498–514.

Characteristics of individual family members and relationships within the family are the second type of variable that may inhibit or facilitate the transmission of political partisanship from one generation to the next. A number of social and psychological studies, for example, have reported that power and affective relationships in the family are related to the acceptance of parents as role models.[20] Studies of specifically political orientations have suggested that acceptance of parental political values is similarly affected.[21] Still others have suggested that the level of politicization in the household is a prime determinant of the rate of parent-student transmission. Finally, sex roles are said to have an effect because of the presumed dominance of the male in political life.

Of these three kinds of characteristics—affectivity and control relationships, politicization, and sex roles—one revealed rather unexpected findings, one showed no impact on transmission rates at all, and only one conformed to our initial expectations. The unexpected conclusions result from an analysis of sex roles, where mothers appeared at least as influential as fathers. Because of the unexpected nature of the findings, a separate chapter (Chapter 6) is partly devoted to examining the relative contribution of mothers and fathers in the transmission of political orientations generally.

Affectivity and control relationships are the characteristics which proved to be unrelated to the degree of parent-student similarity, a finding which presages the negative results of subsequent chapters. These relationships were operationalized in a number of ways in order to measure interaction regarding politics; general interaction; relationships between the mother and father as well as between the parents and children; evaluation of parental control; the current student-parent closeness and whether this feeling had changed over the past several years. Moreover, in line with some earlier findings, we considered the possibility of interaction between these characteristics and levels of politicization.[22] But even among highly politicized families affection and the location of power do not consistently alter the level of congruency between student and parent partisanship. An implication of this is that

[20]William H. Sewell, "Some Recent Developments in Socialization Theory and Research," *The Annals*, 349 (September 1963), pp. 163–81; Glen H. Elder, Jr., "Parental Power Legitimation and Its Effects on the Adolescent," *Sociometry*, 26 (March 1963), pp. 50–65; Elizabeth Douvan and Martin Gold, "Modal Patterns in American Adolescence," in Lois and Martin Hoffman (eds.), *Review of Child Development* (New York: Russell Sage Foundation, 1966), Vol. II, pp. 469–528.

[21]Russell Middleton and Snell Putney, "Political Expression of Adolescent Rebellion," *American Journal of Sociology*, 68 (March 1963), pp. 527–35; Robert E. Lane, "Fathers and Sons: Foundations of Political Belief," *American Sociological Review*, 24 (August 1958), pp. 502–11; Eleanor E. Maccoby, Richard E. Matthews, and Anton S. Morton, "Youth and Political Change," *Public Opinion Quarterly*, 17 (Spring 1954), pp. 23–39.

[22]Middleton and Putney, "Political Expression of Adolescent Rebellion."

differences in the modes of interaction among families of higher and lower strata or of different races or religions do not in general affect the transmission of partisan orientations. The source of the variations observed earlier among demographic groups must be sought elsewhere.

The saliency of politics for family members has a predictable and rather hardy impact on the similarity of parents' and students' partisanship. The more interested and involved the family members are, the greater the congruency of student and parent attitudes. Examples based on two different measures are found in the first and fourth columns of Table 2.3. In the first column we show that the students' own reported levels of interest[23] help determine their similarity with their parents. The figures in the fourth column show that the frequency of husband-wife conversations about politics[24] has the same effect. In each case the effect is most noticeable among the lowest group.

Since we have available to us the seniors' perceptions of their parents' partisanship, it behooves us to probe into these findings somewhat further. Specifically, the explanation for the findings just reported may be in the accuracy of perceptions of students in varying environments. That is, where political interest is high or conversations are frequent, students may perceive their parents' partisanship more accurately. The politically interested students readily pick up or perhaps seek out cues about their parents' feelings, and in a home where politics is discussed freely, cues are likely to be made more obvious and more often. If perceptual accuracy varies in this fashion, it alone may explain the decrease in the student-parent correlation among less politicized families. Children may adopt their "perceived parents' " partisanship equally at all levels of politicization, but the poorer accuracy of some students leads to a reduction in the true student-parent correlation.

In part this intricate process is just what happens. This is most obvious when the students' own political interest is the control variable. The student-"perceived parent" correlations given in the second column of Table 2.3 show that students at all levels of interest mirror their parents to the same degree. However, the third column of figures reveals the de-

[23]As a measure of political interest throughout the book we will use a question which asks respondents how often they "follow what is going on in government and public affairs — most of the time, some of the time, only now and then, or hardly at all." Often we will refer to these responses as indicating High, Medium, and for the last two categories combined, Low interest.

[24]We will make frequent use of the question on husband-wife political conversations and a similar one on student-parent conversations. They come from the parent and student questionnaires respectively. The exact wordings are: "Do you and your (wife) (husband) ever talk about any kind of public affairs and politics, that is, anything having to do with local, state, national, or international affairs? (If Yes) Is this very often, pretty often, or not very often?" "Do you ever talk about public affairs and politics with any of the following people: First with members of your family? (If Yes) How often would you say that is — several times a week, a few times a month, or once or twice a year?"

TABLE 2.3
LEVELS OF POLITICIZATION AND SIMILARITY OF STUDENT AND PARENT PARTISANSHIP

Interest in Public Affairs	Student-parent correlation	Student-"perceived parent" correlation[a]	"Perceived parent"-parent correlation[b]
Low	.38 (301)	.58 (279)	.51 (274)
Medium	.48 (778)	.57 (693)	.60 (680)
High	.49 (771)	.58 (718)	.61 (708)

Husband-Wife Political Conversations	Student-parent correlation	Student-"perceived parent" correlation[a]	"Perceived parent"-parent correlation[b]
Not at all	.32 (310)	.46 (284)	.48 (275)
Not very often	.45 (429)	.56 (395)	.55 (394)
Pretty often	.49 (526)	.60 (475)	.62 (470)
Very often	.54 (349)	.61 (334)	.64 (330)

[a] The correlation between the student's partisanship and the perception of the parent's partisanship.
[b] The correlation between what the student perceives to be the parent's partisanship and the parent's own reported partisanship; i.e., this is a measure of the accuracy of students' perceptions.

creasing accuracy of the less interested students. These two properties, the steady reflection of perceived partisanship and the declining accuracy of the perceptions, combine to give the results, already noted, in the first column of the table.

The data in the second part of the table show that perceptual distortion is not the sole explanation of varying rates of parent-student transmission. The correlations in column five do show a steady decline, so that where parental political conversations are less frequent, students are less likely to take on what they believe to be their parents' views. Still, the differences in the student-"perceived parent" correlations are not as great as the true differences. The extremes in the former case differ by .15, while in the latter case they differ by .22. Thus the declining accuracy of perceptions observed in column six does not create, but rather magnifies the variations in student-parent similarity.

In general the pattern observed for husband-wife political conversations is probably more frequent than that using the students' political interest. It is at least true that inaccuracy is usually accompanied by a large decline in the student-"perceived parent" correlation. In the case of mothers, for example, in which the accuracy of student reports was rated from one (perfect accuracy) to four (three or more steps off the diagonal of the 7 x 7 matrix), the correlations between student and "parent" partisanship are .69, .57, .47, and .24 respectively. For fathers the correlations are very similar—.68, .61, .51, .29. Whichever pattern is more frequent, however, it is instructive to know that patterns like those in Table 2.3 do occur. In either case the variations in family transmission patterns are in large part due to declining accuracy of perceptions among less politicized families. Such students are rebelling against or unintentionally straying from their parents' orientations less often than meets the eye, and in some cases no more than children in highly politicized families.

Having now dealt with demographic variables and characteristics of individual family members and the interaction among them, we consider briefly the effects of two other factors. The first of these is the parents' vote in the 1964 presidential election between Lyndon Johnson and Barry Goldwater. The impact of the parents' vote may be particularly important if one focuses on the way in which partisanship develops. For young children, the presidential vote along with other behavior around election time may be taken as the best indicators of the parents' partisan attitudes. Other indicators, such as expressions of partisan opinions, may be much less salient or meaningful to children. Moreover a youngster has not accumulated a set of experiences from which to judge the normality or frequency of one kind of vote or other partisan act. This lack of relevant experiences may be especially important for Independent parents, for

Independence is not easily conveyed in a single election.[25] If this reasoning is correct, parental voting has its greatest impact on young children. Still, high school seniors do not have the strong partisan ties that will develop later, so that some residual impact of the parents' voting should be observed.

In this context the force exerted by the parents' voting behavior seems quite significant. Relevant data are presented in Table 2.4. Although there are no data from other years with which to make a comparison, the retention rate, say, of 57 percent among Republicans who voted for Goldwater seems very much greater than the 38 percent rate among Republicans voting for Johnson. The effect of the vote is particularly large among Democratic parents who voted for Goldwater, where the retention rate drops to only 24 percent. There were very few such Democrats, of course, as the N's at the bottom of the table indicate. But it seems as if a parental vote contrary to a strong national trend has particular potency for changing the partisan loyalties of children. Among Independent parents the impact of a Democratic vote was slightly greater than that of a Republican vote. Overall, however, the effect among Independent parents fell in between the impact on the two partisan groups.

The net effect of parental voting should not, of course, be overestimated, and it may be salutary to compare Table 2.4 with Table 2.2. Since most Democrats voted for Johnson, the left-most column of the earlier table is very similar to the left-most column in Table 2.4. And even though many Republicans also voted for Johnson, the right-most columns

TABLE 2.4

STUDENT PARTY IDENTIFICATION BY PARENT PARTY
IDENTIFICATION, BY PARENT'S 1964 PRESIDENTIAL VOTE

| Students | Parents | | | | | |
| | Voted Dem.[a] Party ID | | | Voted Rep. Party ID | | |
	Dem.	Ind.	Rep.	Dem.	Ind.	Rep.
Democrat	70%	37%	21%	24%	13%	10%
Independent	25	52	42	42	56	33
Republican	5	11	38	34	31	57
Total	100%	100%	100%	100%	100%	100%
	(808)	(277)	(151)	(75)	(130)	(325)

[a]Thirteen percent of the parents are nonvoters who are grouped by the preference they expressed for Johnson or Goldwater. Separate analysis of nonvoters and voters showed no major difference in the impact on students.

[25]Even among the seniors, the identification of Independent parents was less accurately perceived than that of partisan parents. See Niemi, "Collecting Information about the Family," p. 478.

of the two tables are quite similar. Also the overall retention rate among Independent parents is almost identical to both the figures in Table 2.4. These similarities suggest that current voting behavior is a marginal rather than major determinant of the seniors' partisan ties. This same conclusion is reached if one calculates the net contribution of parents' voting behavior to rates of defection from parental partisanship. A very generous estimate suggests that voting behavior resulted in the defection of about an additional nine percent of the students (out of 41 percent who defected).[26]

At the same time that one minimizes the net effect, it should be emphasized that when conflict between partisanship and voting does occur, the seniors prove to be quite malleable. When parents preferred one party but voted for the other, only about a third of the students followed the parents' partisanship. Moreover, when the students defected, fully a quarter went all the way over to the other party rather than adopting an Independent stance. It seems likely that if seniors are this malleable, younger students are even more susceptible to the shifting influence of voting behavior and other partisan cues. For young children, relatively high partisan instability in the face of conflict is a predictable result.

A second specific influence on students' partisanship is the perceived partisan position of their friends. In many cases, of course, reinforcement or at least no conflict exists; 37 percent of the students felt that their friends' partisanship was the same as their parents', and another 30 percent of the students described their friends as about evenly split between Republicans and Democrats. Nevertheless, this leaves a third of the students for whom there was a conflict between the parents' and friends' loyalties. Almost half of these conflicts—15 percent of all students—were a combination of Republican and Democratic loyalties, while the remainder were a mixture of Independents and partisan forces.

That friends' partisanship has a considerable effect on students' own loyalties can be observed in Table 2.5. To interpret this table it is helpful to use as a standard of comparison the situation in which the respondents perceived their friends to be about equally split ("half and half"). Presumably the friends exerted little pull on these students. Note, incidentally, that these entries are very similar to the overall figures in Table 2.2. If every other column is compared to the relevant column of the "half and

[26]Referring to Table 2.4, one might reasonably assume that of the 63 percent defectors from Republican parents who voted Democratic, *at least* 43 percent would have defected anyway (since 43 percent defected even when the parent voted Republican). Thus voting behavior may have contributed to the defection of 20 percent of the children of these 151 parents. Making similar calculations for the other groups, we find the following figure for the net contribution of parental voting: $[.20\ (151) + .46\ (75) + .24\ (277) + .20\ (130)]/1766 = 157/1766 = .089$. This calculation is very liberal since it takes no account of defections prevented when voting reinforces parental partisanship.

TABLE 2.5
STUDENT PARTY IDENTIFICATION BY PARENT PARTY IDENTIFICATION, CONTROLLING FOR PARTISANSHIP OF STUDENTS' FRIENDS[a]

Students	Dem. Parents			Rep. Parents			Ind. Parents			Half & Half Parents		
	Dem.	Ind.	Rep.	Dem.	Ind.	Rep.	Dem.	Ind.	Rep.	Dem.	Ind.	Rep.
Dem.	75%	39%	18%	48%	25%	7%	24%	6%	6%	65%	28%	12%
Ind.	21	45	35	30	54	24	75	91	92	27	53	40
Rep.	4	16	47	22	21	69	2	4	2	8	20	48
Total	100%	100%	100%	100%	100%	100%	101%	101%	100%	100%	101%	100%
	(478)	(175)	(155)	(121)	(69)	(157)	(38)	(34)	(25)	(254)	(146)	(142)

[a]Includes students who said they were sure of their friends' partisanship and those who were unsure but "guessed." Separate analysis of the sure and unsure respondents revealed no major discrepancies.

half" portion of the table, it shows that the perceived friends' partisanship does exert a force over the partisan tendencies of students. Retention rates go up and defection rates go down when the friends' identification is consistent with parental partisanship. Just the opposite is true when a conflict exists. The force exerted by Independent friends appears to be the greatest, for vastly increased proportions of students emerge when friends are perceived as non-partisan. This may be due to the fact that few students perceived their friends as mostly Independents, since it was a volunteered response. Probably only those who felt relatively sure about their perceptions gave this answer.

Here, in contrast to the parents' voting behavior, we have a better way of estimating the net effects of the friends' partisanship on deviations from parental loyalties, and the results are enlightening. By assuming that the figures in the "half and half" portion of Table 2.5 represent the absence of friends' influence, we can estimate both the additional defection arising from conflict situations and the reduced defection resulting from reinforcement of parental loyalties. When this is done, the net impact of friends' loyalties is judged to be a nearly two percent *decrease* in overall defection.[27] Our results here thus underscore the twin points made in connection with parents' voting behavior. The overall effect of friends' partisanship is small, and it perhaps even contributes to less defection than would otherwise occur. This is due to the fact that these forces most often reinforce parental partisanship. However, when the forces do conflict, there is a considerable pull away from the partisan attitudes of parents.

Parental Homogeneity

The effects of parental agreement across a wide array of issues will be considered in Chapter 6. In addition, a detailed analysis of partisanship can be found elsewhere.[28] For present purposes, suffice it to say that the effect of parental homogeneity on student-parent similarity is definitely in the expected direction, but the correlation with homogeneous parents (.57) is not as much above the figure for the total population (.47) as might be anticipated. When parents are homogeneous,[29] one's predictive ability is not vastly increased over the predictive power gained by relying on data from a single parent. The explanation for this, while perhaps not

[27]The calculation involved is: $[-.10 \ (478) + .07 \ (175) + .01 \ (155) + .17 \ (121) - .02 \ (69) - .21 \ (157) + .42 \ (38) - .38 \ (34) + .46 \ (25)]/1794 = 33/1794 = .018.$

[28]M. Kent Jennings and Kenneth P. Langton, "Mothers versus Fathers: The Formation of Political Orientations among Young Americans," *Journal of Politics*, 31 (May 1969), pp. 329–58.

[29]Operationally, parents are considered homogeneous if the values for the mother and father fall along the main diagonal of a square matrix representing a cross-tabulation of mother and father values on a given variable. Otherwise they are heterogeneous. Pairs are eliminated if there is missing data for either parent.

obvious, is simple and involves us again with distributional matters. It is simply the case that with seven-tenths of the parents being homogeneous, one is most often dealing with a family in which the parents agree. Thus overall comparisons are largely made up of homogeneous cases, and measures of student-parent similarity based on the total sample or on the homogeneous portion differ by only a moderate amount. In any event, both the student-mother correlation (.40) and the student-father statistic (.35) are decidedly lower when the parents differ.

STUDENT-PARENT CANDIDATE PREFERENCES

Many of the seniors whom we interviewed were eligible to vote in the subsequent presidential election of 1968. By inquiring into student preferences in the election preceding the interviews, and by ascertaining parental voting behavior, something can be learned about the sources of incipient voters' candidate preferences. In particular, we are concerned with the similarity of student and parent candidate preferences and with the impact of partisanship on student preferences. The interplay of parental preferences and student partisanship will also be noted.

The correlation between student preferences and parental voting behavior is .59, indicating a rather high degree of correspondence between the parents' behavior and student voting intentions.[30] There are two chief reasons why this correlation is not even higher. One is again the matter of perceptions. On the basis of the students' perceptions of their parents' voting behavior, the correlation is raised to .68, so that students are somewhat more similar to how they *think* their parents voted. The second factor tending to reduce the overall correlation is that students, compared to parents, leaned in a Democratic direction. As a result, when the parent voted for Johnson, students followed suit almost all of the time (93 percent); but when the parent favored Goldwater, many fewer students followed this lead (64 percent).[31] Here, unlike the case of party identification, the differential pull of the Democrats lead to an overall edge for them in the aggregate distribution. Seventy-four percent of the students reportedly would have voted for Johnson, whereas 68 percent of the parents claimed to have done so.

The deviation of students from a Goldwater preference can be explained in part by the weaker partisan ties of the students. It has been

[30]Student-parent correlations are based on pairs in which the parent voted. However, use of parental preferences for the nonvoters barely affects the statistics. No attempt was made to determine which students would actually vote.

[31]Overall, 83 percent of the students preferred the candidate for whom their parent voted.

convincingly shown that the longer one identifies with a party, the stronger the ties to the party become.[32] A slight extension of this reasoning would lead one to expect that at the same expressed level of partisanship students are actually less tied to their party loyalties and can more readily express a preference for the expected winner. This is in fact what happens. Among all partisan and Independent groups (except for strong Democrats, where the difference is .5 percent), a higher percentage of students than parents "voted" for Johnson. In a Republican year, of course, we would expect students to swing in a Republican direction to a greater extent than parents.[33] In spite of this constant shift in favor of the Democratic candidate, the correlation between partisanship and voting preference is roughly the same for students (.45) and parents (.52). For both samples partisanship works the same way, sharply differentiating respondents according to their propensity to vote in one direction or the other.

One interesting implication of these findings is that the eighteen-year-old vote is likely to increase the amount of electoral swing, contributing disproportionately to the winning side, especially in landslide elections.[34] Another consequence might be to make it easier for a third party to pull voters away from the major parties. However, the eighteen-to twenty-year-old group is small enough compared to the rest of the electorate that the effects will be very small.

Significantly, student voting preferences among parts of the population are related to parents' votes in much the same way as party identification. One of the chief findings regarding partisanship was the relationship of family politicization to actual and perceived student-parent similarity. Those finds are reproduced almost exactly in the expressions of candidate preference. When the students' political interest is controlled as in the left side of Table 2.6, the actual student-parent correlation dips convincingly as interest decreases. The student- "perceived parent" correlation, however, is nearly constant, and the drop in the true figures is due to the increasingly poorer perceptions among the less interested. Also shown in the table is that the frequency of husband-wife political conversations has the same complex effect that it had on partisanship. The student-"perceived parent" correlation does decrease as conversations become less frequent, but the drop is much less than the decrease in the true correlation. This difference is a result, of course, of the less accurate perceptions among less politicized families.

[32]Campbell, et al., The American Voter, pp. 161–65.

[33]A similar finding is reported in Philip E. Converse, "Of Time and Partisan Stability," Comparative Political Studies, 2 (July 1969), pp. 139–71, at footnote 4.

[34]However, this did not happen in 1972, since young voters were slightly more in favor of McGovern than were older voters.

TABLE 2.6
LEVELS OF POLITICIZATION AND SIMILARITY OF STUDENT AND PARENT CANDIDATE PREFERENCES

Interest in Public Affairs	Student-parent correlation	Student-"perceived parent" correlation[a]	"Perceived parent"-parent correlation[b]	Husband-Wife Political Conversations	Student-parent correlation	Student-"perceived parent" correlation[a]	"Perceived parent"-parent correlation[b]
Low	.49 (240)	.70 (207)	.70 (198)	Not at all	.45 (240)	.59 (212)	.74 (196)
Medium	.56 (646)	.65 (569)	.83 (532)	Not very often	.54 (342)	.65 (298)	.77 (280)
High	.65 (626)	.70 (559)	.84 (535)	Pretty often	.59 (456)	.66 (394)	.82 (383)
				Very often	.72 (295)	.78 (273)	.86 (262)

[a] The correlation between the student's candidate preference and the perception of the parent's preference.
[b] The correlation between what the student perceives to be the parent's candidate preference and the parent's own reported preference.

From the analysis of party identification, we would also expect more or less deviation from parents' behavior depending on the degree of conflict in the student's environment. One obvious way in which conflict can arise is when the students' own partisanship tends in a direction opposite that of the parents' voting behavior. When this occurs, we would expect greater deviation from parental voting behavior than when student partisanship and parental voting are consistent. A test of this hypothesis bears out our reasoning. If one uses the Independent students as a baseline, it is apparent both that consistency increases student-parent similarity and that inconsistency decreases it. For example, only 16 percent of the Republican students deviated from a parental preference for Goldwater compared to 49 percent of the Independent students and 68 percent of the Democratic students. Similarly, barely three percent of the Democratic students deviated from a parental vote for Johnson, while 12 percent of the Independents and 26 percent of the Republican students did so. Along with the greater attraction for the students of Johnson over Goldwater, these figures show clearly the effects of consistency and conflict.

A second way in which conflict can develop for students is when the mother and father vote for different candidates. We have come to expect this sort of conflict to be infrequent, but when it occurs, to lower dramatically the degree of correspondence between adolescents and parents. In voting behavior the nature of the variable in a sense compels such a reduction in student-parent similarity. The variable we are working with is dichotomous, so that if parents acted differently, a student must agree completely with one parent and disagree with the other. Hence, unless one parent consistently has greater influence, both the student-mother and student-father correlations will be quite low. Also, the correlations with each parent will have the same value but different signs. That each parent does have some influence (positive or negative) over the student is indicated by the low value of the correlations—$+.09$ for students and their mothers and $-.09$ for students and fathers. In percentage terms, the students in these heterogeneous homes preferred Johnson less than students in homogeneous "Johnson families" but more than those in purely "Goldwater families." Where the parents were homogeneous, the student-parent correlation (.63) is about the same as for the sample as a whole.

In sum, students' candidate preferences are much like their parents'. Deviations from parental behavior occur for the same reasons that departures from the parents' partisan attitudes arise. These reasons are chiefly the poorer perceptions that accompany lower degrees of political interest, various kinds of environmental conflict, and the temporal advantage accruing to one party or the other in a particular year.

PARENTAL AWARENESS OF STUDENT PARTISANSHIP

An interesting and hitherto unconsidered aspect of socialization in the family is parental awareness of childrens' developing political orientations. Though much has been written about the role of the family in political socialization, there has been virtually no attempt to obtain a parent's-eye view of the process. Do parents know what their children's political views are? Or more basically, do they even know that their children are developing political ideas? Such questions have not been explored even though they may tell us a great deal about the amount of and type of family influence on pre-adult political attitudes.

These questions are very broad, of course, and consideration of their full breadth is well beyond the scope of the present analysis. We can, however, dip into a narrow aspect of the whole topic. The parents in our sample were asked about the partisanship of their high school senior. From this we can determine the extent to which parents report awareness of the partisan coloration of their children. This will allow us to infer the degree of manifest attempts at partisan socialization.[35]

A large minority of the parents cannot identify their children's partisan preferences. Altogether 37 percent of the parents were unable to locate their child along the partisan spectrum, even though the question was designed so that parents had to volunteer this response.[36] Parents expressed their lack of awareness in different terms. Twenty-six percent simply said that they did not know how the student felt, while another 11 percent said the student "hasn't decided yet."[37] The wording is suggestive. The "hasn't decided" response, if taken literally, suggests that parents know something about the student's feelings. They know either that the student has simply not thought about partisan politics enough to judge the parties or that he or she has consciously considered the merits of the parties but has been unable to arrive at any decision (including the decision that the parties are about the same). The "don't know" or DK response suggests a genuine lack of awareness on the part of the parent. Whatever partisan attitude, if any, the student has, the parent is ignorant of it.

Despite the plausibility of these interpretations, no distinction between "hasn't decided" and DK responses will be made below. Although

[35]A more extensive analysis of parents' reports, with a methodological emphasis, is found in Richard G. Niemi, *How Family Members Perceive Each Other* (New Haven: Yale University Press, 1974), Chapter 4.

[36]The question also included a preface to discourage the response that "he isn't old enough to worry about politics yet." The question was: "Although your (son) (daughter) isn't old enough to participate in politics much, do you think (he) (she) would consider (himself) (herself) a Republican, a Democrat, an Independent or what?"

[37]By their own reports, only one percent of the students are undecided about their loyalties. Less than one-half of one percent said they were uninterested in politics or apolitical.

further investigation is clearly warranted, with follow-up questions or interviewer probes to clarify parents' responses, we are not yet convinced that the phrasing of the answer implies different levels of parental awareness. On the one hand, it is possible that for some parents a DK response really indicates that the parent thinks the student has not made any partisan choice. On the other hand, some parents may use the "hasn't decided" response because it is less embarrassing than saying "I don't know." In any event, comparison of the relative frequency of the two responses in numerous subgroups of the population did not reveal any meaningful differences. The ratio of one response to the other is usually quite stable, and the rest of the time fluctuates in an inconsistent pattern.[38]

The relationships between a number of socio-political traits and the proportion of parents unable to identify their children's partisan feelings are given in Table 2.7. As expected, parents are most often unable to

TABLE 2.7

PROPORTION OF PARENTS WHO DO NOT KNOW THEIR
OFFSPRING'S PARTY IDENTIFICATION, WITHIN CONTROL CATEGORIES

Control Category	Proportion Don't Know[a]		Control Category	Proportion Don't Know	
Offspring's Party Identification			Interest in Public Affairs (Parent)		
Strong Dem.	34%	(359)	Very low	50%	(138)
Weak Dem.	38	(457)	Low	44	(251)
Ind. Dem.	37	(274)	Medium	37	(586)
Ind.	51	(242)	High	34	(936)
Ind. Rep.	45	(158)			
Weak Rep.	36	(258)			
Strong Rep.	18	(143)	Interest in Public Affairs (Student)		
Region			Very low	48%	(47)
Northeast	40%	(464)	Low	42	(267)
Midwest	38	(581)	Medium	38	(804)
South	38	(542)	High	35	(795)
West	36	(328)			
			Race		
			White	37%	(1717)
			Black	44	(199)

[a]Includes parents who responded "don't know" and "hasn't decided yet."

[38]In the remainder of the chapter "don't know" or "DK" responses refer to parents who said they do not know their children's partisan attitudes and those who said that the students had not made up their minds.

classify Independent students, but the pattern of DK's within categories of the students' party identification is less regular and not as strong as supposed. Parents label Independent Democrats just as often as weak Democrats, and both of those nearly as often as strong Democrats. On the Republican side the variations are monotonic and sharper, but even then over a third of the weak identifiers were not labelled by parents. The erratic pattern of DK's within party identification categories is partially due to the effects of other variables given in the table. Blacks, for example, who are labelled by parents less often than whites, tend to raise the proportion of DK's among strong Democratic identifiers but not among other students. Among white strong Democrats, the proportion of DK's drops to 31 percent. Parent and student political interest also contribute to the erratic pattern. In particular, it helps account for the small number of DK responses among parents of strong Republican identifiers. Strong Republicans are considerably more politicized than any other group, which makes their partisan attachments more salient. It ought to be observed, however, that a rather uneven pattern of DK's within party identification categories is maintained for all levels of political interest.

The level of political interest of family members is itself significantly related to the proportion of parents who do not know their children's party identification. Fully a third of the parents are unable to label their children when either the parent or student is highly interested, but this is much less than the 50 percent DK rate among the least interested respondents. It should also be noted that the frequency of student-parent political conversations and of husband-wife political conversations were also related to the proportion of DK responses. As the frequency of either type of conversation increased, the proportion of DK's decreased steadily. One other measure of parental involvement, the campaign activity index, was not monotonically related to the proportion of DK's, but it did show that parents who were very inactive were able to label their children's feelings much less often than parents who were more highly involved.

Of the other variables examined, none reveals the expected relationship to parents' claims of knowledge. There is a difference in the proportion of DK's between whites and blacks, for example, but the direction is mildly surprising. It might have been expected that black parents would say that their children were Democratic (as 96 percent of them are) even if they really did not know. The tendency to assume that students are Democrats might also have been expected to lower the proportion of DK's in the South, but regional differences are minimal. Almost no differences at all are observed among parent and student sex combinations. Parents are no less likely to know their daughters' than their sons' partisan feelings and mothers label their children as often as fathers. Finally, there are no meaningful differences in the proportion of DK responses for families of various sizes and for younger or older parents.

CONCLUSION

The findings just reported on parents' perceptions of students' partisanship offer an interesting and in some ways ironic conclusion to our analysis of party identification. As we have stressed so many times, partisanship is unlike other political stimuli in the degree to which it is a permanent, salient, generalized posture toward the political world. As such, students should and probably do know more about their parents' party ties than about most other aspects of parental political attitudes and behavior. Parents should and do know something about their children's partisanship, whereas it is likely that they know very little about their children's other political orientations. Partly owing to these perceptions, we should also expect the similarity of students and parents to be greater for partisanship than for most other political matters. And we know that this is true.

In spite of all this, the findings regarding parents' reports of their students' partisanship lead us to conclude, first of all, that the process of socialization into partisan orientations is often carried on at a nearly subconscious level. It is not much of an exaggeration to say that parents socialize their children despite themselves. Certainly the parents who do not know their children's party identification and those who think that their children have not yet made up their minds are not intentionally directing the development of their children's political ideas. If they were attempting to exercise deliberate influence, the children's current feelings would be the first information they would seek. For the two-thirds of the parents who do attribute a party identification to their sons or daughters, the possibility that they are consciously directing their children's learning cannot be ruled out entirely. However, this possibility can be discounted on other grounds. The fact that parents do not often accurately perceive their children's preferences suggests that they have a very shaky basis for attempting to influence them.[39] That parents have not always conveyed their own preferences to their children also suggests a lack of effort on their part. Among most parents the process of political socialization is not a pressing concern.

Secondly, and perhaps more surprisingly, we conclude that parents by and large do not care what their children's partisan orientations are.[40]

[39]Among parents who gave a partisan or Independent preference for the students, the correlation with the students' own reports of their party identification was .57.

[40]This is similar to the conclusion reached by Almond and Verba, *The Civic Culture*, p. 135, that "overwhelming majorities of the respondents of both parties [in the United States but not in other countries] expressed indifference regarding the partisan affiliations of the future mates of their children."

This seems to follow directly from the first conclusion. If their children's partisan attitudes were important to parents, they would make a greater attempt to influence their development in desired directions. But if parents are mostly indifferent to the party loyalties of their children there is no particular reason for them to be even aware of what they think. It might be argued that parents *seem* unconcerned because they assume that children simply follow in parents' footsteps. There is some validity in this argument since parents did bias their views of students attitudes toward their own feelings. But the proportion of DK's and the extent of the bias hardly support the conclusion that parents assume children accept their views unquestioningly. Hence, many parents must be relatively indifferent to the partisan orientations of their children.

We hasten to add that the lack of deliberate efforts to direct the socialization of youths in partisan directions does not mean that such efforts are lacking on all political and social matters. Parents are concerned about their children's attitudes regarding basic societal rules, such as obeying the law or being loyal to one's country. At times there are also less consensual topics on which parents try to influence children's views. One thinks, for example, of civil rights, which for some is a moral or religious as well as a social concern. When contemporary events bring such an emotionally charged issue to the fore, parents may feel called upon to guide their children's views as much as possible.

An additional qualification of the present conclusion is that parents' lack of concern about children's partisan attitudes, as well as political attitudes more generally, is not unlimited. Parents may be totally indifferent about their children's political views—so long as they do not become_____(Socialists, Communists, John Birchers, Ku Klux Klansmen, SDSers, pacifists, etc.). The blank is filled in variously by different people. For some the bounds of political acceptibility may be very narrow and for others rather wide. But for most parents we suggest that there are limits between which they attempt to guide their children. The limits may be fuzzy, of course, and they certainly change over periods of history. Moreover, in many and perhaps most cases, parents have to provide little explicit direction to guide their children along the desired paths; the efforts of other socialization agencies and the example of parents' own attitudes and actions are a sufficient force. Nevertheless, parents do try to insure that their children develop within certain bounds.

Within these bounds, however, the development of children's partisanship is frequently a laissez-faire operation. That the correspondence between students' and parents' partisanship is as high as it is under these conditions attests to the strength of family socialization in this area of pre-adult political development.

CHAPTER THREE

Opinions on Public Policy Issues

Iᴛ ᴍɪɢʜᴛ ʙᴇ argued that specific public issues are too transitory to warrant a prominent place in the study of political socialization. As Hyman noted over a decade ago, the "mere socialization of the child into a particular attitude or even a cluster of attitudes is bound to be an inadequate mechanism to provide the individual with a fully prepared view to meet future political issues in adult life. The world is ever changing and the specific events that will emerge in the political arena in future decades cannot all be anticipated. The individual would thus have to face some problems *de novo*."[1]

While recognizing this limitation on the analysis of current policy questions, we should not ignore their role in the process of political socialization. Perhaps the chief reason, Hyman's generalization notwithstanding, is that some issues are extremely long-lived. A current example is the racial problem, which has already been manifest for decades and shows no signs of an early retreat. Particular aspects of the problem, e.g., busing to achieve school integration, may ebb and tide, but the underlying problem survives for a long time. What this means, of course, is that before such an issue is resolved, those who were pre-adults when the issue first arose will form a moderate to large segment of the adult pool of opinions and votes. Indeed, the attitudes taken by the incoming generation may be a clue as to how long the controversy will last as well as what the resolution is likely to be.

A second point is that the attitudes of the young may provide an indication of the likelihood and the direction of change along major policy dimensions. Socialization studies have often been criticized for emphasizing continuities rather than discontinuities. Analysis of the differences between parents' and children's views of current policies, and projection of these differences to some future time, can help us break out of excessive concern for the preservation of political views and facilitate the prediction of future trends.

[1]Herbert Hyman, *Political Socialization* (Glencoe: Free Press, 1959), pp. 74–75. An interesting test of whether basic orientations learned early in life help determine future issue positions is undertaken by Donald D. Searing, Joel J. Schwartz, and Alden E. Lind, "The Structuring Principle: Political Socialization and Belief Systems," *American Political Science Review*, 67 (June 1973), pp. 415–32.

Third, the impact of issues on shaping wider political orientations should be stressed. The Vietnam war is a case in point. There seems little doubt that the debate which has swirled about this conflict has had a tremendous impact on young people's views of the political system in general. Consideration of specific public policy issues also provides another vantage point from which to view parent-to-child transmission of political values. The extent to which our findings about intergenerational transmission can be generalized depends in part on the number and breadth of orientations that we consider. Thus for the sake of completeness alone we want to consider current issues. In addition, the fate of particular controversies and the prospects for change in societal views are partly dependent on how these attitudes are formed.

In this chapter, then, our focus will be on several contemporary public policy issues. While no one set of issues is representative of all others, those included cover various types of concerns—for example, abstract versus concrete, domestic versus foreign or international relations, highly salient and less visible, and very contentious as well as noncontroversial matters. This diversity lends a welcome degree of generality to our findings.

STUDENT AND PARENT OPINIONS

Comparison of student and parent opinions requires that each generation have reasonably well-formed attitudes on specific policy items. From previous work we know that a small but noteworthy portion of adults admit to being uninterested in any given issue.[2] In our own case, from five to 14 percent of the parents said they were not interested enough to have an opinion about prayers in public schools, the federal role in school integration, and whether the U.S. should stay in the United Nations.[3]

[2] Philip E. Converse, "The Nature of Belief Systems in Mass Publics," in David E. Apter (ed.), *Ideology and Discontent* (New York: Free Press, 1964).

[3] The exact questions are:

(1) Some people think it is all right for the public schools to start each day with a prayer. Others feel that religion does not belong in the schools but should be taken care of by the family and the church. [Here a screening question was inserted and those who were interested were asked the following.] Which do you think—schools should be allowed to start each day with a prayer or religion does not belong in the schools?

(2) Some people say that the government in Washington should see to it that white and Negro children are allowed to go to the same schools. Others claim that this is not the government's business. [Screening question.] Do you think that the government in Washington should see to it that white and Negro children go to the same schools or stay out of this area as it is none of its business?

(3) Some people say that the United States should get out of the United Nations because it's not doing us or the world any good. Others claim that we should stay in the United Nations because it is helpful to us and the world in general. [Screening question.] What do you think—should we stay in because it's helpful or get out because it's not helpful?

The screening question reads: Have you been interested enough in this to favor one side over the other?

TABLE 3.1
STUDENT AND PARENT OPINIONS ON PUBLIC POLICY ISSUES

Issue	In Favor of (Agree)	Depends	Opposed to (Disagree)	Total[a]	
Prayers in public schools					
Students	67%	4	29	100%	(1786)
Parents	80%	5	16	101%	(1785)
Federal role in school integration					
Students	71%	10	20	101%	(1907)
Parents	59%	13	28	100%	(1748)
Stay in United Nations[b]					
Students	87%	9	4	100%	(1712)
Parents	86%	9	5	100%	(1565)
Allow speeches against churches					
Students	86%	*	14	100%	(2058)
Parents	72%	*	27	99%	(1909)
Elected Communist can hold office					
Students	36%	1	63	100%	(2054)
Parents	28%	*	71	99*	(1884)
American government is best for all[c]					
Students	54%	*	46	100%	(2055)
	*Less than ½ of 1 percent				

[a]Based on those interested enough to have an opinion (for the first three items).

[b]"In favor of" this item means that we should stay in the United Nations even if "things didn't go our way." Those saying "stay in unless things go against us" are in the "depends" category.

[c]This item was asked of students only.

Among the students, the comparable figures ranged from six to 16 percent. In this respect, then, the two generations are very similar, with students only a little less likely to have formed an opinion.

Differences begin to emerge, however, when we view the distribution of opinions for these and other issues. Of the six items shown in Table 3.1,[4] one shows near unanimity and, of course, high agreement across parent and student samples. Even with the proviso that things might not go our way, less than 15 percent of either sample approved withdrawal from the United Nations. This attitude, of course, is not inflexible, and if things really did go against U.S. interests, greater support for withdrawal

[4]The additional items called for agreement or disagreement with the following statements: "If a person wanted to make a speech in this community against churches and religion, he should be allowed to speak." "If a Communist were legally elected to some public office around here, the people should allow him to take office." "The American system of government is one that all nations should have."

would undoubtedly develop. But under normal or even moderately bad circumstances, support for continued membership will remain very high.

For a second item no parent comparison is available. However, the student distribution alone suggests that many seniors emerge from their high school classrooms with an exaggerated picture of the virtues of the American style of government. Responsibility for this view can no doubt be laid on frequent public rhetoric as well as the ethnocentric tendencies running through so many social studies textbooks.[5] This aspect of citizenship training has long been observed, but it is very persistent and, to judge by the seniors, still rather effective.

Four of the questions, then, show some degree of controversy and important student-parent differences. Three of these deal directly or indirectly with matters of civil liberties. In all three the students take a more libertarian stance than their parents. The change is particularly impressive for the question about speeches against churches and religion, for the students are approaching the level of consensus found for abstract generalizations about democracy.[6] Conversely, widespread agreement among the older generation on the school prayers issue did not prevent a significant shift in attitude among the younger population.

It might be argued the two issues just cited are somewhat ambiguous in that each contains two obvious components. On the one hand there is the civil liberties concern with protection of the rights of minority viewpoints. On the other hand, each could be viewed simply from the standpoint of being pro- or anti-religion. Since the younger generation tends to be less religious, this factor alone could account for the student-parent discrepancy. To deal with this possibility we used evaluations of the Bible as a control for attitude toward religion in the schools. In each of the four control categories, for both questions, students still gave the more libertarian response more often than parents (see note 14).

The evidence is thus persuasive that the seniors are considerably more libertarian in outlook than are their parents. Less apparent, however, is whether this difference is a function of generational or life cycle processes. It may be that the newer generation will persist in this edge, especially on the school prayer question, which has been raised to the level of a constitutional question. Or it may be that when thrust into the adult world of politics, these youthful predilections will erode. This is espe-

[5]C. Benjamin Cox and Byron G. Massialas, *Social Studies in the United States* (New York: Harcourt, Brace and World, 1967), pp. 178–85.

[6]James W. Prothro and Charles M. Grigg, "Fundamental Principles of Democracy: Bases of Agreement and Disagreement," *Journal of Politics*, 22 (May 1960), pp. 276–94. For similar evidence from elementary schoolchildren and an analysis of the relationship between commitment to principles and specific applications, see Gail L. Zellman and David O. Sears, "Childhood Origins of Tolerance for Dissent," *Journal of Social Issues*, 27 (No. 2, 1971), pp. 109–36.

cially likely if the libertarian rhetoric has been learned by rote in school, without the underlying rationales having been internalized.[7]

The students are also more willing to endorse a vigorous federal role in enforcing school integration. The item about schools is the only question in both the student and parent interviews that asked directly about civil rights, but other evidence also supports the more favorable view by students of black needs and demands. In free-answer material about America's negative assets (Chapter 5), students relatively more often gave a pro-black response. Similarly, students more frequently than parents favorably associate the Democratic party with advancements by black Americans (Chapter 4). All of these differences are most certainly generational in character, and are part of the overall reevaluation of the status of blacks that was well underway by the mid sixties.

The difference in proportions of the two samples favoring federally enforced integration is not large. But we should point out that this is one of the few variables for which we feel confident that a genuine generational shift has occurred. As we scan the orientations that we have already considered, as well as those in the ensuing chapters, we find remarkable aggregate similarity between parents and students, or there is presumptive evidence that the observed differences are at least partly due to life cycle processes. Viewed in this light the shift in support for a strong federal hand in integration is more significant. Moreover, comparison with data from a national cross-section sample in 1964 makes the shift appear considerably larger. The same question was asked in the election survey conducted by SRC in late 1964. In that sample some 48 percent of the adults favored federal pressure for integrating the schools. This overall change from about half of the adults to seven-tenths of the youths —over a fifth of the total population—is highly significant and, of course, very encouraging to those supporting greater governmental pressure.[8]

In addition to the student-parent discrepancies, there is considerable divergence of opinions within each sample. For each issue we have examined the singular and joint effects of a cluster of standard and special variables. Overall the most consistent predictors are the old favorites, political interest and education. However, even these two variables are

[7]Comparison between ours and Stouffer's results certainly shows that a large-scale shift in approval of civil rights for anti-religious speeches occurred between 1954 and 1965. Stouffer found only 37 percent approval of the right of a person to make a speech in the community against churches and religion. However, it is not clear whether this difference is part of a long-term trend or due to the particular climate of the early 1950's. See Samuel A. Stouffer, *Communism, Conformity, and Civil Liberties* (Garden City, N.Y.: Doubleday, 1955), p. 33.

[8]The youth sample, by design, excludes a disproportionate number of lower status individuals in the same age cohort as the seniors. However, since status, here measured by the education of the head of the household, is unrelated to responses to the integration question for both the parent or youth samples, the nature of the youth sample would not seem to bias this comparison.

TABLE 3.2

"SUPERPATRIOTISM" RELATED TO COSMOPOLITANISM SCORES
AND EDUCATION OF HEAD OF HOUSEHOLD

| Cosmopolitanism | Elementary | | Education of Head of Household | | | | College | |
			Some High School		High School Graduate			
Least 1	93%[a]	(22)	73%	(11)	53%	(11)	84%[b]	(18)
2	96	(28)	65	(13)	48	(13)		
3	79	(28)	43	(10)	72	(29)	67	(14)
4	76	(96)	73	(49)	56	(83)	39	(60)
5	70	(88)	58	(58)	50	(95)	39	(60)
6	65	(99)	54	(122)	46	(176)	39	(167)
Most 7	64	(72)	60	(60)	40	(95)	30	(128)

[a]Entries are the percentage agreeing that all nations should have the American form of government.
[b]The two lowest categories are combined because of small N's.

unrelated to certain of the specific issues, and several other factors such as region and religion have a particularly potent effect on some of the attitudes. Hence the issues are discussed one at a time, except for the two civil liberties items which are taken up together.

"Superpatriotism" shows some of the liveliest variation of all the opinions discussed. Political interest and education of the parents have a rather marked negative effect on agreement that all nations should have the American form of government—with correlations of $-.14$ and $-.23$, respectively. As one would expect, seniors with little political interest and having parents with an impoverished educational background are much more inclined to take this hyperbolic position. About as strong as these two factors is the relationship between superpatriotism and cosmopolitanism $(-.17)$.[9] Individuals with narrow, parochial outlooks strongly concur that everyone else should adopt our system, while those with a broader perspective apparently recognize some of the difficulties inherent in so sweeping a judgment.

The impact of political interest or education and cosmopolitanism are also cumulative; and the combined effects of these variables isolate groups of seniors with widely differing viewpoints. Shown in Table 3.2 are the proportions taking a superpatriotic position when education and cosmopolitanism are controlled. There are few deviations from a perfect pattern despite the small number of cases in some cells, and the effects of each variable stand out clearly. So strong is the joint contribution of these variables that there is nearly unanimous agreement at one extreme and

[9]Cosmopolitanism, or localism–cosmopolitanism, will be used throughout the book. It is measured by "unfolding" rank-orders of interest in international, state, and local affairs. See M. Kent Jennings, "Pre-Adult Orientations to Multiple Systems of Government," *Midwest Journal of Political Science*, 11 (August 1967), pp. 291–317.

only 30 percent concurrence at the other. To the extent that this attitude is promoted by elementary and high school courses, the effect of the curriculum is sharply mediated by characteristics of the students and their families.

When we turn to the civil liberties items we find, first of all, that parental education is a good predictor of these attitudes. This is not surprising, since it is a repetition of the findings for earlier years by Stouffer and by Prothro and Grigg.[10] The relationship is stronger in the adult population, although in the case of speeches against religion this is an artifact of the near-consensus among the students. Interestingly, political concern is a partial surrogate for education with respect to these questions. But for both issues, for each of the samples, the correlation of opinion with interest is smaller than the statistic involving education. Nor are the effects of the two predictors cumulative. Thus, while community leaders in the Stouffer study scored higher on tolerance measures even with education controlled,[11] mere interest in politics does not seem adequate to heighten sensitivity to the rights of others.

Additional factors also influence civil liberties attitudes. Unlike Stouffer's finding of the mid fifties, region plays no role in the distribution of such feelings.[12] Religion, however, does affect the responses to these questions. Jews much more often than others take a civil libertarian position.[13] The only instance in which this does not occur is among students on the question of speeches against churches and religion. It should be recalled, however, that students' responses to this item were so onesided that greater than average agreement is unlikely because of error if nothing else. Moreover, where differences do occur, they persist given a control for education.

The more libertarian attitude taken by Jews has little effect on the overall population because of the small size of the Jewish minority. In contrast, religious fundamentalism has smaller individual effects but has a greater overall impact on questions involving religious freedom.[14] Fun-

[10]Stouffer, *Communism, Conformity, and Civil Liberties*, p. 90; Prothro and Grigg, "Fundamental Principles of Democracy," p. 285.

[11]Stouffer, *Communism, Conformity, and Civil Liberties*, pp. 90, 104. McClosky shows that political activists are more tolerant than the general public, but no control is imposed for education. See Herbert McClosky, "Consensus and Ideology in American Politics," *American Political Science Review*, 58 (June 1964), pp. 361–82.

[12]Stouffer, *Communism, Conformity, and Civil Liberties*, Chapter 5.

[13]This was also found by Stouffer, *Ibid.*, p. 143.

[14]Fundamentalism was measured by asking respondents about the Bible as follows: "Here are four statements about the Bible (Interviewer hands card to Inverviewee) and I'd like you to tell me which is closest to your own view. The statements are:
1. The Bible is God's Word and all it says is true.
2. The Bible was written by men inspired by God but it contains some human errors.
3. The Bible is a good book because it was written by wise men but God had nothing to do with it.
4. The Bible was written by men who lived so long ago that it is worth very little today."

damentalism, measured by attitude toward the Bible, is negatively related to approval of speeches against churches and religion. This is true of both samples although, as with education, the two are more closely related in the parent data. For both sets of respondents, education and (absence of) fundamentalist religious beliefs reinforce each other. Thus the least approval of anti-religious speeches comes from individuals with a strong Biblical faith and relatively little education for themselves or their parents. The lop-sided character of the student responses can be seen from that fact that in this extreme group, 79 percent of the seniors still give verbal support to this particular use of free speech. Nonetheless, agreement with this position increases as parental education rises and Biblical faith deteriorates, with the result that every one of the 46 seniors at the other extreme supports free speech against churches.[15] At the adult level the contrast is sharper; at the one extreme little more than half (55 percent) of the parents lend their acceptance to anti-religious speeches, while on the other end, support is very high (93 percent).

The school prayer issue is unlike the topics we have taken up so far. The desire for prayers in schools is not an extreme position that one abandons as soon as the complexities of the situation are explained or when one understands the difficulties of enforcing such a position. And while it involves a civil liberties question, it evokes more feeling than does the question of speeches against churches. Thus it would be surprising if it were not related to characteristics of the students and their parents in different ways than the previous issues.

The first such observation is that education and political interest are only minimally related to attitudes on the school prayer issue. In their place, religion and region occupy the position of good predictors. The religious differences are much like those noted for the free speech item. First, Jews are strikingly different from the remainder of the population. Whereas high proportions of Protestant (73 percent) and Catholic (61 percent) students favor school prayers, less than a third (31 percent) of the Jews feel this way. All of the percentages are inflated in the parent sample, but Protestants (83 percent) and Catholics (80 percent) are still much more inclined to accept prayers than are Jews (47 percent).

Secondly, the stronger one's religious fundamentalism, the more likely one is to support prayers in the schools. But the nature of this relationship is that of a step-function. This can be seen clearly in the percentages table on the following page. As one moves from the first to the second category, support for school prayers tapers off, but not by much. Similarly, between the third and the tiny fourth group there is but a small shift. In the middle, however, there is a considerable drop in the number backing

[15]This figure is based on seniors with college-educated parents and who endorse either of the two least reverent statements about the Bible.

Interpretation of the Bible	Percentages in Favor of School Prayers			
	Students		Parents	
God's Word	73%	(807)	85%	(961)
Some human error	65	(847)	77	(700)
Not inspired by God	20	(64)	54	(72)
Irrelevant today	15	(13)	49	(12)

prayers in schools. This gap is particularly large in the student sample, a fact which will be commented on more extensively below.

Regional differences on attitudinal questions are seldom as impressive as those found here. Oftentimes regional variations are small and/or limited to South-non-South breaks, and can sometimes be traced to attributes derivative of the region's political make-up. In contrast, consider the proportions of students that favor school prayers in each of the four major regions of the U.S.: South, 86 percent; Northeast, 68 percent; Midwest, 62 percent; West, 38 percent. The Northeast and Midwest are near the proportion for the population as a whole and do not differ much from each other (although the Midwest is consistently lower for parents as well and when controls are imposed—see below). The South and West, on the other hand, stand apart as the extremes of support for and opposition to prayers in schools. Differences among the parents are smaller, but the same ordering obtains: South, 89 percent; Northeast, 84 percent; Midwest, 78 percent; West, 60 percent.

Importantly, the extremes observed here are precisely those found by Stouffer for attitudes toward civil liberties. In his study the South was easily the most prone to suppress nonconforming behavior and opinions while the West was most supportive of the freedom and rights of others. The Northeast and Midwest were in between, although their ordering was the reverse of that found here.[16] The underlying causes of Stouffer's and our regional variation may be much the same. In the South, issues like school prayers may be more often viewed in terms of the values involved, be it religion, segregation, the American or Southern way of life, and so on. A threat to these cherished values should be opposed even if individual rights are sometimes forfeited in the process. In the West, and to a lesser extent in the other two regions, the same issues are more often viewed as matters of individual rights and privileges. Hence, if some people object to prayers in public schools, they should not be made to engage in them; the matter of religious values does not enter as clearly into this calculation. Thus, although we have argued that this issue is not solely one of civil liberties, it may be so viewed by a larger proportion of the Western population.

[16]Stouffer, *Communism, Conformity, and Civil Liberties*, Chapter 5.

If this explanation is correct, it should at least be the case that regional differences remain when religious variation is controlled. There are two such tests for the persistence of regional effects. In the first one we divide the samples according to religious identification and region. The following figures for the student sample show that each variable has a residual impact on attitudes toward school prayers when controlling for the other one:[17]

Percentages in Favor of School Prayers

Region	Protestant		Catholic		Jewish	
South	89%	(499)	78%	(51)	54%	(15)
Northeast	76	(200)	69	(167)	32	(47)
Midwest	66	(376)	59	(116)	0*	(13)
West	35	(147)	43	(112)		

*The Midwest and West are combined because of small N's.

It is particularly clear that Jews hold distinctive attitudes from Protestants and Catholics and, more to the point, that the earlier regional differences are maintained within each group of co-religionists. The figures for the parent sample yield rather similar results, although with the overall favoritism of parents toward school prayers, Protestants and Catholics from the South and Northeast differ by very little, showing about 90 percent support in each case.

The second test for the persistence of regional variation is made by controlling for attitude toward the Bible. Upon doing so we continue to find striking effects of both region and religious attitude among both adults and youths. Even though the number of cases in the cells showing little confidence in the Bible is now quite small, the results are remarkably consistent. To some extent, then, our explanation of regional differences receives added support. At the very least the analysis indicates that region, religious identification, and fundamentalism all contribute greatly to both student and parent feelings about the propriety of student prayers.

The remaining two orientations can be dealt with summarily since the group variations are small, or large but exactly as expected. On the matter of school integration, for example, black students (90 percent) and parents (78 percent) are more favorable than their white counterparts (68 percent and 57 percent, respectively). Equally pedestrian is the observation that Southern whites (53 percent among students and 40 percent among parents) are less in favor of this activity than are whites outside the South (77

[17]"Protestant" includes a fairly wide range of denominations which differ significantly from one another. The control for region captures some of this variation, although additional variation is still found among specific groups.

percent and 67 percent). Beyond these obvious differences, however, no meaningful patterns were apparent. Even educational background does not discriminate between those on opposing sides of this issue.

On the UN question the picture is one of widespread support in nearly all parts of the population. It was noted earlier that overall political interest was a good predictor of concern about this particular issue; but among those with some feeling about the issue, general political interest did not differentiate pro and con attitudes. Cosmopolitanism does make some difference, with locally oriented students and parents slightly less favorable toward the UN. At times when support for the international body was less one-sided, this geo-political orientation was probably a powerful determinant of one's position. At the present time, however, upwards of 80 percent of even the localists would not advocate withdrawal from the international body.

Patterning of Intergenerational Change

A review of the material for all of the policy questions reveals that student and parent patterns are mostly the same. Moreover, the correlations that we have observed are not consistently higher for either generation. Nevertheless, there are some intergenerational changes within segments of the population that are worthy of note. These changes are of two kinds. The first type occurs when the opinions of students as a whole are more one-sided than parents'. A good illustration of what happens is provided by the proportions supporting freedom for speeches against churches and religion. We noted in Table 3.1 that an aggregate shift of 14 percent occurred between responses of the two samples. But the figures in Table 3.3 show that this change was far from uniform throughout the population. In highly educated families, in which the parents already strongly supported this use of free speech, little generational change is apparent. The reasons, of course, are not hard to come by. Given the level of parental support, the student proportion could have risen by a maximum of but 14 percent. With only the assumption that some error

TABLE 3.3

PARENT AND STUDENT SUPPORT FOR FREEDOM OF SPEECHES AGAINST CHURCHES AND RELIGION, BY EDUCATIONAL LEVEL

Education of Head of Household	Parents		Students		Change
Elementary	56%	(477)	82%	(481)	+26%
Some high school	71	(366)	85	(367)	+14
High school graduate	75	(559)	87	(563)	+12
College	86	(501)	92	(502)	+6

finds its way into these data, the maximum change is unlikely to occur. Then too, the students "going against the grain" of responses for their parents' educational level are likely to be highly resistant to pressures in the direction of the norm. Thus a low rate of change is to be expected. At the opposite extreme, among those least educated and correspondingly least inclined to grant this instance of free speech, the change amounted to a quarter of the student total. Parents with a high school education are in between initially, and their children change at rates between the extremes. The pattern we observe here is repeated for the same issue when controlling for political interest and for the interpretation of the Bible. That is, change between parent and student generations varied inversely with the degree to which parents' opinions were one-sided.

This type of intergenerational change is significant for at least two reasons. First of all we see graphically how a characteristic can be a good predictor at one time or in one generation but a less adequate predictor in other circumstances. The variable rates of change have the effect of reducing the differences between segments of the younger generation. In the example in Table 3.3, a 30 percent difference between the extreme groups of parents is reduced by two-thirds among the students. As a result of this shift there is a substantial reduction in the relationship between the predictor and dependent variable—in the example, from .22 among the parents to .09 for the students.

A second point is that the aggregate parent-student change reveals only part of the story about changes in groups within the population. Thus what appears to be a "moderate" generational difference may in fact be anything from a barely noticeable shift to a huge gulf, depending on what part of the population one considers. In the present example there is only a slight difference of opinion between well-educated parents and their offspring; among the least educated the divergence grows to the point that we might interpret it as a "generation gap." If this same pattern were to occur for multiple attitudes, we would expect a serious intergenerational rift—but concentrated in certain parts of the population.

In circumstances such as these, a parallel situation at the individual level probably accompanies the aggregate pattern. That is, some types of parents will agree with their own children more often than will others. Here, for example, highly educated parents and their children overwhelmingly share the same opinion (81 percent of the time). Among the parents reaching high school this figure drops to 68 percent, and it goes even lower among those with an elementary education (51 percent).[18]

[18]Note that these percentages depend heavily on the distribution of the adult sample (which is partly the point); one cannot infer from these figures that the parent-student correlation decreases with each drop in the educational level. Indeed the parent-student correlations are similar in this example for all four education levels.

This individual pattern, too, is suggestive of greater conflict in selected portions of the population.

On the basis of the kind of intergenerational change that we have been discussing, deviant cases may be especially telling. One such case is found in black and white attitudes on the school integration question. We have previously observed that black parents favor enforced integration more than whites (78 percent versus 57 percent); the figures in Table 3.1 also recorded the 12 percent increase between adults and students. If the pattern for the free speech issue characterized the integration question, the generational difference should be greater for whites than for blacks. In fact, the shift is virtually the same for both groups—11 percent for the former and 12 percent for the latter. Thus even though the distribution of attitudes was more skewed among the black parents, the change in attitudes between generations kept pace with that among whites. Unlike the previous case, then, there was no reduction in group differences in the younger generation. The only alteration was that black students were highly unified in support of integrated schools (90 percent) while whites were still divided (67 percent in favor).

The second major type of intergenerational change is in some ways just the opposite of that considered so far. In this case the *parents'* responses are more one-sided, which means that students as a whole shifted *away from* the position taken by a majority of the adults. Figures already provided give us two examples of how this change altered parent-student comparisons among population groupings. In the first case we can compare the proportions of students and parents favoring school prayers among those offering varying interpretations of the Bible (see p. 71). For the first two groups, in which parents are more united in favor of school prayers, there is a decrease of 12 percent in the corresponding groups of students. In the two groups which find parents already divided, this intergenerational change is much larger (34 percent). These changes are step-like rather than linear, but they still suggest a much sharper generational cleavage among groups already divided at the adult level (and in this respect are similar to the previous case). Unlike the earlier example, however, the effect here is to *heighten* the contrast between groups within the youth generation. Whereas parents who were poles apart in their Biblical views differed by some 36 percent on the school prayer matter, comparable students differed by about 58 percent.

The control categories based on the Biblical authenticity question involve a subtle shift from the prior example in which education was the control. Namely, students and their parents are each grouped according to their own responses, which may differ; hence the respondents in the "God's Word" category are not all student-parent pairs.[19] However, in a second comparison using the school prayer issue, we again have mostly student-parent pairs.[20] In this case (see p. 72) we found parents most extreme in the South and, indeed, there was a change of only three percent between the two generations. Next in line were the Northeast and Midwest, in which the distributions were not too different from one another. In both of these areas the change amounted to 16 percent. Adults in the Western states showed the least consensus about the school prayer issue. Correspondingly, the intergenerational change was the greatest (22 percent). Since we are dealing with student-parent pairs, we can also look at individual pairs as we did in the first example. As expected, the proportion of students and parents who agree is highest in the South (80 percent), where the aggregate change was the least. In the next two regions, agreement rates follow the bias of the parental responses, and are 72 percent and 64 percent in the Northeast and Midwest, respectively. Finally, the agreement level in the West drops to 50 percent.

The explanation of this second major pattern of change probably lies in the type of contacts made by individuals in each control group. Although considerable investigation would be necessary to substantiate this hypothesis, it seems likely that students, say, in the South would encounter in their homes, schools, and circles of friends and acquaintances relatively more individuals in favor of school prayers. The position taken by most parents would thus be reinforced by day-to-day contacts. In areas where the parent generation is closely divided on the question, students would much more often encounter the opposing view. In the course of repeated exposure, conversion to that viewpoint is a more likely prospect.

In any case the two patterns that we have observed illustrate an important point about student-parent differences. Both types of change result in a greater parent-student discrepancy in some parts of the population than in others, and differences between student groups are considerably larger or smaller than corresponding differences among parents. The effects are also carried over to student-parent pairs as we have seen. Parents and their children may have a considerably greater or lesser likelihood of agreeing with each other if they belong to some groups than to others. Put more dramatically, the location and extent of the generation gap cannot be judged from overall figures alone.[21]

[19]A similar case involves the proportions of students and parents in favor of seating a duly elected Communist. When a control is made for political interest, change increases as the division among parents rises.

[20]Because of a few boarding schools in the sample, a small percentage of students and parents currently resided in different regions.

[21]This theme is carried forward in Chapter 11, where we undertake a more extensive analysis of parent-student similarities and differences. For evidence along these lines using more recent soundings, see Daniel Yankelovich, Inc., *Generations Apart* (New York: Columbia Broadcasting System, 1969).

STUDENT-PARENT SIMILARITY

Of the five policy issues for which we have responses from both samples, two stand out as likely candidates for strong currents of influence from parents to children. The questions on prayers in schools and on federally enforced school integration involve visible population groupings and are topics of more than usual prominence at both the national and local levels. Moreover, they are especially relevant here given that the populations under consideration have a direct interest in the schools. Thus we can expect that parents' opinions are themselves more stable on these issues than on less salient ones, and that children are more sensitive than usual to parental viewpoints. We should find, then, at least a moderately high degree of similarity between parents and students on these items.

The correlations between parent and student opinions are given on the left side of Table 3.4. Viewed in context with other coefficients that we have generated (see especially Chapter 6), these correlations substantiate the considerable prominence of these topics for the seniors and their parents. Many of the other correlations—including those for more global concepts such as political trust and cosmopolitanism and for specific behaviors such as media usage—are well below the figures for these two school-related measures.[22] By the same token, however, parent-student similarity on these issues is well below that found for party identification. In addition, if such salient issues produce correlations of this magnitude, it is likely that more remote and abstract matters result in considerably lower degrees of correspondence.

The latter point is well illustrated by the correlations for the second pair of issues. The right side of Table 3.4 gives the coefficients for the civil liberties items. In this case the similarity between parents and their offspring is very low. These issues carry neither the immediacy nor the concreteness of the school prayer and school integration questions. As such, we would expect parental responses to evidence less stability and clarity, so that there is no firm position for the student to identify.[23] Nor are these subjects likely to be the basis of dinner-table conversations. Hence, what feelings the parents do have tend not to be communicated to children in the family. Finally, we have noted that adult attitudes on these issues cannot be readily predicted from a knowledge of their more

[22]Note that on the prayer issue students are more often like parents who are *in favor of* school prayers. Despite this, there is a decline in the proportion of students compared to parents favoring school prayers. This is similar to the situation observed in Chapter 2 regarding defections from Democratic and Republican parents, and it can be explained on the same basis.

[23]When speaking of response instability we are influenced, of course, by Converse's analysis in "The Nature of Belief Systems in Mass Publics."

TABLE 3.4

RELATIONSHIP BETWEEN STUDENT AND PARENT OPINIONS ON FOUR POLICY ISSUES

Students	Federal Role in School Integration[a] Parents			Prayers in Public Schools[a] Parents			Elected Communist Can Hold Office Parents			Allow Speeches against Churches Parents		
	Pro	Depends	Con	Pro	Depends	Con	Pro	Depends[b]	Con	Pro	Depends[b]	Con
Pro	83%	64%	45%	74%	62%	34%	45%	—	32%	88%	—	82%
Depends	7	17	14	3	8	7	1	—	0	0	—	0
Con	10	18	41	23	30	59	53	—	67	12	—	18
Total	100%	99%	100%	100%	100%	100%	99%	—	99%	100%	—	100%
	(961)	(202)	(453)	(1253)	(68)	(238)	(528)	—	(1337)	(1376)	—	(523)
	$\tau_b = .34$			$\tau_b = .29$			$\tau_b = .13$			$\tau_b = .08$		

[a]Based on pairs in which both the parent and student were "interested enough" to give a pro or con response.
[b]Ten or fewer cases.

general orientations. All of these factors depress the level of parent-child correspondence.[24]

With these four issues we have only begun to tap the variety of policy concerns that one might wish to consider. Nonetheless, we have probably seen most of the range of parent-student issue similarity that is found in the general public. The correlations for the integration and prayer issues probably approach the apex for such figures, while there are undoubtedly many abstract, complex, or obscure issues for which parents and children resemble each other hardly at all. Note incidentally that these moderate to nonexistent relationships occur despite the important ways in which children "necessarily" resemble their parents. Children of high school age are mostly of the same religion as their parents, usually reside in the same locality and region, and share a common social status. In spite of what appear to be powerful forces pushing in the direction of homogeneity, parent-student pairs resemble each other moderately only when issues are especially prominent.

If some further evidence of the absence of a powerful association between parents' and students' attitudes is needed, it comes from a comparison of whether or not individuals even had an interest in the prayer and integration issues. If we divide the samples into those with and those without an opinion, the correlation between parent and student responses is .03 for the prayer issue and .01 (whites only) for the integration question. In other words, whether the seniors have opinions about these matters is entirely independent of whether their parents express an interest in them. Note, moreover, that lack of association in this respect has not been allowed to reduce artifically the amounts of parent-student agreement observed above. The correlations in Table 3.4 are based on pairs in which both the student and parent expressed an opinion. This reduces the base to 82 percent and 89 percent of the total for the prayers and integration issues, respectively. The moderate parent-student correlations must be further interpreted with this in mind.

Variations in Student-Parent Agreement

As we consider parent-student similarity in population groupings, we can immediately concentrate on the two most salient items. The correlations for the civil liberties issues, as well as the UN question, do vary, although in what appear to be a random fashion. Almost all of the correlations are positive, but the variations follow no particular pattern and are often different for the two separate topics.

[24]The correlation for the UN question is also very low, although it is somewhat misleading because of the extremely skewed response. The correlation is .11, but 79 percent of the students and parents (who take a position) feel the same way about the issue. This is a higher percentage than for either the prayer or integration question.

For the prayer and integration issues, on the other hand, sizeable, consistent differences emerge. Initially we can point to differences by the education of the head of the household. In contrast to the findings in the previous chapter, however, parent-student similarity is greatest in less-educated families, and drops off as educational achievement rises. For the prayer issue the correlations are .35, .37, .25, and .18 for families in which the head has an elementary, partial high school, complete high school, or college education, respectively. The figures for the integration matter are, in the same order, .38, .37, .35, and .30. Why should opposing patterns appear for partisanship and specific issues? One suggestion comes from the likewise contradictory patterns found when controlling for student and family politicization. We found in Chapter 2 that interest and involvement were positively and strongly related to parent-student transmission of partisanship, whereas here the level of politicization does not appreciably alter the degree of similarity between parent and child. It appears that in some instances interest and involvement stimulate higher parent-student correspondence. Since these factors are positively correlated with education, this effect is great enough to create a positive association between education and generational similarity. When politicization has no effect, however, parents and their children are most alike in less well-educated families.[25]

Family interaction patterns also regulate the degree of parent-student congruity. We consider first the dimension of affectivity or attachment. As predicted by previous studies, similarity is highest when the student and parent get along well, and it declines along with the quality of the parent-child relationship. The pattern is especially strong for the school prayer issue, as the following parent-student correlations show:

Student and parent are:	School Prayers	School Integration
Very close	.34	.36
Pretty close	.26	.33
Not very close	.11	.29

Similar findings occur for the other dimension commonly used to characterize the family—power or control relationships. For example, when students reported on parental regulation of their activities, those citing an "average" amount of influence were more like their parents than those reporting little supervision (for both issues) or much control (for school prayers only). Analogously, when the seniors were asked to evaluate the amount of control, those judging it to be about right were more closely allied with their parents' opinions than those who felt that parents had too

[25]There remains, of course, the question of why higher politicization increases parent-student similarity in some cases but not in others. Looking ahead to Chapter 4, it appears that the effect is observed primarily where partisan orientations are involved.

much or too little control. (Again the latter is true for school prayers only.) The findings reported here are true at all levels of politicization. Even when the family is relatively lacking in political interest, students who had more satisfying relationships with their parents more often adopted the parents' views.

We have noted elsewhere, and have seen again in the chapter on partisanship, that family interaction patterns are often unrelated to the flow of attitudes from parent to child.[26] What is it that causes the effects of family patterns to be evident on these issues but not on other orientations? One possibility is the *salient* and *emotive* nature of these issues. Race, religion, and schools all touch deep reservoirs of feelings, attachments, and prejudices. As such, affective relationships in particular should cause variation in parent-student correlations. Opinions and orientations striking less deep-seated emotions could be expected to show less relationship with affective attachments to parents. Since most political matters are somewhat remote from the everyday concerns of the general public, we would expect only a limited number of orientations to bear any relationship to affective features of the family. If correct, this explanation helps account for the narrow range of orientations for which family interaction is an important determinant of parent-student transmission rates.

Substantial variations in student-parent similarity also occur along regional lines. Unlike the differences due to educational and family characteristics, regional variations are not important because region itself is necessarily the explanatory variable, nor even because we expect numerous regional differences for other issues. Rather, this pattern further illustrates certain features of the transmission process when parents' own attitudes vary widely among groups. First of all, we can observe clearly the effects of "social climates." Student opinions are shaped not only by their own parents' feelings, but also by the position taken by other adults in the environment. Thus parent-student similarity is greatest when the parents' attitudes are consistent with the majority position in that arena. For example, among Southern parents, who as a whole were highly in favor of school prayers, 87 percent of the students in "pro-prayer" families adopted this position; of the small group of parents opposing school prayers, only 33 percent of the students went along with this position. Similarly, nearly all black students agreed with parents who for some reason took an opposing viewpoint.

A second observation bears on several points made earlier. We noted the varying amounts of intergenerational change in population segments and commented that the magnitude of the parent-student correlation

[26]M. Kent Jennings and Richard G. Niemi, "The Transmission of Political Values from Parent to Child," *American Political Science Review*, 62 (March 1968), pp. 169–84.

does not necessarily correspond to the degree of change as measured there (footnote 18). The regional variations on the prayer issue offer an excellent case in point. In terms of the percentage sharing the same attitude, students were most like their parents in the South; yet the parent-student correlation was only .14—a lower statistic than in any of the other areas. In light of the previous paragraph on the influence of social climates, this apparent anamoly becomes reasonable. Students in the South were heavily in favor of school prayers regardless of their parents' viewpoint. Thus the correlation, which is reduced by deviations from parents with either opinion, is lowered while the skewed parental distribution keeps the percentage agreement inflated.[27] The correlations for the other regions do not make such dramatic examples, but they do vary in ways not predictable from the degree of percentage change between the older and younger generations.

These examples caution us against attributing great influence to the parents because a high percentage of students agree with them. It may be that in some cases students are more influenced by older cohorts in general than by their own parents in particular. In such cases parents who oppose a majority opinion will often find that their children take a different view. More to the point, however, is that among parents who hold a majority opinion, students who agree with them may derive their opinion not from the parent but from a larger part of the adult environment. Parental influence may thus be relatively small not only in the face of aggregate uniformities as we have seen so often, but even when large proportions of student-parent pairs hold identical views.

Despite this caveat, our purpose here is not to deny the existence of strong channels of influence between parent and child but to find out just when and how these channels are operative. Two further analyses counter the somewhat one-sided picture that has been presented thus far. The first deals with the now familiar consideration of the homogeneity of the mother's and father's views.

The picture is complicated slightly by the differences between concrete and more abstract issues. For the latter, parental homogeneity does not improve upon the low student-parent correlations observed earlier. It is true that students and parents are more similar in homogeneous than in heterogeneous families, but all of the correlations are quite close to zero.

---

[27]This description may be clarified by examination of the table on which it is based. The percentages for and against school prayers are given by columns and (in parentheses) by the total. For ease of presentation the "Opposed" and "Maybe" responses have been combined:

		Parents			
		Pro		Con	
	Pro	87%	(78)	67%	(12)
Students					
	Con	13	(8)	33	(3)

For the two salient issues, however, parental agreement substantially raises the level of student-parent congruity over that for the entire sample. The correlations rise to .40 for the school prayer issue and to .48 for the question on school integration. These statistics are in sharp contrast to those for heterogeneous families, where the correlations regarding school prayers are .20 for student-mother pairs and .03 for student-father pairs. On the integration issue the corresponding figures are .11 and .00. As we have observed for some other orientations, girls seem especially sensitive to the effects of parental homogeneity. The correlations for girls and their parents are greater than those involving boys on all four issues, with the average difference being .12. Overall, then, the precise level of student-parent agreement depends on at least the saliency of the issue and the sex of the students involved. But the major point is clear. Under conditions of parental homogeneity student-parent congruity on prominent, specific issues may reach the relatively high levels heretofore reserved for partisanship and voting intentions.

A second way of establishing the conditions underlying strong parental influence is to look at the specific questions within the context of a broader opinion orientation. While our interview schedule was not designed with this in mind, there is sufficient material to do this for four of the policy items (excluding the UN question). What we want to do is to characterize parents in terms of the strength and consistency of their opinions about a broad issue-area. Controlling for this characterization, we can then take another look at parent-student similarity on specific issues for what it tells us about the intrafamily transmission process.

Let us consider, for example, students who are developing their own attitude toward school integration. One source of ideas is their parents' feeling about this question. But in many cases the parents' position will not be altogether clear. In this event the students may infer their parents' attitude partly on the basis of the parents' general attitude regarding racial matters. If the parents are in fact consistent, the students' inferences are correct, and they will follow the parents' lead a certain proportion of the time. But suppose the parents are for some reason generally anti-black but in favor of school integration. Then students who base their perceptions on the parents' general orientation will be incorrect about the parents' attitude on the specific question. Presumably such students will take an anti-school integration position more often than students of consistent parents favoring integration, thereby reducing the level of agreement with the parents. A similar process would take place if the parents were generally pro-black but opposed to school integration.

An alternative process can take place when parents' opinions are known. It may be quite evident that parents are pro-school integration, while at the same time they do not take a consistently pro-black position.

In this event, the clear stimuli observed by the students for the one issue is clouded by the parents' seemingly contrary position on similar matters. Here again, then, there is reason to believe that students will adopt the parents' position less often than when parents take a consistent stand on the entire range of an issue-area.

We do not have enough information to characterize the parents' overall attitude concerning racial problems, but we do have a second question about integration. Parents were asked: "Which of these statements would you agree with?—'White people have a right to keep Negroes out of their neighborhoods if they want to,' or 'Negroes have a right to live wherever they can afford to, just like white people.' " A follow-up question determined whether they felt "strongly" or "not very strongly" about the position. Using this single question and its follow-up as a surrogate, we can classify the parents into four groups, given in order of most to least favorable to blacks: strongly pro-black, weakly pro-black, weakly pro-white, and strongly pro-white. In each of these groups parents may be for or against integration, making eight categories in all. But since those in the two middle categories have strong but inconsistent attitudes (strongly pro-neighborhood integration but against school integration) and are difficult to rank, we have combined them. However, the addition of two categories for parents who said "it depends" gives us a total of nine categories.

As we have suggested, this differentiation helps considerably in specifying the viewpoint adopted by the student. As shown in Table 3.5, which includes whites only, the rate of adoption of the parents' opinion on school integration varies considerably depending on the consistency and strength of the parents' feelings about neighborhood integration. Likewise, adoption of the alternative view depends heavily on both parental viewpoints. As pointed out in detail in footnote b to Table 3.5, the middle categories show that the effect of inconsistent parents is about the same as having parents with an ambiguous attitude. Moreover, even for parents with an ambiguous position on the school question, the attitude toward neighborhood integration influences student responses.

The same type of analysis can be made for the school prayer issue. Here we use as another relevant attitude the parents' interpretation of the Bible. Our prediction, of course, is that when attitude on the prayer issue is held constant, the proportion of students in favor of school prayers will decline as the Bible is viewed less divinely. The data in Table 3.6 support this prediction rather well. Only one reversal of the strong trend appears, and that occurs in the middle categories where the ranking is somewhat unclear anyway and where the number of cases is quite small. Thus the students' opinion on the school prayer issue is determined not only by that same opinion among the parents, but by the overall parental view of religion as well.

TABLE 3.5

STUDENT OPINIONS ON SCHOOL INTEGRATION, BY PARENT OPINIONS ON SCHOOL AND NEIGHBORHOOD INTEGRATION[a]

	Parent Opinion								
Neighborhood Integration:	Yes	Yes	No	Yes	No/Yes	No	Yes	No	No
Opinion Strength:	Strong	Weak	Weak	Both	Strong	Both	Weak	Weak	Strong
School Integration:	Yes	Yes	Yes	Depends[b]	Yes/No[c]	Depends[b]	No	No	No
Student Opinion									
Yes	86%	77%	65%	64%	56%	56%	53%	29%	32%
Depends	6	11	5	17	17	18	9	17	16
No	8	12	30	18	26	26	38	54	52
Total	100%	100%	100%	99%	99%	100%	100%	100%	100%
	(426)	(211)	(22)	(99)	(151)	(42)	(82)	(23)	(156)

[a]This table includes only white respondents.

[b]These categories are difficult to place, and one might well combine them with the "inconsistent" category in between them. Our point in separating them is a) to show that having inconsistent parents has about the same effect as having parents with an ambiguous "middle" position and b) that even when parents are unsure about the school issue, their attitude on the neighborhood question influences students' views.

[c]This category contains "inconsistent" parents who combine a strong opinion about neighborhood integration with an opposite view on school integration.

TABLE 3.6

STUDENT OPINIONS ON SCHOOL PRAYERS, BY PARENT OPINIONS AND PARENT
INTERPRETATIONS OF THE BIBLE

Interpretation of the Bible: School Prayers:	God's Word Yes	Human Error Yes	God's Word Depends[a]	Parent Opinion Not Divine God's Word Yes/No[b]	Human Error Depends[a]	Human Error No	Not Divine No
Student Opinion							
Yes	79%	69%	68%	44%	60%	31%	30%
Depends	2	5	7	8	9	6	6
No	19	26	25	48	30	63	64
Total	100%	100%	100%	100%	99%	100%	100%
	(719)	(470)	(30)	(138)	(31)	(99)	(32)

[a]These categories are difficult to place, and one might well combine them with the "inconsistent" category in between them. The parental combination "not divine, depends" is omitted because of too few cases.

[b]This category contains "inconsistent" parents who are opposed to school prayers but view the Bible as God's Word or who support prayers but judge the Bible as not divine. The proportion of students in this category who answered "Yes" is smaller than might be expected on the basis of the other categories because it contains mostly (70%) parents who answer "No" to the question on school prayers.

For the civil liberties items our procedure was quite simple because of the limited data available, but the results are similar to what we have seen so far. Each of the items was used as a control for the other. We reasoned, for example, that if a parent accepted speeches against religion, this attitude was more likely to be perceived and adopted by the student if the parent also supported civil liberties for Communists. Proceeding in this fashion we have three groups of parents—those who take the civil liberties position in both, in only one, or in neither of the two examples. Taking these groups in the order mentioned, we find that 94 percent, 85 percent, and 80 percent of their children accept speeches against religion. Similarly, the proportions saying that a Communist should be allowed to take office are 47 percent, 32 percent, and 14 percent. Once again, then, the data support the inference that students are influenced both by the parents' opinion on the specific question at hand and by the parental position on other related matters.[28]

The importance of this analysis lies in the realization that in all four of the cases that we examined, student attitudes are predicted more accurately when other relevant attitudes of the parents are incorporated. This offers empirical support for the belief that parents influence children

[28]Since there is a religious element in the question on speeches against churches and religion, we also used the parents' interpretation of the Bible as a second control. The result was another monotonic pattern ranging from 91 percent acceptance of speeches (when the parent took a dim view of the Bible) to 81 percent (when the parent took the Bible as God's Word and opposed speeches against religion).

through their entire attitude structure rather than simply via their opinion on isolated issues. This suggests a crucial point: family influence is greater than what is indicated by the parent-student correlations alone. This does not mean that the parent-student correlations are incorrect or necessarily misleading. They do indicate properly what is often a low degree of correspondence between parents and students on particular, fairly narrowly conceived orientations. And this is important. Parents do not pass along attitudes to their offspring by determining children's responses to the variety of particular questions that we could throw at them. And this means that considerable student-parent disagreement may ensue on any particular item. But parents' attitudes as a whole do influence their children's orientations more than is suggested by the statistics showing congruency on single items.[29] Children are the products of their parents even though they are often unlike them with regard to specific orientations.

Our overall evaluation of family influence is therefore a mixed one, but we have come to some definite conclusions. We began by showing that parent-student similarity on specific issues varies widely. But we added to this mundane point that the degree of parent-student congruity depends in large part on the saliency and concreteness of the items, with the correlation near-zero unless the issues are tangible and of unusual prominence. If the issues are indeed real and salient, the correlation becomes moderate, particularly it seems, among less well educated families, where the parent and student are close, and above all, when the mother and father share a common viewpoint. In addition, we observed significant variations by region, which demonstrated that high levels of parent and student similarity (in percentage terms) are sometimes accompanied by relatively low levels of parental influence. This possibility is an important theoretical and practical point. Finally, we showed that detecting family influence must not be limited to examining the transmission of single, isolated ideas. This last point is critical for it is an indication that there is more to family influence than meets the eye. Future assessments of the role of the family in the political socialization process must take account of these less obvious influences.

ISSUES AND PARTISAN DEFECTION

One of the reasons for studying opinions on policy issues is because of the effect that these opinions have on other political orientations and on

---

[29]This point, of course, applies to orientations in other chapters as well as the questions discussed here. In Chapter 2, to take an obvious example, the parents' vote in 1964 affected the students' partisanship. When the effect was to pull the student away from the parents' partisanship, the influence of the vote actually lowered the parent-student correlation for party identification.

political behavior. In research on voting, for example, there is a continuing concern over the role of issues in moving voters away from their "standing commitment" to vote for one party or the other.[30] Here most of our attention will be directed toward a related and in some ways a prior question. Do issue-positions of young people help determine their partisanship and their intended voting behavior by altering the pattern of parent-to-child transmission of party ties and ballot habits?

To make this kind of test we narrowed our concern to only one of the issues treated above. In the 1964 election the posture toward civil rights issues was a major delineator of Republican and Democratic policy positions.[31] This prompted us to use the integration question as a measure of the impact of issues on parent-student transmission processes. Just in passing we should note that this attitude does create the expected defections from partisanship in the 1964 vote among both generations. Republicans, for example, voted for Johnson to a greater degree if they were in favor of a strong federal role in school integration. Similarly, Democrats defected more readily if they took the opposing view.

An initial test for the effects of issue-position is made by dividing the student-parent pairs by whether the student was for or against school integration. Those in the "depends" category were eliminated.[32] In these groups the student-"parent" correlations for party identification (i.e., using students' perceptions of the parents) were .57 and .58, respectively. Hence there was virtually the same amount of *overall* defection from the parents' partisanship. What was needed, however, was an indicator of how much the students moved from their parents' identification in a Democratic direction and how much in a Republican direction. This was accomplished with a simple integer scoring method. Among parents who were strong Democrats, children were considered to have moved 0, 1, . . . , 6 steps from the parent if they (the students) were strong Democrats, . . . , strong Republicans, respectively. Among weak Democratic parents, students could score −1 if they were strong Democrats or 1, . . . , 5 if they were Independent Democrats, . . . , strong Republicans, respectively. This procedure was repeated for each of the seven groups of partisan parents. If we divide each score by the number of parents in the category from which it was derived, we get an indication of the movement away from each set of partisan parents. We can also add up all the "deviation scores" and divide by the total number of parents, thus getting

[30]Numerous references are given in Gerald Pomper, "From Confusion to Clarity: Issues and Voters, 1956–1968," *American Political Science Review*, 66 (June 1972), pp. 415–28.

[31]For empirical evidence that party differences were perceived by the mass electorate, see Philip E. Converse, Aage R. Clausen, and Warren E. Miller, "Electoral Myth and Reality: The 1964 Election," *American Political Science Review*, 59 (June 1965), pp. 321–36, esp. p. 329.

[32]We also limit this analysis to whites.

an overall score. It is apparent that by our convention positive scores indicate movement in a Republican direction and negative scores indicate a Democratic direction.

Now if the students' attitudes do have an impact on the deviation from parental partisanship, the scores for students who are opposed to integration should be more positive (i.e., more in a Republican direction) than the scores of the other students. We say "more positive" rather than "positive" for two reasons. In the aggregate, students are slightly more Democratic than they perceived their parents to be. Thus a very small negative score would indicate movement toward the Democrats, but less movement in this direction than for the population as a whole. Secondly, the scores can be considerably affected by the distribution of party identifiers among the parents. This does not affect the comparison when students are divided solely by their civil rights attitudes, but it will affect some comparisons below.

For the initial test these caveats turn out to be unnecessary. For the students opposed to integration the score is .074, meaning that those students as a whole moved slightly toward the Republicans. In contrast, the students in favor of integration scored −.157.[33] This result supports the conclusion that students' issue-positions altered the parent-to-student transmission process in a direction consistent with these attitudes.

However, this is not a very demanding test. We must ask at least for a control on the parents' vote in 1964. We showed in Chapter 2 that the parents' most recent vote did influence the degree to which the child took on the parents' partisanship. It is also the case that among the students opposed to integration there is a heavier-than-average concentration of parents who voted for Goldwater. Perhaps it is the Goldwater vote rather than the students' own issue-positions that pull these students in a Republican direction. A similar argument holds, of course, for students in favor of integration.

In order to control for this possibility, the student-parent pairs were first divided according to the parents' vote. These groups were then divided by the students' attitude on the integration question, and defection scores were calculated. The results for both Johnson and Goldwater voters separately support the earlier conclusion. When the parent voted for Johnson, the student scores were .571 when the students opposed integration and .027 when they favored it. The fact that both scores are positive—showing movement toward the Republicans—is a result of the

[33]One can also make predictions based on comparisons within specific categories of partisans—e.g., where the parent is a strong Democrat and the student is for versus against integration. Also one can contrast the deviation from strong Democratic parents and strong Republican parents when the students attitude on integration is held constant. Of 13 such predictions (seven with partisan categories and six holding integration attitudes constant) nine are in the predicted direction.

fact that most parents in this group are Democrats. Among Goldwater voters the student scores are −.287 for students opposed to integration and −.619 for students favoring it.[34] (Parallel reasoning accounts for the negative scores.) Even when we control for the effects of parental voting, then, the students' attitude on the integration issue helps determine the direction in which their partisanship deviates from that of their parents.

Much the same situation exists with regard to student deviations from parental voting behavior. The deviation of students' intended votes depends in part on student attitudes on the civil rights question. Because of the dichotomous nature of the vote we can look directly at the percentages without calculating deviation scores. Consider, for example, the preferences of students whose parents voted for Johnson. If the students were opposed to integration, some 17 percent stated a preference for Goldwater. This figure is a considerable jump over the seven percent who preferred Goldwater while favoring integration. Looking at the students whose parents preferred Goldwater, we find that 20 percent of those opposed to integration would have voted for Johnson, in contrast to a much larger 48 percent of those supporting integration. Once again the effects of another variable—student partisanship in this case—might be confounding our results. Controlling for this, however, we still find large differences in deviations from the parents' vote depending on the students' opinions on the integration question.

Our findings in this section should not be exaggerated. There are in fact many students who deviate from their parents' partisanship or vote in a direction contrary to what we would predict from their civil rights attitude.[35] Moreover, many who deviated in the "right" direction may have done so for reasons quite apart from the integration issue. Nevertheless, the net deviations are in the direction predicted on the basis of the students' opinions on this specific policy item.

This pattern of deviations from parental partisanship helps maintain the consistency of party identification and issue-positions. Though opinions on specific issues are perhaps only a minor determinant of students' party affiliations, the role they play in altering the parent-student transmission process contributes importantly to keeping a modicum of ideological distinction between the parties at the mass level. In addition, we are reminded, as Key so strongly counseled in regard to voting behavior, that not all of the development of party identification should be attributed to

[34]Due to the limited number of cases in some categories, there are only ten predictions that can be made within partisan categories or holding constant the integration attitude and which have at least 15 cases on which to estimate the deviation scores. Of these, six are in the predicted direction.

[35]On the other hand, it should be emphasized that some students *who failed to deviate* from their parents' partisanship or vote probably did so because this attitude or behavior coincided with their issue preferences.

irrational or subconscious motivations. To a degree—at least by the late adolescent stage—children do alter their partisan feelings and their candidate preferences to accord with their attitudes on salient issues. To this extent the development of partisanship is a "rational" response to their viewpoints on specific issues.[36]

[36]V. O. Key, Jr., *The Responsible Electorate* (Cambridge: Belknap Press, 1966); see also Arthur S. Goldberg, "Social Determinism and Rationality as Bases of Party Identification," *American Political Science Review,* 63 (March 1969), pp. 5–25.

CHAPTER FOUR

Political Knowledge and
Conceptual Sophistication

H OW KNOWLEDGEABLE are high school seniors about public affairs and politics? This blunt question is asked often and in a variety of practical and theoretical contexts. It was frequently raised, for example, in discussions of the eighteen-year-old vote. Proponents argued that high school graduates knew as much as or more about politics than many adults and that with several additional years of disenfranchisement their knowledge probably deteriorated anyway. Opponents countered that recent graduates knew many facts about our government and political system, but they lacked a kind of knowledge and understanding that comes only with experience.

More general, if less practical, interest in the level of high school students' knowledge has been generated with regard to major concerns of political socialization. For example, what are the timing and sequence of learning about politics? We know from previous studies that children learn a good deal during the elementary years, and we have some indication of the order in which they learn about political phenomena.[1] But how much have students learned by the time they finish their secondary schooling? Are they in fact as knowledgeable as adults or do they fail to absorb much political information until they are active participants in the political arena? A related concern is the source of students' political information. To what extent does the family dispense information as well as influence attitudes?

Going somewhat beyond mere possession of information is the question of how sophisticated high school seniors' political views are. This question is critical from a number of viewpoints. Are socialization agents, and schools in particular, successful in teaching more than isolated facts? Since the retention of old information and acquisition of new ideas is partly dependent on the existence of some sort of framework or organizing concepts, the ability of students to retain what they learn while in school and to continue learning afterwards is greatly assisted by the development of ideological perspectives. Similarly, value judgments are

---

[1]Robert D. Hess and Judith V. Torney, *The Development of Political Attitudes in Children* (Chicago: Aldine, 1967), pp. 23–26; Fred I. Greenstein, *Children and Politics* (New Haven: Yale University Press, 1965), pp. 57–63.

more easily made and justified if held as a part of an integrative framework of beliefs.

Of particular concern here is whether students have learned to view the political parties in a systematic way. Do they understand and use some general concept, such as the familiar liberal-conservative dimension, to understand and to evaluate party differences? If so, is this level of sophistication a result of family influences or must its sources be sought elsewhere? If not, does comparison with parents suggest that more sophisticated views will accrue with age and experience?

The questions concerning us in this chapter, then, are how far has the acquisition of political knowledge and sophistication progressed by the end of high school, and what part do the family and other conditioning factors play in the development that has taken place.

POLITICAL INFORMATION

To assess the amount of factual political information held by students and parents, six questions were asked of both samples. While six items can barely begin to tap a respondent's total political knowledge, the questions are diverse enough to afford some interesting conclusions. Moreover, since the items form a cumulative scale (see below), we have greater confidence that they are assessing a knowledge dimension.

The percentages of students and parents answering each question correctly are given in Table 4.1. The questions obviously varied greatly in difficulty, since as few as one in four and as many as nineteen in twenty gave correct answers. On the whole neither the students nor parents had a decided advantage over the other. The students gave substantially more correct responses to two of the questions and considerably fewer right answers on two more. On the remaining two items, parents were slightly more often correct on one, and the two samples were tied on the other.

While students and parents have approximately equal amounts of factual knowledge, as measured, there is a sharp difference in their knowl-

TABLE 4.1
STUDENT AND PARENT RESPONSES TO INFORMATION QUESTIONS

Question	Percentage Giving Correct Answer			
	Students		Parents	
Governor of their state	88%	(2062)	93%	(1920)
Country with WW II concentration camps	83	(2062)	83	(1916)
Was Franklin Roosevelt a Dem. or Rep.	64	(2063)	93	(1923)
Length of senator's term	50	(2048)	29	(1916)
Number of justices on supreme court	38	(2062)	23	(1918)
Country Tito is leader of	27	(2059)	43	(1914)

edge of certain topics. The students, first of all, seemed to be more knowledgeable about governmental structure and, presumably, the mechanics of governmental operations. On both of the questions concerning organization of the government, the students gave correct answers much more often than parents. On the other hand, of the three questions with historical relevance, two of them were answered better by parents. This is true of the question about Tito, even though he was by no means only of historical interest in 1965. The exception is the matter of concentration camps during World War II. We suppose that the story of the concentration camps is told so often in the classroom and over the mass media that many students become aware of them. On the sixth question, naming the governor of the state, nearly all students and parents were correct.[2]

These differences in areas of expertise can be attributed to the past experiences of students and parents. Considering the emphasis placed on memorization of figures, dates, and places in so many high school courses, one would expect students to be more aware of such facts than parents.[3] While parents have been forgetting their school lessons, however, they have been experiencing, learning, and retaining knowledge of individuals and events important in their lifetimes. The most striking example of this is the almost universally correct identification by parents of President Franklin Roosevelt as a Democrat. The direct experience of these parents, many of whom were themselves high school students in the 1930's, fixed the identification in their minds better than any school lesson they might have had.[4] That a higher proportion of parents also identified Marshall Tito is probably due to repeated exposure to him over a long period of time. Though a contemporary figure in 1965, whom students might have encountered in their texts or in the mass media, Tito was not as familiar to the students as to their parents.

Since the question of the students' political knowledge was often raised in connection with the eighteen-year-old vote issue, we might draw some conclusions about this from our findings. It appears certain that students are capable of voting in the sense that their knowledge of formal governmental operations, at the national level at any rate, is at least as great as that of parents. However, our findings suggest the importance of other

[2]Comparison with New Haven figures suggests that knowledge of the governor's name grows by 12–14 percent between eighth and twelfth grade. See Greenstein, *Children and Politics*, pp. 58–59.

[3]See Byron G. Massialas, "American Government: We Are the Greatest!," in C. Benjamin Cox and Byron G. Massialas (eds.), *Social Studies in the United States* (New York: Harcourt, Brace & World, 1967), pp. 167–95.

[4]Actually the percentage of students correctly identifying the party of FDR may overestimate the number who were sure of their answers. Some 23 percent of the students (three percent of the parents) said that FDR was a Republican. If as many students "guessed" that he was a Democrat, the proportion actually knowing drops below a half.

considerations as well. Parents appear to have built up a reservoir of knowledge about past experiences. To the extent that these experiences are partisan in nature, they are likely to have made parents' partisan loyalties more resistant to change. Students, with what appears to be a highly restricted historical knowledge of partisan figures, switch their loyalties more easily. This is, of course, the same point made in Chapter 2, but here we add that the knowledge learned (or perhaps we should say not learned) by young people is a likely contributor to their partisan instability. Thus rather than posing the question of whether eighteen-year-olds have sufficient knowledge to vote intelligently, one might better ask about the consequences of adding to the electorate a group of individuals with the particular kind of knowledge they possess.

The Impact of the Family

In order to assess the relationship between student and parental political knowledge, a Guttman scale was constructed for use in addition to the individual items. For students all seven items scaled (CR = .92); for parents, the question on the length of Senate terms did not scale, so a six-item scale is used (CR = .93). The different numbers of items in the scales obviously affect the distributions of the samples, but more importantly, this has little effect on the student-parent correlations.

Using these cumulative scales, it is evident that both students' and parents' levels of knowledge are correlated with measure of intelligence or schooling, and politicization. Political interest, for example, yields a .30 correlation with parental knowledge and a .24 figure with student knowledge. Similar figures hold for other measures of politicization. The parents' education shows a .22 correlation with their knowledge, while the students' grade average has a .25 correlation with the knowledge scale. These findings are as expected, but they are important to observe in anticipation of the data presented below on relative transmission rates.

Sex differences have often been absent in our results, but previous suggestions of differential knowledge are substantiated here. The sex difference appears to be somewhat greater for parents than for students, as indicated by the following figures:

Political Knowledge

	Low						High	Total
	1	2	3	4	5	6	7	
Boys	3%	4	11	25	16	14	27	100% (1063)
Girls	5%	9	17	24	15	11	18	99% (997)
Fathers	1%	1	6	35	32	25		100% (1093)
Mothers	2%	3	16	44	21	13		100% (1360)

It may be that the school has temporarily dampened the typical male superiority in political knowledge. Nonetheless, the male edge among students is maintained for every question and among those at every grade average level.[5]

The overall parent-student correlation for political knowledge is .25 (Table 4.2). In talking about parental impact on student information we are not suggesting that positive correlations necessarily show that the specific pieces of information tapped by our questions are being transmitted. That may occasionally be the case. More significantly, however, we are arguing that homes where the parents have higher levels of information are likely to be homes where the atmosphere is conducive for the child's acquisition of political facts.

TABLE 4.2

RELATIONSHIP BETWEEN STUDENT AND PARENT
POLITICAL KNOWLEDGE

Student Knowledge[a]	Parent Knowledge[a]					
	Low 1	2	3	4	5	High 6
Low 1	26%	23%	8%	5%	2%	0%
2	28	16	17	6	3	1
3	9	10	13	17	14	8
4	5	14	29	25	27	22
5	17	22	14	17	17	8
6	10	8	13	12	11	14
High 7	5	7	6	17	25	45
Total	100%	100%	100%	99%	99%	98%
	(34)	(41)	(237)	(782)	(492)	(337)
$\tau_b = .25$						

[a]Knowledge was measured by a six- or seven-point Guttman scale, as described in the text.

Compared with other orientations observed throughout the book, there is a moderately strong impact of parents on the political knowledge held by their children. However, the correlations for the individual items vary, and in a rather suggestive pattern. The highest correlations by a considerable margin are for the two items involving international considerations— $\tau_b = .31$ for the question on concentration camps and .28 for the identification of Tito. In general it may be that this kind of subject-matter is less often emphasized in school, so that parents' information (or lack of it) is a greater determinant of students' knowledge. If this is the case, however, the story of World War II concentration camps

[5]Merelman shows the male advantage increasing from sixth to twelfth grade, where it is substantial. Richard M. Merelman, *Political Socialization and Educational Climates* (New York: Holt, Rinehart, and Winston, 1971), pp. 124–25.

is an exception. This would not be surprising, since the story of the Second World War, and of the atrocities committed by the enemy, are often taught as a part of American history. Topics relating to international and comparative politics, but which do not play a monumental part in American history, are taught much less frequently. In general, then, knowledge of these topics is subject to greater influence of the family and of the students' own interests.[6]

The lowest student-parent correlation is for the one item concerning partisan politics—the party of FDR (.09). This low figure shows that partisan information, as opposed to party identification, is poorly passed on from one generation to the next. It is, in fact, a foreshadowing of results later in this chapter. For the remaining three items the correlations cluster in the middle, .13 for the Senate term and .16 for the others. Parental influence is small but noticeable.

In Chapters 2 and 3 we observed a sharp gradient in the student-parent correspondence when controlling for parental education; but in the first case student-parent similarity was greatest among the highly educated, while in the other instance the pattern was reversed. Here, the pattern is similar to that for specific issues, as indicated by the student-parent correlations among families in which the head has an elementary, partial high school, complete high school, or college education, respectively: .21, .22, .15, .16. Though the difference is small, the impact of the parents on students' knowledge is greater at the lower levels of parental education. One implication of this is that the correlation for the entire cohort of seventeen- and eighteen-year-olds would be slightly higher than for our student sample. More importantly, the pattern observed here may be indicative of more academic matters, while for more strictly political phenomena, levels of politicization (which are positively associated with education) affect parent-student transmission sufficiently so that overall similarity is greatest in well-educated families.

As in Chapter 3, we also note here the absence of any relationship between politicization and student-parent similarity. Politicization makes no difference, whether measured in terms of overt activities or professed interest or whether based on student or parent responses. As we noted earlier, measures of politicization are themselves related to respondents' political knowledge, but they do not in this case alter the rate of parent-student transmission. The same holds true for respondents' sex. Males of both generations were shown to be more knowledgeable then females, but student-parent similarity is nearly the same regardless of the sex mix under consideration.

[6]Some confirming evidence of this last point will be presented below. The two "international" items along with the question on FDR are influenced by some particular characteristics of the students (e.g., their religion), while the remaining items are not.

To this point we have shown that student and parent knowledge levels are moderately correlated, suggesting that parents directly and indirectly affect the political knowledge of their children. Political knowledge, however, like knowledge of most any sort, is related to the students' academic ability. As noted, the correlation of the students' grade average with the political knowledge scale is .25. Knowing this and the fact that parental knowledge is also correlated with student grade averages, it is worthwhile asking whether students are affected by their parents' knowledge level above and beyond the impact of the students' own academic ability. In other words, is the previously observed student-parent correlation for political knowledge maintained when controlling for the students' grade average?

The results of such a test are the following correlations for students with grade averages of A, B, C, and D or F, respectively: .39, .18, .23, .46. Whether the strong curvilinear pattern of the correlations is significant is an interesting question, but not the major point here. What is crucial from the standpoint of our question is that parents seem to have a moderate to large impact on students' political knowledge even when grade average is controlled. Thus parental knowledge appears to be a relatively important predictor of the amount of political information possessed by pre-adults.

In addition to the impact of parents and of the student's own abilities, other student characteristics often contribute to knowledge levels. In some cases these are general orientations to the political world (e.g., cosmopolitanism) which influence a broad range of political ideas. In others some characteristic exercises on idiosyncratic influence on knowledge of particular events or situations (e.g., the impact of one's religion on awareness of concentration camps). Both kinds can be illustrated using student data. One wide-reaching influence was observed when we considered the effects of a cosmopolitan outlook on the ability to answer correctly the two questions of international import. Even when controlling for degree of political interest and grade average, the more cosmopolitan students were considerably more likely to identify Marshall Tito and the location of World War II concentration camps.[7] Significantly, cosmopolitanism was *not* related in a consistent fashion to the other information questions. The state governor, for example, was not better known by the more local- and state-oriented respondents. Knowledge of international and comparative politics thus seems peculiarly subject to the influence of student interests, perhaps because it requires efforts beyond absorbing strictly American history and politics.

Two potentially far-reaching effects are observed for the lone piece of

[7]M. Kent Jennings, "Pre-Adult Orientations to Multiple Systems of Government," *Midwest Journal of Political Science*, 11 (August 1967), pp. 291–317.

partisan information. One relationship is the causally ambiguous connection between partisan attitudes and knowledge. About two-thirds of the partisans of either a Democratic or Republican stripe were able to identify Franklin Roosevelt's party. A similar number of Independents leaning toward a party gave a correct answer. Of the "pure" Independents, however, a somewhat reduced proportion (55 percent) were correct. Whatever the causal sequence involved, the lower partisan knowledge of Independents has its roots in pre-adult years.

The level of sophistication that respondents bear toward party politics is also related to their knowledge of our one partisan item. The sophistication measure will be explained in detail later in this chapter. Basically it measures the extent to which the respondent is familiar with the liberal-conservative dimension and the placement of the two parties on it. Since the students' recognition of this dimension is clearly related to their political interest and grade average, each of these variables was controlled in testing for the relationship between sophistication and responses to the question on FDR. Even with these controls, respondents who were familiar with the liberal-conservative terminology were from 10 to 30 percent more often able to identify Roosevelt's party. As with party identification, the precise causal sequence is unclear. But it is likely that for some students a more truly ideological view of the parties permits them to remember more information of a partisan nature. For these students, a sophisticated political viewpoint may be a major factor in their knowledge of the entire sphere of party politics.

Illustrative of more specific characteristics affecting students' political knowledge is the impact of religion on awareness of World War II concentration camps. For obvious reasons we would expect Jews to have a heightened awareness of the existence of these camps. Controlling for religion and grade average suggests that this is true. Except for "A" students, of whom over 92 percent in each religious group gave a correct answer, from 10 to 25 percent more Jews than Catholics or Protestants were able to indicate the site of these camps. If one were to assess political knowledge with a much wider array of questions than we used, many factors such as the one noted here would arise. These specific characteristics rooted in the child's experiential history must be recognized as one source of political knowledge.

For our last look at the sources of student political knowledge we turn to the set of student-mother-father triads that have proved so useful in previous chapters. Once again parental homogeneity is a prime determinant of student-parent similarity. Among parents with identical scores on the knowledge scale, the student-parent correlation is .38, with the effect being slightly greater on boys (.42) than on girls (.36) These figures contrast with a student-mother correlation of .24 and a student-father correlation of .27 among families with heterogeneous parents.

The observed effect of parental homogeneity in determining student-parent similarity is noteworthy because of the nature of the knowledge variable. In the case of an attitude, such as party identification, it is readily apparent how a student can be influenced by both parents. Some students consciously adopt one parent's feeling or behavior while others are cross-pressured into a neutral or semi-neutral position. Presumably, however, one does not consciously opt to be smart like one parent or dull like the other parent. Nor does the knowledgeable student feel cross-pressured because of being more like one parent than the other (although the dull student may feel such pressures). This might lead one to expect that students would be less affected by both parents in the development of their knowledge and to be influenced chiefly by the more knowledgeable parent.

Such reasoning appears to be incorrect, for student political knowledge is indeed influenced by the level of each parent. A further indication of this, in addition to the correlations above, is found if we correlate the student's knowledge level with an average of both parents' scores. The correlation of .33 is higher than the figure given above for a single parent (.25) or the figure derived by using only the score of the more knowledgeable parent (.31). While the differences are not large, they do reveal that in learning facts and figures as well as attitudes and behavior, the full parental environment contributes to the development of the pre-adult. And awareness of this full environment affords us a better understanding of pre-adult knowledge and other orientations.

IDEOLOGICAL VIEWS OF THE POLITICAL PARTIES

In addition to knowledge of isolated political facts, we are interested in respondents' belief systems—the way in which political ideas are bound together, constrained, and organized. In the politics of the United States as well as some other countries, one of the predominant belief systems in recent times has been the liberal-conservative dimension. Placed on this dimension one finds legislative and executive policies, judicial decisions, political parties, and an assortment of political actors. Here our concern is limited to an awareness and understanding of such a dimension with respect to the political parties and to placement of the Democratic and Republican parties on it. Where respondents are unaware of this dimension, the analysis focuses on other party differences that are cited.

Some justification for our emphasis may be required, inasmuch as it is fashionable these days to talk of a realignment of the party system and of the political ideologies surrounding them. No longer would the long-familiar issues arising out of the Depression era dominate political controversies. Hubert Humphrey briefly revived them toward the end of the 1968 campaign, but that was only a temporary anachronism. Along with the demise of the old issues, the customary ideological view in which Democrats, save for the Southerners, were liberals and Republicans were conservatives needed to be discarded. At the operational level of voting, this revised view seemed justified, since a very conservative candidate (old view), George Wallace, was receiving about half of his non-Southern support from Democrats—i.e., those who were supposed to be liberals (old term).[8] The 1972 campaign revealed further inroads on the traditional issues, although they were certainly not absent.

While one senses a good deal of truth to the idea that the dominant issues are rapidly changing, ideological coinage will no doubt change less drastically. "Liberals" and "conservatives," we expect, will be around for a long time, although the meaning attached to them and the groups associated with each label may vary substantially as time goes by. Indeed our own data will suggest this. Moreover, if the liberal-conservative dimension is retired, some other ideological scheme is likely to take its place, so strong is the need for some simplifying characterization of the complex world of politics. Thus it makes good sense to examine the way in which pre-adults view the political parties. What we have to say about the liberal-conservative dimension is likely to be substantially correct for a replacement.

The initial question in the interview relating to party differences was a straightforward one: "Do you think there are any important differences in what the Republicans and Democrats stand for?" If the respondents said "No" or "I don't know," the interviewer went on to a more suggestive question to be analyzed in the next section. If the respondents said "Yes," they were asked what the differences were. Coding of these responses will be explained below.[9]

One of the most telling figures is the first datum to confront us. A slight majority of both students and parents said that there were no important differences between the parties! Additional small percentages said they did not know if differences existed, and a few more said there were differences, but they did not know what they were, which is surely an indicator of little active use of the knowledge that there are differences.

[8]Philip E. Converse, Warren E. Miller, Jerrold G. Rusk, and Arthur C. Wolfe, "Continuity and Change in American Politics: Parties and Issues in the 1968 Election," *American Political Science Review*, 63 (December 1969), pp. 1083–105; Seymour Martin Lipset and Earl Raab, "The Wallace Whitelash," *Transaction*, 7 (December 1969), pp. 23–35, especially p. 26.

[9]Part of the analyses below will be reminiscent of the "levels of conceptualization" study in *The American Voter*. However, the question used here is much less probing than the series of items used in that analysis. Hence we should expect more respondents who see no party difference than the 22 percent of *The American Voter* sample whose responses had no issue content. The coding of the differences that are cited, while bearing some resemblance to the levels of conceptualization, is a scheme devised and explained by Philip E. Converse, "The Nature of Belief Systems in Mass Publics," in David E. Apter (ed.), *Ideology and Discontent* (New York: Free Press, 1964).

TABLE 4.3

PERCEPTIONS OF NO DIFFERENCES BETWEEN THE POLITICAL PARTIES[a]

Interest in Public Affairs	Students		Parents	
Very low	84%	(50)	82%	(139)
Low	75%	(293)	76%	(250)
Medium	69%	(582)	71%	(577)
High	57%	(834)	58%	(914)

Education of HOH	Students		Parents	
Elementary	74%	(496)	71%	(474)
Some high school	68%	(363)	68%	(361)
High school grad	65%	(556)	70%	(558)
College	55%	(473)	56%	(484)

Race	Students		Parents	
White	67%	(1825)	67%	(1692)
Black	52%	(190)	62%	(191)

[a]Entries are the combined percentages saying there is no difference between the parties, "don't know," and there is some difference but they do not know what.

Combining these three groups, we find that very nearly two-thirds of the students and parents (66 percent in each case) are unable to cite any party differences in response to a neutral question.

Two points stand out here. First, these figures must surely be taken with the proverbial grain of salt. That many of these respondents see some, however vague, difference between the parties is obvious from the distribution of the electorate on the levels of conceptualization measure. Still, they see nothing so general as to constitute a major distinction between the two primary political combatants. Second, parents do not have an edge on students in their awareness of distinctions between the political parties. Some party-related differences have been found between prospective new voters and long-active parents—in the strength of their partisanship, for example. But in the proportion observing some party difference, as in the overall recall of political facts, neither parents nor students hold a decided edge.

In both samples there are marked variations among subgroups in the proportion citing no differences. As seen in Table 4.3, the respondents' political interest, race, and parental education have a considerable effect. Nonetheless, even among college-educated parents and their youth, and among the highly interested respondents, over half fail to cite a way in which the parties differ significantly. The lower proportion of blacks denying a party difference stands out sharply since they are on the average less politically interested and from less well educated families. As we shall see below this is attributable to the perceived role of the parties in supporting blacks' own group interests.[10]

If we next pair individual students with their parents, little of a positive nature is revealed about the sources of students' views. The student-parent relationship, shown in Table 4.4, yields a correlation of only .10. While we have not yet begun to look at the type of party differences cited, it is already clear that cognitive images of the parties—as opposed to the affective view captured in party identification—are derived directly from parents to only a small degree. It is true that the type of party difference cited by the parent makes it more or less likely that the child will report a difference. But even among parents who mention what we will call below a philosophical difference, children have only a 50–50 chance of naming some distinguishing feature of the parties.

Student-parent correspondence varies systematically, although in no case is the similarity more than moderate. Family politicization evidently alters the impact of the parental viewpoint, since the student-parent correlation goes up with an increase in either husband-wife or student-parent political conversations. For example, in families with least fre-

[10]Male-female differences are minimal, with adult women slightly less often making any partisan distinctions.

TABLE 4.4
STUDENT REPORTS OF PARTY DIFFERENCES BY PARENT REPORTS

Students	Parents		
	No Party Differences[a]	Some Party Differences	
No party differences[a]	69%	58%	
Some party differences	31	42	
Total	100%	100%	
$\tau_b = .10$	(1224)	(627)	
Parent Totals	66	34	(1883)
Student Totals	66	34	(2029)

[a]See note to Table 4.3.

quent to most frequent conversations between the mother and father, the statistics are $-.01$, $.06$, $.11$, and $.16$, respectively. In line with this variation, greater student-parent similarity is found as one moves up the education ladder. In families in which the head of the household received a grade school education or less, students' and parents' views are independent $(-.01)$. Among families where the head has some high school or a completed high school education, the correlations are positive but still small ($.10$ and $.08$, respectively); and among the college-educated the degree of similarity is moderate ($.17$). The appearance of these patterns indicates that perceptions of party differences are most often learned from parents when the family is highly politicized and of relatively high status. This is unlike the pattern found earlier in this chapter for knowledge of political facts, but it appears to be characteristic of partisan orientations.

Transmission of perceptions of political party differences is weakest from fathers to their children. The father-student correlation is near zero for both boys and girls, while the mother has a noticeable impact on sons ($.14$) as well as daughters ($.18$). Party politics may be a man's game in some respects, but mothers appear to have an important role in shaping party images as well as party preferences (see Chapters 2 and 6).

Further evidence of the limited impact of the family can be seen in the effects of parental homogeneity. When one parent reports a party difference and the other does not, the student-parent correlation is indeed low; $.06$ with mothers and $-.06$ with fathers. But when both parents report a difference or both do not, the correlation increases only slightly to $.10$, which is no higher than for the single-parent data. As is frequently true, girls in homogeneous families are more like their parents than are boys. Not that girls respond very much like their parents. It is just that boys' perceptions of the existence of party differences are nearly independent of parental views. Only in certain small subsets of the population—such as when students converse frequently with homogeneous parents, where the correlation is .24—does information about the existence of party differences seem to filter down through the family. In general, transmission of ideas from parents to students plays only a small role in the development of party images.

Types of Party Differences Cited

From the third of the students and parents who perceived a party difference, a wide array of responses was received. To cope with this variety, a code of five major and over 100 detailed categories was used. The categories form a "priority code," wherein the "best" responses (as defined below) were coded first. Hence if all the responses could not be recorded, those which were least adequate were left off. Also, in many of the distributions given below, and in the next section, each respondent is classified according to his best answer.

In accordance with our interest in the ideological nature of perceived party differences, highest priority was given to responses classified as "broad philosophical" differences.[11] Included here are responses referring to the parties' *attitude toward change; posture toward social welfare programs, socialism, and free enterprise; stand on the power of the federal government;* and *attitude on the relationship of individuals and government.* Also included are *unexplained uses of the terms "liberal," "progressive," "conservative," "reactionary," "moderate."* The second major category includes references to groups which are aided or hurt by the policies of one party or the other. Such references deserve high priority in that the respondent does see the parties as being beneficial or detrimental to a general class of individuals.

The final three categories are referred to much less often. Next in order, after group references, come responses about domestic fiscal and monetary policies (spend too freely or not enough, spend us into debt, reduce debt, balance budget, bring sound money, cheap money). These are followed by mentions of single domestic issues, ranging from social security to federal aid to education to farm policy to civil rights. The last of the major categories is foreign policy. Finally, a few statements which could not be coded elsewhere, are put together in a "miscellaneous" category, which has the lowest priority of all.

The distributions of students and parents on this priority code are given in Table 4.5. In order to keep a perspective on the total number of students and parents we are talking about, the distributions are percentaged on the basis of those who mentioned some party difference and on the total sample base. Probably the most notable feature of these distribu-

[11]This is the same code used by Converse for the 1960 election study data, and our description of it is a paraphrase of his. Converse, "The Nature of Belief Systems in Mass Publics," p. 220.

TABLE 4.5
STUDENT AND PARENT REPORTS OF POLITICAL
PARTY DIFFERENCES

	Students		Parents	
Broad philosophy	47%[a]	16%	36%	12%
Group interests	29	10	44	14
Fiscal and monetary issues	6	2	14	5
Specific domestic policies	9	3	3	1
Foreign policy	7	2	1	1
Miscellaneous	3	1	1	0
Total	101%	34%	99%	33%
	(701)	(2029)	(634)	(1883)

[a]The first column of figures for students and parents is based on those who mentioned some party difference (34 percent of the students and 34 percent of the parents). The second column is based on the total student or parent sample.

tions is the larger percentage of students than parents who cite a broad philosophy difference between the parties. A quick interpretation suggests that the newer generation looks beyond narrower aspects of party differences and gets to the philosophical roots of these surface manifestations. Yet there are problems with such an interpretation. For one thing, views of the parties are highly correlated with education, so that part of the student-parent discrepancy is due to the nature of the student sample. If we eliminate parents with less than a high school diploma, the percentage citing a broad philosophical difference resembles the student figure much more closely. Secondly, while students have the terminology at hand to describe a philosophical difference between the parties, their understanding of it is evidently poorer than parents'. For example, we will note in the next section that students more often are confused about just which party it is that is more conservative and which is more liberal.

Evidence for this latter point also comes from an examination of the specific differences proclaimed by students and parents. For this and later similar comparisons, we combine all the responses in a major category, whether or not the individual gave a "higher" or "lower" response as well. Students and parents giving a broad philosophy response are distributed as follows:

	1	2	3	4	5	6	Total
Students	36%	17	11	23	6	7	100% (496)
Parents	21%	11	26	19	10	13	100% (353)

1. Undefined terms
2. Acceptance or resistance of change, the status quo
3. Socialism vs. capitalism; social welfare concerns
4. Centralization and states' rights
5. Individual dignity and initiative
6. Other

Large numbers of individuals in both samples used undefined terms in describing the parties. But the proportion is substantially higher in the student sample. We suppose that many students have heard these terms in some context or other and learned that they are associated with the two parties. What the labels mean, however, is often unclear.

Differences in emphasis can also be seen in the remaining distribution of broad philosophy responses. Without longitudinal data we cannot be positive of our interpretation, but the differences are very suggestive. Students are relatively more concerned about the parties' attitudes toward change and new ideas, and whether the parties are quick or slow to respond to current problems. This is befitting of a group concerned with a variety of new, intricate social problems.[12] Parents, on the other hand, more often describe the parties in terms of their perceived stands on private enterprise, socialism, and social welfare programs. For most students, we assume, these are not very lively issues.

The other differences in the overall student and parent distributions (Table 4.5), together with detailed analyses of the responses, suggest that a significant shift in the images of the parties was underway by the mid-60's. Group interests obviously declined as a major delineator of party positions. And just as striking are the changes in the types of groups mentioned. While this in itself might be attributed to the same lack of experience with the party system noted above, there are equally striking changes in the types of groups mentioned—these shifts comport well with our notions of the changing salience or significance attached to various groups, suggesting a generational rather than a life cycle explanation.

Interestingly, most of the changes were in the image of the Democratic party. For example, among the parents, 45 percent of the group references mentioned working (little, common, laboring) people or unions. This figure drops to 26 percent among the younger generation. In contrast, references to favoritism toward big business (industry, Wall Street) or rich people were virtually the same in both the parent (32 percent) and student (31 percent) generations.[13]

Other changes in group references also affect images of the Democrats and are mostly in their favor. Few individuals saw benefits from one of the parties to blacks or other minority groups, but the percentage is clearly higher among students (7 percent) than parents (2 percent). The remaining change is in the number of respondents who were struck by the absence of benefits to select groups (no catering to special interests, good for the majority), or, alternatively, by the divisive nature of one of the

[12]Admittedly one of the difficulties here is knowing whether this concern is characteristic of the current generation or of young people of nearly any generation.

[13]"Erroneous" references (Democrats are for rich people) or negatively worded references (Republicans are *against* unions) were coded, but inspection shows such references to be rare.

parties. Barely 11 percent of the parents mentioned such a response, while among the students 26 percent reported this difference between the parties. Parents and students did agree, by margins of seven to one, that Democrats are less divisive than Republicans.

Changes in responses about domestic issues add further evidence of an alteration in the images that the newer generation has of the parties. Generally, fiscal and monetary issues—often references to national or personal prosperity—are less frequently mentioned by students while other domestic problems receive relatively more emphasis (Table 4.5). Especially revealing are the particular nonfiscal problems cited:

	1	2	3	4	5	6	7	8	9	10	Total	
Students	47%	14	6	2	8	4	1	0	4	16	102%	(130)
Parents	14%	11	6	23	14	13	3	4	4	7	98%	(83)

1. Civil rights
2. Medical insurance
3. Poverty program
4. Social welfare programs
5. Social security
6. Tariffs, free trade
7. Minimum wages
8. Prohibition
9. Misc. aid to education, farm policy, etc.
10. Other; no specific category appropriate

Easily the most often mentioned issue for the students is civil rights. Forty-seven percent of the references to domestic policy are in this one area. The same issue attracts only 14 percent of the parents' responses. The items in which parents lead are uniformly those that were critical years before our survey was undertaken. In fact, a few parents are still given to mentioning the perceived party position on Prohibition. Not the least important point is that double the number of student responses could not be classified in any of the categories provided. No one issue received a lot of mentions,[14] but a series of new policies and problems are getting increased attention.

Variations in the reported type of party differences fall along the same lines as the proportion citing any difference. In particular, there are considerable changes in the percentages reporting broad philosophy differences on the one hand and group interests on the other hand. The greatest variation, understandably, occurs when controlling for the education of the head of the household. Among parents with an eighth grade education or less, the proportion giving a broad philosophy explanation drops to a low point of 14 percent; this figure jumps to 24 percent among those with some high school education, to 35 percent among those completing high school, and to 59 percent of the college students. Group interest citations run in the opposite direction, ranging from 54 percent among the least educated, to 55 percent and 48 percent as education rises, and then plummeting to 24 percent of the highly educated respondents. For the student sample, the proportions run in the same direc-

[14]Care was taken in the coding stage to identify responses made by more than a few individuals, and new categories were established when such responses were found.

tions, although the gradient is not as steep, no doubt because at the time of the interview all of the seniors themselves had the same amount of formal education. Still, controlling for parental education, the percentages noting broad philosophy differences are 28 percent, 37 percent, 52 percent, and 57 percent from lower to higher education, respectively. Group references again run in reverse order 45 percent, 37 percent, 20 percent, and 22 percent. Obviously, one's education and, among young people, one's parents' education, have a great deal to do with the perception and active use of political party descriptions that are general in scope and philosophical in nature. The degree of political interest is also related to perception of broad philosophy differences, but the relationship is not as strong as with education.

One other relationship is worth noting. Our earlier comments about belief systems suggest that the presence of organizing concepts such as are contained in the broad philosophy responses should make it easier for individuals to retain specific bits of information about political matters. Thus we should find a positive correlation between the type of party differences cited and the amount of political information held by the respondent. Such is the case for both students and parents, but with an important difference. The correlation for parents (.27) is considerably higher than that for students (.14).

The lower figure for pre-adults is what we would expect if students are learning material by rote or without regard to organizing concepts which might facilitate retention of and active use of the material. Some students appear to be quite knowledgeable by the facts and figures presently at their command, but they are not equipped with integrative frameworks capable of handling all of this material. As time goes by, individuals who have learned or will learn some conceptual way of approaching political affairs will probably learn and remember many specific data, whereas those without a general scheme will learn little more in the way of specific facts and will forget more of what they presntly know. Thus the correlation will rise as the students move further along the life cycle.

Turning finally to the impact of the family, we find additional evidence that ideological views of political parties must come for the most part from the school, the media, and other nonfamily sources. Of the various measures we examined, perhaps the best indicator is that only seven percent of all students and parents actually report the same class of party differences. Broadly ideological views of the parties, like perceptions of party differences in general, do not stem directly from parental views.

RECOGNITION OF A LIBERAL-CONSERVATIVE DIMENSION

In the preceding section we were concerned with the unaided description of party differences. To tap the wider circle of individuals who would recognize the liberal-conservative distinction when it was brought to their attention, the terms were explicitly introduced in a series of further questions. All respondents were asked, "Would you say that either one of the parties is more conservative or more liberal than the other?" If the answer was "Yes," the respondent was asked which party is more conservative and then asked, "What do you have in mind when you say that the Republicans (Democrats) are more conservative than the Democrats (Republicans)?" Responses to the latter question were recorded using the same detailed code described in the last section.

Among respondents answering "No" to the opening question, we wished to sort out those who were skeptical about party differences from those who did not actually comprehend the terms. Thus, these respondents were asked, "Do you think that people generally consider the Democrats or the Republicans more conservative, or wouldn't you want to guess about that?" This question sifted out an additional group who were able to give a response. To probe the accuracy and depth of a response given after this much hinting, a question was asked parallel to the "meaning" question above: "What do people have in mind when they say the Republicans (Democrats) are more conservative than the Democrats (Republicans)?" Coding was done as above. Among those unwilling to hazard a guess, it was assumed that they were completely unfamiliar with the terms, and no further questions were asked about this subject.

Using responses to this series of questions, we adopted Converse's scheme of distinguishing five strata varying in the extent of "recognition and understanding" brought to bear by the respondents. The lowest rung is made up of those who could not "guess" what most people thought about liberal-conservative differences between the parties. Just above them are individuals who said that one party is more conservative, but who were unable to supply any meaning for the terms. This group is in an ambiguous state; they have some inkling of a party difference and judge the Republicans to be the conservative party more often than not—64 percent versus 36 percent for the Democrats—but they are apparently unable to verbalize even the narrowest aspect of that difference. In any event, even the two lowest strata together (53 percent of the students and 45 percent of the parents) constitute a somewhat smaller proportion than those who initially cited no party differences (Table 4.4). Prompting, as expected, has uncovered an awareness that was previously hidden.

In the middle stratum we begin to find meanings attached to the liberal and conservative tags. However, respondents at this level distinguish themselves by the erroneous ways (according to usual definitions) in which they match parties, labels, and meanings. A number of them, for example, say the Democrats are more conservative. Others make more elegant errors, such as calling the Republicans more conservative because they are more favorable toward change. Coding for errors was very lenient, so that for responses for which it was very difficult to judge the associations involved, correct matching was assumed.

In the two highest categories, respondents defined the ideological labels in a reasonably appropriate way and correctly pinned them on the parties. The difference is that definitions of those in the second level were relatively narrow or concrete (references to groups, domestic, foreign, and miscellaneous issues), while definitions given by persons in the top stratum were general and abstract (broad philosophy responses).

Student and parent distributions across these five strata of recognition and understanding are given at the bottom of Table 4.6. Perhaps the first observation is that parents more often show some recognition of the liberal-conservative dimension; in each of the three lowest strata one finds fewer of the adult generation. This is interesting in light of the fact that equal proportions of youths and parents failed to report any party difference when the question contained no aids. Apparently a greater number of parents have heard the terms sufficiently often that they are more or less meaningful when brought to their attention. When encountered, fewer parents leave the terms undefined and fewer make errors in matching them with the parties. At the same time, the interpretation parents give the liberal-conservative dimension is narrower and less abstract than that given by students. The parental focus on group benefits and fiscal matters accounts for this considerable difference.

Both student and parent samples show a strong correlation between the level of recognition and understanding and such attributes as the educa-

TABLE 4.6

PARENT-STUDENT CORRESPONDENCE ON RECOGNITION AND UNDERSTANDING OF THE LIBERAL-CONSERVATIVE DIMENSION

| | Parents Recognition and Understanding[a] | | | | | |
| | None | | | | Broad | |
Students	1	2	3	4	5	
None 1	44%	43%	33%	33%	29%	
2	18	17	20	13	12	
3	14	12	14	13	9	
4	8	8	7	16	12	
Broad 5	16	20	25	26	38	
Total	100%	100%	99%	101%	100%	
$\tau_b = .16$	(314)	(534)	(176)	(203)	(632)	
Parent Totals	34	11	10	28	17	(1892)
Student Totals	37	16	13	10	24	(2026)

[a]Descriptions of the categories are given in the text.

tion of the respondents or their parents and the respondents' political interest. These are the same correlates observed for active use of ideological terms in differentiating the parties. Sex differences are small among the students, but mothers are found much more frequently in the lower three categories than are fathers.

Turning to the student-parent pairs, we find that there are several ways in which we might examine the similarity of parents and their children. No matter what the method, however, the evidence provides further support for the conclusion reached in the previous section: transmission of ideas from parents to their children accounts for little of the party imagery of the students as a whole. For example, comparing their placement on the five strata of recognition and understanding, the correlation between parents and students is .16. Examination of Table 4.6 on which this figure is based, shows that even among parents in the highest category, half of the students do not recognize the terms or are unable to define them or match them properly.

Variations do occur in the degree of parent-student correspondence, but the correlation rises significantly above that for the total population only when parents are homogeneous. In these families—about a third of the total—the student-parent correlation is .31, with boys (.34) more like their parents than girls (.26). In contrast, the student-mother correlation is .19 and the student-father correlation is .11 when the parents are not homogeneous. Thus, where each parent reinforces the other, in matters of knowledge and sophistication as well as in attitudinal orientations, students resemble their parents more closely, and our ability to predict the student's position is enhanced accordingly.

KNOWLEDGE, POLITICAL PARTY DIFFERENCES, AND PARTISANSHIP

We have reserved for the final section of this chapter an analysis of certain relationships between political knowledge, perceptions of political party differences, and partisanship. Two major questions will briefly concern us. First, we ask whether knowledge and sophistication affect the degree of correspondence between parent and student party identification. Second, we ask whether defection from partisanship in voting or projected voting is observed among parents and students of varying levels of knowledge and conceptual clarity.

It has often been pointed out that partisanship develops in most children before they attain even a modicum of knowledge about what the parties stand for and how they differ from each other.[15] Given this developmental sequence, the impact of student learning, when it does

[15]Hess and Torney, *Development of Political Attitudes in Children*, Chapter 4; Greenstein, *Children and Politics*, Chapter 4.

occur, would seem to be marginal at best. Still, our analysis in Chapter 2 suggested that some changes in partisanship take place during the late elementary and high school years, and these changes may be stimulated by newly gained wisdom about parties and politics. If this is true, we would be particularly likely to find increased deviations from parental partisanship among the students who are the most knowledgeable about politics and the most skilled at understanding political ideas.

The student-parent correlations for party identification are given in Table 4.7, controlling for student political knowledge, reports of party differences, and recognition of the liberal-conservative dimension. In each case students who are "low" on the control variable deviate relatively more than others from parental attitudes. This particular finding is partly spurious, owing its existence to the fact the "low" students also tend to be those with less interest in politics, with attendant consequences observed in Chapter 2. Though spurious, it is still significant that the greatest student deviation from parental views occurs among those with the least knowledge and understanding. Indeed, this is another commentary on the relatively weak role of political learning in accounting for student partisanship.

More to the point of our above reasoning is that for two of the three controls in the table, there are indications of a curvilinear pattern in the degree of student-parent correspondence. Students who are most knowledgeable and those with rather sophisticated notions of party differences deviate from parental partisanship to a greater extent than those in the middle categories.[16] Quite unlike the "low" students, defections from parental views in these cases are probably due in part to political learning in the high school years. The knowledge gained about parties and politics presumably leads some students to reassess their own partisanship, with a resulting drift away from parental partisanship. Thus while development of knowledge and conceptual skills concerning the parties does not have a large overall effect on students' partisanship (the differences in the correlations are not large nor perfectly consistent), a slightly disproportionate amount of defection apparently is stimulated among the most politically alert students.

Party images and political knowledge have fairly little impact on deviation from parental attitudes, but they may still have a considerable impact on projected political behavior of pre-adults. Knowledge of the parties develops extensively during the high school years, so that by the time individuals cast their first ballots, their view of the parties may well

[16]The recognition variable purposely accommodates a larger and less select group of respondents in the topmost category, and the curvilinear relationship may be obscured because of it. Although there is a fairly strong correlation (.28) between the recognition variable and the unaided reports of party differences, the top recognition category does contain a fair number of students who originally claimed that the parties do not differ.

TABLE 4.7

STUDENT-PARENT PARTISANSHIP, CONTROLLING FOR STUDENT
KNOWLEDGE AND SOPHISTICATION

Political Knowledge	Student-Parent Party Identification Correlation		View of Party Differences	Student-Parent Party Identification Correlation		Recognition and Understanding	Student-Parent Party Identification Correlation	
Low 1	.35	(73)	No differences	.44	(1191)	None 1	.43	(679)
2	.41	(118)	Foreign policy	.52	(44)	2	.43	(281)
3	.44	(262)	Domestic policy	.56	(54)	3	.41	(233)
4	.52	(461)	Fiscal policy	.59	(40)	4	.50	(192)
5	.47	(286)	Groups	.44	(183)	Broad 5	.55	(436)
6	.47	(228)	Broad phil.	.47	(292)			
High 7	.44	(423)						

interact with their partisanship in determining how they will vote. Since the seniors have not actually voted, our test cannot be as strict as we would like. Nevertheless, we can use students' reports of how they would have voted in 1964 to get a tentative answer to our question. Parents' votes will be examined for their intrinsic value and to establish a baseline for judging the student data.

The election of 1964 was a Democratic landslide, and relatively few Democrats deviated from their avowed partisanship by voting for Goldwater. Perhaps for this reason, there is no pattern to the deviations by Democratic parents or students when controlling for knowledge and sophistication. In all categories about 90 percent or more of the respondents cast a Democratic ballot.[17] Among Republicans a much larger proportion deviated from their partisanship, and some patterning becomes evident. However, differences in defection rates occur only between groups that vary grossly in knowledge or conceptual skills. For example, respondents who cited some party difference defected less than those who reported no difference; but there is no clear pattern among those stressing broad philosophy, group references, fiscal policy.

Defection rates for groups of parents and students are shown in Table 4.8. For each of the three controls, those who ranked lowest deviated much more frequently than the remainder of the samples. The consistency of this pattern suggests that it will indeed be characteristic of the younger generation as it moves into the electorate and that it will continue in evidence as this generation gets older. Although our finding is of a coarser nature, it is highly reminiscent of the relationship reported in *The American Voter* between the "levels of conceptualization" and defection

---

[17]In addition, the "lower" categories are more heavily populated with blacks, who voted overwhelmingly Democratic in 1964 regardless of their knowledge and awareness.

TABLE 4.8
DEFECTION RATES FOR PARENT AND STUDENT REPUBLICANS, BY LEVEL OF KNOWLEDGE AND SOPHISTICATION

Political Knowledge	Percentage Defecting from Party Identification		View of Party Differences	Percentage Defecting from Party Identification		Recognition and Understanding	Percentage Defecting from Party Identification	
	Students	Parents		Students	Parents		Students	Parents
Less	54% (106)	47% (40)	No difference	46% (354)	37% (314)	None Minimal	50% (193)	53% (112)
More[a]	34%[b] (430)	29% (482)	Some difference	25% (180)	21% (202)	or greater	34% (389)	24% (408)

[a]"More" is categories 1–3 for parents and 1–4 for students. "Less" is 4–6 for parents and 5–7 for students.

[b]The entries are the proportion of Republicans voting for President Johnson (or students saying they would have voted for him) in 1964.

rates among Democrats in the second Eisenhower election.[18] We are led to conclude, as that study did, that people who are rather uninformed about politics contribute disproportionately to fluctuations in the partisan division of the vote. We can add here that such a pattern, at a gross level at least, is characteristic not only of Democrats or of the generation of the 1950s, but continued at least to the mid sixties. It describes as well the new generation of American voters, and is a result of forces well underway before individuals even enter the electorate.

Taken together these findings indicate a curious but no longer surprising relationship between political acumen and party identification. We did detect what appears to be a small impetus toward greater defection from parental partisanship among the most highly informed students. But the major effect of increased political knowledge seems to be a strengthening of attachment to one's party, and often, a greater affinity with one's parents' partisanship. How ironic it is that the attempt to create intelligent, informed, unattached voters often results in strengthening the very attachments that one is working against.

CONCLUSION

The findings of this chapter complement those of other chapters in several respects, and they derive some of their importance therefrom. First, the present chapter deals to some extent with ideological perspectives about politics rather than with orientations of an affective nature or with perceptions of specific, concrete, or immediate objects, issues, and behavior. One of our main conclusions in this regard is that parents have little direct impact on students' conceptual apparatuses. Nonetheless, there are small pockets of students, e.g., in highly politicized families with homogeneous parents, in which the effects of parental attitudes are marked. From a political point of view such small pockets may be quite important for they may contain the party cadres of the future.

Second, the current results complement those in other chapters by observing party-related matters from an additional point of view. Previously we have looked at them indirectly in terms of issues about which the parties take stands and directly with party identification. Here we looked at images of the parties across the two generations. A result of this fresh perspective is to point out even more clearly than before the unique nature of party identification. For even though partisanship itself is strongly passed on from one generation to the next, party images are not. Or to put it even more pointedly, partisan similarity persists in the face of changing partisan images.

More generally, this result throws into bold relief the strong effect of more or less institutionalized identifications, or at least of simple, readily

[18]Campbell, *et al.*, *The American Voter*, p. 264.

understood, and reasonably apparent affiliations, on the transmission of political orientations from parents to their children. That this is not limited to politics is suggested by the striking difference between the high similarity of parents and students on church identifications and the much lower agreement on attitudes toward the Bible.[19] In religion as in politics, where parties, factions, institutions, or even individuals capture the loyalty of large numbers of persons, a relatively high rate of transmission to the next generation is likely—provided that object itself remains in high esteem.

Finally, this chapter clearly illustrates some different aspects of the political learning process. In dealing with political information, for example, it became apparent that cues from parents were mediated and supplemented by conditions of social structure—sex, religion, and historical experiences. By the same token, the relationship between knowledge and academic achievement suggests the importance of cognitive abilities and motivation. The linkage between cognitive development and political sophistication was aptly illustrated by the fact that students (like parents) with greater knowledge and understanding of politics defected less often from their party—shored up as they were by firmer knowledge and greater understanding of the party system.

[19]M. Kent Jennings and Richard G. Niemi, "The Transmission of Political Values from Parent to Child," *American Political Science Review*, 62 (March 1968), pp. 169–84.

CHAPTER FIVE

Citizenship Roles Within
the System

Dᴇꜰɪɴɪɴɢ one's relation to the political community is an important stage in the development of the political self. Just as the individual develops a repertoire of expectations and skills with respect to other individuals, so too with respect to political institutions. Since the dawn of civilization humanity has had to contend with various forms of organized authority relationships, but it is only with the advent of the modern nation-state that these relationships have been so shot through with questions of civic obligation and participation, national loyalty and support, and the common good.

Given the fact that children are born into a political system which more or less holds binding power over them, what kind of eventual resolution do they make with that system in terms of their citizenship role? On the one hand, what sorts of obligations are entailed by citizenship? Most particularly, what amount and forms of participation are considered appropriate or requisite? On the other hand, to what degree is loyalty and support offered—especially support which is not dependent on immediate rewards? These are the concerns that underlie this chapter.

We address ourselves to five main topics. First, as they stand on the threshold of maturity what are the twelfth graders' idealized conceptions of the good citizen in American society? How strong is the civic obligation norm? Second, pervasive feelings of political efficacy have been singled out as requisites of healthy democracies. What is the state of efficacy among the seniors, and to what may this state be attributed? A third subject hinges on the forecasting of civic participation. Since high school students have traditionally been excluded from the principal roles of manifest political activity, it becomes especially important to know how they see themselves behaving in the future. Are there ways in which these projections are wedded to contemporary behavior, and what does this tell us about the evolution of the political self as citizen in the system? The fourth topic takes us into the area of legality and support. How trusting are the seniors and what are the sources of their trust? Finally, we return to the domains of obligation and participation to consider a specific political issue, in this instance a suffrage issue. Even though the issue has been resolved subsequent to the date of field work, the episode provides an illustration of how the specific application of obligation and participation norms is tempered by various socialization forces.

THE GOOD CITIZEN

We begin our discussion by portraying the general image held of the good American citizen by the high school seniors and their parents. Although a number of approaches could have been used to elicit an image of the good citizen, we relied upon an open-ended question which allowed individuals to construct their own idealized version. As shall be presently demonstrated, this tactic yields a large variety of specific responses which can then be aggregated into a smaller number of broad categories. In addition, the variation of responses even among adolescents and their parents—to say nothing of teachers and principals—indicated that more structured approaches might have circumscribed unduly the respondents' choices. The question ran as follows: "People have different ideas about what being a good citizen means. Tell me how you would describe a good citizen in this country—that is, what things about a person are most important in showing that he is a good citizen?"

Both the students and parents proved quite voluble in their replies, with the former averaging 2.7 coded responses and the latter 2.6. Of course, the volubility is in part a function of how finely one codes, and we usually elected finer rather than coarser content analysis. However, the descriptions were distributed across a wide spectrum of traits so that even if only broad coding categories had been utilized the level of verbosity would have been marked.

Turning to the substantive attributes of model citizens, it is clear that the 1965 graduating class saw them predominantly in their political roles. Whether we consider the results in terms of all respondents or all responses, the manifestly political side of the good citizen stands out. Thus nearly three-fourths of all students' responses dealt either with political participation or allegiance. Not that nonpolitical attributes are completely overlooked by the seniors. In fact, about one-third of them refer to a cluster of attributes we call "social-interpersonal behavior," and a similar proportion aver that the good citizen is a person of high moral and ethical standards. Nor should it be argued that these clusters are necessarily apolitical in all their guises. Helping people or leading an honest life may well have direct political implications. In the more conventional sense, however, participatory and allegiant modes vis-à-vis the political system would ordinarily become parts of the input, conversion, and output process associated with American political life. It is these modes which mark the students' depiction of the ideal American.

Broadly speaking the four major clusters shown in Table 5.1 can be adapted to the Almond and Verba trilogy of participant, subject, and

TABLE 5.1
GOOD CITIZENSHIP DESCRIPTIONS AMONG STUDENTS AND PARENT

	Percentage of Respondents		Percentage of Responses	
	Students	Parents	Students	Parents
Participation in System				
(a) no level specified				
Votes	37.8%	27.2%	14.0%	10.4%
Interested, pays attention	21.9	11.7	8.1	4.5
Active in general	18.4	6.5	6.8	2.5
Informed voting	8.0	4.8	3.0	1.8
Works to improve country	4.9	3.6	1.8	1.4
Miscellaneous	4.8	2.2	1.8	0.8
(b) local level specified				
Active, takes part	19.2	20.1	7.1	7.7
Works to improve locality	4.6	5.2	1.7	2.0
Votes in local elections	3.8	3.7	1.4	1.4
Active in school affairs	1.1	3.1	0.4	1.2
Miscellaneous	1.6	0.7	0.6	0.3
Subtotal	126.1%	88.8%	46.7%	34.0%
Allegiance to System				
Obeys laws	28.2	34.2	10.4	13.1
Loyal to government	16.4	7.0	6.1	2.7
Willing to help country	9.5	4.5	3.5	1.8
Will fight for nation	6.4	1.3	2.4	0.5
Honors nation's symbols	4.4	2.0	1.6	0.8
Pays taxes, doesn't cheat	3.4	3.1	1.3	1.2
Doesn't downgrade nation	2.6	1.6	1.0	0.6
Miscellaneous	2.9	1.2	1.1	0.4
Subtotal	73.8%	54.9%	27.4%	21.1%
Social-interpersonal Behavior				
Tolerant of others	10.4	13.1	3.8	5.0
Helps other people	9.5	14.2	3.2	5.3
Gets along with people	4.3	12.2	1.6	4.6
Kind, considerate	4.3	7.8	1.9	3.2
Good family person	3.0	9.1	1.1	3.5
Good neighbor	2.5	8.5	0.9	3.2
Miscellaneous	1.4	0.4	0.5	0.2
Subtotal	35.4%	65.3%	13.0%	25.0%
Moral-ethical Behavior				
High integrity, principles	7.5	5.0	2.8	1.9
Religious, church-going	5.2	16.6	1.9	6.4
Honest, trustworthy	5.1	10.4	1.9	4.0
Moral, clean	4.6	8.2	1.7	3.2
Improves oneself	4.2	4.5	1.6	1.7
Hard worker, does his best	3.9	4.6	1.1	1.7
Miscellaneous	4.4	1.5	1.6	0.6
Subtotal	34.9%	50.8%	12.6%	19.5%
Don't know	0.6	1.3	0.2	0.5
Totals	270.8%	261.1%	99.9%	100.1%
	(2060)	(1922)	(5581)	(5012)

parochial orientations.[1] We have tampered somewhat with the subject classification and refer to this as allegiance to the system. Participation and allegiance taken together comprise manifestly political conceptualizations of the good citizen. Parochial orientations—those without obvious political content—are subdivided into behaviors and attributes resting directly on interpersonal transactions and those residing essentially in intrapersonal behavior. In some respects, this last cluster echoes the creed of the Protestant ethic.[2]

Within the political realm, the participant mode overshadows that of the subject or allegiant orientation. This converges with the conclusion of Almond and Verba that the civic culture of the United States is one which shades more toward the participant than subject role, in contrast to Great Britain.[3] No doubt the years of repetitious schoolroom exhortation to participate, as well as public rhetoric and "get out the vote" campaigns, have had some effect in heightening the participant role for young adults as they prepare to leave high school. Exercising the franchise is a particularly apt medium by which Americans demonstrate their citizenship according to the reports of the high school seniors. If, as some have said, free elections are a *sine qua non* of democracy, then a large share of American youngsters enter adulthood pretty well convinced that taking part in those elections is a *sine qua non* of good citizenship.

Some appreciation for the participation ethos of the twelfth graders can be gained by comparing their imagery with that of their parents. First, it may be observed that the parochial orientations loom much larger among parents than their offspring. Whereas 45 percent of the parental responses fall in the two parochial dimensions, the same is true for only 26 percent of the students'. In Chapter 10, we take up in some detail the reasons for this disparity. A sufficient note here is that we believe these differences to be largely life cycle in nature, and that the high school cohort will move toward emphasizing more of the parochial values as they move through the years. The essential point for the moment is the greater investment which teenagers put in the political properties of good citizenship.

The second compelling feature of the comparisons is that even though both parents and youth stress activism more than allegiance, the gap between the two modes is greater amongst the students. While it might be thought that parents would be even more impressed with the concept

[1]Gabriel Almond and Sidney Verba, *The Civic Culture* (Princeton: Princeton University Press, 1963), Chapter 1.

[2]A different and much more fully explicated handling of responses to the root question is taken up in George Levenson, "The Public Responsibilities of Private Man," (unpublished Ph.D. thesis, University of Michigan, 1971). See also his "The School's Contribution to the Learning of Participatory Responsibility," in Byron Massialas (ed.), *Political Youth, Traditional Schools* (Englewood Cliffs: Prentice-Hall, 1972), Chapter 9.

[3]Almond and Verba, *The Civic Culture*, Chapter 14.

that good government involves high participation—having been besieged over the years to demonstrate their concern for policy outcomes—the more idealized version comes through with greater clarity in the younger years. In sum, the emerging adults not only start out with a good citizen imagery heavily infused with political properties in an absolute sense; they also begin with an imagery more thoroughly infused in this vein than that possessed by the older generation.

Now it might be charged that what we have portrayed are largely clichés which are the product of classroom and media indoctrination. Give the schoolchildren certain stimuli and they give the appropriate, canned reply. The danger of receiving such trite verbalizations has led some investigators to employ projective and hypothetical techniques to elude the catechismal response.[4] Yet it is highly unlikely that one moves any great distance away from an experiential base by simply posing hypothetical situations, for the individual still must cast about for some way of relating the past accumulation of thoughts and behavior to the posed situation. And one runs the risk of beginning to tap imaginative and problem-solving skills rather than internalized values.

But let us assume that these good citizen portrayals are largely clichés. Does this decrease their currency as normative standards held by young Americans? We think not, for the stuff of much politics is wrapped up in slogans and clichés. People act on the basis of clichés. If it is simply a cliché that the good citizen votes, for example, it is nevertheless true that for most periods in American history this is the one consciously political act that people have felt compelled to perform. If it is simply a cliché that loyalty to country is a hallmark of good citizenship, it is also true that most Americans at most times have been basically loyal, even during such times as the Depression and the late 1960s when criticism abounded. So as these seventeen-and eighteen-year-olds stood on the verge of adulthood they were armed with a series of norms or "clichés" which would serve as reference points. The norms might not be honored, they might be reshuffled, they might contain internal inconsistencies, and they might be replaced by some others, but they nevertheless signified the core of the idealized citizen.

This section has demonstrated that the seniors of 1965 invested the ideal citizen with a remarkable number of political characteristics; and within the political domain the participant culture stands out. In the next two sections we take up two aspects of the participant way of political life. As we do this it will become apparent that some fairly sharp demarcations

---

[4]Foremost among these researchers are Joseph Adelson and his collaborators. For examples of their innovative research see Joseph Adelson and Robert P. O'Neill, "The Growth of Political Ideas in Adolescence; the Sense of Community," *Journal of Personality and Social Psychology*, 4 (September 1966), pp. 295–306; and Judith Gallatin and Joseph Adelson, "Individual Rights and the Public Good," *Comparative Political Studies*, 3 (July 1970), pp. 226–42.

may be detected among the young if the stimuli are presented more in terms of one's own perspectives and expectations rather than in terms of an ideal model. Nevertheless, the hovering presence of the heavily politicized ideal citizen should not be forgotten for it provides both a rough gauge to which maturing citizens will compare themselves, and also a model to which they may at times aspire.

POLITICAL EFFICACY

Of all the qualities inherent in the notion of democratic citizenship none is perhaps so critical as that denoting the self-perceived ability of citizens to cope with the political system and to have some impact on its performance. Such self-perceptions are vital for two reasons. First, the belief that one is efficacious is related to taking part in politics. Persons encumbered with a sense of inefficacy are less likely to try to influence governmental processes which have an effect on them or on those relevant to them. While the prospect of negative sanctions and the presence of differential opportunity costs will mediate the efficacy-activity nexus, the crucial importance of a feeling of political efficacy cannot be denied. In the measure that democracy strives to achieve a full participatory life for all strata of the *polis*, the development of efficacy becomes a major requirement in the socialization of the young. Obviously the distribution of political efficacy across the polity has implications for the allocative functions of the political system as well as portraying something of the political richness of individual lives.

There is a second sense in which the emergence of political efficacy is vital. Political efficacy ordinarily implies a relationship between the individual and the government. To feel efficacious is to feel that the government will be responsive to the efforts of individuals and collectivities. To feel efficacious is to subscribe to a political norm. As Easton and Dennis state:

> As a norm [efficacy] refers to the timeless theme of democratic theory that members of a democratic regime ought to regard those who occupy positions of political authority as responsive agents and that the members themselves ought to be disposed to participate in the honors and offices of the system.[5]

Easton and Dennis go on to argue that support for this norm is, in effect, support for the regime. This, in turn, helps lead to the persistence of regimes. Political efficacy thus takes its place in the systems approach to politics as a key input into the system. One does not have to adopt the full panoply of the systems approach to agree that the distribution of political competence in the populace is an important indicator of support for the regime.

[5]David Easton and Jack Dennis, "The Child's Acquisition of Regime Norms: Political Efficacy," *American Political Science Review*, 61 (March 1967), pp. 25–38. The literature on efficacy is voluminous. See note 4 in the Easton and Dennis article for references, as well as Ada Finifter, "Dimensions of Political Alienation," *American Political Science Review*, 64 (June 1970), pp. 389–410.

A feeling of political efficacy begins to emerge as early as the third grade on the American scene. At this stage, feelings of low efficacy predominate over those of high. With each succeeding grade, however, the efficacious spirit rises and at a rapid rate. By the time they reached the eighth grade, over half of the children in the University of Chicago study were in the high bracket of a trichotomy of high, medium, and low. Just as important, there was a marked increase over the grades in the cognitive ability of the children to respond meaningfully to statements tapping the efficacy dimension.

We confront our high school seniors, then, in the firm knowledge that at least the ideas which lie behind the concept of political efficacy are by no means foreign to them. The next section will include a discussion of how the student's sense of efficacy intertwines with other relevant political orientations. For the remainder of the present section we concentrate on aggregate student-parent comparisons and on an analysis of student-parent pairs.

Our measures of student political efficacy are not as replicable from adult and childhood studies as one might desire. Because of methodological problems uncovered during the pre-testing, we decided to drop two of the four questions comprising the standard SRC political efficacy scale. Of the two remaining questions the students were asked one in an unchanged form, and another was changed only by referring to parents instead of oneself in the question wording (see below). Parents were given the standard four items.[6] We will present data based on comparisons of responses to the two comparable items as well as scale scores based on four items in the case of parents and two in the case of students.

The only way to obtain an aggregate match-up of students and parents is to take their responses to the two common items:

	Percent Giving Efficacious Answer	
	Students	Parents
"Voting is the only way that people like my father and mother[a] can have any say about how the government runs things."	67	50
"Sometimes politics and government seem so complicated that a person like me can't really understand what's going on."	41	28

[a]"me" was substituted in the parent interview.

[6]The remaining two items are:
(1) I don't think public officials care much what people like me think.
(2) People like me don't have any say about what the government does.

Surprisingly, perhaps, the students exceed their parents in giving an efficacious reply to these two stimuli.[7] Part of the answer to this advantage would seem to lie in the twelve years of schooling during which the students have heard repeatedly that the idividual citizen can have an impact on the governmental process in a variety of ways and that, complicated though the government may be, it is still possible for the average citizen to make sense out of it. Alternatively, if children have not been indoctrinated with the factuality of these matters, they have at least been instructed that this is the way matters *should* be. In addition to the schools, other agents have, of course, repeated this theme throughout the child's lifetime. Beyond this, however, the student has also had little opportunity to test these feelings of efficacy. Conversely, the parents have had ample opportunity to test their efficacy and it must be assumed that in some cases they have found the results wanting.

Another key to the student advantage lies in the established relationship between education and political efficacy. All the students are, by definition, high school graduates (strictly speaking, they were going to be in a matter of days or weeks). And approximately one-half of them planned to attend a four-year college after graduation. Among parents, on the other hand, two-fifths had not received the high school diploma. Although we will not go into the matter in detail until Chapter 11, it may be noted that relative education makes a dramatic difference in the aggregate comparisons. The greater the students' expectations about exceeding their parents' education the greater is the student advantage in efficacious postures. In large part the overall margin of the student generation derives from those cases in which the students expect to outstrip the parents' educational achievements.[8]

These findings are intuitively appealing, but exactly what processes dictate them are not sharply defined. Perhaps the most reasonable explanation rests in the symbolic and tangible rewards attached to upward mobility. Planning to go beyond the educational achievements of one's parents signifies a worthy accomplishment in the American scheme of values. As such, the student may develop a sense of self-esteem as well as one of some mastery and control over the environment. This may, in turn, generate a fairly substantial gap between child and parents with

[7]Using somewhat different measures, Jack Dennis also found parents lagging behind their eleventh grade offspring in political efficacy. See his "Political Learning in Childhood and Adolescence: A Study of Fifth, Eight, and Eleventh Graders in Milwaukee, Wisconsin," Madison, University of Wisconsin Research and Development Center for Cognitive Learning, 1969, p. 27.

[8]While the relationship between education and political efficacy is always strong in survey studies, this does not necessarily mean that continually rising levels of education will —regardless of external events—yield continually rising levels of efficacy. On this point see Philip E. Converse, "Change in the American Electorate," in Angus Campbell and Philip E. Converse (eds.), *The Human Meaning of Social Change* (New York: Russell Sage Foundation, 1972), Chapter 8.

respect to the norm and psychological disposition summed up in the term political efficacy. For the child doing less well than the parents, these conditions are clearly lacking. Of course this does not necessarily mean that the student will be burdened with a sense of low efficacy. It simply means that compared with one's parents the mobility and achievements will be less and the resulting gap on efficacy correspondingly narrowed.

Anticipatory socialization would also account for the systematic changes across levels of relative education. Upwardly mobile students begin to identify with the target strata. These strata are, by definition, higher than those occupied by their parents. Since there tends to be a steady increase in efficacy at every major educational gradient, upwardly mobile students are identifying with target strata which typically possess greater efficacy than is true of their parents' own strata. By taking on the trappings and norms of the target strata, the students are anticipating their own futures. As the relative educational advantage of students over parents decreases (and reverses in relative terms), the target strata become much more like those already occupied by the parents. Children of college graduates who are quite certain of becoming college graduates themselves are not upwardly mobile. Their absolute sense of efficacy may well exceed that of the upwardly mobile students. But the difference between these potential college graduates and their parents is virtually nil. They are anticipating no more than what inhabitants of their parents' strata have already achieved.

Although contributing less to the overall difference in student versus parental efficacy scores, the factor of race also figures prominently in intergenerational comparisons. Again, this is a topic reserved for full discussion in Chapter 11. Suffice it to say at this point that 1) the student advantage over parents is more marked among black than white families; and 2) the cross-race differences between blacks and whites are smaller in the student than in the parent generation.

It has been widely assumed that efficacious parents produce efficacious offspring. The assumption rests partly on the occurrence of major and minor family political dynasties, and partly on the fact that since higher status people are more efficacious—and since status is to some extent inherited—the children of higher status parents should also feel efficacious. Support for the assumption is, at first glance, of meager proportions according to our data. Taking the two statements common to both samples, we find correlations of .14 and .08 for the "have any say" and "can't really understand" statements, respectively. These are obviously not of a magnitude to suggest a pervasive current of political efficacy flowing between parent and child.

Our measurement of parental political efficacy can be improved by adding the two other standard efficacy items to the two already under consideration. Responses to these four items form a Guttman scale with a

C.R. of .93. Similarly, the responses to the two student items were "scaled" with a C.R. of .94. Table 5.2 presents the overall marginals and the cross-tabulations for the student-parent pairs. Inspection of the percentages leaves little doubt that there is some positive correspondence between parents and their children. And the pattern exhibits a graceful monotonicity. Yet the strength of the association is not at all strong. As with the single item comparisons, we must conclude that parental efficacy is but a weak predictor of student efficacy.

Standing apart from the majority of other political orientations considered in this volume, the magnitude of the relationship is not exaggerated among girls. To the contrary, the highest similarity for any sex pairing is that for boys and fathers (.20). What seems to lie at the root of this exception to our general findings is the sense of mastery and control over the environment embedded in the efficacy measure. Typical imagery in the United States, and indeed in most societies, invests the male with more comprehension and control over his environment than is true for the female. In our own study we found empirical correlates for the imagery, inasmuch as husbands held a net advantage of 15 percent over their wives on the political efficacy measure. Similarly they held an 11 percent advantage in terms of personal efficacy. Since the growing boy acquires a sense of these societal norms, it is probable, *ceteris paribus*, that he more often selects the father rather than the mother as the model for emulation. This would be so even if the father actually is less efficacious than the mother. While girls could conceivably do likewise, a strong cross-sex pull would be required. Some suggestion of the ambivalent modelling operative for girls comes from observing that the two lowest parent-child correlations involve pairs which include daughters.

TABLE 5.2
STUDENT-PARENT POLITICAL EFFICACY

Students	Parents Low Efficacy 1	2	3	4	High Efficacy 5	
Low efficacy 1	32%	27%	26%	18%	16%	
2	37	35	34	41	35	
High efficacy 3	31	38	40	41	49	
Total	100%	100%	100%	100%	100%	
	(261)	(302)	(415)	(446)	(491)	
$\tau_b = .11$						
Parent Totals:	14	16	22	23	26	(1922)
Student Totals:	23	36	41	(2056)		

Notwithstanding the enhanced association between boys and fathers, the general picture for the paired relationships is still modest. An immediate attack on our findings is that great measurement error is involved. We freely acknowledge that such a complex concept as political efficacy is not easily tapped by eliciting reactions to a few statements in an interview situation. Our assessment of the students' efficacy is particularly vulnerable since it relies on only two items. To the degree that measurement error is involved the true parent-child correspondence is understated. Evidence to be presented below suggests, however, that the measure articulates in a predictable fashion with other political orientations. We shall see also that under certain circumstances the parent-child congruity reaches impressive heights.

Another possible explanation for the loose parent-child relationship is that other parental characteristics help shape the child's sense of efficacy. This is undoubtedly true, but the way in which this happens is elusive. For example, let us take parental education. As stated before, education is rather strongly related to efficacy among adults. Therefore, should we not expect to find the children of better-educated parents to be more efficacious? Taking the education of head of household as the parental indicator, it turns out, as expected, that the higher the education the more efficacious the child. But this relationship is weak (.13), and is, in fact, not significantly different from that obtained by taking the parents' efficacy score. Similarly with occupational status of the head of household; while positive, the relationship still reaches a level of only .15. Finally, the subjective social class identification of the parents bears a predictably positive relationship to the child's efficacy, but again the magnitude is modest (.17). Similar results are obtained by examining the single items rather than the scale scores.

We conclude, therefore, that none of the traditional social structure variables does an appreciably better job of predicting the students' sense of political efficacy than does the parents' own sense of efficacy. A caveat should be entered at this stage. Since the study design intentionally excluded dropouts, a large segment of the bottom tail of the conventional socio-economic status classification is missing from the analysis. That segment would undoubtedly contribute more variance to the overall relationship between parental social class and student efficacy. That is, by deleting the lower social strata we have constrained the possible contribution social class could make to the relationship. While this restriction potentially affects virtually all of our findings on student-parent pairs, its effects are probably more severe than usual in the case of efficacy.

We noted previously that the relative education of the student-parent pairs was impressively related to the students being more efficacious than their parents. Educational juxtaposition may be used in another fashion to illustrate the transmission process within the family. Parent-student pairs are arrayed along lines of educational similarity, regardless of whether the departures from similarity are in an upward or downward direction. Thus we have three categories: St=P, St≠P, St≠≠P. In effect this means taking a student-parent education matrix and designating cases along the diagonal as St=P; cases slightly off the diagonal become St≠P; and those furthest off represent the greatest dissimilarity and are designated St≠≠P.

On the basis of knowledge that education is associated with efficacy, the prediction is that the greater the educational similarity the higher the efficacy relationship between parent and child. The results bear out the prediction. Laid against the overall τ_b of .11 is the .17 where St=P, .09 where St≠P, and .06 where St≠≠P. Clearly the less alike the parent and child in education, the less alike is their political efficacy. Notice that these figures say nothing about the direction of efficacy, but rather refer only to an increasing difference. While the magnitude of the association for the St=P cases is not nearly as high as one would like for demonstrating parent-to-student flows, the declining associations for the other cases indicate that the theoretical point is well conceived.

As the previous analysis suggests, the articulation between the political efficacy of parents and their offspring varies somewhat according to some elements of social stratification and the particular sex combinations involved. By far the most important source of variation, however, is the degree of symmetry between mother and father. Parental pairs included in the subset of student, mother, and father triads were divided into those with identical scores on the efficacy measure (30 percent) and those with divergent scores.

The correlation between efficacy scores for students and homogeneous parents is .26. When compared with the student-parent correlation of .11 for single parents, that involving like-minded parents represents a sizeable jump. There is virtually no difference for triples embracing girls versus boys. In contrast to the situation involving only one parent, however, the relationship is not as smoothly monotonic. Much of the impact of agreeing parents comes among those who are the most efficacious. Faced with two parents who feel highly efficacious, it is a rare student who does not likewise feel quite efficacious: only 6 percent score low, 20 percent medium, and 74 percent score in the high category.

The reason for this pronounced tendency at the upper end of the efficacy continuum lies in the kind of behavioral cues associated with a feeling of mastery over the environment. To feel efficacious means ordinarily to manifest certain signs of control and competence. When growing children see both parents exhibiting such signs they are particularly apt to develop a sense of mastery themselves by sheer dint of repetition and reinforcement. By contrast children with two parents of low efficacy receive fewer cues unless the parents flagrantly flout their inefficacy. The latter condition seems unlikely for the most part since it is in the nature of inefficacy to be passive and nonexpressive. Added to this is the fact that most other forces in the children's environment are pushing them toward a belief that they should be efficacious. These forces help countermand the presence of two inefficacious parents. Conversely, these forces help bolster the effect of two extremely efficacious parents.

The impact of homogeneous parents is even more markedly revealed by looking at the pattern for one of the two statements identical to both student and parent interviews. Of the two items the most sensitive and least ambiguous one is that stating that voting is the only way to influence the conduct of the government. For students with homogeneous parents on that belief the student-parent correlation is .31. Compatible with a recurrent pattern, this figure is appreciably higher for girls (.41) than for boys (.23). Expressing more vividly the substantially greater impact on girls are the percentage figures. Eighty-six percent of the daughters whose parents responded in an efficacious vein to the statement responded in the same way. By contrast only 47 percent responded efficaciously if both their parents were inefficacious. The pattern is the same though of lesser magnitude for sons.

Working with the homogeneous parents not only demonstrates the cumulative effects on the child; it also supports our belief that the measures of political competence employed have no small measure of validity. Were this not so, it would be difficult to account for the rising levels of parent-student symmetry as conjugal similarity increases.

Additional ammunition for this contention as well as further insights into the transmission process are observed by taking note of the triples marked by parental disagreement. Standing in contrast to the .26 correlation involving homogeneous parents are those for heterogeneous parents: .12 between students and fathers and .05 between students and mothers. Conflicting parents set up an ambiguous or contradictory set of cues for the child, with the net result being much less agreement between child and either parent than in the homogeneous situation. Again, if the efficacy measures were completely lacking in verisimilitude one would hardly expect this difference across the two sets of triads.

An exceptional feature to the results among heterogeneous triples is the higher association with father rather than mother. A more typical finding in our study is that where parents diverge the child more often is aligned with the distaff rather than male parent. While the difference in the present instance is not large, its departure from the common pattern bears some interpretation. In part, the present finding echoes what we found in looking at students and single parent pairs, where it was noted that the highest association was between boys and their fathers. It was held that because of the sex-linked aggressiveness and environmental control features embedded in the concept of efficacy fathers would more often be the more significant model, especially for boys. Much the same argument applies here. Given disagreement among parents, the child would more often resemble the father because of the sex-linked properties of efficacy.

PROJECTED PARTICIPATION

As most every schoolboy and schoolgirl knows, the pre-adult years in the United States are laden with exhortations about one's eventual role as an active citizen. The school years are described as the period during which the individual will acquire a set of tools and predispositions with which to become a participating member of the adult political order. Until that time is reached, citizenship roles traditionally consist almost exclusively of law-obedience, spectator behavior, and the psychic benefits of identifying with the polity. Some entry into the participative mode is accepted with the advent of the eighteenth birthday, for by law people may participate in certain "adult" political activities at this juncture. Now that the voting age has been lowered to eighteen still greater entry will be achieved at that age, and it seems inevitable that a number of other activities heretofore barred will become available. Some activities will have to be deferred until age twenty-one or, in the case of many public offices, until a more advanced age.

Some exceptions to the foregoing staging have always been present of course. Children have for decades worn campaign buttons and engaged in other sorts of minor electoral efforts. And it has not been uncommon for high school students—under the impetus of politicized parents or energetic teachers—to take part in a more vigorous fashion in electoral politics. Recent years have witnessed—perhaps for the first time—considerable politicization of high school youth, especially in the arena of nontraditional and confrontation politics. Just how sustained this penetration will be is uncertain; nor is it really clear what proportion of high school students are now actively trying to affect political outcomes. In any event the conception of participative modes was certainly a delayed one as of 1965 and it seems likely that for most high school seniors today their roles as active contributors are still cast more in terms of what they will be, rather than what they are.

It is with this background in mind that we approach the subject of how our high school seniors view their future role in the polity. While the citizenship role is multidimensional, as we have seen, our concern will be with the anticipated level of overt participation in public affairs. Rather than attempting to derive an objective estimate of future participation based on contemporary, concrete behavior of the student, we shall rely upon subjective estimates. Subjectivity is preferable in this context because it connotes the level of internalization of the participative norm. In this sense, it reflects the success of family, school, and the larger society in implanting a generally approved norm.

The measure used is built upon two subjective questions, one with a definite futuristic cast, the other placed in the present. One asked the student to estimate, looking ahead to when he was "on his own," whether he expected to be "very active," "somewhat active," or "not very active" in public affairs and politics. On the grounds that contemporary, subjective involvement contributes to future role expectations, the second question gauged present self-appraised interest in public affairs, ranging from following such matters most of the time down to hardly at all. Responses to these two questions were, not suprisingly, related to each other $\tau_b =$ .27), but at a sufficiently modest level to permit their incorporation into a combined index reflecting the answers to both questions. The resulting index scores are arrayed along a five-point continuum with a distinctive bell-shaped curve: very low = 9 percent; low = 17 percent; average = 34 percent; high = 30 percent; very high = 10 percent.

In searching for the familial antecedents of a student's subjective probability of participation, we covered a sizeable range of parental social and political traits. Included among the latter were parental participation in electoral campaigns, school affairs, and community activities. While virtually all the relationships met our hypotheses in terms of the sign of the associations, none really proved exceptionally determinative. Most of the correlations lay between .05 and .15. This was true of both bivariate and multivariate analysis. So unyielding were the patterns that even for students with homogeneously participative parents in the subset of triples the association was just barely improved over that with a single parent.

Contrary to popular stereotyping scarcely any differences exist according to the student's sex or race. It has been found that in elementary school boys are more interested than girls in political figures and in politically related events. Similarly, at the adult level, men consistently outpace women in most forms of politicized behavior—although the secular trend shows the gap narrowing and at the upper educational brackets the differences have vanished. But in terms of anticipated behavior, high school boys score only a shade higher than their female classmates (43 percent vs. 37 percent in the two highest categories of the measure). As late as the last year of high school, then, sex-typing does not affect appreciably the envisioned participatory role. Later on the coeds may well be the victims, and the boys the beneficiaries, of sex-related norms as they pertain to political life.[9]

It is also significant that race proves so poor an indicator of differences. What small difference there is, in fact, favors the blacks over the whites (42 percent vs. 39 percent in the two highest categories). This is all the more surprising when we recall the white edge in political efficacy, for, as we shall see, efficacy does contribute to projected participation. Despite decades of closed political opportunities and discrimination of the rankest sort, the black youths contemplate as much or more future activity. Perhaps that constitutes the very source of their determination. With so much ground to make up and so many inequities to rectify, the black youths more than compensate for the formal and informal obstacles to participation and for the somewhat lower levels of traditional political resources which will be at their command.

These findings by family traits, sex, and race as well as an awareness of the developmental processes of political learning led us to look upon projected participation as a product of the individual's unique experiences and synthesizing processes. Obviously every person is a result of unique experiences, and ultimately the mental processing of stimuli and the varied behaviors all become infinitely complex across individuals. Yet in terms of political learning it is patent that the growing child readily adopts almost wholesale some parental attributes while others represent an amalgam of forces in the socialization field. Our own study indicates that partisan preference stands at one end of the continuum of political orientations readily passed from parent to child. Standing at the other end of the continuum are those orientations which the young virtually carve out for themselves.

By this we mean that some political orientations are acquired in a building block fashion. Whereas little prior knowledge or experience is necessary for children to "receive" the party identification of their parents, the acquisition or development of such orientations as political efficacy, cynicism, cosmopolitanism, and good citizenship is not only a more diffuse process but also much more learner-initiated. A sequence of steps or building blocks may be visualized in the formation of these orientations. Figures and institutions must be initially cognized and evaluated, partly on the basis of prior nonpolitical referents. These initial cognitions and evaluations usually undergo testing and modification based on new incoming stimuli as filtered by the child's own experiential history and mental capacities. After each new block, the developing child is

[9]Richard Merelman reports a twelfth grade edge for boys over girls of 18 percent to six percent in terms of a desire to run for office later in life. But girls scored as high or higher on the *norm* of participation. See his *Political Socialization and Educational Climates* (New York: Holt, Rinehart, and Winston, 1971), pp. 124–28.

prepared to move on to another stage. As a consequence the sources of a particular orientation may lie much more in the surrounding blocks than in more remote and indirect foundation blocks such as the values and actions of the parents. This is particularly so for orientations which cross the child's horizon later rather than earlier in life.[10]

Fortunately, the grounds for these conclusions can be based upon more than speculation and inductive reasoning. If the norm of projected participation emanates more from an experiential base and from internal synthesizing, then it should be observable by tapping some of these forces. We can begin this exploration by reexamining the topic of the last section, political efficacy.

As noted previously a feeling of political efficacy is conducive to overt participation in the political system. Considering parents, for example, we noted a correlation of .23 between political efficacy and a campaign index and one of .18 between efficacy and a combined index representing participation levels in school and community affairs. Given these levels of articulation among parents we may fully expect a similar set among their offspring. There is, indeed, a moderately good relationship between projected participation and political efficacy in the younger generation (.22). The limits of the relationship are constrained somewhat by the fact that one-third of the cases lie in the middle category of the projected behavior index, while two-fifths of the cases lie in the "high" category of the political efficacy measure. Had we been able to stretch out each of the measures into more discrete categories, it seems likely that the relationship would be even stronger.

This association is by no means a function of some hidden cause such as parental education or occupational status. When the cross-tabulations are repeated holding each of these variables constant, the correlations remain remarkably consistent. Thus the argument—that the degree to which a young person's sense of efficacy leads toward a participative mode is a phenomenon which is both interior and developed by the self—acquires more support.

Political efficacy refers to a specific relationship between the individual and the political system. It stands in contrast to personal efficacy. There are a variety of measures of self-esteem or self-images, several of which are presented in Rosenberg's work with young adults.[11] Our own measure refers to the degree of self-confidence the individual has. No particular individual-systemic interactions are necessarily involved. It is, rather,

[10]The argument developed here was inspired, in part, by Roger Brown's eloquent presentation in his *Social Psychology* (New York: Free Press, 1965), Part Three, "The Socialization of the Child."

[11]Morris Rosenbesrg, *Society and the Adolescent Self-Image* (Princeton: Princeton University Press, 1965).

a self-image denoting a level of opinion strength; that is, whether the individual holds definite opinions and the degree of confidence he has in them. A three-item scale with a C.R. of .93 was fashioned from a battery of six force-choiced questions submitted to the students.[12] We shall refer to the measure as personal efficacy, with the understanding that it refers specifically to opinion strength.

Just as a sense of political efficacy leads toward a participative stance, so too might we expect personal efficacy to operate similarly. Such is the case: the higher one's level of opinion strength the higher the level of projected participation (.21). What seems to be at work is an extension of one's own personal sense of worth and self-confidence on to the larger panorama of the polity. Well before they will be active participants in the system, high school students exhibit the connection between what might be called self-mastery and the expectation of trying to master or help control political events. Again our confidence in this linkage is buttressed by the fact that neither the educational nor occupational class of the household head exerts any significant effect on the basic relationship.

Since both political and personal efficacy have an affinity with expected participation, it becomes important to know what their joint effects are. Does one override the other, do they act in a cumulative or multiplicative fashion? Rather than combining the two measures into a composite index—and thereby gaining parsimony but sacrificing specificity of effects—the link between personal efficacy and expected participation was examined at each of the three levels of political efficacy. To simplify the presentation of the results, we extracted the proportion of students scoring in the two highest categories of the projected participation measure. Since there are three political and four personal efficacy conditions, values for twelve cells were extracted. The results are presented in Table 5.3.

Two major points emerge. First, both types of efficacy have staying power. Within each level of political efficacy the higher the personal efficacy (excepting ties), the higher the percentage of subjective participation. By the same token, within each level of personal efficacy the higher the political efficacy, the greater the expected activity.

A corollary finding of equal significance is the cumulative nature of the joint influences of each efficacy dimension. Although not shown in Table 5.3, the plot of the cell entries would match rather closely the plotting if

[12]The items are:

(1) When you make up your mind about something is it pretty hard to argue you out of it or do you change your mind pretty easily?

(2) Some people have strong opinions about a good many things. Other people are more in the middle of the road. Which kind of person are you?

(3) When you get into an argument, do you usually get your way or do you often give in?

additive effects were postulated. That is, the effects of each separate row condition (personal efficacy) are similar for each column in that row and vice versa. Another way of saying this is that the more the student has of each type of efficacy the higher is the projected participation. When balanced against the overall average of 40 percent envisioning high activity, the range of scores illustrates very well the cumulative impact of the two dimensions.

Personal and political efficacy, while apt indicators of future visions of participation, are not rooted in concrete behaviors. They denote self-images more than anything else. Vital as they apparently are in generating a predisposition for later behavior, they are only part of the set of experiences through which adolescents carve out their own images of their future roles as citizens. Common sense as well as assumptions of anticipatory socialization would lead us to expect that the more politicized the students are now the greater political role they envision for themselves later. And in accordance with our model of self-development, this association should persist in the face of parental traits.

For pre-adults, one of the most sensitive indicators of politicization is the frequency of political discourse. Reading about, listening to, and watching programs dealing with public affairs and politics are activities which many are required to do; they are to some extent also passive. Talking with someone about political matters requires sustained effort, both as listener and talker. Furthermore, teenagers have traditionally had many more important matters to discuss than the state of the world. A conversation index was built from the students' estimates of how frequently, in terms of how many days in the week or month, they discussed public affairs and politics with members of their families and how often with friends outside the classroom. Merging the two response patterns resulted in a five-point index of conversation frequency.

TABLE 5.3

JOINT EFFECTS OF PERSONAL AND POLITICAL EFFICACY ON PROJECTED
POLITICAL PARTICIPATION

Personal Efficacy	Political Efficacy					
	Low		Medium		High	
Low 1	17%[a]	(68)	23%	(124)	34%	(103)
2	21	(151)	32	(230)	34	(207)
3	25	(169)	44	(276)	58	(314)
High 4	29	(92)	44	(115)	67	(212)

[a]Entries represent the percentage in the cell scoring in the two highest categories of the projected political participation measure.

TABLE 5.4

RELATIONSHIP BETWEEN FREQUENCY OF POLITICAL CONVERSATIONS
AND PROJECTED POLITICAL PARTICIPATION

Political Conversations		Projected Participation				
		Low 1	2	3	4	High 5
Rare	1	30%	12%	7%	4%	2%
	2	24	23	22	11	7
	3	30	43	34	35	26
	4	14	18	29	38	43
Frequent	5	2	4	8	12	22
Total		100%	100%	100%	100%	100%
		(209)	(390)	(614)	(519)	(323)

$\tau_b = .31$

As anticipated, the rate of political conversations is positively linked to projected activity (Table 5.4). Compared with the two efficacy measures, in fact, conversation frequency shows a much better fit. Nor is the linkage a function of parental education and occupation, for the correlations are maintained at handsome levels when these measures are controlled.

We observed earlier that both political and personal efficacy predicted projected participation, but that political efficacy proved somewhat the stronger of the two. But the two taken together exerted a generally cumulative effect on projected behavior. The effects of conversational frequency and political efficacy may be combined in the same fashion. Here we shall test the additive model more specifically by comparing predicted values with those actually obtained. Figure 5.1 contains the plottings for each set of values, assuming additivity. While the full range of the conversation index is employed, the political efficacy scores have been dichotomized into high and low.

With one noticeable exception toward the lower left side of the graph (the "High Efficacy," "Very Low Conversation" combination), the obtained values match very closely the predicted ones. Another way of viewing the lines in the figure is to note what happens to students of a given political efficacy level as their conversation frequencies rise. As each succeedingly higher range of conversation frequency is encountered, the expectations of later participation increase visibly. The same pattern unfolds as we move each given conversation range through the low and high levels of efficacy.

Adding personal efficacy to the matrix complicates the analysis considerably. Nor are the results unequivocal. Yet the central message stands out, especially for those students with moderate to high opinion strength. Typically, personal efficacy works in an additive fashion with political efficacy and conversation frequency. Thus 80 percent of the students with high political efficacy, high personal efficacy, and high conversation frequency have expectations for high political participation. From this zenith the expectations decrease until fewer than 10 percent predict such participation among those with low scores on the three measures. In effect, the plottings of Figure 5.1 would be elongated still more with the addition of personal efficacy.

Overall, however, conversation frequency and political efficacy have a more consistent and stronger impact on the subjective probability of participation. This finding has two important meanings. First, it says that "political" variables are key barometers in forecasting expected adult

Figure 5.1

Predicted and Actual Values of High Projected Political Participation, by Political Efficacy-Conversation Frequency Combinations

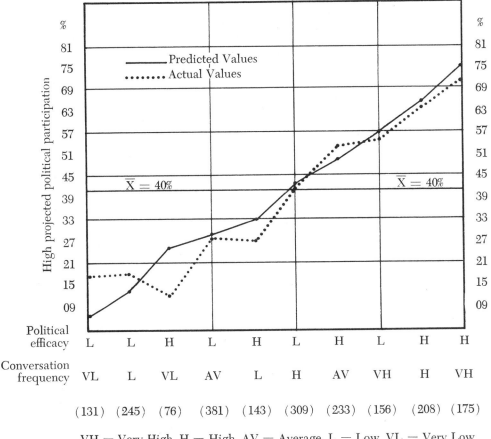

Political efficacy	L	L	H	L	H	L	H	L	H	H
Conversation frequency	VL	L	VL	AV	L	H	AV	VH	H	VH
	(131)	(245)	(76)	(381)	(143)	(309)	(233)	(156)	(208)	(175)

VH = Very High, H = High, AV = Average, L = Low, VL = Very Low

political participation. By the time children reach the age of seventeen or eighteen they have already acquired unique political personalities. This configuration enables them to process political stimuli and to anticipate, with varying degrees of success, their own political futures. We are arguing that this self-designated future role becomes anchored in certain *political* habits and frames of mind rather than in antecedent conditions. Not that the antecedent conditions were unimportant in fixing the anchor zones. Instead, the anchor zones, rather than the antecedents, become the points of departure for such emerging orientations as political participation.

A second meaning is that both concrete behaviors and internalized norms condition the students' outlook on their future roles. It is not enough to note that the norm of political efficacy bears on projected participation, although it is reassuring to find the relationship. Modifying and reinforcing this linkage in a fundamental way is the concrete, contemporary act of talking politics. By acting out or applying, however obliquely, the qualities residing in the norm of political efficacy the more politicized students move toward the "participant orientation" of citizenship. Conversely, those less efficacious students who seldom have political dialogues apparently forecast for themselves more of the subject or possibly parochial modes of citizenship behavior. What we wish to stress here are the twin, interrelated functions of beliefs *and* actions in forming the image of the future political self. Needless to say this image will be realized in varying degrees of success for these youths as they progress through the life cycle. If our results are any guide, however, the precursors of participation are well-grounded in personal and political efficacy and in pre-adult versions of political behavior.

POLITICAL TRUST

With the aid of hindsight it is obvious that the levels of political trust observed among both students and parents in 1965 would not be repeated in later years. That there has been a sharp decline in rates of political trust has been firmly documented elsewhere.[13] In light of this rapid change, which affected both older and younger generations, we will examine aggregate levels of trust only briefly. Then we will turn our attention to the student-parent pairs. While the massive changes in trust indicate that extrafamilial sources are very important in the development of this orien-

[13]Arthur H. Miller, "Political Issues and Trust in Government: 1964–1970," paper presented at the 1972 Annual Meeting of the American Political Science Association, Washington, D. C., September, 1972; Paul Abramson, "Political Efficacy and Political Trust among Black Schoolchildren: Two Explanations," *Journal of Politics*, 34 (November 1972), pp. 1243–75; Jerald G. Bachman, *Youth in Transition* (Ann Arbor: Institute for Social Research, University of Michigan, 1970), pp. 25–31.

tation, parent and student levels could still be highly co-related—i.e., the most trusting students, relatively speaking, might come from families in which parents are most trusting, again relatively speaking. To provide some contrast in our analysis, we will also take a brief look at student and parent personal trust.

Our measure of political trust for both students and parents is a Guttman scale of five items dealing with the conduct of the national government.[14] The coefficients of reproducibility are .93 and .92 for parents and students, respectively. In the parent sample a similar procedure was used to construct a measure of interpersonal trust or trust in people (CR = .94).[15] For students the same three items did not meet our scaling criteria, although similar items have scaled for other youth samples.[16] Because of our concern for comparability between students and parents, we utilize a four-point index for students which is nearly identical to the scale for parents. The political and interpersonal trust items differ, of course, in the focus on government in the former and on people in general in the latter. It is an empirical question, which we shall take up later, as to how closely related these measures are.

There is no absolute standard by which we can determine whether a population is especially trusting or cynical in its political outlook. Work on childhood socialization, however, shows that at least in the late 50's and early 60's young children were nearly devoid of negative feelings about political authority. This contrasted sharply with the frequent negative judgments made by adults.[17] It has also been found that trust decreases

---

[14]The items are:

(1) Do you think that quite a few of the people running the government are a little crooked, not very many are, or do you think hardly any of them are?

(2) Do you think that people in the government waste a lot of the money we pay in taxes, waste some of it, or don't waste very much of it?

(3) How much of the time do you think you can trust the government in Washington to do what is right—just about always, most of the time, or only some of the time?

(4) Do you feel that almost all of the people running the government are smart people who usually know what they are doing, or do you think that quite a few of them don't seem to know what they are doing?

(5) Would you say that the government is pretty much run by a rew big interests looking out for themselves or that it is run for the benefit of all the people?

[15]The items are:

(1) Generally speaking, would you say that most people can be trusted or that you can't be too careful in dealing with people?

(2) Would you say that most of the time people try to be helpful or that they are mostly just looking out for themselves?

(3) Do you think most people would try to take advantage of you if they got a chance or would they try to be fair?

[16]A similar scale was previously used in Morris Rosenberg, "Misanthropy and Political Ideology," *American Sociological Review*, 21 (December 1956), pp. 690–95.

[17]Fred I. Greenstein, *Children and Politics* (New Haven: Yale University Press, 1965), Chapter 3; Robert D. Hess and Judith V. Torney, *The Development of Political Attitudes in Children* (Chicago: Aldine, 1967).

substantially between eighth and twelfth grades, although apparently not reaching adult levels.[18] On the basis of this evidence we should expect to find considerably more trust among the seniors than among their parents. That this is true is borne out by the figures in Table 5.5, which show the weight of the student distribution falling much more on the trusting end of the scale. The students may be retreating from an even more trusting attitude held earlier, but compared to their parents they still see little to be cynical about in national political activity.[19]

Here is a case where the impact of nonfamily agents—notably the school—looms large. The thrust of school experience is undoubtedly on the side of developing trust in the political system in general. Civic training in school abounds in rituals of system support in the formal curriculum. These rituals and curricula are not matched by a critical examination of the nations's shortcomings or the possible virtues of other political forms. Coupled with a moralistic, legalistic, prescriptive orientation to the study of government is the avoidance of conflict dimensions and controversial issues.[20] A direct encounter with the realities of political life is thus averted or at least postponed. Hence, while development of cynicism does grow during the high school years, development of adult levels of distrust awaits contacts with the adult political world.[21]

Trust is not distributed evenly throughout the population, and we shall presently observe some differences among portions of the student and parent samples. The differences are not large, however, and one of our tasks will be to assess the implications of the relative uniformity of trust in all parts of the public. First, let us note the existing differences, for they have an interesting story to tell.

Race is one of the most obvious characteristics that seems likely to differentiate cynical from trusting youths. Blacks and other minority

[18]Sandra J. Kenyon, "The Development of Political Cynicism among Negro and White Adolescents," paper presented at the 1969 Annual Meeting of the American Political Science Association, New York, September, 1969, p. 5; Jerald G. Bachman and Elizabeth Van Duinen, Youth Look at National Problems (Ann Arbor: Institute for Social Research, University of Michigan, 1971), pp. 25–31. One instance in which no developmental trend was found is reported in Jack Dennis, "Political Learning in Childhood and Adolescence," p. 27.

[19]There was unquestionably a significant drop in political trust in the half-dozen years after our interviewing was done, and this ought to be taken into consideration in evaluating the absolute level of responses we report here. Nevertheless, young people still appeared more trusting than adults in 1970. See Bachman and Van Duinen, Youth Look at National Problems, pp. 29–31.

[20]These are old charges but apparently still true. After a survey of the literature on the subject and on the basis of a subjective analysis of leading government textbooks in high schools, Byron G. Massialas reaches similar conclusions: see his "American Government: We are the Greatest!" Social Studies in the United States (New York: Harcourt, Brace & World, 1967), pp. 167–95.

[21]Despite our confidence in the role of the school, it is difficult to pinpoint any one aspect of it as bearing responsibility for the promotion of political trust at the secondary school level. Civics courses, for example, seem to have little effect in this regard. See Chapter 7.

TABLE 5.5

POLITICAL TRUST AMONG STUDENTS AND PARENTS

	Least Trust 1	2	3	4	5	Most Trust 6	Total	
Students	5%	3	13	37	25	17	100%	(2053)
Parents	21%	9	17	33	11	9	100%	(1887)

group members have ample reason to be distrustful of all kinds of political authority. Thus it is surprising to see that black and white students are distributed very similarly on the political trust scale. One detects only a faint degree less trust among the minority-group students ($\tau_b = -.04$). Nor is this finding a "fluke," contradicted by most other evidence. Rather, it seems to have been characteristic of the population prior to about 1966. Since this seems to be a phenomenon which is so obviously time-dependent, and since it has been discussed at length by others, we will not deal with it further here.[22]

We find another small difference in degrees of trust when we divide the population along religious lines. The most significant division both theoretically and empirically is that between Catholics and non-Catholics. Formal authority in the Catholic church is hierarchical and very powerful compared to that of the major non-Catholic churches, despite the dissatisfaction with that authority voiced in recent years. Does the trust in religious authority carry over into the political domain? An initial glance at the distributions of religious groups on the political trust scale would seem to confirm such a transfer of affect. In both student and parent samples, Catholics are noticeably higher in political trust. Further analysis, however, shows that this relationship is spurious, owing its existence to the current impact of partisanship on political trust (see below). Religious differences exist, but religion itself has no direct impact on political trust.[23]

Distrust of politicians and of the political process need not be directed at one party only, and indeed the questions used to measure trust avoid any specific reference to the incumbent administration. Nevertheless a small amount of partisanship is picked up in the political trust scale, inasmuch as election studies have found partisans to be slightly more

[22]Miller, "Political Issues and Trust in Government;" Abramson, "Political Efficacy and Political Trust among Black Schoolchildren;" Bachman and Van Duinen, *Youth Look at National Problems;* and Anthony M. Orum and Roberta S. Cohen, "The Development of Political Orientations among Black and White Children," *American Sociological Review*, 38 (February 1973), pp. 62–74.

[23]The same conclusion about attachment to the country and its authority figures is reached by Hess and Torney, *Development of Political Attitudes in Children*, p. 117.

trusting when their party is in power.[24] Evidence from the parents in our study is in accord with this finding, for adult Republicans in 1965, with their party out of power, were less trusting than Democrats ($\tau_b = .16$). This difference also extends to the younger generation in a slightly weaker form (.12). By the time of high school graduation, if not earlier, evaluation of the political process takes on a slight partisan coloration.

Other characteristics which have served as useful controls in earlier chapters show virtually no relationship to political trust among students or parents. Sex, occupational status, political interest, cosmopolitanism, and region, among others, fail to differentiate the trusting from the cynical.[25] There is some evidence, however, which points to certain personal experiences as sources of political distrust. In Chapter 8 we will show that if students' daily contacts with teachers and administrators are unfavorable, the students are less trusting of national political authorities. Thus some spillover effects apparently occur as a result of unfavorable interaction with nonpolitical authorities (or, if one wishes to consider teachers political authorities, lower level political authorities).

Personal Trust

Personal trust or faith in people is often considered to be a general attitude of which political trust is one specific manifestation. In other words, political trust is thought to be dependent on one's belief in the trustworthiness of people in general. If this is true, there should be a positive association between personal and political trust. And this has indeed been found in some studies.[26] The strength of the association, however, has not often been assessed, nor is the finding universal.[27] In one recent study, factor analyzing the same items used here and with a national adult sample, Aberbach found a τ_b correlation of .16, that is, a positive but modest association.[28]

The evidence from our study leads us to conclude that personal and political trust, at least as presently measured, are distinct attributes which have rather little to do with each other. In part this judgment rests on further support for the weak though positive correlation between the two

[24]Joel D. Aberbach, "Alienation and Political Behavior," *American Political Science Review*, 63 (March 1969), pp. 86–99, at p. 94.

[25]In adult election studies as well, there were (until recently) few background correlates of political trust. See John P. Robinson, Jerrold G. Rusk, and Kendra B. Head, *Measures of Political Attitudes* (Ann Arbor: Institute for Social Research, 1968), p. 633.

[26]Rosenberg, "Misanthropy and Political Ideology;" Robert Agger, Marshall N. Goldstein, and Stanley A. Pearl, "Political Cynicism: Measurement and Meaning," *Journal of Politics*, 23 (August 1961), pp. 477–506.

[27]Litt found the relationship at one education level in a Boston suburb, but not at the other level nor in Boston itself. Edgar Litt, "Political Cynicism and Political Futility," *Journal of Politics*, 25 (May 1963), pp. 312–23.

[28]Aberbach, "Alienation and Political Behavior," p. 92. Calculating τ_c for Kenyon's data, we find a correlation of .21; Kenyon, "Development of Political Cynicism," pp. 8.

measures. For the seniors the correlation was .14 while for parents it is an even lower .10. Moreover, this association is not noticeably and consistently higher among relevant subgroups. For example, we controlled on political interest on the assumption that personal and political trust would be more closely related when respondents were politically interested. Among the students, the correlation does go up to .21 in the top group on political interest, but the statistics do not decrease monotonically with lessened political interest. In the parent sample, the highest correlations are found in the middle two categories. Hence, even when respondents follow political affairs more closely, their general faith in people is only a minor determinant of their political trust.

A second reason for saying that the two dimensions are distinct lies in the correlates of each. A prime case is that of black-white differences. We noted above that racial discrepancies were small for political trust, and that among parents, blacks were actually more trusting. When dealing with personal trust, however, the negative feeling of many blacks, both students and especially parents, is very apparent. Blacks in the mid sixties were quite willing to trust the government, but at the same time they were highly suspicious of the motives of most individuals.[29] This suggests, then, that political evaluations do not spring from judgments about the honesty and integrity of most individuals.

The student and parent distributions reveal another divergence between personal and political trust. While parents are considerably *less* trusting politically than the students, they are slightly *more* trusting in their personal relationships. This holds true for each of the three component items in the personal trust index. This shows again the weak link between the two kinds of trust. In this case the relationship is opposite that for the black-white example. There, black respondents were politically trusting despite highly negative views of ordinary individuals. Here, we find that adults on the whole hold cynical political views while maintaining what appears to be a very high level of personal faith.

Other factors besides race and generation show the same tendency to be correlated with one but not the other kind of trust. The education of the head of the household, for example, which is uncorrelated with political trust, shows a correlation of .08 with personal trust in the student sample, and of .22 in the parent sample. For occupation a similar pattern prevails.[30] Thus individuals from a higher status background are likely to

[29]The same finding is reported by Kenyon, "Development of Political Cynicism," pp. 17–18. Bachman finds essentially the same results, although with differences by region and attendance of integrated or segregated schools; the same results hold for Jews in his data.

[30]The higher correlation with social class among the parents will occur throughout our findings. It is attributable in part to the fact that the students are on the verge of adulthood but have not as yet established their own social class. And education, sometimes used as measure of class, is constant by design among the students.

have more faith in their fellow man, but are just as likely to hold a dim view of the character and ability of political functionaries.

Personal trust is also a moderate predictor of parental views of today's teenagers (τ_b = .18). Trusting parents are more likely to think highly of the current crop of teenagers while cynical parents more often agree that they are "going to the dogs." Not surprisingly, the degree of political trust is nearly uncorrelated with such opinions. A question about consultation on the job by one's employer, which can be interpreted as indicating trust and confidence in his judgments, is mildly correlated with personal trust (.14) and uncorrelated with political feelings. An analogous measure of family trust is likewise more highly correlated with personal than political trust. Finally, several specifically political attitudes and behavior are poorly correlated with beliefs about other individuals though predictive of or dependent on political trust. The matter of teachers' and/or administrators' unfairness is correlated evenly with both kinds of beliefs. Thus personal and political trust seem to lie along distinct dimensions, affecting and being affected by divergent kinds of orientations.

The Impact of Parental Trust

Despite their differences, personal and political trust are similar in one respect. In both cases student scores are but weak reflections of parental values (Table 5.6; personal trust not shown). The minor impact of parents on their children is surprising in light of the generalized character of these variables. Warmth or hostility toward specific, transient political issues and objects might not be shared by family members because their transitory nature prevents the kind of discussion and mutual influence that lead to more uniform outlooks. With trust, however, we have a more pervasive kind of belief system that cuts across particular individuals and

TABLE 5.6
RELATIONSHIP BETWEEN STUDENT AND PARENT SCORES
ON POLITICAL TRUST

	Parents					
Students	Least Trust 1	2	3	4	5	Most Trust 6
Least trust 1	8%	9%	4%	4%	5%	2%
2	4	3	3	3	1	1
3	17	19	13	11	9	12
4	36	35	40	36	36	33
5	22	20	24	29	29	27
Most trust 6	12	15	16	18	19	25
Total	99%	101%	100%	101%	99%	100%
τ_b = .12	(95)	(52)	(246)	(685)	(479)	(321)

objects. What our findings show is that these kinds of general dispositions are subject to heavy undercutting influences outside the family nexus.

In addition to the low overall student-parent correlations, we find little evidence of greater parental impact within selected portions of the population. What evidence does exist points once again to differences between personal and political trust. For the latter variety, the degree of family politicization has some impact on family transmission rates. For example, controlling for the frequency of political conversations between husband and wife, the student-parent correlations are .19, .14, .10, .10, for most to least frequent conversations, respectively. The same pattern holds when we control for the rate of student-parent discourse: .16, .11, .10, .04. Thus, where family political interaction is most frequent, parental trust is somewhat more often passed along to the younger generation. In the case of personal trust, however, no comparable pattern exists.

There is also faint evidence that the transmission of political trust is altered by relationships among family members. When the students report that they are very close to the parent who was interviewed, the correlation between their levels of trust is .14. For students who feel pretty close, the correlation falls off slightly to .11. In the small group of seniors who admit that they are not very close to their parent, the correlation drops to .01. This same pattern, however, is not found for variables which capture other aspects of the parent-student relationship. Moreover, when we control for politicization and family characteristics simultaneously, even the slim evidence above evaporates. In any event, the parental impact on personal trust seems totally unaffected by family interaction. Both kinds of trust are impervious to sex, political interest, and social class, all of which have been analytically fruitful in previous chapters.

Finally, parent-student transmission of only one kind of trust —personal trust in this case—is altered when we consider the mother and father simultaneously. For personal trust, we found what has proved to be the typical response pattern. Among homogeneous parents the parent-child correlation increases, although it is still not very large (.18). It is significantly greater, however, than either the student-mother figure (.12), or the student-father correlation (.00) found when the parents differed. Surprisingly, this pattern does not occur for political trust, where the student-parent statistic is virtually identical for homogeneous parents (.11), and for mothers (.10) and fathers (.11) when they differed.

LOWERING THE VOTING AGE: A SPECIFIC ISSUE INVOLVING THE CITIZEN WITHIN THE SYSTEM

Given the great stress the students attach to voting as the embodiment of good citizenship, it might be expected that the high school seniors were chomping at the electoral bit, impatient to become part of the mass electorate. Surprisingly, this was hardly the case during the mid sixties. As of 1965 slightly less than a majority of the students said they favored lowering the voting age, with the same being true of parents. In looking for an explanation for the division of opinion, we found, in addition to parental positions, three important determinants. Boys more than girls, Southerners more than non-Southerners (especially Westerners), and those projecting an active versus passive political future were all more disposed to support the age reduction. Moreover, these factors tended to work in a cumulative fashion.[31]

Although the eighteen-year-old vote has since become the law of the land, it is instructive to note that the forces helping shape adolescent opinion on this issue of the citizen's role within the system lay in large part outside the guiding hand of the immediate family. Thus, on the average, the region in which students happened to be reared exposed them to a relatively unique political culture vis-à-vis this issue. Similarly, having been born a boy or girl almost predetermined (on the average) a different pattern of socialization which results in net differences on the issue. Both of these variables are ascribed attributes over which the students had no control. Projected participation is of a different order and represents a sampling of the individual's own political self-image, an image-fragment which (we argued above) is wrought in substantial part by the student's own hand. The findings on the suffrage issue suggest the multiple and diverse socialization forces predisposing the adolescent to size up a particular issue one way or another.

There is another respect in which the suffrage issue illustrates the diverse sources of political beliefs. By considering how beliefs on this issue changed after 1965, we can provide a striking instance of events altering attitudes. While very little of the student militancy of the mid to late sixties dealt with the question of suffrage, it nonetheless seems reasonable to suppose that support for lowering the voting age subsequently increased among high school students. If nothing else, the escalation of the Vietnam war after 1965 would point toward this. Substantial numbers of adults as well as pre-adults see an incongruity in voteless young men risking their lives in war. Both World War II and the Korean conflict generated fresh support for a lower voting age, and the Vietnam conflict seemed to be no exception. In fact, a Gallup poll in the spring of 1968 revealed that nearly two-thirds (a new high) of the adult population ostensibly favored the move; this despite the fact that state electorates continued to turn down referenda. High school students should sooner or later reflect these gross changes among adults. It also seems probable that

---

[31]For a fuller discussion, see Paul A. Beck and M. Kent Jennings, "Lowering the Voting Age: The Case of the Reluctant Electorate," *Public Opinion Quarterly*, 33 (Fall 1969), pp. 370–79.

the wave of student activism would eventually have the effect of shifting the modal tendencies of the high school students more in line with those of college students.

We have strong evidence that these probabilities were, in fact, accomplished. We make use of the SRC's 1969 sample of twelfth grade boys, which was asked the identical question on eighteen-year-old voting.[32] Here are the results, for males only:

Favor eighteen-year-old vote
1965 interview respondents   53%
1965 questionnaire respondents   55
1969 questionnaire respondents   81

Although girls would start from a lower 1965 base, and would thus probably not reach the 1969 high for boys, there is little reason to doubt a striking gain among them also.

Here is a classic example of events shaping opinions. The rising politicization of youth since 1965 plus the citizenship role implications of young men fighting in an unpopular war apparently exerted a profound effect of the 1969 cohort, one which is but four years younger than our own sample. Why, it might be asked, did events produce what must be accounted a massive shift on this issue whereas we detected slight 1965–69 shifts on construction of the good citizen role, when we compared the same two cohorts. Similarly, interpolated figures comparing the two cohorts on political and personal trust—while showing a decline on political trust in particular—do not reveal the drastic shifts accompanying the suffrage issue. If the cataclysmic events of the late sixties were traumatic enough to affect teenagers on the question of suffrage, then why not on other matters?

We have, of course, supplied part of the answer in the question. A concrete issue such as the voting age is of a different order than diffuse trust in the government or idealized versions of the good citizen. The latter are qualities which begin to take hold from an early point in the life cycle, are rather continuously reinforced, and would presumably stand high in the hierarchy of what is politically important to the individual. Furthermore, the socialization agents transmitting these orientations ordinarily change their goals and behavior only very slowly. On all counts these orientations of trust and good citizenship would be resistant to marked alteration across an intercohort gap of four years. Even at the intraindividual level these orientations would have greater stability than is true of more ephemeral concerns.

[32]This is the *Youth in Transition* study. We are indebted to Dr. Jerald Bachman for making these data available to us.

An issue such as dropping the voting age claims virtually none of these properties. Even the most generous estimates of when the topic crossed the screen of youngsters, its degree of reinforcement and refinement, its ranking in the hierarchy of important systemic qualities, and the consistency of stance amongst relevant socialization agents would still result in light-year differences between these two types of orientations. It is precisely these differences which apparently made aggregate opinions on the voting age proposition quite vulnerable to change as a result of events from 1965 onward. In the absence of deepseated and important attachments, the infusion of stimuli from the outside world, including some direct propaganda, led to an aggregate shift among twelfth grade boys.

Despite enormous strains within the political system, most of them pushing away from the modalities of the 1965 sample, the 1969 sample moved less with respect to basic matters of social and political trust and citizenship obligations. Of course there were direct benefits for the teenagers in favoring a reduced voting age whereas there were none in terms of the good citizen's duties. But this only serves to illustrate why generalized norms—the good society, the good government, the good citizen—are *relatively* resistant to change over the short run. It is as though the students detached from the general question of the citizen's place within the system the specific question of the eighteen-year-old's place.

Changes in the distribution of opinion on the suffrage issue underscore the emerging politicization of the young in America.[33] The heavy student emphasis on political roles, participant orientations, and political efficacy take on added significance in the light of post-1965 events. Without doubt the twelfth grade cohort in 1965 was favorably predisposed toward the norm of citizen participation in public affairs. By their description of the good citizen they also signified their belief that participative behavior would be worthwhile both for the individual and the political system. Earlier cohorts would probably have evinced a similar set of perspectives. What distinguished the cohorts beginning around the mid sixties was a quickened pace of reality testing. They "shot the gap" between the halcyon days of late adolescence and the workaday political world of concerned adults. Rather than deferring their application of the political

[33]Among the more relevant works in the voluminous literature on the student movement are Kenneth Keniston, *The Young Radicals* (New York: Harcourt, Brace & World, 1968); Julian Foster and Durwood Long, *Protest: Student Activism in America* (New York: William Morrow, 1970); Lewis S. Feuer, *The Conflict of Generations* (New York: Basic Books, 1969); and Philip C. Altbach and Robert S. Laufer (eds.), *The New Pilgrims: Youth Protest in Transition* (New York: David McKay, 1972). A revealing look at the wide differences between college and non-college youth is found in Daniel Yankelovich, Inc., *Generations Apart* (New York: Columbia Broadcasting System, 1969). A useful corrective on the generation gap thesis can be found in Joseph Adelson, "What Generation Gap?," *New York Times Magazine*, (January 18 1970).

efficacy norm they increasingly submitted the norm to punishing tests. The time lag traditionally involved in turning a projected political role into an actual one was foreshortened for thousands, perhaps hundreds of thousands. And whereas the vote has been a customary, time-honored route for active induction into the political process, activities outside the electoral process often took center-stage from the mid sixties onward. Even in the suffrage realm, however, four years produced a massive shift among high school seniors in the proportion advocating a reduced voting age.

The politicization of the young was not without its uncertain and, to many, alarming aspects. Yet placed in the context of the participant political culture of the United States it at least becomes comprehensible. As our own data disclose, the pre-adults were heavily imbued with participative, efficacious norms. When the force of domestic and international events was perceived as impinging dramatically and malevolently on their lives, the norms were brought to the surface. There is nothing terribly uncommon about that in American history. Some of the techniques for implementation were unique, at least in their intensity. What must not be lost sight of, however, is the thorough job of socialization to participation which society has traditionally performed in the United States. In this sense the nation began reaping a harvest of seeds which sprouted early. Just as the elements of nature sometimes produce premature germination, so too the elements of politics provided extremely generous soil for the early flowering of politicized behavior among the young.

CHAPTER SIX

The Consequences of Parental
Agreement Patterns*

P̲ᴀꜱᴛ ᴛʜɪɴᴋɪɴɢ about families and political socialization has often made two interrelated, dubious assumptions. The first is that a single parental or family force shapes the political character of the child. From this point of view either parent may be taken indiscriminantly as a focal point in studying the socialization process. Thus, in accounting for the familial sources of a child's political orientations, the relevant social, personal, and political attributes of the mother and father are not clearly differentiated. At the same time, little consideration is given to the prospect that the attributes of each parent may work together in either a cumulative or interactive fashion to affect the child's political outlook.

Both methodological complexities and research costs have led to research applications of this assumption. The most important result has been to rely on data about a single parent. It is implicitly assumed that little or nothing would be gained by having relevant information about the second parent. Theoretical limitations in the form of attaching overriding importance to socio-economic characteristics common to both parents or to the tendency of one parent (especially the father) to set the tone and style for both have also served to perpetuate the single force view.

To some extent our own analysis of the family's role in socialization has operated under both the prevailing methodological and theoretical constraints. This is reflected in our conventional use of student-single parent pairs. Now for many purposes the monolithic, undifferentiated approach may be quite sufficient and the marginal returns from mother-father-student analysis so slim as to negate the considerable costs of data collection and analysis. Yet we found in previous chapters that knowing the orientations of both parents usually made a significant difference in accounting for the orientation of the student. Clearly, then, the single parental force assumption is limited in its applications.

A second dubious assumption has typically accompanied the first. This is the masculine-dominance assumption. In brief, the reasoning is that fathers supply the basic political character of the parental pair since men are more politicized than women. Wives and mothers presumably take

*Occasional portions of this chapter are drawn from an article by M. Kent Jennings and Kenneth P. Langton, "Mothers versus Fathers: the Formation of Political Orientations among Young Americans," *Journal of Politics*, 31 (May 1969), pp. 329–58.

their cues from their husbands. Concomitantly, men are also viewed as the prime purveyors of political orientation to their children because of the same edge in politicization and the customary sex-typing whereby politics is seen as more appropriate for men than women. The upshot of this assumption (oversight) is that information concerning fathers rather than mothers, or both, is typically taken as an adequate barometer of parental attributes.

The objectives of this chapter are based directly on these twin assumptions. First, we will draw together in systematic fashion results relating to the effects of homogeneous parents; particular attention will be paid to the consequences of student gender. The second objective is to explore in some detail the apparent influence of each parent over the child under conditions of conflicting orientations between the parents. Here the masculine dominance assumption is tested, while at the same time further information is brought to bear on the single force assumption. Since partisanship is such an important and reliably measured orientation, a detailed analysis is presented of the conditions under which a given parent exerts exceptional influence in establishing the child's partisan leanings. Establishing these conditions of differential influence is the third objective of this chapter.

THE IMPACT OF HOMOGENEOUS PARENTS

Throughout the previous chapters we have alluded to a recurrent pattern in the symmetry of parent-student pairs. Almost without exception the similarity between the student and a single parent—regardless of whether that parent was male or female—was exceeded by the similarity between the student and each parent when those parents saw eye to eye or behaved in a congruent fashion. So pervasive was this pattern that it proved to be the strongest and most consistent of factors predicting parent-child similarity.

We may draw these related, but separately presented findings together. Table 6.1 displays four sets of correlations arranged by substantive categories. Most of the specific issues (including partisanship) and the general orientations have been discussed in previous chapters or publications. The group evaluations are obtained by asking people to rate their degree of group approval on a "feeling thermometer" running from 0° to 100°. Spectator politicization refers to the frequency of media usage to follow public affairs and politics.[1] The "good citizen attributes" variable denotes the complexity ascribed to the ideal citizen role.

[1]The importance of group evaluations is discussed in Philip E. Converse, "The Nature of Mass Belief Systems in Mass Publics," in David E. Apter (ed), *Ideology and Discontent* (New York: Free Press, 1964), pp. 206–61. One of the best efforts to bridge media behavior and political socialization is found in Steven H. Chaffee, L. Scott Ward, and Leonard P. Tipton, "Mass Communication and Political Socialization," *Journalism Quarterly*, 47 (Winter 1970), pp. 647–50; 666.

TABLE 6.1
THE EFFECTS OF HOMOGENEOUS PARENTS ON
PARENT-STUDENT SIMILARITY

	Student-Single Parent	Student-Homogeneous Parents		
		Total	Boys	Girls
Issue Positions				
Presidential preference ('64)	.59	.63	.64	.58
Party identification	.47	.57	.58	.58
Integration of schools	.34	.48	.44	.53
Prayers in schools	.29	.40	.36	.44
18-year old vote	.13	.27	.17	.43
Letting Communist hold office	.13	.12	.10	.18
U.S. participation in United Nations	.11	.25	.11	.47
Allow anti-religious speeches	.08	.06	−.06.	.16
Group Evaluations				
Catholics	.28	.38	.34	.44
Southerners	.22	.43	.51	.30
Labor unions	.22	.31	.31	.30
Negroes	.20	.23	.22	.26
Whites	.19	.07	.11	.03
Jews	.18	.20	.29	.09
Protestants	.13	.03	.08	.08
Big business	.08	.13	.14	.19
General Orientations				
Political knowledge	.25	.38	.42	.36
Cosmopolitanism	.17	.26	.16	.52
Political trust	.12	.11	.04	.24
Political efficacy	.11	.26	.27	.24
Recognition of party differences	.10	.10	.10	.13
Good citizen attributes	.03	.16	.08	.27
Spectator Politicization				
Television	.20	.29	.42	.13
Magazines	.15	.35	.34	.37
Main media	.13	.35	.44	.22
Political interest	.12	.12	.12	.12
Newspapers	.11	.29	.21	.35
Radio	.08	.13	.10	.17

The first comparisons are between the overall single parent-student versus the homogeneous parent-student correlations. (Readers may wish to use the former as a gross indicator of parent-to-child transmission rates across a wide variety of orientations.) To make a point noted before, the correlation between students and homogeneous parents is the same regardless of whether the value for the mother or father is taken. This follows from our usual definition and operationalization of homogeneity, i.e., if the values for the mother and father fall along the main diagonal of a square matrix representing a cross-tabulation of mother and father values on a given variable, then that mother-father pair is considered homogeneous.

Comparing columns 1 and 2 reveals the rather powerful effects of parental homogeneity. In 21 out of 28 possibilities the association for homogeneous parents is greater than that for the single parent case.[2] Since τ_b correlations cannot be interpreted in terms of variance explained, it is difficult to state precisely the statistical increments achieved in the homogeneous configuration.[3] Significantly, though, homogeneity displays strong effects within each of the four rubrics—issue-positions, group evaluations, general political orientations, and spectator politicization. Obviously the consequences of homogeneous parents are not localized. Without question, however, having like-minded parents has no appreciable effect on seven of the indicators: political trust, recognition of party differences, letting a Communist hold office, allowing anti-religious speeches, political interest, and evaluations of whites and Protestants.

The pattern uncovered for the Communist and anti-religious speech items is not at all suprising given their well-nigh hypothetical nature. As we noted in Chapter 3, the likelihood of parents successfully passing on the concrete applications of abstract democratic concepts is remote. Pro- or anti-civil libertarianism of the type denoted by these items is simply not anchored in the concrete experiences of either the parents or their offspring. Thus moving from the impact of a single parent to that of two like-minded parents does not improve the transmission levels because the concepts remain sophisticated. Given the high initial ratings of whites and Protestants by both students and parents and the accompanying low variance it is perhaps not surprising that homogeneity does not increase parent-student agreement—though why it should slightly lower the agreement is puzzling. Accounting for the lack of pull from homogeneous parents in the other areas is a more trying question, and one which we cannot answer at this time.

Despite these caveats the overall picture is impressive and will become even more so momentarily. If ever a case could be made for the multiplier effect of complementary socializing agents, homogeneous parents provide a striking example. Although the precise fashion by which this effect transpires is not manifest, it is not difficult to interpret the findings in

---

[2] Some of the measures used are multi-item scales, others the responses to a single question. Breaking down the multi-item measures would increase the number of comparisons but would serve no useful conceptual purpose.

[3] It is also true that the product-moment correlations for these relationships usually run higher than the τ_b figures.

terms of learning by imitation and contagion. With similar models at hand the child is presumably being exposed to repetitive cues not just from one valued model, but from two. Not only does this mean a "double-barrelled" set of cues, it also means the absence of conflicting sets of cues. As we shall see momentarily, the consequences of conflict among parents is deleterious for parent-student agreement. Therefore, the student growing up in a home with like-minded parents stands in the optimal position for taking on parental characteristics.

Specific evidence can be marshalled for the double-barrelled effect. It might be argued that it is simply the lack of conflicting cues which heightens parent-student agreement in the homogeneous situation. A partial test of this argument lies at hand in the presence of the students living in homes with only one parent present (14 percent of the sample). If it is simply the absence of conflicting signals which prompts greater parent-child similarity, then this subset of student-parent pairs should agree at the same rate as the student-homogeneous parent pairs. But the evidence does not support that prediction. Student-parent correlations are nearly always markedly lower in those cases which involve a single parent than in those with two like-minded parents. Therefore, the physical presence of *two* nonconflicting parents appears to make a crucial difference.[4]

A modelling explanation for the general elevation of parent-child agreement seems especially preferred to prominent alternatives in the case of homogeneous parents. One alternative referred to in Chapter 1 was the psychoanalytic approach, wherein the affective and power relationships between parent and child was viewed as leading to certain outcomes for the child. A second alternative was a form of social learning, *viz.*, reinforcement theory. A third alternative, which we labelled resource availability, stems from stratification theory and posits that the different socialization emphases across the social strata lead to differential outcomes.

Certainly our data are not as rich as they should be for rejecting these alternatives in favor of the theory of observational learning. Nevertheless the alternatives usually fail the necessary empirical tests. In the first place, homogeneous parents are simply not particularly different from parents as a whole or, as noted below, from heterogeneous parents. That is, on the measures which we have pertaining to the three alternative explanations, the politically homogeneous parents do look like other parents. In the second place student-parent similarity is not impressive when affective, power, or social background characteristics are taken into con-

---

[4]Ideally we would be able to control for a variety of other factors which might be causing this difference; and the length of time the child has been in the one-parent category should be considered. Unfortunately, the relatively small N's involved and the absence of thorough information prevent the more detailed analysis. On the other hand, it seems unlikely that any such factors would erase the sizeable differences observed.

sideration. For example, if parental pairs are arranged on a family power structure continuum and this continuum is related to a given political orientation among their offspring, the correlation is much lower than when homogeneous parental pairs are arrayed on a given political orientation and this array is related to student distributions on the same dimension. All of this is not to say that power, affect, and differential resources do not condition the articulation between homogeneous parents and children. Rather, it is to argue that it is the sheer presence of parental homogeneity itself which figures most prominently in "determining" student profiles.

We are least able to reject the reinforcement alternative. As suggested earlier, observational learning and reinforcement often work hand in glove in molding the child. To the extent that both parents in the homogeneous situation act to reinforce predispositions in their children which reflect their own similar predispositions, then clearly the likelihood of parent-child congruency rises. What seems very unlikely, however, is that reinforcement *alone* would move the child toward greater agreement with homogeneous parents. To the extent that there is conflict between the outcomes of reinforcement and observational learning processes the symmetry between parents and children will, of course, ordinarily decrease.

Another set of informative comparisons in Table 6.1 consists of columns 3 and 4, where the students with homogeneous parents have been divided according to sex. While there are exceptions, the rule is for daughters to agree more with their homogeneous parents than for boys to agree with theirs. Excluding the four instances of virtual ties, the correlations involving girls are higher in 16 out of 24 cases. So strong is the affinity between daughters and homogeneous parents that in only four instances are the student-single parent correlations not exceeded.

Why should daughters be more vulnerable than sons to the sway of agreeing parents? The answers seem wrapped up in the affective structure of the family and in sex differences regarding the extrafamilial environment. It is instructive to note the greater filial devotion expressed by daughters (see below). Given consonance among parents plus high affective warmth toward either or both parents, girls are apparently under strong conscious and subconscious pressure to go along with their parents. To deviate from agreeing parents who are revered would be a costly psychological breach. If the parents have openly expressed sentiments on an issue, and the daughter has cognized them, the process suggested would be fairly direct. But even if there has been no explicit statement or act of cognition, daughters may well respond to a stimulus more so than boys on the basis of how they *think* their parents would react to the same stimulus.

A complementary contributing factor is the difference between how boys and girls relate to the outside world vis-á-vis the family.[5] Even in adolescence girls remain more home-centered than do boys. They have less freedom than boys, less often have jobs, depend more on the family for advice and entertainment, and think and plan more about their own future families. In general, then, boys are less family-oriented than are girls. Given a boy and girl feeling equally close to their parents, the boy would more often be exposed to a variety of events, transactions, and preoccupations outside the family domicile. With this greater outward orientation, it is perfectly compatible that boys less often reflect the posture of homogeneous parents.

Maintaining Triadic Homogeneity

One final question may be raised about homogeneous parents and their offspring. Homogeneous parents are by no means always successful in fashioning children in their own image. Is it possible to state some conditions under which homogeneous parental pairs are more likely to foster homogeneous triads? Two examples will be offered here, more in the spirit of suggestive explanations than as definitive answers. The first example takes up intrafamilial factors, while the second introduces extrafamilial ones.

Even though both parents, by definition, are like-minded in the homogeneous set, it seems likely that one might be more influential than the other in inducing similar behavior and attitudes in the child. Experimental or observational investigations would be the appropriate devices for assessing the relative impact of homogeneous parents. Given our study design we can only make a small, but suggestive attempt.

Let us take party identification as the political variable to be examined. Altogether, 74 percent of the parents are homogeneously partisan (see definition below). Within this total is a subset (76 percent) representing those students succumbing to their parents' identification, while the other group (24 percent) consists of those who fail to follow their parents. Our analytic effort is to see if there are any prominent familial attributes which help set off these defecting students. That is, given like-minded parents, it is conceivable that one parent may be relatively more influential than the other in preventing the party deviation of the student. In order to examine this possibility we devised indices depicting the relative politicization and education of mothers versus fathers.

[5]The following summary borrows from Elizabeth Douvan and Martin Gold, "Modal Patterns in American Adolescence," in Lois and Martin Hoffman (eds.), *Review of Child Development* (New York: Russell Sage Foundation, 1966), Vol. II, pp. 469–528; and various selections in Eleanor Maccoby (ed.), *The Development of Sex Differences* (Stanford: Stanford University Press, 1966).

Against the backdrop of the generally assumed political dominance of the father in the family it is surprising to see his marginal strength in helping preserve triadic homogeneity. If either parent plays a more impressive role in maintaining the family homogeneity of party preferences, it seems to be the mother and not the father. Evidence for this conclusion emerges upon examining the relative politicization of the parents as determined by campaign activities.[6] As expected, there are more families where the father shows greater politicization. But when mother is the more highly politicized, she has relatively more "pulling power" than father in maintaining the child's loyalty to the parents. The net difference is 12 percent between the case where mother is relatively higher than where the opposite prevails. A similar, though less marked, relation prevails according to relative education. When mother is the more highly educated, triadic homogeneity is more often maintained than when father is the better educated.

Most assuredly the differences revealed by these measures are not large in an absolute sense. They must, however, be placed in the context of conventional notions concerning male dominance. Not only is that view disputed by this evidence; it tends, in fact, to be replaced by one indicating a slight maternal superiority within the family circle. Preliminary work with other political dispositions suggests a similar pattern, but our conclusions are tentative at best.

Having considered the intrafamilial side in helping preserve triadic homogeneity, let us now take up the extrafamilial side. In reporting on the correspondence between homogeneous parents and their offspring little attention has been paid to questions of direction. That is, even though homogeneous parents and their children show moderate to high agreement rates, it is possible that differences exist according to where these parents fall on whatever measure is under attention. Illustratively, homogeneous parents who are high on political efficacy might be more adept at passing on their level of efficacy than are parents with low political efficacy. Indeed, this is a finding reported in Chapter 5. Other results of this nature have also been observed in previous chapters; most lend themselves to ad hoc explanations designed for the particular orientation being examined. There is, however, a set of findings which are susceptible to a more general interpretation; these findings lie in the area of issue-orientations.

[6]This is a slightly modified version of the Milbrath political campaign index. (The change is that respondents were asked to report on activities, except voting, in any public election during the last 10 years.) Taking their index scores, father and mother pairs were then cross-tabulated with three resultant patterns—those where mother had the higher score, those where both were equal (i.e., on the diagonal), and those where father was higher. This is the basic procedure followed for all measures used in this chapter showing the "relative" positions of mothers versus fathers. For the Milbrath index see Lester W. Milbrath, *Political Participation* (Chicago: Rand McNally, 1965), pp. 165–66.

We know that the student's position on various issues does not arise in a vacuum nor simply as a reflection of parental views. One rather rough way in which other forces can be summarized is in terms of national opinion cultures. For each issue of any visibility at all there would be a national distribution of adult opinions. Let us make a simplifying assumption that these issues can be dichotomized into such categories as pro-con, yes-no, approve-disapprove. Except in cases of ties, then, there would be a majority opinion on each issue. Let us go on to assume that these opinion cultures penetrate in greater or lesser degree the student's perceptual screen. If these were the only forces operative, we would expect the student to reflect the (adult) majority stance rather than the minority stance. Especially in the instance of homogeneous parents, however, we suspect that other forces are present. Moreover, we also know that some of the parental pairs will be in the majority cell and the remainder in the minority cell for each issue. The question then becomes: Is the success of homogeneous parents in maintaining triadic homogeneity conditioned by majority opinion cultures?

Since they are all easily dichotomized variables, we may use the issues listed earlier in Table 6.1 (save party identification) to answer the question. There is a rather definite majority opinion ($\geq$ 60 percent) in the entire parent sample on all but the eighteen-year-old vote issue (55 percent); national cross section figures are similar where the same measures are available. Our first step is to divide the parental pairs on each issue according to whether they are in the national majority or minority. Then we look at their offspring, noting whether they are more likely to defect from their parents under one condition or the other. Listed below are the student defection rates for the seven issues:

	Student Defection When Parental Pairs in	
	Minority	Majority
Allowing anti-religious speeches	81%	13%
U.S. participation in United Nations	63	5
Letting Communist hold office	53	34
Integration of schools	39	15
Presidential preference ('64)	34	7
Prayers in school	31	21
18-year-old vote	31	42

Without question the effectiveness of homogeneous parents is visibly altered according to whether they conform with the national majority or minority opinion culture. In most cases the rate of student defection is enormously greater when the parents are at odds with the majority. It is important to note that these results are not artifacts of ideological dimensions. That is, regardless of whether the majority culture is conservative or liberal the students still defect less from majoritarian parents.

Only one exception mars the otherwise consistent results. Student defection is actually greater on the eighteen-year-old vote issue when the parents are in the majority camp. Part of the reason may lie in the rather close national division which existed on the issue at that time, closer than on any of the other issues presented here. A second reason may be that this is an issue of peculiar relevance to adolescents. Processes at work with respect to the other issues may not apply with equal force when the issues are population specific.

Triadic homogeneity flowers, then, when the parents receive support from the larger opinion culture. Again we see the analytic gain achieved by drawing in additional sources of socialization. First, we went from one parent to two. Within the latter we examined the differential effects on boys versus girls. Next we saw how mothers are apparently more instrumental in keeping the child from straying away from like-minded parents. Finally, we have established the critical nature of congruence between homogeneous parents and the political environment as a force in keeping children within the fold. Thus the configuration of several forces, not just one or even two, sharpens our understanding of how students come to acquire their political orientations. Sometimes by changing one element of that configuration, such as whether parents are reinforced or undercut by the larger political culture, the net impact on the student's political beliefs is substantially altered.

THE IMPACT OF HETEROGENEOUS PARENTS

Standing in direct contrast to those situations involving like-minded parents are those where parental disagreement exists. At various points in previous chapters we mentioned that parent-child similarity decreased when that parent was known to disagree with the spouse. In effect, the orientation of the one parent helps countervail that of the other. The present section collates the findings for heterogeneous parents by comparing parent-child correspondence among homogeneous versus heterogeneous couples.

Such comparisons are enriched and extended by the inherent statistical nature of agreeing and disagreeing couples. It will be recalled that the operational definition of heterogeneous parents on any given measure is whether their scores fall off the main diagonal when their scores are cross-tabulated. Since the parents are by definition in a state of noncongruence, parent-child agreement patterns may be observed between the child and *each* parent. This, of course, differs from the case of homogeneous parents because mothers and fathers reach identity and the child's resemblance to each of them is the same. The presence of disagreeing parents enables us to assess student-mother versus student-father correspondence. Inferentially, we may estimate the relative influence of mothers versus fathers in affecting the political coloration of their offspring.

Let us first consider the overall comparisons involving students paired with homogeneous versus heterogeneous parents, disregarding for the moment whether the latter refer to student-mother or student-father pairs. Table 6.2 reveals the attrition of parental influence in parental conflict settings. On every measure save political trust, participation in the UN, and evaluation of whites and Protestants, the correlations involving heterogeneous parents are lower than those for homogeneous parents. And in most instances the differences are large. Thus the parent paired with a dissimilar mate is much less likely to have his/her orientations echoed in the offspring than is a parent paired with a similar spouse.

Is it possible that heterogeneous parents have some properties which distinguish them from the homogeneous ones, and that it is these properties rather than heterogeneity per se which results in lower student-parent congruence? Certainly the possibility must be entertained. The two sets of parent pairs on each of several orientations were compared with respect to a number of socio-economic and family relations characteristics. These included educational levels, occupational status, length of marriage, marital harmony, and political interest. In no instance did noticeable or consistent differences emerge between the homogeneous and heterogeneous couples. While our controls by no means exhaust the possible sources of variation, we are nevertheless satisfied that it is the basic occurrence of either congruence or incongruence which prompts the difference in the accompanying parent-child pairs.

Just as the complementarity of socialization agents helps explain why homogeneous parents have a pronounced effect on their children, so too the discrepancy of socialization agents helps explain the lowered effects of heterogeneous parents on their children. Even though a given child may respect, adore, or emulate one parent more than the other, both parents are significant reference individuals for most children. And even if not highly valued subjectively, both parents loom large in the environment of the child, especially one who has gone through a series of stages climaxing in late adolescence.

When these "significant others" are not in harmony, the chances are high that this disharmony will be transmitted to the child. We use the word transmitted since such disharmony need not be directly perceived in order to bear consequences. For example, the child may not perceive that one parent feels more politically efficacious than the other; but the fact that disparity exists means that two agents are giving off different signals. As a result the child's tendency to reproduce one parent's profile is dampened by the other parent's competing message, *ceteris paribus*. This conclusion flows from the fact that *both* student-mother and student-father correlations are lower among heterogeneous cases than homogeneous ones (recalling that student-mother and student-father results have to be the same among the latter).

TABLE 6.2
PARENT-STUDENT SIMILARITY AMONG HOMOGENEOUS AND
HETEROGENEOUS PARENTAL PAIRS

	Homogeneous Parents	Heterogeneous Parents	
		Student-Mothers	Student-Fathers
Issue Positions			
Presidential preference (64)	.63	.09	−.09
Party identification	.57	.40	.35
Integration of schools	.48	.11	.00
Prayers in schools	.40	.20	.03
18-year old vote	.27	.00	.00
U.S. participation in United Nations	.25	.41	−.35
Letting Communist hold office	.12	.10	−.10
Allowing anti-religious speeches	.06	.03	−.03
Group evaluations			
Southerners	.43	.15	.16
Catholics	.38	.27	.19
Labor unions	.31	.20	.18
Negroes	.23	.17	.10
News	.20	.15	.12
Big business	.13	.07	.09
Whites	.07	.20	−.04
Protestants	.03	.21	.05
General Orientations			
Political knowledge	.38	.24	.27
Cosmopolitanism	.26	.13	.11
Political efficacy	.26	.05	.12
Good citizen attributes	.16	.11	.04
Political trust	.11	.10	.11
Recognition of party differences	.10	.06	−.06
Spectator Politicization			
Main media	.35	.07	.07
Magazines	.35	.17	−.15
Newspapers	.29	.08	.02
Television	.29	.03	.16
Radio	.13	.00	.00
Political interest	.12	−.01	−.03

Very clearly, the likelihood of given parental orientations being exhibited by their high school seniors depends in part upon parental agreement levels. Since parental agreement fluctuates across the range of orientations shown in Table 6.2, the likelihood of strong student-parent correlations does also. That is, the proportion of homogeneous parents varies from a high of around 90 percent to a low of around 30 percent; since homogeneous parents are more successful than heterogeneous ones in passing on political orientations, the absolute numbers of "successful" cases varies dramatically across orientations even if the correlations are the same.

Thus while the theoretical significance of the findings is not necessarily affected by the proportion of homogeneous versus heterogeneous parents on a given orientation, the political significance is affected. If, for example, the proportion of homogeneous couples averaged only 15 percent across the various measures in Table 6.2, we would attach a different significance to the impact of homogeneity than if the average proportion were 50 percent. (In practice the average across all the measures is close to 50 percent.) The criterion we employed for homogeneity is stringent and unyielding, regardless of the type of variable being used. Thus we have calculated the minimum proportion of homogeneity, because we have defined anything off the main diagonal as representing heterogeneity.[7] More generous definitions expand the proportion of homogeneous parents (except for the two-by-two case) but also tend to dilute the category and the operation of the homogeneity principle.

Let us turn now to the question of relative influence according to parental sex. The prevailing view of intrafamilial interaction is that husband-father plays the dominant political role. The fairly slender soundings of the empirical studies supporting this view[8] are buttressed by one's intuitive notions and observations about the place of the sexes in American party politics. As with most occupations, men occupy the elite positions. More significantly, men are also more evident at the cadre and mass public levels. Politics is conventionally thought of as sex-appropriate for men, whereas doubts and ambiguities prevail regarding women. In

[7]Since homogeneity is defined by those pairs occupying the same cells in a square matrix, the likelihood of homogeneity, per se, tends to vary directly with the number of categories in the variable being handled. Illustratively, fewer homogeneous couples are likely to show up on a thirteen-category variable than on a three-category variable, other things being equal. This being the case, it is risky to speak with assurance about the absolute number of homogeneous couples across various political orientations.

[8]See Herbert McClosky and Harold Dahlgren, "Primary Group Influence on Party Loyalty," *American Political Science Review*, 53 (September 1959), p. 762; Angus Campbell, *et al.*, *The Voter Decides* (Evanston: Row, Peterson, 1954), p. 206; Bernard Berelson, *et al.*, *Voting* (Chicago: University of Chicago Press, 1954, p. 102; and Robert Lane, "Fathers and Sons: Foundations of Political Belief," *American Sociological Review*, 24 (August 1959), pp. 502–11; and his "Political Education in the Midst of Life's Struggles," *Harvard Educational Review*, 38 (Summer 1968), pp. 468–94, esp. pp. 479–93.

fact, sex role differentiation has been detected as early as the fourth grade among American school children.[9] Bearing these tendencies in mind, it is perhaps only logical to assume that within families the father will be more determinative of the offsprings' political coloration than will the mother.

On the other hand, there is some evidence which suggests that the above interpretation about male dominance needs reevaluation. First, psychoanalytic theory and clinical work reveal that the normal resolution of Oedipal tendencies prohibits strong cross-sex identification; nonpsychoanalytic theorists have arrived at similar conclusions.[10] Consequently, same-sex rather than father-dominant transmission patterns might prevail. Second, three studies of young people based on limited samples and recall data report findings on the intergenerational transfer of party identification which undermine the father-dominant thesis.[11] Finally, alterations in the social structure and widened educational opportunities suggest that the traditional division of political labor within the family is changing, and that a greater sharing of political roles will occur among the more educated, middle class families.[12]

Inferences concerning the presumed influence of mothers versus fathers may be drawn by comparing the last two columns of Table 6.2. Contrary to popular opinion and the arguments advanced earlier,

[9]Fred I. Greenstein, *Children and Politics* (New Haven: Yale University Press, 1965), Chapter 6; and Robert D. Hess and Judith V. Torney, *The Development of Political Attitudes Among Children* (Chicago: Aldine, 1967), Chapter 8. For evidence pointing to the perpetuation of sex-related differences even among political elites see M. Kent Jennings and Norman C. Thomas, "Men and Women in Party Elites: Social Roles and Political Resources," *Midwest Journal of Political Science*, 12 (November 1968), pp. 469–92; and Edmond Constantini and Kenneth Craik, "Women as Politicians," *Journal of Social Issues*, 28 (No. 2, 1972), pp. 217–36.

[10]On the psychoanalytic see, for example, O. H. Mowrer, *Learning Theory and Personality Dynamics* (New York: Basic Books, 1961). A nonpsychoanalytic rendering is Robert R. Sears, Eleanor Maccoby, and Harry Levin, *Patterns of Child Rearing* (Evanston: Row, Peterson, 1957). This view does not, of course, rule out the likelihood of some identification with the same-sex parent. See Philip E. Slater, "Toward a Dualistic Theory of Identification," *Merrill-Palmer Quarterly*, 7 (April 1961), pp. 113–26.

[11]These studies are: Philip Nogee and Murray Levin, "Some Determinants of Political Attitudes Among College Voters," *Public Opinion Quarterly*, 22 (Winter 1958), pp. 449–63; Eleanor Maccoby, *et al.*, "Youth and Political Change," *Public Opinion Quarterly*, 18 (Spring 1954), pp. 23–29; and John Shelton Reed, "The Transmission of Party Preference by Identification," unpublished paper, 1969. In a study of students in sixteen colleges it was observed that deviation from parental ideological perspectives—on a left-right continuum—was more frequent *vis-à-vis* fathers than mothers. See Russell Middleton and Snell Putney, "Political Expression of Adolescent Rebellion," *American Journal of Sociology*, 68 (March 1963), pp. 527—35. In addition, a recent small study of college students and their parents revealed that on four out of five scale comparisons the congruence between mother and son was slightly higher than that between father and son. See Lucy N. Friedman, Alice R. Gold, and Richard Christie, "Dissecting the Generation Gap," *Public Opinion Quarterly*, 36 (Fall 1972), pp. 334–46.

[12]This topic is taken up in M. Kent Jennings and Richard G. Niemi, "The Division of Political Labor between Mothers and Fathers," *American Political Science Review*, 65 (March 1971), pp. 69–82.

mothers do surprisingly well when pitted against a dissimilar spouse. Of 28 possible comparisons, the correspondence for student-mother pairs is higher than that for student-father pairs in 19 cases, with 3 being dead heats and 6 showing at least a minimal advantage for fathers. Only in two instances—television usage and efficacy—does the student-father exceed the student-mother by more than .05. But student-mother results exceed student-father results by that much in 14 instances! Assuming that the conflict situation provides the acid test of differential parental influence, mothers undeniably emerge as victors.

Although mothers do well throughout the range of orientations listed in Table 6.2, close inspection shows that their greatest strength comes in orientations possessing a valence quality. Specifically, 8 measures under "Issue-Positions" and at least 4 under "Group Evaluations" all show a modest to moderate edge for mothers. Measures listed under the other rubrics yield mixed and generally less marked differences by parental sex. Given the stated tendency in valence dimensions, it seems desirable to approach the data from another angle, in part to ensure against the possibility that the mothers' superiority is not simply reflecting marked differences in the opinion structures of mothers versus fathers.

One way of doing this is to work with the dichotomous issue-orientations—excluding party identification. We may think of these as producing sets of bi-polar parental pairs, since by definition the heterogeneous parents take opposite sides on these issues. To assess the pull of mothers versus fathers a series of tables taking the following form was constructed:

	Mother pro Father con	Mother con Father pro
Student pro		
Student con		

Parent and student positions on the issues are ordered such that a positive correlation indicates that the student agrees more with mother than with father.

Across the seven issues the correlations range from .03 to .23. Although these are by no means strong correlations, they are compatible with the findings presented in Table 6.2. They are, moreover, perfectly suitable for rejecting the father-dominant model of value transmission. Controlling for sex of the student results in patterns for each sex which echo almost without exception the picture for students as a whole. In general, however, the relationship is somewhat stronger among girls than boys.

These relationships do not take into account the direction of the parent and student responses. It is possible that the consistent edge of mothers over fathers could result from high student-mother agreement when mother responds one way and father the opposite (e.g., mother pro, father con), but not for the reverse situation (mother con, father pro). But regardless of the combination, mothers have the edge, slight though it may be. For example, if mother is pro and father is con, the proportion of pro students is higher than when father is pro and mother is con.

A concrete example of what this finding means lies in its relationship to majority opinion cultures. As mentioned earlier, there is a national adult majority position on each of the seven issues which could affect basic parent-student agreement patterns, particularly if the mother typically sided with the majority. As indicated, though, when mother takes the majority position on the issue she draws more student agreement than does father when he takes that position. Conversely, she also gains more agreement in the minority position than does father when he is in the minority.

The Corollaries Of Differential Influence—The Case Of Partisanship

As documented previously, nowhere does parent-child congruity reach higher levels than in the case of party identification. So strong is this relationship, compared with others, that one tends to overlook the fact that it is far from perfect. Similarly, the marked husband-wife accord on party identification ($\tau_b = .59$, using the seven-point party identification measure) still falls far short of unity. From this information alone we know that students are not necessarily found in homes where partisan harmony reigns between their parents. And the previous section (Table 6.2) revealed that agreement with both mother and father declined remarkably under conditions of parental disagreement, with the fathers suffering more in this process than mothers. What we wish to do now is to probe much more intensively this question of partisan conflict in the family and its consequences for children. By doing so, we may illumine the more general processes involved when children confront learning situations in which the parents, as agents of socialization, have conflicting stances.

In this analysis we take the seven-point party identification measure and collapse it into three components—strong, weak, and "leaning" Republicans; strong, weak, and "leaning" Democrats; and "pure" Independents (i.e., those who do not lean toward either party). Each member of the family triad of student, mother, and father is classified in that fashion. Three patterns emerge when the three members of each triad are compared. First are the 57 percent where all members have the same general preference. Second are the 17 percent where mothers and fathers are homogeneous, but the child deviates. Third are the 26 percent where the mother and father disagree, and the child agrees with one or neither of them. It is this last set with which we are concerned. It is worth noting in passing, however, that these figures demonstrate that the family circle is by no means monolithic in its partisan attachments. By considering only triples, this diversity is actually understated. Expanding the family constellation to include other children would yield even more complex structures. Compared with most other political orientations, however, this complexity would take on the appearance of simplicity.

Taking the triads with disagreeing parents, 40 percent of the students side with mother, 35 percent with father, and 25 percent with neither, a finding in accord with the correlational differences (Table 6.2). Thus the mother has a slight edge, contrary to long-standing impressions. We have commented elsewhere on the surprising finding and the historical changes which have prompted it.[13] Rather than dwell on that point, our task here is to summarize the regularities which accompany siding with the mother, father, or neither. Although the evidence is irregular at this stage, it does appear that the factors underlying the differential impact of mothers versus fathers in the partisanship arena also operate in other domains.

We have observed from time to time that transmission rates are only sporadically aligned with whether the child is male or female. Nevertheless, in considering a broad range of orientations it seemed that girls were more often in accord with homogeneous parents; and we have just noted in the foregoing section that mothers seemed to be more influential under conditions of parental heterogeneity. Partly because of space limitations, we have seldom asked the question of whether boys are more likely to side with fathers and girls more so with mothers when there is conflict between the parents. That is, is there a same-sex pattern of affinity under conditions of conflicting parental cues?

Panel 1 of Table 6.3 reveals that there is indeed a modest same-sex pattern, with girls more often being aligned with mothers and boys more so with fathers. Whether these are "conscious" same-sex choices is problematic. The students do not necessarily wind up agreeing with the same-sex parent as a result of a deliberate choice in the face of a recognized conflict. As we shall see later, parental disagreement is not always attributed when present, and is not always present when attributed. With the coming of the new feminist movement it is quite possible that girls may more consciously opt for the mother's position and that boys will also be drawn in that direction as the traditional sex-typing breaks down. If that were to happen it would accelerate a trend already present in these 1965 data. This follows from the fact that while same-sex affinity is operative among both boys and

[13]Jennings and Langton, "Mothers versus Fathers."

girls, it is considerably stronger for the latter. Whereas the net advantage of fathers over mothers is but 6 percent for boys (column 3 less column 1), the net advantage of mothers over fathers is 17 percent for girls (column 1 less column 3). Each parent may receive some advantage from same-sex imitation, but mothers are the chief beneficiaries.

Another possible explanation for why the conflicted child agrees with one versus the other parent may lie in the reservoir of affective ties between parents and children. If children perceive a parental division of opinion, it seems probable that they will side with the parent toward whom they feel closest simply because they associate favorable objects with that parent. Even if they do not actually perceive the conflict, the cuetaking mechanism would still seem to be such that cues from the more favorably viewed parent would be received and internalized more frequently.

Because of the dearth (and most probably very unusual surrounding circumstances) of cases where the child feels closer to father than mother, our analysis will be restricted to the two situations where 1) affect toward each parent is equal, and where 2) the mother is viewed the more warmly.[14] The data indicate that emotional ties do make a difference (Table 6.3). The closer the feeling toward mother the more often her preference is shared; the less close to her the more often the father's preference is shared. Moreover, this relationship is much stronger than that for the preceding analysis along sex lines. Again, it should be noted that while both mothers and fathers benefit from the process, the former achieve slightly higher gains.

Since partisanship is a distinctly political variable, it might be argued that certain political properties of the parents should be operative in pushing the conflicted child in one direction or the other. Very often in political socialization inquiries (and other political studies for that matter) there is an attempt to account for political behavior with nonpolitical variables—to the exclusion of patently political characteristics. What we have called the resource availability (social stratification) approach and certainly the psychoanalytic approach would fall into that category. These are weakly represented by the first two variables we considered, sex and affective relationships.

Social learning theory as represented by the reinforcement and observational approaches would allow for a more explicit use of political variables as explanations for other political orientations. In the case at hand, for example, one might immediately suggest that when the children confront disagreeing parents, they will veer toward that parent holding the belief most dearly. In the first place the more intense parent is likely to be more aggressive in signal giving; thus there is "more" for the child to imitate and

[14]Both girls and boys feel closer to their mothers, although the pattern is stronger among girls.

TABLE 6.3
AGREEMENT BETWEEN PARTY IDENTIFICATION OF PARENTS AND
OFFSPRING AMONG PARENTS WITH HETEROGENEOUS IDENTIFICATIONS

Characteristic	Student's Party Identification Same as:			
	Mother	Neither	Father	
Student Sex				
Girls	47%	22	30	(56)
Boys	33%	28	39	(73)
		$\tau_b = .13$		
Relative Closeness to Parent				
Closer to mother	51%	19	30	(48)
Equally close to each	26%	30	43	(69)
		$\tau_b = .22$		
Partisanship Level of Mother versus Father				
Mother higher	56%	15	29	(41)
Equal	40%	31	29	(35)
Father higher	26%	30	43	(53)
		$\tau_b = .29$		
Campaign Activity Level of Mother versus Father				
Mother higher	59%	13	28	(23)
Equal	41%	22	38	(55)
Father higher	30%	34	36	(52)
		$\tau_b = .31$		

observe. In the second place, other things being equal, the least costly way to reconcile the conflict is to adopt the posture which the more intense parent holds. The child runs fewer risks of injured feelings by doing so. If both parents have equal intensity, then the child will use some other decision rule.

Inasmuch as the party identification measure has an intensity dimension built into it, we may classify the heterogeneous couples into three categories: 1) mother is more intense; 2) father is more intense; or, 3) they are equal in intensity. As Table 6.3 shows, the students are very much affected by differential levels of partisan intensity. When mother has the greater adherence, the students slide toward her preference; similarly, when father has the greater adherence, the movement is toward him. While the principle operates for each parent, it does so more strongly for mothers. The father's net advantage is 17 percent when he is the more partisan, whereas the mother's net advantage is 27 percent when she is the more partisan. Tempering this somewhat is the fact that in absolute numbers there are more instances of higher father intensity.

The importance of intensity is highlighted by comparing the overall relationship (as indicated by the correlations) with that for sex and relative closeness to parents. Clearly, the political variable is more pronounced than the nonpolitical ones. The importance of manifestly political characteristics is underscored if we turn to relative rates of campaign activities.[15] Students gravitate toward the parent who is more active politically. As with relative degrees of partisan intensity, the explanation would seem to lie in the greater emission of cues from the more active parent as well as from the "least injury" reasoning of the students. Even though each parent shares in the imitation benefits to be gained from greater activity, it is obvious that mothers do so much more than fathers: the net advantage for fathers is only 6 percent whereas that for mothers is 31 percent. Again, this must be tempered by the fact that there are over twice as many instances wherein fathers are more active than their wives than vice versa.

Two main conclusions flow from these findings about the bases of the differential strength of each parent when they disagree politically. First, there are processes which do enhance the likelihood that one versus the other will more often be "reproduced" in the profile of the offspring. The linkages formed by same-sex identification and filial attachments work to benefit one versus the other parent. In addition to these nonpolitical variables are those more explicitly political. Here it became apparent that the more politicized parent is the one winning whatever implicit or explicit contest may be going on for the preferences of the child. Moreover, the impact of these political characteristics is, in an absolute sense, more visible than the nonpolitical ones.

While it is significant that both mothers and fathers benefit from the processes described above, there is no question that the students' likelihood of agreeing with mothers is more affected by just where the mothers stand vis-à-vis their husbands on these measures. For each of the four measures mothers are the greater beneficiaries when they occupy the higher or preferred position. But this gain is most noticeable for the politicization measures. What seems to happen is that when her activity and intensity levels increase the mother becomes a much more visible and salient source of political information. She reaps corresponding benefits as her relative position improves. This is only partially true for fathers, and the major reason is that the child more often adopts a position independent of both mother and father as the latter becomes more politicized. As mother's politicization level becomes relatively high, traditional habits of sex-typing are attenuated. She is seen as having political views in her own right and she presumably tests and exercises them in the family circle. Should the secular forces at work in society result in an even greater proliferation of politically dominant views, one would expect maternal strength in the transmission process to wax rather than wane.

[15]Intensity and activity are but weakly related among these parents—$\tau_b = .10$.

We may use this somewhat greater variability of distaff influence to illustrate the cumulative nature of the processes whereby the child swings toward one or the other parent. It was determined that each of the variables continued to make a contribution to the agreement patterns when multivariate analysis was used. That is, their effects were not "washed away" by controlling for the other variables involved. This suggests that cumulative effects are operative. Some examples will illustrate how the characteristics add up to push the child very much toward one parent or the other. Here the percentage agreeing with the mother's partisan preference will be taken as the dependent variable.

We noted previously that both relative closeness to mother and mother's relative level of partisanship were positively related to taking mother's party identification. If the variables are combined, as in the top half of Table 6.4, the effect is to produce a rather extraordinary range. Thus when the child feels closer to mother and mother is the more partisan parent (upper left cell), nearly two-thirds of the students agree with her. At the other extreme, when the child feels equally close to each parent and father is the more partisan (lower right cell), agreement with mother is reduced to about one-sixth. Clearly each of the two characteristics has some impact, but the cumulative effects are perhaps even more impressive.

Another example combines student sex and the relative campaign efforts of mothers and fathers. While both variables continue to exhibit "indepen-

TABLE 6.4

AGREEMENT BETWEEN PARTY IDENTIFICATION OF MOTHER AND OFFSPRING AMONG PARENTS WITH HETEROGENEOUS IDENTIFICATIONS, UNDER TWO SETS OF CONTROL CONDITIONS

Relative Closeness to Parent	Partisanship Level of Mother versus Father		
	Mother Higher	Equal	Father Higher
Closer to mother	64%[a] (17)	50% (14)	40% (17)
Equally close to each	34% (23)	31% (21)	16% (25)

Student Sex	Campaign Activity Level of Mother versus Father		
	Mother Higher	Equal	Father Higher
Girls	70% (8)	50% (24)	38% (24)
Boys	53% (15)	33% (31)	23% (28)

[a]Cell entries show the percentage agreeing with mother out of the N for that cell, which is given in parentheses.

dent" effects within each level of the other, the cumulative pattern is striking. In fact, assuming the independent variables are uncorrelated, the value for each cell comes extremely close to the expected value dictated by the additivity model.[16] As a practical matter the results mean that girls in families where mothers are the politicos are about three and one-half times more likely to acquire their mother's preference than are boys in homes where father is the more politically active.

PERCEIVED DISAGREEMENTS

An essential contention in our treatment of heterogeneity has been that disagreement between parents has an immediate importance for the child even if such differences are not explicitly recognized. Nevertheless, the question of perceptions should not be discarded. If nothing else, a perceived difference has more subjective meaning to a person than does a "real" difference. An individual can intentionally act on the basis of perceived discrepancies to try to resolve them, ignore them, or favor one position over the other. And a "real" difference that goes unnoticed works its influence only by indirection. So we may ask of our triples: What is the incidence of child-perceived parental disharmony, and how does the child reconcile perceived differences? Are these reconciliations consistent with the patterns found for real differences? Material for answering these questions is confined to the area of party identification.

Students see less discrepancy than actually exists among their parents. In the case of partisanship there are some 129 instances (26 percent) of heterogeneous parental pairs. There are only 72 (14 percent) similar cases of student-perceived heterogeneity. By inference, one way in which offspring resolve parental disagreements is simply not to recognize that they exist. Nonrecognition may be a function of no cues, of course, but it can also stem from ignoring such cues. In any event it would seem that fewer adolescents actually have to confront the question of parental division than would be necessary under conditions of full information.[17]

We can look behind these aggregate patterns to the relationships among individual students and their parents. That is, we can establish how often students correctly identify conflict between their parents. There are two

[16]As it turns out these two variables are absolutely uncorrelated, as are most of the pairs formed from independent variables. Working with the grand mean, row means, and column means the predicted values for each cell in the two panels of Table 6.4 were calculated. The size of the errors ranged from 0 to 3 in the second panel with an average of 1.5. In the first panel the additive process is somewhat less strong; the range of errors is 0 to 11, with an average of 4.

[17]The tendency to underestimate true parental differences also characterizes student reports of parental political interest, voting turnout, and direction of the vote. See Richard G. Niemi, *How Family Members Perceive Each Other* (New Haven: Yale University Press, 1974), Chapter 3.

prominent ways in which this can be done. First, we can take the proportion of perceived disagreements which reflect "actual" disagreement. This results in an overlap of 54 percent; out of all students who perceived a disagreement, 54 percent of their parents actually were in disagreement. While this proportion may not appear to be inordinately high, it yields a better success ratio than does the other procedure. In this case we take all those parents who have a self-revealed difference, and then ascertain what proportion of their offspring correctly identify this conflict. Here the correct perception figure is 34 percent.

Under both tests there is a large amount of misperception and error. Such error must be placed, however, in the context of *all* perceptions being made. Overall, 64 percent of the student-parent pairs represent agreement between the parents' actual party identification combination and the students' perception of it. Moreover, this agreement is particularly high at either end of the party identification spectrum, wherein lie the bulk of the cases. Thus, 83 percent of the Democratic parental pairs and 81 percent of the Republican parental pairs were correctly identified. Within the interior combinations these percentages drop off rather markedly; and it is these latter combinations, of course, which contain the instances of parental discrepancy. Where the cues are double pronged and in the same direction, then, students do exceedingly well. It is among the more ambiguous, and probably unstable constellations, where their batting averages taper off. To this it should be added that even among the parental pairs themselves there is some discrepancy between one spouse's revealed party preference and the mate's perception of that identification. Using even the liberal conventions we have employed (all three categories of each party being considered as identifying with that party) it turns out that 19 percent of the husbands incorrectly identify their wife's party identification and 14 percent of the wives commit a similar error with respect to their husband's identification.

We may now perform the same set of operations for comparing students with their (perceived) heterogeneous parents as was done previously, but our analysis will be confined to two major points. First, which parent do students side with when they perceive parental discord? Second, what is the effect of sex pairings on these patterns?

Our earlier discussion revealed that mothers held an edge in gaining offspring agreement on party identification. Working with student perceptions, however, this small advantage is reversed. When parental differences are perceived, 45 percent of the students agree with father, 35 percent with mother, and 20 percent with neither. Comparable figures are 35 percent, 40 percent, and 25 percent when parental disagreement is defined in terms of parental self-reports. An immediate conclusion to be drawn here is that the traditional modes of sex-typing are more operative when the child actually believes there is conflict between parents. Given conventional public manifestations of sex appropriate behavior, the child perhaps seizes upon the "maleness" of politics to resolve the choice somewhat more often in the father's direction. To some extent these findings might appear to undermine our earlier reasoning about the slippage of traditional sex roles in the political socialization process. It should be reemphasized, however, that the adoption of a preference in the context of conflicting preferences held by relevant others is not necessarily contingent upon explicit recognition of such divergencies.

There is, in any event, a nice reconciliation of the somewhat different findings. Previously we observed a moderate same-sex pattern, whereby students with conflicting parents showed a slight tendency to agree with the same-sex parent. This pattern is much more evident when dealing with the perceptual data, as these figures reveal:

	Student's Party Identification Same as:				
Student Sex	Mother	Neither	Father	Total	
Girls	53%	13	33	99%	(30)
Boys	24%	24	52	100%	(42)
Total	35%	20	45	100%	(72)

$$\tau_b = .25$$

Our overall (Total) figures now become explicable. The same-sex pattern is, in the first place stronger for boys than girls, with a "mother-father" net difference of 28 percent for boys and 20 percent for girls. This is one reason the overall totals favor fathers. A more important factor is that boys comprise nearly three-fifths of the total subset perceiving parental disagreement. Thus they contribute disproportionately to the overall picture of student-parent agreement, and since boys favor their fathers over their mothers by a substantial margin, this inflates the overall percentage of students siding with fathers. If boys and girls contributed equally to the table, the total figures would read: mother = 38 percent, neither = 18 percent, and fathers = 42 percent. Father's edge would still remain, but at an attenuated level.

Perhaps the most significant point, nevertheless, is the strong same-sex pattern. The correlation of .25 compares with one of .13 when dealing with parent-revealed differences in party identification. It seems safer to conclude that affinity with the same-sex parent provides the rule of thumb decision-making principle, rather than the principle of deciding in terms of what society recognizes as more sex-appropriate. In the vernacular, when the chips are down the child more often than not goes with the same-sex parent.

CONCLUSION

As the previous four chapters and the first portions of this chapter demonstrate, the range of similarity between parents and their children is vast. It simply will not do to talk about the transmission of political orientations as though there were only one set of orientations and as though the processes were always the same. In the concluding chapter of this book we will set out some reasons why so much variability exists. Thus the readers who, at this point, desire an overall assessment of the parental role in shaping the political character of the adolescent may want to glance ahead to the final chapter.

Our primary purpose in this chapter was to illustrate how the configuration of socialization agents affects in a powerful fashion the person being socialized. The evidence assembled here shows the workings of the principles of homogeneity and heterogeneity. Almost without exception the child is more likely to reflect one parent's orientation when that orientation is also shared by the other parent. Similarly, the child is less likely to reproduce one parent's orientation when that orientation is not shared by the other parent. Thus the likelihood of any sort of parental tradition being passed on from one generation to the next is very much a function of the content which each parent brings to that transmission process. It is also clear, however, that homogeneous parents are no guarantee that the child will reproduce the parental disposition. To the contrary, there are several instances in which homogeneity has only a modest "lifting" effect. Again, we shall address in the final chapter the reasons for that in the context of an overall assessment of the parental role.

We have found it useful to account for the operation of the homogeneity-heterogeneity principles in terms of the tenets of observational learning. Indeed, it becomes difficult to account for the kinds of findings displayed without resorting to a theory based on the processes of imitation, copying, and identification. At the same time, the great range in the relationships suggest that observational learning can take us only so far. There are a number of orientations for which—in the family setting at least—the theory would appear to be inadequate. Variations in reinforcement, cognitive development, and the affective and power domains of the family undoubtedly play a substantial role here.

There are also strong reasons for believing that parents are by no means the only sources of political learning for the growing child. They may not even be the most important. Their influence with respect to some orientations is severely conditioned by the nature of other agents and forces in the child's environment. We obtained some inkling of that conditioning by observing the greater "success" rate of homogeneous parents when they were in step with the prevailing national mood versus when they were running against the grain. In Part III we will explore much more widely and deeply the question of how the parent's role in political socialization is mediated, bolstered, and undercut by the other major institutional source of political learning—the educational system—as well as by the more informal mechanisms of the peer group.

III   THE IMPACT OF THE EDUCATIONAL SYSTEM

CHAPTER SEVEN

Effects of the High School Civics Curriculum

CO-AUTHOR: KENNETH P. LANGTON*

THE FOUNDERS of the American republic stressed the importance of education to the success of democratic and republican government. Starting from its early days the educational system incorporated civic training. Textbooks exposing threats to the new republic were being used in American schools by the 1790s. By 1915, the term "civics" became associated with high school courses which emphasized the study of political institutions and citizenship training.[1]

Throughout this period to the present, however, there has been controversy over the objectives, content, and impact of government courses. While most educators can agree that the development of good citizenship is important, the "good citizen" is something of an ideal type whose attitudes and behavior vary with the values of those defining the construct. Yet when the literature on the development of civics is examined a few consistent themes appear. The civics course should increase the student's knowledge about political institutions and processes, make him a more interested and loyal (but not superpatriotic) citizen, and increase his understanding of his own rights and the civil rights of others. The literature also implies that good citizenship does not exist in vacuo; it means active political participation as well as loyalty and interest.[2]

*This chapter is based on an extension and revision by M. Kent Jennings and Richard G. Niemi of an article by Kenneth P. Langton and M. Kent Jennings, "Political Socialization and the High School Civics Curriculum in the United States," *American Political Science Review*, 62 (September 1968), pp. 852–67. Citations of this chapter should list the authors in this order: M. Kent Jennings, Kenneth P. Langton, and Richard G. Niemi.

[1] For a short historical background and bibliography on the civics curriculum in American high schools see, *inter alia*: I. James Quillen, "Government Oriented Courses in the Secondary School Curriculum," in Donald H. Riddle and Robert S. Cleary (eds.), *Political Science in the Social Studies* (36th Yearbook, National Council for the Social Studies, 1966), pp. 245–72; and Franklin Patterson, "Citizenship and the High School: Representative Current Practices," in Patterson, *et al.*, *The Adolescent Citizen* (New York: Free Press, 1960), Chapter 5.

[2] See for example: Educational Policies Commission, *Learning the Ways of Democracy: A Case Book in Civic Education* (Washington: National Education Association of the United States, 1940), Chapter 1; and Henry W. Holmes, "The Civic Education Project of Cambridge," *Phi Delta Kappan*, 33 (December 1951), pp. 168–71. The most ambitious effort to formulate and assess the level of citizenship skills and qualities is the recent National Assessment program. See National Assessment of Educational Progress, Report 2, "Citizenship: National Results," and Report 6, "1969–1970 Citizenship: Group Results for Sex, Region and Size of Community" (Washington: U.S. Government Printing Office, November, 1970 and July, 1971, resp.).

It is apparent that curriculum, teachers, school climate, and peer groups all may contribute to the political socialization process; but the relative contribution of each is unclear.[3] Attempts to assess the actual impact of the school in general, and the curriculum in particular, have produced controversial and inconsistent results.

At the high school level the outcome of research on the association between curriculum and political socialization has been mixed. Moreover, the conclusions of these studies are often hampered by their lack of generalizing power to broader universes of students and by the rather restricted nature of the dimensions being studied.

In a quasi-experimental study of three Boston-area high schools, Litt found that while civics courses had little impact upon students' attitudes toward political participation, these courses did affect students' "political chauvinism" and "support of the democratic creed."[4] Experimental pedagogical methods have also resulted in some observable short-term cognitive and affective changes.[5] However, other studies of the relationship between formal courses in social studies and politically relevant attitudes report either inconclusive or negative results. The early New York Regents' Inquiry on Citizenship Education, which found that the quantity of work done in social studies was not reflected in changed "citizenship" attitudes, was later echoed by the Syracuse and Kansas studies of citizenship[6] and data from the Purdue Opinion Panel.[7]

Almond and Verba asked adult respondents in their comparative study to recall if any time was spent in their school teaching about politics and government. They compared the level of subjective political competence of individuals who reported that time was spent in their school teaching about politics with those who reported that it was not. The authors conclude that the data show "a relatively clear connection between manifest political teaching and political competence in the United States, Britain, and Mexico."[8] They conclude that manifest teaching about politics can

[3]For a general discussion of this problem see: James S. Coleman, "Introduction" in James S. Coleman (ed), *Education and Political Development* (Princeton: Princeton University Press, 1965), pp. 18–25.

[4]Edgar Litt, "Civic Education Norms and Political Indoctrination," *American Sociological Review*, 28 (February 1963), pp. 69–75.

[5]See, e.g., C. Benjamin Cox and Jack E. Cousins, "Teaching Social Studies in Secondary Schools and Colleges," in Byron Massialas and Frederick R. Smith (eds.), *New Challenges in the Social Studies* (Belmont: Wadsworth, 1965), Chapter 4; and Robert E. Mainer, "Attitude Change in Intergroup Programs," in H. H. Remers (ed.), *Anti-Democratic Attitudes in American Schools* (Evanston: Northwestern University Press, 1963), pp. 122–54.

[6]Patterson, *et al.*, *The Adolescent Citizen*, pp. 71–73; Roy A. Price, "Citizenship Studies in Syracuse," and Earl E. Edgar, "Kansas Study of Education for Citizenship," *Phi Delta Kappan*, 33 (December 1951), pp. 175–81.

[7]H. H. Remmers and D. H. Radler, *The American Teenager* (New York: Charter, 1962), p. 195.

[8]Gabriel Almond and Sidney Verba, *The Civic Culture* (Princeton: Princeton University Press, 1963), p. 361.

increase an individual's sense of political competence, but that this is less likely to happen in nations (like Germany and Italy) whose educational systems have been dominated for much of the life span of the respondents by anti-democratic philosophies.

In addition to the mixed findings of various studies, there is also some question as to the potential of the secondary school for political socialization. It is possible that by the time students reach high school many of their political orientations have crystallized or have reached a temporary plateau. Early research on the political socialization of American pre-adults argued that the elementary school years are the most important for the formation of basic political orientations.[9] It is also possible that the high school civics courses to which students are exposed offer little that is new to them, that they simply provide another layer of information which is essentially redundant.

Granting either or both of these points one should, perhaps, not expect dramatic movements simply on the basis of one or two courses. However, some incremental changes should be visible. One might also hypothesize differential incremental effects according to some central characteristics of the students, their families, the school, the curriculum, or the political orientations themselves. Before examining these questions in detail, we will first observe the place of the social studies and civics courses in the landscape of American secondary education.

High School Students And Exposure To The Social Studies

The reason for dwelling on the social studies courses lies in the formal civic education responsibilities vested in them and the inherent nature of the course content. While civic education undoubtedly occurs in nonsocial studies classes also (to say nothing of other parts of the school environment), it is patent that the major thrust of the civic education curriculum rests in the social studies. American educators have long given the social studies a prominence in the secondary school not found in most other nations. A fairly basic pattern was established in the early part of the twentieth century, a pattern which has shown remarkable longevity. World History, American History, and American Government or Problems of Democracy have been the stock in trade for a number of decades. Yet new courses have crept into the curriculum and new content has been latched on to old course titles. And for all the uniformity, schools do differ in what they make available to their students.

[9]Robert D. Hess and David Easton, "The Role of the Elementary School in Political Socialization," The School Review, 70 (Autumn 1962), pp. 257–65; David Easton and Robert D. Hess, "The Child's Political World," Midwest Journal of Political Science, 6 (August 1962), pp. 229–46; Robert D. Hess and Judith V. Torney, The Development of Political Attitudes in Children(Chicago: Aldine, 1967); and Fred I. Greenstein, Children and Politics (New Haven: Yale University Press, 1965).

Just how much social studies do the students receive and what kinds of courses do they take? By taking the experiences of the high school seniors as they are preparing to graduate we can construct an outline which will answer those questions. During our interviews with the twelfth graders they indicated which social studies courses they had actually taken (or were presently enrolled in) during grades 10–12. We allocated the courses into ten broad categories, as shown in Table 7.1. Most of the categories are self-explanatory, but two need clarification. American Problems includes the familiar Problems of Democracy course, plus such occasional titles as Contemporary Problems, Social Problems, and Problems of American Life. Specialized World History embraces courses outside the standard World History course as, for example, European History, Asian History, and World Cultures. A course title is not a foolproof guide to the content of the course, but there appears to be general congruence between course titles and the type of textbooks employed and topics covered.

Table 7.1 contains two types of information about social studies in the United States. The first column indicates the precentage of seniors who were attending schools where the various courses were part of the curriculum, either as a requirement or elective. There is a great range, with American History being ubiquitous and World History, American Government, and Economics being found in over three-fifths of the schools attended by the seniors. At a somewhat lower level are American Problems, specialized World History, Geography, and Sociology. Finally the "newcomers" of Psychology and International and Comparative Politics were available to less than one-fifth of the students.

Laid against these offerings are the percentages of students who had actually taken such courses (column 2). It is a rare student who gains a diploma without encountering American History. Beyond this subject, however, coverage is considerably less comprehensive, with World History, American Government-American Problems, and Economics exhibiting moderate strength. Of this latter group, Economics has probably shown the most gain during the post-World War II period. Sociology, though christened as the queen of the social sciences, is still seldom found in the high school student's repertory. This is even more true of Psychology—by all odds the largest of the behavioral sciences at the professional and academic levels. What emphasis contemporary students receive on international relations and world politics has to come through other courses, for there are precious few students who take (or have available) courses specifically designed for this. The low percentage for Geography is primarily a function of the fact that most students now take Geography during either the eighth or ninth grades.

TABLE 7.1

A COMPARISON OF SOCIAL STUDIES OFFERINGS VERSUS EXPOSURES
DURING GRADES 10–12, FOR HIGH SCHOOL SENIORS

Course	Percent Attending School Offering Course (2063)	Percent Who Have Taken Course (2063)
American History	98	98
World History (general)	80	53
American Government	62	43
Economics	65	30
American Problems	42	27
World History (specialized)	31	16
Sociology	30	12
Geography	30	06
Psychology	16	06
International and Comparative Politics	13	05

In sum, what the high school student of the sixties was receiving in the way of social studies bore the heavy imprint of the traditional pattern. Whereas the college curriculum during the past decades was heavily infiltrated by the behavioral sciences, the secondary schools responded only very slowly to changing intellectual and practical interests. For the student going on to college, this gap may not be crucial because it can be bridged during the college years. Of more concern are those not going further and those who have already left school. In essence, the dominant type of "social change" they will have had is History and American Government. Although recent trend data are not handy, it does appear that the classic configuration of course exposure is beginning to erode. And it is likely that the traditional courses are undergoing alteration, though surely not rapidly or vigorously enough to suit the critics of the traditional curriculum and the proponents of the "new" social studies.[10]

Another way of approaching the diet of social studies is to look at the sheer volume of courses consumed by the students. Overall the mean was 3.08, and the mode was three courses. Clearly one cannot charge the American educational system with depriving its consumers of a goodly quantity of social studies.

[10]Edwin Fenton, The New Social Studies (New York: Holt, Rinehart, and Winston, 1967); Howard Mehlinger, "The Study of American Political Behavior," (an occasional paper from the High School Curriculum Center in Government, Indiana University, mimeo. 1967); John S. Gibson, New Frontiers in the Social Studies–1, 2 (New York: Citation Press, 1967); Byron G. Massialas and C. Benjamin Cox, Inquiry in Social Studies (New York: McGraw-Hill, 1966); and Donald W. Oliver and James P. Shaver, Teaching Public Issues in the High School (New York: Holt, Rinehart, and Winston, 1966).

To this point we have dealt with all the social studies. For political socialization inquiries it is defensible for some purposes to restrict the courses to those in the American Government-American Problems area. This is not because important aspects of value and skill acquisition may not transpire in other social studies courses. Rather, it is the American Government and Problems courses that are directly oriented toward achieving these political skills and values. These are the classic "civic education" courses.

Schools offering American Government usually do not offer a Problems course, and vice versa. Whereas the American Government courses focus heavily on the forms, structures, backgrounds, and traditions of American political life, the Problems courses emphasize a wider scope of socio-political activities, are more contemporary in nature, and are typically organized around major problems in American public life. Because of the different emphases and formats of the two courses, it has been advanced that they will have differential effects.

Altogether 68 percent of the students had taken one or the other of these two courses, with 43 percent having had an American Government course and 27 percent a Problems course. As in the case of the total number of social studies courses there are also differences in the degree of exposure to civics courses. Perhaps the most striking variations are by region and metropolitanism. Over four-fifths of the students in the West and Midwest, about two-thirds of the Southerners, but slightly under two-fifths of the Northeastern residents had experienced such a course. Similarly there is an inverse relationship between the metropolitan configuration and course exposure—the more metropolitan the area the less likely will the student have taken the course. Beyond these spatial characteristics the only other discriminating characteristic is the academic calibre of the school (in terms of college prep proportions). Students in schools at each extreme less frequently took a civics course than those in the middle ranges.

Disguised in the overall patterns are some contrasts between taking American Government versus American Problems. For example, Southern students took the Government course over the Problems course at a ratio of about 5:1. Northeastern students, by contrast, were much more exposed to the Problems than to the Government course, the ratio being about 4:1. Similarly, public school pupils more often found themselves in American Government whereas the nonpublic students were more frequently in American Problems. A final illustration is that black students—primarily because of their concentration in the South—had the Government course more often than did whites, even though whites had a slightly higher overall rate of exposure.

Since civics courses tend to be required if present in the school curriculum, one must assume that the spatial variations are functions of state and school system practices rather than being indicative of any special passion for or against the courses on the part of students. Indeed, there is specific information on the latter point suggesting that the social studies are not as onerous as some critics have claimed. The seniors were asked which subjects they liked best and which they liked least. Of the subject areas taken by virtually all students—English, social studies, mathematics, and physical or biological sciences—social studies courses ranked slightly below English as the best liked, but slightly ahead of both math and the sciences. On the other hand, math was judged the least-liked subject, followed by English, social studies, and the sciences. Compared with the other major subject areas, then, the social studies do moderately well in terms of student enthusiasm.

THE EFFECT OF CIVICS COURSES

Now that the distribution of civics exposure has been described we can turn to the crucial question of their impact. That is, are a student's political values, cognitions, and skills affected by course exposure. Course exposure here means having taken none (32 percent of the sample), one (59 percent), or more than one (9 percent) civics course. Since a civics course is usually taken by requirement, we may assume that no self-selection bias is at work. The possible biases introduced by the differential exposure noted in the previous section appear not to affect the findings reported below.

In selecting the dependent variables for this analysis, we attempted to touch on many of the consistent themes in the "civics" literature which are germane for political science. Rather than examine only one or two variables, we have elected to pursue a wide variety so that the possible variations in effects may be uncovered. The dependent variables are as follows:

1. *Political knowledge and sophistication*—For better or worse, performance on factual examinations is a prime way in which the success of a course and teacher is evaluated. The political knowledge scale discussed previously (Chapter 4) will be employed as an indicator of factual learning. Another measure, touching more directly on political sophistication, is the index of recognition and understanding of political party differences (Chapter 4).

2. *Political interest*—A hallmark of the "shoulds" of political education in the United States is the shaping of citizens to take an active

interest in political affairs. Although numerous studies of adults suggest that the schools and other socializing agents fall short of the goals envisioned by the authors of civics textbooks, it is nevertheless possible that these achievements would be even less impressive in the absence of intensive inculcation in the civics courses. Among many alternative measures of interest available in the interview protocols, we shall rely on the answers to the straightforward inquiry about how closely students follow public affairs (Chapter 2, footnote 23).

3. *Spectator politicization*—A more direct measure of interest in political matters is the degree to which students consume political content in the mass media. If the civics curriculum spurs an interest in politics, it should be reflected in greater media consumption. Separate soundings of the students' behavior vis-à-vis television, newspapers, and magazines will be used in testing this hypothesis.

4. *Political discourse*—Even more dramatic evidence of the success of the civics experience would be an upsurge in the adolescent's level of politically tinged dialogue. In view of the fact that there are relatively few ways in which the high school senior can (or does) assume active political roles, the frequency of political conversations is not an improbable surrogate for forms of adult level political activity. For present purposes the student's report of the frequency of political discussion with peers will be used.

5. *Political efficacy*—The belief that one can affect political outcomes is a vital element of political behavior, and Easton and Dennis have demonstrated the rising sense of efficacy as the child progresses through elementary school.[11] Much of civic education's thrust is toward developing a sense of civic competence. Efficacy is expressed by the students' scores on the two-item index (Chapter 5).

6. *Political trust*—While trying to create interest in politics and a sense of efficacy, the civics curriculum almost inevitably tries to discourage feelings of mistrust and cynicism toward the government. Indeed, cynicism seems in part to be antithetical to a feeling of civic competence. The five-item scale is employed here (Chapter 5).

7. *Civic tolerance*—Considerable discussion exists in the citizenship literature on the necessity for inculcating norms of civic tolerance. Even though the curriculum materials and the teachers often fail to grapple with the complexities of these norms, a proper and necessary role of civics courses is seen as creating support for the "Bill of Rights," due process, freedom of speech, recognition of legitimate diversity, and so forth. In

---

[11]David Easton and Jack Dennis, "The Child's Acquisition of Regime Norms: Political Efficacy," *American Political Science Review*, 61 (March 1967), pp. 25–38.

order to probe the effect of exposure to civics courses on these types of beliefs, a three-item civic tolerance scale is utilized.[12]

8. *Participative orientation*—Instilling a propensity toward participation in public life becomes especially evident as a civic education goal as the adolescent approaches legal age. In particular, one might hypothesize that the participation ethic would displace an orientation that is more basic and formed early in life such as loyalty to country. Responses to the open-ended question tapping the students' view of the "good citizen" form the basis of the participative orientation measure (Chapter 5).

Before turning to the findings it will be instructive to consider some of the factors which could affect the relationship between exposure to civics and the outcome variables. For example, one could argue that a positive association between exposure and political knowledge may only be found among students from less-educated and less-politicized families. This "sponge" theory maintains that children from more culturally deprived families are less likely to be saturated with political knowledge and interest in the family environment; therefore they are more likely to be affected by the civics curriculum when they enter high school. Conversely, one might hypothesize that it is children from the more highly educated family who are most likely to have developed the minimal learning skills and sensitivity to politics which would allow them to respond to civics instruction.

The academic quality of the high school could also affect the efficacy of the civics curriculum. A school that sends 75 percent of its seniors on to a four-year college might be presumed to have a significantly different and better academic program than a school that sends only 15 percent of its students.

Since we are focusing on civics courses rather than history courses—taken in moderate to heavy amounts by virtually all high school students—we also want to be sure that we are measuring the independent effect of the civics curriculum and not the interactive effect of the history courses. One can easily think of other possible predictor variables: grade average, sex, political interest.

The problem of multiple predictors clearly calls for a form of multivariate analysis. We chose the Multiple Classification Analysis Program (MCA).[13] This program is useful for examining the relationship of each of

---

[12]The following three agree-disagree questions formed a Guttman scale with a CR of .95:
  (1) If a person wanted to make a speech in this community against religion, he should be allowed to speak.
  (2) If a Communist were legally elected to some public office around here, the people should allow him to take office.
  (3) The American system of government is one that all nations should have.

[13]Frank Andrews, James Morgan, and John Sonquist, *Multiple Classification Analysis* (Ann Arbor: Institute for Social Research, University of Michigan, 1967).

several predictors to a dependent variable at a zero order level and while the other predictors are held constant. Eta coefficients and partial beta coefficients indicate the magnitudes of the relationships for zero order and partial correlations, respectively. The program assumes additive effects and combines some features of both multiple regression and analysis of variance techniques. Like regression procedures using dummy variables, the program allows predictor variables in the form of nominal as well as higher order scales and it does not require or assume linearity of regression.

In the subsequent multivariate analysis seven variables were held constant while the independent effect of the civics curriculum was examined: 1) academic quality of the school;[14] 2) grade average; 3) sex; 4) student's political interest;[15] 5) the number of history courses taken; 6) parental education; and 7) parental politicization (discussion of politics within the family). Information on the latter two variables was derived from parent interviews.

Findings For The Whole Sample

One of the first points to be established here is that scant differences emerge in the dependent variables as a consequence of whether the student had taken a more traditional American Government course or the more topically oriented, wider ranging American Problems course. There is a consistent, though quite small tendency for students taking the former course to consume more political content in newspapers, magazines, and on television, and to discuss politics with peers more frequently. But compared with students taking the American Problems course they more often stress the loyalty (48 percent versus 37 percent) rather than the participation aspect of good citizenship behavior. Aside from these rather meager differences, students taking the two major types of courses are virtually indistinguishable in terms of their political orientations. Knowing this, we may proceed with some confidence to treat them (and those taking a sprinkling of other courses) together and to focus our analysis primarily on the amount of exposure, *viz.*, none, one, or two courses during grades 10–12.

An overview of the results offers strikingly little support for the impact of the curriculum. It is true that the direction of the findings is generally consonant with the predictions advanced above. That is, the more civics courses the students have had the more likely they are to be knowledgeable, to be interested in politics, to expose themselves to the political

[14]School academic quality is based on the percent of seniors going on to four-year colleges or universities in each school. This information was obtained from school sources.

[15]When political interest was examined as a dependent variable in the MCA analysis it was, of course, dropped as a control variable.

content of the mass media, to have more political discourse, to feel more efficacious, to espouse a participative (versus loyalty) orientation, and to show more civic tolerance. The possible exception to the pattern is the curvilinear relationship between course taking and political trust. Thus, the claims made for the importance of the civic education courses in the senior high school are vindicated if one considers only the direction of the results.

However, it is perfectly obvious from the size of the correlations that the magnitude of the relationships is extremely weak, in most instances bordering on the trivial. The highest positive eta coefficient is .06, and the highest partial beta is but .11 (for political knowledge).[16] At the same time the impact of the two family level traits—parental education and political discourse—is ordinarily much greater than that of course exposure. Our earlier anticipation that course taking among older adolescents might result in only incremental changes is borne out with a vengeance. Indeed, the increments are so miniscule as to raise serious questions about the utility of investing in government courses in the senior high school, at least as these courses are presently constituted.[17] Furthermore, when we tested the impact of the history curriculum under the same control conditions it was as low or lower than the civics curriculum[18]

Another spectre haunts the apparent meager contribution of the curriculum. It proved possible to allocate those students who had taken civics courses into the precise years of exposure—tenth, eleventh, or twelfth grades. Although the bulk of the students took such a course during their last year in high school (86 percent), there are a significant number having done so during grades eleven (8 percent, N=109), and ten (6 percent, N=84). Taking these distributions as a recency of exposure

[16]For convenience partial beta coefficients will be referred to as betas or beta coefficients. The beta coefficient is directly analogous to the eta, but is based on the adjusted rather than the raw mean. It provides a measure of the ability of the predictor to explain variation in the dependent variable after adjusting for the effects of all other predictors. This is not in terms of percent of variance explained. The term beta is used because "the measure is analogous to the standardized regression coefficient, i.e., regression coefficient multiplied by the standard deviation of the predictor and divided by the standard deviation of the dependent variable, so that the result is a measure of the number of standard deviation units the dependent variable moves when the explanatory variable changes by one standard deviation." Andrews, et al., Multiple Classification Analysis, p. 22.

As mentioned earlier, the MCA program assumes additive effects. While some interaction may be present, a close scrutiny of the statistical analysis makes it doubtful if the impact is particularly large.

[17]Employing nonprobability samples in the United States, Sweden, West Germany, England, and Italy, two researchers reached the conclusion that civics courses have little or no impact anywhere. Russell F. Farmen and Dan B. German, "Youth, Politics and Education" in Byron G. Massialas (ed.), Political Youth, Traditional Schools (Englewood Cliffs: Prentice-Hall, 1972), Chapter 12.

[18]In a preliminary analysis the impact of taking social studies courses as a whole was examined. The number of social studies courses taken accounted for little difference in the students' orientations.

indicator, we then compared the respective students' scores on our various measures of political orientations. The results show almost without exception that the more recent the exposure the more likely will the students' scores be in line with the predictions made on the basis of the goals of civic education. Another way of saying this is that virtually all of the small contribution that the curriculum makes in yielding positive results emanates from those students who were (in most instances) just finishing their civics course as the school year headed into its final weeks.

Here we see in operation some well-known properties of the memory curve. As one moves away in time from the original information input, the retention of that information deteriorates unless reinforcement is provided. It appears that for those students exposed at the tenth and eleventh grades reinforcement had been lacking and, conversely, those currently taking the course were still in an environment of fresh stimuli and reinforcement. If one were to project the assumed erosion at work amongst the earlier-exposed students onto their later-exposed classmates, then the conclusion is that the latter will also undergo information loss.

The expectation, then, is that if one had reinterviewed the later-exposed students a year or two later their performance would have resembled that of their earlier-exposed peers. Weighted against this projection, however, is the prospect that some of the students might receive reinforcement or new information during college or, less likely, in noncollege settings. Even though deterioration might have set in, the original input from the civics courses might be quickly recouped and perhaps intensified. We cannot, of course, provide the answers to such problematic occurences with the data at our disposal. The best that one can say is that in the very short run the curriculum exerts what little effect it has on those under current exposure.

It could be argued that the inclusion of a key variable, viz., the quality and type of teaching, would produce differential effects among those students who have taken one or more courses. This may be true, and the role of teachers will be examined in Chapter 8. Another factor which might elicit differential patterns among students taking such courses is the content of the materials used and the nature of the classroom discourse. This contingency confronts the considerable uniformity in curriculum materials and the domination of the textbook market by a few leading books.[19]

Do these findings mean that the political orientations of pre-adults are essentially refractory to change during the senior high school years? This

[19]See James P. Shaver, "Reflective Thinking, Values, and Social Studies Textbooks," *School Review*, 73 (Autumn 1965), pp. 226–57; Frederick R. Smith and John J. Patrick, "Civics: Relating Social Study to Social Reality," and Byron G. Massialas, "American Government: We are the Greatest!," both in Cox and Massialas, *Social Studies in the United States*, Chapters 6 and 9.

possibility cannot be easily dismissed. Certainly pre-high schoolers have already undergone, especially in the American context, several years of intensive formal and informal political socialization. They may have developed, by the time they reach secondary school, a resistence to further formal socialization at this stage in the life cycle. But there is also an alternative explanation. If the course work represents information redundancy, there is little reason to expect even modest alterations. By redundancy we mean not only repetition of previous instruction, though there is surely a surfeit of that. We mean also redundancy in the sense of duplicating cues from other information sources, particularly the mass media, formal organizations, and primary groups. Students not taking civics courses are probably exposed to these other sources in approximately the same doses as those enrolled in the courses. Assuming that this is the case, and that the courses provide relatively few new inputs, the consequence would be lack of differentiation between course takers and noncourse takers.

For these reasons it would be well to look at courses and teachers that do not generate information redundancy. That is the virtue of examining the finer grain of teacher performance and course content, as proposed above. Another strategy, and one to be adopted in the remainder of this chapter, would be to look at subpopulations of pre-adults where redundancy might be less frequent than for pre-adults in general. Less redundancy could be occasioned either by infusion of new information where relatively little existed before, or by information which conflicts with information coming from other sources.

Among the universe of subpopulations one could utilize, perhaps none is as distinctive as that of the black minority. The unique situation of blacks in American social and political life and the dynamics now at work have been well documented.[20] Because of cultural differences between the white majority and the black minority, the frequent exclusion of blacks from socio-political life, the contemporary civil rights ferment, and the less-privileged position of blacks in our society, it seems likely that information redundancy should occur less often among the black adolescents. Therefore, the student sample was divided along racial lines.

[20]In addition to such classics as Gunnar Myrdal's *An American Dilemma* (New York: Harper & Bros., 1944), see more recent works: Thomas F. Pettigrew, *A Profile of the American Negro* (Princeton: D. Van Nostrand, 1964); Kenneth B. Clark, *Dark Ghetto* (New York: Harper and Row, 1965); Lewis Killian and Charles Grigg, *Racial Crises in America* (Englewood Cliffs: Prentice-Hall, 1964); Donald R. Matthews and James W. Prothro, *Negroes and the New Southern Politics* (New York: Harcourt, Brace & World, 1966; Dwaine Marvick, "The Political Socialization of the American Negro," *The Annals*, 361 (September 1965), pp. 112–27; William C. Kvaraceus, *et al.*, *Negro Self Concept: Implication for School and Citizenship* (New York: McGraw-Hill, 1965); and L. L. Knowles and Kenneth Prewitt (eds.), *Institutional Racism in America* (Englewood Cliffs: Prentice-Hall, 1969).

FINDINGS FOR THE BLACK SUBSAMPLE

Although the black portion of the sample is not as large as one might desire for extensive analysis (raw N = 186, weighted N = 208), it is sufficiently large to permit gross comparisons with white students of similar social characteristics and also permits some analysis within the black subpopulation. The subsample size and the fact that the drop-out rate is appreciably higher among blacks than whites underscores the admonition that this subsample should not be extrapolated to the black age cohort in general. It should also be noted that the subsample contains twelve respondents classified as nonwhites other than black.

Demographically, the black students are located disproportionately in the South (55 percent versus 25 percent for whites) and come from more disadvantaged backgrounds than do the whites. The latter is true despite the fact that the backgrounds of black students who have persevered through high school are undoubtedly less deprived than are those of their cohort who dropped out. Social status differences between blacks and whites are more pronounced in the South than in the North.

Black and white students have taken civics courses in approximately the same proportions (blacks 63 percent, whites 68 percent). When the association between the civics curriculum and the dependent variables discussed above was reexamined within both racial groups, some intriguing differences appeared. These caused us to reassess the place of the civics curriculum in the political socialization of American youth.

Political Knowledge

White students score more highly on the knowledge scale than do blacks; and when parents' education is controlled the differences persist at all levels. Civics courses have little effect on the absolute political knowledge level of whites (beta = .08). The number of courses taken by blacks, on the other hand, is significantly associated with their political knowledge score (beta = .30). The civics curriculum is an important source of political knowledge for blacks and, as we shall see later, appears in some cases to substitute for political information gathering in the media.

Although the complex multivariate analysis holds parental education constant, it does not allow us to observe easily the singular role of this crucial socialization factor upon the relationship between curriculum and political orientations, especially when interaction effects are present. Therefore, contingency tables were constructed, with parental education controlled, for all relationships between the number of government courses taken on the one hand, and each political orientation on the other. All instances in which education makes a distinctive imprint are reported.[21] For the case at hand—political knowledge—controls for parental education did not alter the effects of the curriculum among either whites or blacks.

In another attempt to measure political knowledge as well as ideological sophistication, students were asked which political party they thought was most conservative or liberal. Each party has its "liberal" and "conservative" elements, but studies of roll call voting in Congress as well as the commentary of the politically aware place the Republican party somewhat to the right of the Democrats. Forty-five percent of the students said that the Republicans were more conservative than the Democrats. Thirty-eight percent confessed to not knowing the answer.

In answering this question students were faced with a problem not of their own making. It can be presumed that some respondents made a random choice (i.e., guessed) to extricate themselves. One gauge of the frequency of guessing is how often the Democrats were assigned a conservative position (17 percent). If we make the reasonable assumption that this form of random guess is symmetric around the midpoint of the response dimension, we can say that an additional 17 percent of the students guessed "correctly" by putting the Republicans in the conservative column. Accordingly, we may deduct 17 percent from the 45 percent who said Republicans were more conservative, leaving 28 percent who are able to connect the conservative label to the Republican party.[22]

We are less interested in the absolute number of students who are able to connect symbol with party than with the role the civics curriculum plays in this process. Again we see that course work has little impact on white students while the percent of blacks who "know" the parties' ideological position increases as they take more civics courses (Table 7.2).

TABLE 7.2

CIVICS CURRICULUM EXPOSURE AND KNOWING THE IDEOLOGICAL POSITION OF THE REPUBLICAN AND DEMOCRATIC PARTIES, AMONG BLACK AND WHITE STUDENTS

Number of Civics Courses	Adjusted Percentage of Correct Responses			
	Black		White	
0	0%	(72)	29%	(543)
1+	19%	(122)	31%	(1184)

[21] Parental education was used as a summary control variable because we felt that it best captures the tone of the whole family environment as well as other sources of socialization.

[22] We have borrowed this method of adjusting "correct" answers from David Butler and Donald Stokes, *Political Change in Britain* (New York: St. Martin's, 1969), p. 207.

These findings using both measures of political knowledge offer an excellent example of redundancy in operation. The clear inference as to why the black students' responses are "improved" by taking the courses is that new information is being added where relatively less existed before. White students enrolled in the courses appear to receive nothing beyond that to which their nonenrolled cohorts are being exposed. This, coupled with the great lead which whites in general already have over the black students, creates greater redundancy among whites than blacks.

One should not deduce from these results that the white students have a firm grasp on political knowledge; as Table 7.2 and other data indicate, they clearly do not. Rather, white students have reached a saturation or quota level which is impervious to change by the civics curriculum. From their relatively lower start the black students' knowledge level can be increased by exposure to the civics curriculum.

Political Efficacy and Political Trust

Almost twice as many black students as white scored low on the political efficacy scale. When the effect of parental education is partialed out the racial differences remain at each educational level, although they are somewhat diminished. Interestingly enough, the difference in the percentage of those who scored low is less between black and white students whose parents have had only an elementary school education (13 percent) than between black and white students whose parents have had a college education (24 percent).

The number of civics courses taken by white students has little perceptible effect on their sense of political efficacy (beta = .05). Among blacks, though, course exposure is moderately related to a sense of efficacy (beta = .18). As can be seen in Table 7.3, this is particularly true for blacks from less-educated families. The strength of the relationship decreases significantly among higher status students. Course taking among the lower status blacks acts to bring their scores into line with their higher status cohorts. There is but a faint trace of this pattern among white students.

Although black students at all levels of parental education feel less efficacious than their white counterparts, it must be concluded that without the civics curriculum the gap would be even greater. As in the case of political knowledge, we have another illustration of less redundancy at work among the black subsample. For a variety of reasons the American political culture produces a lower sense of efficacy among black youths compared with whites. But by heavily emphasizing the legitimacy, desirability, and feasibility of citizen participation and control, the civics course adds a new element in the socialization of low and middle status black students. Since those from the less-educated families are more

TABLE 7.3

CIVICS COURSE EXPOSURE AND POLITICAL EFFICACY AMONG BLACK
STUDENTS, BY PARENTAL EDUCATION

Number of Civics Courses	*Elementary*[a] Political efficacy				
	Low	Medium	High	Total	
0	64%	20	16	100%	(18)
$\gamma = .56$					
1+	30%	27	43	100%	(39)
	High School Political Efficacy				
	Low	Medium	High		
0	56%	20	24	100%	(41)
$\gamma = .36$					
1+	34%	27	39	100%	(62)
	College Political Efficacy				
	Low	Medium	High		
0	32%	32	36	100%	(15)
$\gamma = .02$					
1+	37%	19	44	100%	(24)

[a]Parental education was set by the highest level achieved by either parent. "Elementary" means neither parent exceeded an eighth grade education; "high school" that at least one parent had one or more years of high school training; and "college" that at least one parent had one or more years of collegiate experience.

likely to be surrounded by agents with generally low efficacy levels, the curriculum has considerably more effect on them than on their peers from higher status environments. Leaving aside the possible later disappointments in testing the reality of their new-found efficacy, the black students from less-privileged backgrounds are for the moment visibly moved by course exposure.

While blacks as a whole are less politically efficacious than whites, they are not at the same time more politically cynical. This relatively low level of political cynicism among blacks may have seemed ironic even in 1965, but it was consistent with their view of the "good citizen" role (discussed later). The high school civics curriculum has only a slight effect upon the trust levels of whites (beta = −.11) and none among blacks (beta = −.01). Perhaps this difference means that the cynicism of the latter may be somewhat less responsive to curriculum content. Data gathered from

1967 onward, however, indicate that black pre-adults were becoming less trusting at a faster rate than whites, suggesting that the blacks were very responsive to an awakened sense of political realities.[23]

Civic Tolerance

One of the abiding goals of civic education is the encouragement and development of civic toleration. Blacks as a whole score lower on the civic tolerance scale than do whites. When parental education is controlled the racial differences remain at each educational level, although they are moderately attenuated. Again, as with political efficacy, the differences in the percentage of those scoring low is less between black and white students whose parents have had only an elementary school education (18 percent) than between black and white students whose parents have had a college education (28 percent). What we may be witnessing is the result of black compensation for the white bias in American society—a bias to which higher status blacks may prove most sensitive.

The number of civics courses taken has little effect on white students' civic tolerance scores (beta = .06), with somewhat greater impact being observed on those from homes of lower parental education. There is, however, a moderate association between exposure and black students' sense of civic tolerance (beta = .22). The more courses they take, the higher their level of tolerance. Blacks are more intolerant even when educational controls are introduced, but the civics curriculum appears to overcome in part the environmental factors which may contribute to their relatively lower tolerance. The items on which the civic tolerance measure is based all have to do with the acceptance of diversity. Aggregate student and parent data suggest that these items tap a dimension of political sophistication less likely to be operative in the black subculture. To the extent that the civics courses preach more tolerance, the message is less likely to be redundant among the blacks than the whites. Unlike political knowledge and efficacy, though, course taking exerts its main effect on black twelfth graders from better-educated families, thereby suggesting that a threshold of receptivity may be lacking among those from lower status families.

Politicization—Interest, Discussion, and Media Usage

Students were asked about their interest in public affairs and how often they discussed public affairs and politics with their friends outside class. There is little difference between racial groups among those who expressed high interest in politics or said they discussed politics weekly or more

[23]Paul Abramson provides a compendium of the research and a theoretical interpretation of black-white differences in his "Political Efficacy and Political Trust among Black School-children: Two Explanations," *Journal of Politics*, 34 (November 1972,) pp. 1243–75.

often with their friends. Nor did controls for parental education uncover aggregate racial distinctions. Moreover, the civics curriculum appears at first glance to have little impact upon these two indicators of politicization among blacks (beta = .15 and −.07, respectively) or whites (beta = .06 and .04). Yet an examination of Table 7.4 indicates that curriculum effect is differentially determined by the educational level of the black students' parents (in contrast to a lack of variation among whites). The differential effect may account for the low beta coefficient in the multivariate analysis.

As blacks from less-educated families take more civics courses their political interest and frequency of political discussion with peers increases. Since less-educated parents ordinarily evince lower states of politicization, one could explain this in terms of nonredundant information spurring an upsurge in student politicization. Students from higher status families, however, actually appear to undergo depoliticization as they move through the civics curriculum.

In their excellent social and psychological inquiry into the personality of the American black, Abram Kardiner and Lionel Ovesey observed that it is the higher status blacks who are most likely to identify and have contact with whites and their culture.[24] But due to their race, the disappointments are more frequent and their aspirations more likely to founder on the rock of unattainable ideals.

Because of their parents' experiences, the higher status black students may have received a more "realistic" appraisal of the institutional and social restrictions placed upon black participation in the United States. Upon enrolling in the civics course, they find at least two good citizen roles being emphasized. The first stresses a politicized-participation dimension. The second emphasizes a more passive role: loyalty and obedience to authority and nation. If they have absorbed from their parents the

TABLE 7.4

NUMBER OF CIVICS COURSES TAKEN AND POLITICAL INTEREST AND DISCUSSION WITH PEERS AMONG BLACK STUDENTS, BY PARENTAL EDUCATION

(Gamma correlations)

Parental Education	Political Interest	Political Discussion
Elementary	+.31	+.20
High school	−.18	−.31
College	−.21	−.36

[24]Abram Kardiner and Lionel Ovesey, *The Mark of Oppression* (Cleveland: The World Publishing Co. [a Meridian Book], 1962).

TABLE 7.5
NUMBER OF CIVICS COURSES TAKEN AND POLITICAL MEDIA USAGE
AMONG BLACK AND WHITE STUDENTS

(Partial beta coefficients)

Media	Black	White
Newspapers	−.17	+.07
Television	−.21	+.04
Magazines	−.10	+.10

probability of restrictions, the participation-politicization emphasis in the curriculum may have little impact upon the higher status black students. Redundancy is low because the information conflicts with previous learning. The "reality factor" causes them to select out of the curriculum only those role characteristics that appear to be more congruent with a preconceived notion of their political life chances. As we shall see later, higher status black students' perception of the good citizen role is compatible with the above interpretation.

Students were also asked how often they read articles in newspapers or magazines or watched programs on television that dealt with public affairs, news, or politics. In the aggregate, students from each racial grouping employ newspapers and magazines at about the same rates; but black students use television more often than do whites, and at all levels of parental education. The civics curriculum has a different impact upon political media usage among whites and blacks. Table 7.5 shows that for white students there is a consistent—but very weak—association between taking civics courses and use of the media as an access point to political information. Among blacks there is a consistently negative but somewhat stronger association between the civics curriculum and political media usage. Observing the same relationship within contingency tables under

TABLE 7.6
NUMBER OF CIVICS COURSES TAKEN AND POLITICAL MEDIA USAGE
AMONG BLACK STUDENTS, BY PARENTAL EDUCATION

(Gamma correlations)

Media	Elementary	Parental Education High school	College
Newspapers	−.07	−.36	−.28
Television	−.39	−.42	−.17
Magazines	−.27	−.07	−.42

less severe control conditions, the civics curriculum continues to have a negative—although fluctuating—impact upon political media usage among blacks at *all* levels of parental education (Table 7.6).

Negative correlations among blacks might be explained on at least two dimensions: substitution and depoliticization. A civics course may increase a student's political interest while at the same time acting as a substitute for political information gathering in the media. This is what appears to be happening among blacks from less-educated families. Negative associations between course work and media usage suggest that the former may be substituting for political information gathering in the media. But as we saw before, there is a significant increase in political interest among lower status blacks as they take more civics courses. The lack of depoliticization in this group was further confirmed by the positive correlation between the civics curriculum and discussing politics with one's school friends (Table 7.4).

The case of the higher status black seems to be of a different order. Negative correlations between the civics curriculum and media usage may indicate substitution, but what is even more apparent is the general depoliticization of higher status blacks as they move through the curriculum. The more courses they take the less likely are they to seek political information in newspapers, magazines, and television. In addition there is also a decrease in their political interest and propensity to discuss politics with their friends.

Citizenship Behavior

Interjecting race adds a special complexity to the relationship between the civics curriculum and the student's belief about the role of a good citizen in this country.

When asked for their conception of the good citizen (based on first responses only), 70 percent of the whites and 63 percent of the blacks fell along two general dimensions: loyalty and political participation. Within these two response dimensions there are distinct racial differences. Sixty-one percent of the black students focus on loyalty rather than participation. Only 41 percent of the white students, on the other hand, see the good citizen role as being one of loyalty rather than political participation. When we probe the relationship between taking civics courses and citizenship orientation some interesting differences are revealed. More civics courses mean more loyalty and less participation orientation for blacks. In Table 7.7 there is a 24 percent difference in loyalty orientation between those blacks who have taken no civics courses and those who have taken one or more. Civics course work has a slightly opposite effect among white students.

TABLE 7.7

CIVICS CURRICULUM EXPOSURE AND GOOD CITIZENSHIP ATTITUDES
AMONG BLACK AND WHITE STUDENTS

| Number of Civics Courses | Blacks Stressing | | |
	Loyalty	Participation	Total
0	51%	49	100% (41)[a]
1+	75%	25	100% (85)
	Whites Stressing		
	Loyalty	Participation	
0	46%	54	100% (395)
1+	39%	61	100% (803)

[a]These N's are lower than corresponding N's in other tables because those respondents not mentioning either loyalty or participation in their first response are excluded from the base.

In other words, while the civics curriculum has little impact upon the white student's view of the good citizen role, it appears to inculcate in blacks the role expectation that a good citizen is above all a loyal citizen rather than an active one. Yet when we look at this same relationship among blacks under the more severe multivariate control conditions, we observe that the size of the beta coefficient ($-.10$) is not large.[25] While it is predictably negative (i.e., loyalty orientation increases with course work), the magnitude of the coefficients reduces our confidence in the earlier contingency table.

The difference in findings may be the result of moving from a relatively simple bivariate analysis with no controls for other possible intervening variables to a more sophisticated mode of multivariate analysis under more rigorously controlled conditions. This undoubtedly accounts for part of the difference, but we also found, as before, that the civics curriculum has a differential effect upon blacks depending on the educational level of their parents.

Black students whose parents have some secondary school or college education increase their loyalty orientation by 36 percent and 28 percent respectively, as they take more civics courses (Table 7.8). Blacks from less-educated families, however, increase their participation orientation much like white students. Due to the small N for black students who have taken no courses and whose parents have an elementary school education or less, this relationship should be treated quite cautiously. Although differences between blacks from different levels of parental education

[25]The beta coefficient for white students is $+.07$.

have been mentioned before, the most one would want to say here is that the civics curriculum seems to increase the loyalty orientations of higher status blacks while having a slightly opposite effect among lower status ones.

A number of interpretations can be placed on these findings. Both loyalty and participation are emphasized in the civics curriculum, and for white and lower status black students the dual emphasis has about equal effect. But as we noted earlier, higher status blacks may have received from their more active parents a "realistic" appraisal of the institutional and social restrictions placed upon black participation in American politics. Consequently, the participation emphasis in the curriculum has little impact. The reality factor may cause higher status blacks to select out of the curriculum only those role characteristics which appear to be most congruent with a preconceived notion of their political life chances.

Another rationale for the findings might be found in the relative fulfillment of white and black needs to belong, to be accepted in this society. If we assume that the black is cut off from many of the associational memberships and status advantages that most whites take for granted, then this unfulfilled need to belong and to be accepted is probably greater than that of the white counterparts. This may be particularly true of the higher status blacks and their parents. Because of their relatively higher education in the black community, they have had more

TABLE 7.8

CIVICS CURRICULUM EXPOSURE AND CITIZENSHIP ATTITUDES AMONG BLACK STUDENTS, BY PARENTAL EDUCATION

Number of Civics Courses	Elementary		Total	
	Loyalty	Participation		
0	83%	17	100%	(6)
1+	63%	37	100%	(28)
	High School			
	Loyalty	Participation		
0	54%	46	100%	(24)
1+	90%	10	100%	(41)
	College			
	Loyalty	Participation		
0	32%	68	100%	(11)
1+	60%	40	100%	(17)

contacts with whites—contacts which, because of their race, have led to more frequent rebuff. The one association not explicitly denied blacks is that of being a loyal American. It is entirely possible that the psychic relief higher status blacks receive in "establishing" their American good citizenship is greater than that of their white counterparts or their lower status racial peers. As a consequence, the loyalty emphasis in the curriculum may have the most impact on the higer status black.[26]

Regional Effects

The black students (like all blacks) are located disproportionately in the southern part of the United States. Because of possible cultural differences we thought it advisable to control for region as well as parental education. Therefore the black subsample was divided into South and non-South with controls for high and low parental education employed in each region.

When controlled for region as well as parental education, the effects of the civics curriculum upon political knowledge, interest, discussion, television-newspaper-magazine usage, and loyalty-participation orientations were consistent with the results for the black subsample as a whole in all except two cases. Among the seven variables discussed above there are 28 cases (two for each region because of the education control or four for each variable) in which a possible deviation from the black subsample as a whole could occur. Due to the small marginals and the fact that there were 26 consistent findings, we attach little conceptual significance to these two exceptions.

In both regions the civics curriculum continued to be negatively associated with political media usage at all educational levels, except for newspaper reading among higher status students outside the South. The relationships are slightly stronger in the South than in the non-South. The differential consequences of parental education were remarkably consistent across both regions. As before, civics courses had a negative effect upon the political discussion (and political interest in the South) of higher status blacks while having a positive impact upon lower status blacks. Finally, in both regions the civics curriculum continued to have its greatest negative effect on the participatory orientations of black students from the more educated families.

There appeared to be different regional effects on only three of the dependent variables. The first of these was political trust. In the South course work decreases trust slightly among high and low status blacks while in the North political trust increased as the student was exposed to

---

[26]After completing his comprehensive codification of the black culture and circumstances in America, Gunnar Myrdal maintained that blacks in this country were "exaggerated Americans," who believed in the American creed more strongly than whites.

the civics curriculum. However, in both regions the outcome of taking a civics course is to make the students from the better-educated family relatively less trusting than their lower status peers. Exposure to civics also means a slight decrease in civic tolerance among high and low status southern blacks. This is also true of lower status blacks outside the South. For all three cases the magnitude of the relationships are quite small, the highest being a gamma of $-.14$. It is only among higher status nonsouthern blacks that a stronger, positive relationship develops—$+.39$.

The political efficacy of lower status students in the South was increased much more by the civics curriculum (.64) than was the efficacy of their higher status peers (.32). This is consistent with the picture for the entire subsample. However, while there was positive relationship between exposure and increased efficacy among higher status students in the non-South, there was negative relationship among lower status students. We are at a loss to explain this negative sign other than point to the small frequencies which may account for this departure.

CONCLUSION

A number of studies in the United States and other countries have stressed the importance of education in determining political attitudes and behavior. The person with only a primary school education is a different political actor from the person who has gone to high school or college. Yet direct evidence demonstrating the effect of college and high school curriculum upon the political beliefs and behavior of students is scarce and generally inconclusive.

Our findings certainly do not support the thinking of those who look to the civics curriculum in American high schools as a major source of political socialization. When we investigated the student sample as a whole we found not one single case out of the ten examined in which the civics curriculum was significantly associated with students' political orientations.

Although the overall findings are unambiguous, there is reason to believe that under special conditions exposure to government and politics courses does have an impact at the secondary school level. When white and black students were observed separately, it became clear that the curriculum exerted considerably more influence on the latter. On several measures the effect was to move the black youths—especially those from less-educated families—to a position more congruent with the white youths and more in consonance with the usual goals of civic education in the United States. Among white students from less-educated families this pattern was barely visible. With respect to some quasi-participative measures, taking a civics course served to depress black performance, especially among those from better-educated families. In virtually all instances the black students were much more affected by taking such courses than were the whites, regardless of whether the results were positive or negative.

We argued that one explanation of the singular consequence of the curriculum upon black students is that information redundancy is lower for them than for white students. Because of cultural and social status differences, the black students are more likely to encounter new or conflicting perspectives and content. The more usual case for whites is a further layering of familiar materials which, by and large, repeat the message from other past and contemporary sources. Even though the political behavior of black youths has changed dramatically in the last five years, there are still strong grounds for suspecting greater curriculum effects among blacks. A recent longitudinal study of a Detroit-area high school, for example, indicated that black students were more affected by variations in social studies curricula and classroom climate than were white students.[27]

It is conceivable that other subpopulations of students are differentially affected by the curriculum; that variations in content and pedagogy lead to varying outcomes; or that there will be delayed consequences from course exposure. In the main, however, one is hard pressed to find evidence of any immediate course impact on the bulk of the students. The programmatic implications of this conclusion are forceful. If the educational system continues to invest sizable resources in government and civics courses at the secondary level—as seems most probable—there must be a radical restructuring of these courses in order for them to have any appreciable result. Changes in goals, course content, pedagogical methods, timing of exposure, teacher training, and school environmental factors are all points of leverage.[28] Until such changes come about, one must continue to expect little contribution from the formal civics curriculum in the political socialization of American pre-adults.

[27]Lee H. Ehman, "An Analysis of the Relationships of Selected Educational Variables with the Political Socialization of High School Students," *American Educational Research Journal*, 6 (November 1969,) pp. 559–80.
[28]Essentially the same conclusions have been reached by the American Political Science Association's Committee on Pre-Collegiate Instruction. See its report in *PS*, 4 (Summer 1971). The report also contains references to curriculum innovation programs. For an ambivalent assessment of the social studies curriculum by a selective sample of white, middle class students see: Richard Remy, "High School Seniors' Attitudes toward Their Civics and Government Instruction," *Social Education*, 36 (October 1972), pp. 590–97, 622.

CHAPTER EIGHT

Social Studies Teachers and
Their Pupils

CO-AUTHOR: LEE H. EHMAN*

O F ALL high school teachers those in the social studies are perhaps the most maligned. This dubious distinction rests on two main bases. First, the very nature of their subject matter makes social studies teachers obvious targets in the community. They may easily stray into areas of sensitivity and controversy, thereby arousing the enmity of parents and other interested parties. Closely connected with this danger is the fact that these teachers also deal with topics about which laymen often feel remarkably informed. Whereas parents would seldom challenge the performance of a high school chemistry teacher on strictly professional and pedagogical grounds, such instances are not at all rare with respect to social studies teachers. This is especially so if questions of value judgments are at issue. And in truth, knowledge about government and political history—the great core of the social studies curriculum—is probably not as narrowly distributed as, for example, knowledge about the physical and biological sciences.

Another source of malignment emanates from more professional audiences. The training and preparation of social studies teachers is less stringent and professional than that in the other major sectors of the secondary school curriculum. This lack is most vividly demonstrated in the tendency to employ members of the physical education staff as social studies instructors. School administrators who would never think of putting a football coach into a chemistry class have few qualms about situating him in an American History or civics course. Thus professional critics of education as well as professors in the collegiate level analogues to the social studies (e.g., historians, political scientists, economists) often express disdain for the general run of social studies instruction found in the nation's high schools.[1] Ironically, one of the oft-cited reasons for the

---

*Citations of this chapter should list the authors in this order: M. Kent Jennings, Lee H. Ehman, and Richard G. Niemi.

[1] See e.g., Martin Mayer, *Social Studies in American Schools* (New York: Harper and Row, 1964); Byron Massialas, *Education and the Political System* (Reading: Addison-Wesley, 1969), Chapter 6; and Franklin Patterson, *et al.*, *The Adolescent Citizen* (New York: Free Press, 1960), various chapters dealing with the relevant disciplines.

teachers' ineffectiveness is that they are constrained by community pressures; and it is these same pressures which constitute the community's disparagement of the social studies teachers.

On the one hand, then, is the accusation that the teachers are too effective, that they either poison the minds of adolescents or tread into areas best left untouched. Even if the lay challenge is that the teacher is misinformed, there is still the tacit assumption that what the teachers say and do is carrying great weight with their students. The other criticism, however, implies that the social studies teachers are relatively ineffective because of the quality of their training and teaching. From this perspective the teachers are either unsuccessful in trying to impart worthwhile learning or, worse yet, they really have little comprehension about what is worthwhile.

It is not our purpose in this chapter to portray the social studies teacher as either hero or villain. We can, however, use these malignments as a backdrop for discussion. We present material allowing for at least a partial assessment of the teacher's place in the political socialization of their charges. The analysis relies heavily on the use of student-teacher aggregate and pair data, just as in looking at the familial impact we examined students and parents in conjunction. In assessing the contribution of teachers it will also be necessary to allow for the prior and simultaneous effects of parents.

Since the composition of the teacher sample assumes considerable importance for our analysis, we begin with a brief description of that sample. Social studies teachers are obviously not the only nor even perhaps the most important teachers having a potential impact on the political orientations of young people. Yet they are the ones charged with the civic instruction of adolescents, and if one is to assay the intended effects of the educational program one must certainly focus on these teachers. Ideally we would have interviewed other teachers also, but resources prohibited that luxury.

Having decided to restrict ourselves to social studies teachers, we still have very difficult choices to make, because interviewing all the teachers to whom the students had been exposed during grades 10–12 was still an uneconomic allocation of resources. While the major criterion was the maximization of student-teacher pairs over the three-year period, a number of other factors were also employed. The specific details are presented in the Appendix. Altogether, it proved possible to interview 317 teachers out of 321 selected (raw N). Teachers were assigned sampling weights in the same fashion as were students and parents from the same schools; the weighted teacher N is 385.

The selection scheme resulted in our being able to interview at least one teacher for over nine-tenths of the students in 84 percent of the schools. This meant that all but 6.6 percent of the students could be paired with at least one teacher. Discarding that small proportion, the final results showed that 26 percent of the students were paired with the teacher from one course, 38 percent with the teacher from two courses, 28 percent with three, and 8 percent with four or more. The average number of course-teachers per student is 2.2. While it would have been ideal to have had even more teachers, we feel reasonably confident that the teacher sample accurately reflects the population of social studies teachers to which the students were exposed. Comparing the overall mean of 3.1 social studies courses per student with the mean of 2.2 course-teachers per student indicates that we obtained surprisingly broad coverage from the 317 teacher interviews. Furthermore the variety of courses taught by the teachers matches rather well the variety of courses taken by the students as a whole.

It should be emphasized that this is not a probability sample of all social studies teachers in the sampled schools. A concise definition of the teacher sample is that it represents those social studies teachers bearing the heaviest load of social studies teaching during grades 10–12 for a national sample of twelfth graders. Thus we have the teachers to whom the students had been most exposed.

For background purposes a few social and occupational characteristics of the sample may be noted. One-half of the teachers hold Masters degrees, 74 percent are males, 94 percent are white, 78 percent spend from 90–100 percent of their teaching time in the social studies, and 69 percent live in the community in which they teach. Slightly over one-half have been teaching ten years or longer. Despite the fact that this sample is characterized by heavy teaching in the social studies, 30 percent of the males have some coaching responsibilities also. Out of all courses which the teachers reported having taught during the past three years 32 percent were in American History, 23 percent in American Government and Problems of Democracy, 22 percent in World History, 10 percent in Economics, and 13 percent in a sprinkling of other social studies courses.

An especially important characteristic of teachers is the type of training they have experienced. There is a considerable literature—much of it speculative and hortatory—about the consequences of differential teacher preparation.[2] In another place we demonstrated that collegiate major exerted a telling effect on the willingness of teachers to express themselves politically within and outside the classroom.[3] We distinguish five collegiate majors: education,[4] social studies, history, social sciences, and a catch-all of "others." The distinction between social science and social

---

[2]One of the better works in this thicket is James D. Koerner, *The Miseducation of American Teachers* (Baltimore: Penguin Books, 1965).

[3]M. Kent Jennings and Harmon Zeigler, "Political Expressivism Among High School Teachers: The Intersection of Community and Occupational Values," in Roberta Sigel (ed.), *Learning About Politics*, (New York: Random House, 1970), pp. 434–53.

[4]This includes physical education majors also.

studies majors is crucial, with the former including the classic disciplines of political science, economics, sociology, psychology, and anthropology. Teachers with social studies backgrounds ordinarily majored in that area—versus, e.g., mathematics or English—as a specialty in their preparation for a teaching career. Education and social studies majors usually matriculate in departments, divisions, or colleges of education. They typically encounter less of the academically demanding and mind-expanding environment of a liberal arts college and are, rather, exposed to a more unified set of values.[5]

The undergraduate majors for the teacher sample are given below, along with the major field for those having M.A.'s:

	Undergraduate Major	Graduate Major
History	35%	40%
Social studies	24	8
Education	13	41
Social sciences	11	8
Other	17	4
	100%	100%

What is perhaps most impressive about these figures is the paucity of social science majors at the undergraduate and graduate levels. Even though over one-half of the teachers were giving courses outside history, and even through a majority of the students had taken courses in addition to history, still a bare fraction of the teachers had any major work in the social sciences. The other side of the coin is the domination by history and education, especially if one equates education and social studies majors, at the undergraduate level. Nor does the picture improve appreciably if we consider undergraduate minors also, since only 20 percent of the teachers had a social science minor. To return to a similar point made in the previous chapter, the social sciences are still but weakly represented among those social studies teachers with whom the students have most class contact.

In discussing the effects of the social studies courses we noted that students do not disdain such courses. Contrary to popular reports, the students actually register rather favorable reactions to such courses. Much the same can be said for the teachers. A student rating of from extremely good to extremely poor was obtained for every teacher named

[5]See Koerner, *Miseducation of American Teachers*, Chapters 4–5; and Egon G. Guba, Philip W. Jackson, and Charles E. Bidwell, "Occupational Choice and the Teaching Career," reprinted in W. W. Charters, Jr., and A. L. Gage (eds.), *Readings in the Social Psychology of Education* (Boston: Allyn and Bacon, 1963), pp. 271–78.

by the student. Out of all ratings 34 percent were "extremely good," 39 percent "good," 19 percent "fair," 6 percent "poor," and 2 percent "extremely poor." The scores ran even higher for teachers of the American Government and Problems of Democracy courses. Whatever we may conclude about the teachers' impact on the students, it will not be easy to trace the reasons to negative evaluations of the teachers.

ASSESSING TEACHER IMPACT

Previous inquiries about high school teachers' influence on their students' political attitudes and beliefs are not only scarce, but also typically offer indirect evidence. They are indirect in the sense that the effects of *courses*, rather than *teachers* is usually the operative question. Litt's study is of this type,[6] and the previous chapter in this book falls into that mold. Still relatively rare are studies such as the one by Ehman, wherein teaching style and the amount of controversial issues discussed were used in assessing certain political orientations of the students.[7]

Yet teachers are also disseminators of political values and skills in their own right, impart cultural norms with political overtones (e.g., competition as a way of life), and help provide a microcosmic model of a society and polity by the manner in which the classroom functions (e.g., authoritarian versus democratic modes). It is with respect to the latter point that the public schools—especially those at the elementary level—have been recently castigated by both hostile and friendly critics.[8] Although most of the apparent "damage" has already been consummated by the time the student reaches senior high school, we will touch briefly on this topic. Our major focus, however, will be on teachers as disseminators of values and skills.

In the area of political socialization the major research claim for teachers as prime sources of youths' political orientations comes from the Hess and Torney work with elementary schoolchildren. These investigators utilized responses from schoolchildren ranging from grades 2–8. They also had available responses to many of the same questions from teachers found in these schools. By comparing the aggregate mean scores from both samples they could see whether children were becoming more

[6]Edgar Litt, "Civic Education, Community Norms, and Political Indoctrination," *American Sociological Review*, 28 (February 1963), pp. 69–75.

[7]Lee H. Ehman, "An Analysis of the Relationships of Selected Educational Variables with the Political Socialization of High School Students," *American Educational Research Journal*, 6 (November 1969), pp. 559–80.

[8]See *inter alia*, Edgar Z. Friedenberg, *Coming of Age in America* (New York: Vintage Books, 1965); Jonathan Kozol, *Death at an Early Age* (Boston: Houghton Mifflin, 1967); John Holt, *How Children Fail* (New York: Pitman, 1967). Perhaps the most significant critique from the "establishment" is Charles Silberman, *Crisis in the Classroom* (New York: Random House, 1970). There are, of course, innumerable polemics and diatribes against the contemporary school system.

like teachers the longer they were in school. It turned out that in most instances the student scores were indeed moving toward convergence with the teacher scores, so that eighth graders had political profiles quite similar to those of teachers. From this Hess and Torney were led to conclude:

> The extent of congruence in responses support [*sic*] the conclusion that the school is a powerful socialization agent in the area of citizenship and political behavior. . . . Where dissimilarities [of aggregate teacher and student means] occur, there is likely to be specific participation by socializing agents and institutions of the community other than the school.[9]

Now it would be foolish to say that the schools or teachers are unimportant in shaping the political lives of their wards. At the same time one must be extremely careful in detailing just how that shaping comes about. Although we have presented aggregate profiles for teachers, students, and parents elsewhere,[10] we refrained from making the same sort of inferences which Hess and Torney applied to comparable data. A number of reasons can be advanced for this decision, and they would appear to apply to the general set of such data.

(1) Making such inferences from aggregate data is a form of ecological fallacy. Simply because two related *aggregates* behave similarly across a range of phenomena is not a sufficient statistical reason to assert that related units at the *individual* level will behave similarly.

(2) The reasons for parallel behavior may be a response to forces common to each sample. Thus by the time they are in the eighth grade the students may be responding to community and mass media forces in a fashion similar to that of teachers. Or they may both be responding to common forces within the school, such as curriculum materials, ritualistic behaviors, or school behavioral norms established by the administration.

(3) A related, but distinct trap in making inferences from aggregate comparisons is that the students may be developing in the direction of the other adults with whom they have had most contact, viz., their parents. Here the aggregate comparisons of students, parents, and teachers are most instructive. They show that students are sometimes more like teachers, and sometimes more like parents. Out of all the measures we examined, teachers perhaps have a slight edge, but clearly not of the magnitude to warrant the conclusion that students are usually more like teachers than parents. Faced, then, with aggregate comparisons in which

[9]Robert D. Hess and Judith V. Torney, *The Development of Political Attitudes in Children* (Chicago: Aldine, 1967), p. 114.

[10]M. Kent Jennings and Lee H. Ehman, "Political Orientations of Teachers, Students, and Parents" (unpublished paper, 1972).

students resemble both teachers and parents one would be hard-pressed to infer (allowing for the moment the legitimacy of such inferences) that teachers were more instrumental than parents in shaping children. This seems particularly so since the students have had a much more sustained history of exposure to their parents compared with their teachers.

A better method of making inferences from the similarity or difference in political orientations between groups such as students, parents, and teachers is through the use of paired statistics, in contrast to the use of aggregate statistics. We want to make inferences concerning the strength of association between attributes held by linked pairs of individuals drawn from two different groups. We would like to know, for example, whether political trust scale scores vary systematically between students and their own parents and between students and their own teachers. We also want to know which association is stronger, and therefore which source has the greater apparent power in shaping and maintaining political orientations.

Since we are interested in the linkages between students and their particular teachers and parents, it is necessary to match up students with their parents as well as with teachers to whom they have been exposed. Essentially we create a set of student-parent-teacher triples, just as formerly we utilized student-mother-father triples. So that all triples will be complete, any student for whom either a parent or teacher was not interviewed is deleted from the analysis. When more than one teacher was interviewed and attached to an appropriate student, the value or weight of each resulting student-teacher pair was divided by the number of all teachers attached to the student.[11]

In the case of parents this matching procedure is defensible because of the relative continuity and limited numbers (two) involved. But with teachers, the continuity is short-lived for specific teachers and the numbers of teachers who have given the child social studies instruction is much greater than two if we stretch the education years back to elementary and junior high grades (to say nothing of the influence of other teachers). How then, can we have much confidence in the student-teacher pairs and the student-teacher-parent triples as units of analysis?

Although we recognize full well the imperfect nature of the data, there are still several reasons why it is better to proceed with what our resources allow rather than not making the effort at all. First, we make the same argument as that advanced in the previous chapter, viz., despite the

[11]As in the case of students with more than one parent this actually means that given students' data records appear on a tape at a rate equal to the number of teachers they had. Since some students have a multiple number of both parents and teachers the number of records to be passed over in computer analysis becomes large—4,206—and the length of records quite long since all records are of uniform length. When weighted appropriately the number of adjusted, analytic student-parent-teacher cases utilized is 1,778, built on a raw N of 1,483 students as the base.

influence of other teachers it is the social studies teachers who are charged with civic education; therefore, one wants to assess, if possible, their effects. Given the temptation to infer individual level relationships from aggregate comparisons, it is especially important to bring to bear whatever data are available to test the reasonableness of such inferences.

Second, even though there is a range in the number of teachers paired with any given student, this does not make any appreciable difference in the relationships. For example, there might have been some bias operating such that students matched with only one teacher were distinctive from those matched with two, three, or more. To check against this possibility separate student-teacher correlations were calculated under the varying conditions of number of teachers per student: one, two, three or more. Virtually all of the differences were trivial and in the few instances where this was not true there was no regular shape in the differences.

A third reason is that, limited though the student-teacher contact may be as represented in our study, it is still more than minimal. Most students have year-long courses from the same teacher. Classes meet every day, the subject matter is relatively narrow, and the teacher has ample opportunity to emit all sorts of stylistic and substantive cues. Casual conversations with students will reveal that they develop definite images of the teacher both as a "person" and as a "teacher." Since we have at least one and in the large majority of cases two or more teachers for each student, we are dealing with a substantial amount of student exposure. Assuming that our measures tap relevant dimensions of socialization, we believe there is a sufficient experiential base to tap teacher impact on students.

An additional argument here is that the amount of exposure to a given teacher is underestimated by considering only student, course-teacher pairs. Students often have the same teacher for more than one course. Out of all students paired with at least one course-teacher, some 31 percent had the *same* teacher in one other course, and 5 percent in two or more other courses. From another perspective, out of all students paired with two or more course-teachers, some 43 percent had the same teacher in one other course, and 7 percent in two or more other courses. These instances of repeated exposures add strength to our contention that student contact with the teachers is more than trivial.

If the comparison of marginals among the three groups was used as the only basis for inferring the relative strength of parents' and teachers' influence on the political orientations of high school seniors, we would expect the teachers to have as much or more influence than parents. But when we examine the paired comparisons summarized in Table 8.1 this general conclusion becomes clearly unwarranted. Nineteen different

TABLE 8.1
STUDENT-TEACHER AND STUDENT-PARENT CORRELATIONS ACROSS A RANGE OF POLITICAL ORIENTATIONS

Correlation Pair and Type	Party Identification	School Integration	School Prayer	Cosmopolitanism	Political Trust
Parent-Student					
Zero-order	.58[a]	.34	.30	.20	.15
Partial	.58	.32	.28	.20	.15
Teacher-Student					
Zero-order	.09	.24	.21	.06	.09
Partial	.02	.20	.18	.05	.09
Multiple R	.59	.40	.35	.21	.18

Correlation Pair and Type	Partisan Intensity	Political Efficacy[b]	Civic Tolerance[b]	18-Year-Old Vote	Main Media	Good Citizen (Political)
Parent-Student						
Zero-Order	.17	.12	.15	.12	.12	.05
Partial	.17	.11	.15	.11	.12	.05
Teacher-Student						
Zero-order	-.01	.11	.07	.11	.03	-.01
Partial	-.01	.11	.07	.11	.03	-.01
Multiple R	.18	.16	.16	.16	.13	.05

Correlation Pair and Type	Catholics	Southerners	Labor Unions	Negroes	Jews	Whites	Protestants	Big Business
Parent-Student								
Zero-order	.36	.29	.29	.26	.22	.18	.14	.12
Partial	.36	.26	.29	.26	.22	.17	.14	.12
Teacher-Student								
Zero-order	.02	.20	.04	.08	.10	.08	.04	-.00
Partial	.02	.15	.02	.05	.09	.06	.04	-.00
Multiple R	.36	.32	.29	.27	.24	.19	.14	.12

[a]Product-moment correlations

[b]See footnote 12.

political measures[12] are included in the table. In no instance is the zero-order correlation higher for teacher-student than for parent-student pairs. Customarily the parent-student edge is sizeable. So fragile are the teacher-student ties that three of the correlations assume a negative sign.

The partial and multiple correlations tell much the same story. Partials were calculated for each pair holding constant the value of the other agent, parent or teacher as the case might be. Teacher-student match parent-student partials in only two instances. And the parent-student values usually represent less of a drop from the zero-order values than is true for the teacher-student pairs. Multiple correlations were also computed, so that the joint effects of teacher and parent orientations could be assessed. If there is very much teacher influence over and above that of the parents the multiple R should jump over the level of the parent-student correlation. Moving across the various measures in Table 8.1 reveals that noticeable increases occur in only four or five instances. Taken together, the zero-order, partial, and multiple coefficients all demonstrate the greater similarity between students and their parents versus students and their teachers.

Dawson and Prewitt discuss the teacher as one in-school political socialization agent.[13] After splitting the teachers' socialization function into manager of the authoritarian-democratic social classroom climate and disseminator of political values, they further divide the dissemination function according to the nature of the value. Their review leads to the conclusion that consensus values—adherence to the democratic creed, the good-citizen role, political trust—are transmitted by the teacher, while more partisan political orientations are disseminated by nonschool agents, rather than the teacher.

The present data do not conform well with their speculations. As we have seen in this pair-wise analysis the teacher-student relationships for the "consensus values" are slight, and certainly smaller than the parent-student relationships. When looking at the party identification dimension the Dawson and Prewitt prognostication holds up. But the correlations for the specific issue items present contradictory evidence, as they can easily be grouped with the "partisan" rather than "consensus" values. Strictly in terms of correlations, teachers appear to have some impact on students' views in the controversial areas of racial integration and religion in the

[12]All of these measures have been presented earlier in the book, but there are some inconsistencies across samples. The political efficacy measure varies across the three samples because it is based on responses to four items among parents, and two among teachers and students. The civic tolerance index is comprised of the "communist take office" and "speeches against religion" items plus—for the students and teachers—responses to the statement: "The American system of government is one that all nations should have."

[13]Richard Dawson and Kenneth Prewitt, *Political Socialization* (Boston: Little, Brown, 1969), pp. 159–60.

schools. Similarly the evaluations of some of the socio-political groupings contain at least as much trace of teacher impact as do the consensus type measures.

Clearly, one would not want to press this line of thinking too far. The consensus type values employed are limited in number and breadth. They also have limitations in that they may simply tap degrees within broad zones of consensus values. Illustratively, even though teachers apparently exert very little impact on the level of political trust among students, they may nevertheless be passing on attitudes which result in a net decision by students to trust the government rather than sabotage it. That is, there may be thresholds beyond which teachers have little impact. Once having brought the students up to a minimal, but decisive level of trust (not tapped by our measures), there may be little room for further elaborations.

By the same token the behavioral norms of good citizenship cover a wide field. After having inculcated certain parameters of permissible versus nonpermissible behaviors teachers may generate few additional effects. Thus children are taught in school that criminal behavior is outside the pale of good citizenship, and it is true that virtually no instances of such "deviant" prescriptions crop up in the student protocols. On the other hand, a variety of behaviors and dispositions are stamped with normative approval, and exactly which ones are most salient to students may depend on idiosyncratic features belonging to the student as well as the interview context.

Another reservation about the impact of teachers is the possibility that the most important years are the elementary ones. By using secondary school pupils and teachers we may have passed by the crucial, formative years of teacher impact. Such would be particularly true in the case of consensual values, which seem to emerge early and are constantly reinforced.

One can advance these caveats, but they still leave intact a major hurdle in trying to show teacher effects. All of the arguments brought forth for teachers can also be presented for parents, other children, the mass media, and events as socializing agents. In the absence of longitudinal or experimental evidence it is impossible to demonstrate that the case for teachers is *sui generis*. Falling back on our "snapshot," nonexperimental data leads, as we have seen, to the conclusion that teacher impact varies from nonexistent to weak.

The Effects of Like-Minded versus Disagreeing Parents and Teachers

One of the most consistent and telling findings of Part II was the additional explanatory power generated by taking into account both parents rather than only one in trying to account for the student's political character. We found repeatedly that the student was much more likely to have a given attribute when both parents shared that attribute than when the parents differed. For convenience we labelled these two situations as homogeneous (or congruent) and heterogeneous (noncongruent). The basic operation at work seemed to be a cuetaking, imitative process whereby the two agreeing agents provided the child with a much more explicit, heavier, and nonconflicting barrage than that represented by two disagreeing agents who tended to push the child either toward the middle or more toward one parent (more often the mother) than the other.

If this process accurately describes the operation of dual agents within the home, may it be extended to a home and nonhome set of socialization agents? More specifically, may we expect student-teacher and student-parent similarity to be affected by the congruency existing between the student's parents and teachers? There are some reasons to doubt this. As stressed above, the teacher(s) attached to each student represent only a small fraction of all teachers to whom the student has been exposed. Moreover, these teachers have had much less sustained, repetitive contact than have the parents. The strong affective structure of the family is also largely absent in the classroom. Whether parent and teacher are alike or unalike, then, may have little bearing on strengthening the teacher's role in either bolstering or undercutting parental influence; by the same token this juxtaposition may have little impact on the basic levels of similarity among student-teacher pairs.

To repeat our argument, however, if social studies teachers are to mean anything as learning agents, some traces should be observable in the data. Nor is it that farfetched to expect the homogeneity-heterogeneity principle to be visible at least in the home versus school situation. This is particularly plausible in terms of how teachers might affect the consonance between parent and child. On the one hand, there is some evidence that teachers reflect the values of the community, thereby fortifying the familial impact and, in terms of the present context, increasing the level of student-parent similarity. On the other hand, there are at least strong popular suspicions that teachers are different than the community, thereby undercutting the parental efforts and, in our terms, lowering parent-student similarity. Under *either* condition the hypothesis is that the parent-teacher configuration will either raise or lower the grand student-parent correlations. The same arguments can be made regarding the effects of parent-teacher configurations on student-*teacher* correlations—that the teachers have more apparent influence when the parents are in agreement with them, and less when parents are at odds with them.

The procedures for establishing homogeneity levels between the students' parents and teachers are basically the same as those used in the case of student-mother-father triples. A square matrix containing the values of the teacher-parent pairs attached to a given student is formed for each orientation under consideration. Values along the diagonal represent agreement, or high homogeneity. Because of the large number of cases involved, two levels of nonhomogeneity can be used. Those values immediately off the diagonal represent moderate heterogeneity, those furthest off extreme heterogeneity (low homogeneity). Thus three levels of parent-teacher congruency are established.

Four measures were selected to test the hypothesis. Two of these involve schools, the school prayers and school segregation issues. Results from the partial and multiple correlational analysis demonstrated that these were two areas in which teachers appeared to make a definite contribution to the student scores. The other two measures are party identification and partisan intensity, areas in which teachers seemed to have almost no impact. Table 8.2 contains the results across the four measures. To facilitate comparisons involving the student-mother-father triples, the ordinal statistic τ_b is used; the pattern would be quite similar for the equivalent product-moment correlations. (Comparisons between the grand correlations using τ_b versus product moment correlations can be made by matching column one of Table 8.2 with the corresponding values in Table 8.1.)

Considering first the two school issues, it is readily apparent that the principle of homogeneous effects is operative among the student-teacher-parent triples. Both the initial gross correlations involving students and their teachers and students and their parents receive a very handsome increase when the subset of students attached to highly homogeneous parents and teachers is considered separately. By the same token the initial relationships decline under conditions of little or no homogeneity. On the school integration issue the decline by homogeneity levels is monotonic for both pairs, but on the school prayer issue this applies only to student-teacher pairs.

Although the homogeneity principle operates with respect to both teachers and parents, it is clear that student-teacher similarity is more sensitive to the principle than is student-parent similarity. The gain shown for highly homogeneous student-teacher pairs is greater than for student-parent pairs, necessarily so since they start from a lower base and reach the same level. Similarly, the range of student-teacher correlations is much greater than for students and parents.

Results for the two partisanship measures are in one way like those for the issue topics. Obviously the initial congruence between students and their teachers starts out at a low, even negative, level. Partisanship is not a fruitful area for showing teacher influence. Of more importance right now, however, is the fact that as one moves down the range of parent-

TABLE 8.2

CORRELATIONS AMONG STUDENT-TEACHER AND STUDENT-PARENT
PAIRS UNDER VARYING CONDITIONS OF HOMOGENEITY BETWEEN
PARENTS AND TEACHERS[a]

	No Controls	Controlling for Parent-Teacher Homogeneity[b]		
		High	Medium	Low
School integration issue				
Student-teacher	.24	.52[c]	.12	−.15
Student-parent	.34	.52	.22	.15
School prayer issue				
Student-teacher	.21	.46	.08	−.16
Student-parent	.29	.46	.07	.16
Party identification				
Student-teacher	.08	.36	−.02	−.38
Student-parent	.46	.45	.32	.48
Party intensity				
Student-teacher	−.03	.15	−.04	−.32
Student-parent	.16	.15	.11	.32

[a]Correlations are rank order τ_b coefficients.

[b]Homogeneity refers to the level of agreement between each student's parents and teachers on the issue in question.

[c]For all measures except party identification the high and low homogeneity entries for student-teacher versus student-parent pairs will be identical, but with opposite signs in the low homogeneity case. This is because high homogeneity means *identity* of values between the accompanying teacher-parent pairs and low homogeneity means complete lack of identity in a dichotomous situation (yes-no, no-yes combinations). The operations for party identification included a slight departure from the above.

teacher homogeneity the student-teacher correlations undergo a dramatic monotonic decrease. Coupled with the same patterns for the two school issues, these latter findings show that any potential impact of teachers on students in valence matters is mightily constrained by the accompanying configuration of parent-teacher symmetry.

Other results are not of a piece with those for the two issues. High homogeneity between parents and teachers does *not* improve student-parent agreement. Stated another way, students are not more likely to resemble their parents on partisanship matters simply because their parents and teachers agree. The opposite, of course, was true on the two issues and for all of the student-teacher findings. Not only does the principle of homogeneous effects break down on this score; it also falters because the *highest* levels of student-parent congruence occur when parents and teachers are in *disagreement* (low homogeneity). These findings defy any easy explanation. We would not expect them to occur very often.

Partisanship occupies a unique place in the socialization process, and the lines of transmission are not easily tampered with. What we suspect is the play of some special factors in the low homogeneity situation such that either the teachers or the parents (or both) stand well apart from the dominant partisan climate in the community.

Surveying the four sets of correlations in Table 8.2 yields another insight into the nature of school and home as transmission agents. Students with parents and teachers in a low homogeneity configuration are faced with diametrically opposing preferences. The "medium" category is simply a less dramatic case. Just as we noted toward which parent the child seemed to gravitate when parents disagreed, so too we can easily see toward which agent the child leans when parent and teacher are at odds. The answer is unequivocal, with the student-parent pairs displaying positive signs and the student-teacher pairs negative ones (see footnote c, Table 8.2). Certainly this would be expected in the instance of partisanship, albeit the extent of the parent margin is surprising.

The two issues probably provide a more common sort of result. Many students are apparently veering toward neither agent, perhaps subconsciously splitting the difference between the two. Even though the magnitude of the associations is modest, it is manifest that in each instance the student more often goes toward the parent rather than the teacher. If one thinks of this as a cross-pressures situation, then the victor is more likely to be the parent than the teacher. The pull of familial associations steeped in affective bonds is stronger than whatever intellectual or other attachments the students might have for the teachers. To this may be added the fact that we have included but one parent in the analysis. Particularly where the parents are like-minded the "effects" of teachers will be even more diluted.

TEACHER CHARACTERISTICS AND STUDENT ORIENTATIONS

In seeking out the impact of teachers on their students we have followed the same theoretical framework which guided most of our efforts directed toward determining the effects of parents on children. By ascertaining the degree to which there is student-teacher similarity on a variety of orientations we have been testing how much socialization takes place via modelling processes and direct transmission of orientations. Although we believe these to be generally useful conceptualizations of how parents and teachers help mold the child's political world, it is patent that agents help shape orientations in other ways also. For example, authority structures within the family and the classroom have been posited as key sources because of transference mechanisms. Similarly, it is argued that the child may apply to the political world other, nonpolitical things learned from various agents.

There are at least two ways in which we might expand upon the basic model used in looking at teachers' effects on students. One would be to maintain the basic approach of examining student-teacher congruency but exerting physical controls for important properties of the teacher. For example, we might reexamine the correlations between students and their teachers within categories of presumably important classifications, e.g., teacher sex, race, level of personal trust, classroom style, or feelings about teenagers. Given the low initial correlations between students and teachers it would require rather powerful processes for such separate analysis to yield rich results. This could happen, of course. An essentially bleak bivariate correlation coefficient can be made to stretch from significant negative to significant positive associations when subsets are considered.[14]

Legitimate and insightful though such a procedure would be, our additional work with the teachers takes a different turn. Instead of using teacher properties as mediating or intervening variables, we will use them in the more direct sense of independent causes, or variables. Illustratively, we might posit a connection between the teacher's regard for students and the students' feelings of political efficacy, on the grounds that how one is treated by those in authority makes a difference in the development of one's sense of mastery over the political environment.[15]

Three major sets of teacher characteristics were employed in this undertaking. "Background" variables included the teacher's race, sex, highest degree, undergraduate major, years teaching experience, and level of personal efficacy. In-school variables included how the teacher felt about handling controversial topics in the classroom, perceived goals of the social studies program, support of in-class expressivism by teachers, hours spent in extracurricular activities with students, and frequency of talking about public affairs with students. Out-school variables included election activities, membership in civil rights organizations, and support for out-of-class political expressivism by teachers.

Each of these measures was cross-tabulated with the various student political orientations. With rare exceptions the results point toward virtually no consequences whatever. In some of the few instances where this is not true there are artifactual or confounding ingredients. For example, teacher's race seems to have some consequences, but on closer examination it turns out that there is a strong correlation between race of student

---

[14]An example of this in the present study occurs when looking at the incidence of grievances redressed by upset parents of high school seniors. See M. Kent Jennings, "Parental Grievances and School Politics, *Public Opinion Quarterly*, 32 (Fall 1968), pp. 363–78.

[15]For a more detailed and essentially bleak look at how the teachers might have been affecting the participation ethic of their students see George B. Levenson, "The School's Contribution to the Learning of Participatory Responsibility," in Byron Massialas (ed.), *Political Youth, Traditional Schools* (Englewood Cliffs: Prentice-Hall, 1972), Chapter 9.

and teacher (r = .72, treating race as a dummy variable). Thus any effects of teacher's race are confounded by the same-race linkages of students and teachers.

How do these sorts of relationships compare with the earlier ones, wherein the student-teacher pairs were examined for congruency on given orientations? While it is undeniably true that many of the correlations uncovered by the earlier analysis were woefully deficient in demonstrating teacher impact, they tend to be higher than any plausible ones contained in the present mode of analysis. This is most especially the case where the student-teacher pairs had at least a modicum of similarity, as on the two school-related issues. Other aspects of the teacher —background, in-class, or out-class characteristics—seldom perform any better in correlational terms than do teacher counterparts to student orientations. In sum, the models of imitative behavior and direct transmission do just as well, and usually much better, than do those resting on more indirect, complex models of socialization.

Having made this claim we should be quick to reiterate that it is obviously based on less than a full treatment of the problem. Other types of data and study designs are necessary. Within the limits of our own data we have not been able to perform the level of complex analysis necessary to render a fully adequate answer to the question of how high school social studies teachers socialize their charges.

One example of a different approach is to rely more on the students' perceptions of teacher attributes as important conditioners of political learning. Let us take feelings of political trust as an example. It could be hypothesized that if students trust school authorities they would tend to generalize this feeling to other authorities, in this case the national government. To test this notion various questions about school fairness were put to the students. They were first asked about treatment of students in general: "Do the teachers in this school generally treat everyone fairly, or are some treated better than others?" (The response that it depends on the teacher was coded here as indicating some unfairness.) Then a question was asked about the interviewee in particular: "Do you feel that you have ever been treated unfairly by any teachers here at this school?" Finally, we asked about the school administrators: "What about the principal, vice-principal, counsellors, and people like that? Do you feel that you have ever been treated unfairly by any of them?"

From these questions a "school fairness" index with four categories was formed according to the number of responses indicating no unfairness. This index has a small, but significant positive relationship with political trust (τ_b = .10). While meager, this result is one of the few rising above absolutely no relationship among all of those involving political trust. Cumulatively, a variety of such experiences with school personnel may contribute to the development of trust or distrust of political leaders and institutions.

Additional support can be marshalled for the argument that student perceptions of fair school treatment foster political trust. When combined with parental political trust these positive school experiences exercise a cumulative effect on the students' level of political trust. They exert a similar force on personal trust. In Figure 8.1 we have plotted the mean student political and personal trust scores, controlling for parental trust and the school fairness index. The bottom two categories of the fairness index are collapsed to avoid diminishing N's. For any level of parental political trust (top half of figure), student trust increases as teachers and administrators are preceived to be fairer. Especially prominent is the salutary effect of "high" school fairness on students coming from homes with distrustful parents. Conversely, if school fairness is held constant, student political trust follows parent levels in 12 of the 15 possible instances. In the lower portion of the figure only one point representing student personal trust is "out of place." For each type of trust, then, parental attitudes and encounters with school authority combine to help determine student levels of trust.

In such fashion the impact of high school teachers may be seen as operating in a more indirect form than the ones which we have explored. Yet there is nothing in the magnitude of these or other relationships uncovered in our work to support popular sociological views. To take the instant case, for example, popular critics of the authority system argue that the adolescents' feelings about how they are being treated will inevitably transfer to more generalized feelings toward political institutions. But if this process approached the level brandished by the critics, then one would expect far livelier performance from the measures of school fairness which we have just utilized. It would seem that such "teacher effects" operate at the margins rather than at the vitals of adolescent political learning.

Conclusion

We have been concerned more in this chapter than in previous ones with methodological complexities in the study of political socialization. Specifically, we have addressed the risks involved in making individual level assumptions from aggregate data. While not gainsaying the usefulness of aggregate comparisons, it is patent that making inferences from them about the impact of specific teachers on specific students is indefensible. Students reveal a remarkable lack of congruence with their own teachers over most of a sizeable range of political perspectives. Moreover, even though congruency with parents is by no means uniformly impressive on these same perspectives, the magnitudes of the student-parent

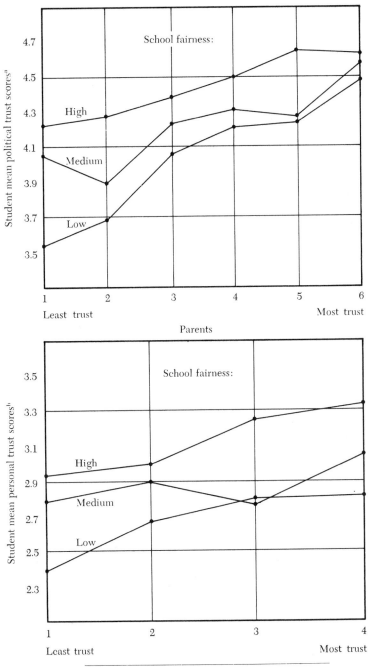

Figure 8.1

STUDENT TRUST BY PARENTAL TRUST AND FAIRNESS OF SCHOOL PERSONNEL

[a] For each point, N ranges from 40 to 289.
[b] For each point, N ranges from 34 to 504.

similarities usually dwarf those for student-teacher combinations. Both the absolute and relative influence of teachers is, therefore, drastically diminished compared with casual interpretations from aggregate profiles. Not surprisingly, methodological considerations have a singular bearing on substantive findings.

Methodological considerations also led us along another path. One was to repeat the form of analysis used so successfully with the student-mother-father triples, substituting in this case student-teacher-parent triples. Although a limited set of political orientations was examined, it appears that the same principles operative at the family level also extend to the family-teacher level. Homogeneity among parents and teachers pushes the child in the direction represented by that homogeneity, whereas heterogeneity more often results in the child adopting intermediate positions. Again, it is the configuration of multiple socialization forces which sharpens our understanding.

We began this chapter by noting the unenviable position of social studies teachers in the high schools. They are criticized both for being too effective and too ineffective. The former argument usually takes the form of conservatives charging that the teachers plant liberal or radical ideas in the youngsters' minds; but it is by no means unheard of in recent years for liberal parents to charge the teachers with being too conservative, especially on matters of dissent and civil rights. The charge of ineffectiveness typically comes from those who believe little at all is being learned in the classroom or what is learned is simply repetitive of what has been learned earlier or elsewhere.

Our attention has focused very much on political attitudes and states of mind; relatively little attention has been given to behavior and cognitive processes. Thus we do not know whether teachers are having any impact on how the students come to handle political stimuli, how they process political materials, or how they search for political answers. Some teachers, still a minority apparently, do stress modes of inquiry, problem solving, and theoretical posture rather than internalization of events, names, rules, and institutional functions.[16] Quite clearly our work has not tapped the problem solving and processing side of political socialization.

Within the realms we have explored, however, it is obvious that the fears of those investing teachers with too much influence are unwarranted. Much as the investigation of course exposure revealed, the analysis of teacher exposure shows relatively few consequences flowing

[16]Our own data are quite suggestive on this point. When asked to describe the general goals of the social studies curriculum in their schools only one in five of the teachers mentioned goals which could, using generous definitions, be allocated into the critical thinking and value analysis modes. See Lee H. Ehman, "Normative Discourse and Attitude Change in the Social Studies Classroom," *High School Journal*, 54 (November 1970), pp. 76–83.

from the social studies classroom. By the time they are in their latter years of high school, students appear to be remarkably resilient to what must be termed conventional modes of teaching and teacher behavior. Traumatic events and longer term forces within the school and outside the school may shake the students, but the social studies classroom remains an unlikely source of such events and forces.

CHAPTER NINE

The Political Texture of
Peer Groups

CO-AUTHOR: SUZANNE KOPRINCE SEBERT*

IN THE PREVIOUS two chapters we dealt with the more formal, pedagogical side of the educational system. But schools are not just settings for academic learning. Rather, schools are dynamic social systems which involve, among other things, frequent peer group transactions and extracurricular activities. In this chapter we take up this other side of school life in an attempt to see how it conditions the political character of late adolescents.

Adolescence is a time of trial and experimentation, a time during which, to use Erickson's overworked term, the search for "identity" quickens.[1] It is also a time when the child is increasingly drawn away from the family hearth. If for no other reason than by creating physical propinquity, the school serves as a prime setting for the unfolding of these adolescent tendencies. The adolescent's organizational life exists primarily within the school, most friendship ties are made and broken with school acquaintances, particular fields of competence and excellence are usually exhibited under school sponsorship, and vocational and heterosexual interests flower within the context of the school.

As generations of parents, social observers, and adolescents themselves have been aware, the focal point of adolescent social life consists of networks of friends. Sometimes these are tightly closed nets and remain relatively stable throughout the high school years. Other times they are more permeable and the composition undergoes frequent change. But to have friends, to be in a group, to belong, to not be rejected are hallmarks of the adolescent period. Erickson postulates that the friend or peer group is especially crucial at this age because it serves as a mechanism for the resolution of identity crises. Reinforcement and feedback are provided, rules may be tried on an experimental basis, and independence of parental identification is fostered through the medium of peer relations.[2]

---

*Citations of this chapter should list the authors in this order: Suzanne Koprince Sebert, M. Kent Jennings, and Richard G. Niemi.

[1]Erik H. Erickson, *Identity: Youth and Crisis* (New York: Norton, 1968).

[2]*Ibid.*, Chapter 3. For one of the rare empirical applications of Ericksonian concepts to the political sphere see Jon Pammett, "Personal Identity and Political Activity: The Action-Trudeau Campaign of 1968." (unpublished Ph.D. thesis, University of Michigan, 1971).

The peer group is particularly important for children in modern societies, where most nuclear families are small and live physically apart from other relatives. Children in such situations grow up having primarily nonfamilial friends who do not necessarily share common values and loyalties with them as would siblings and cousins. The importance of peer relations is emphasized at adolescence when the individual is of an age to begin abandoning dependence on the family of origin, but discouraged by the cultural patterns of modern societies from marrying and assuming adult roles. In these transitional years the peer culture provides a supplementary point of reference for the individual who is seeking self-definition and a set of independent values.

Although there is some evidence about the importance of friends in the development of the political self at the collegiate level, we know virtually nothing about whether and how friends help shape the political self at the secondary school level.[3] In this chapter we turn to a direct examination of students and their small circles of close friends. Our approach will be essentially that which usually characterized our assessment of parent and teacher impact, viz., utilizing the degree of concordance between students and their friends as a basis for inferring observational learning. At the same time, we will employ procedures to test the adequacy of the inference.[4]

A question frequently asked about adolescents and their peers is whether parents or friends have the greater influence on the individual during these years. The conclusion most often reached is that adolescents perceive parents and friends as competent guides in different areas of judgment. The main source of differential influence depends upon the type of issue being considered.[5] When a decision involves status in the

[3]The most comprehensive summary at the collegiate level is found in Kenneth Feldman and Theodore Newcomb, *The Impact of College on Students* (San Francisco: Jossey-Bass, 1969), Vol. I and II, especially pp. 243–48. Two of the few explicit attempts at the secondary level are Kenneth P. Langton, "Peer Group and School and the Political Socialization Process," *American Political Science Review*, 61 (September 1967), pp. 751–58; and David Ziblatt, "High School Extracurricular Activities and Political Socialization," *The Annals*, 361 (September 1965), pp. 21–31.

[4]In light of the frequent claims made for the beneficial effects of extracurricular activities on students' social and political attitudes, we also analyzed the relationship between various forms of in-school and out-of-school participation and the student's attitudes. The analysis was too lengthy to be included here. Suffice it to say that almost nothing was found that would indicate the kinds of effects claimed. Although we studied participation in student government, in athletics, in music and debate programs, in various kinds of clubs, and even students' subjective feelings of belonging to "leading crowds," group involvement accounted for little variation in the socio-political views of students. Indeed, participation was not even allied to "nonpolitical" indicators such as personal efficacy and personal trust. It would seem as if the potential contribution of such participation is redundant in much the same way that civics classes are. That is, few values, skills, and behaviors are derived from participating in school groups that are not picked up elsewhere.

[5]See, e.g., Clay V. Brittain, "Adolescent Choices and Parent-Peer Cross-Pressures," *American Sociological Review*, 28 (June 1963), pp. 385–90; Matilda W. Riley, John W.

peer society, peer influence predominates. When the decision can be perceived as involving status in the larger adult society to which the teenager ultimately aspires, parents are the main source of guidance. Disconcertingly, the evidence for this conclusion comes primarily from inquiries asking adolescents upon whom they would or do rely. Direct comparisons between the values of friends and parents as they bear on the individual are rare. Fortunately we are in a position to provide such direct comparisons, and in the final section of this chapter we take up in detail the relative and combined impact of parents and friends on the political orientations of twelfth graders.

UTILIZING SOCIOMETRY

For the present analysis, a subset of thirteen schools was utilized out of the original group of ninety-seven.[6] The selected schools are in ten states in the eastern half of the United States, four in the South and six in the Northeast and Midwest. One school is Catholic, the others are public. Two of the schools are largely black; one of these is a rural Southern school, the other is an urban school. Three of the schools are located in counties of less than 10,000 people; four in counties between 10,000 and 50,000; one in a county between 50,000 and 100,000; four in counties over 100,000; and one in a city of two million.

The sizes of the senior classes of the schools range from 30 to 495. Compared with the full sample of schools, this subset is somewhat biased in favor of smaller schools. A total of 2,080 seniors were included in this phase of the study. No claim is made that these seniors statistically represent those in the United States as a whole. The schools themselves, however, do represent a range of the kinds of high schools which are found across the country.[7]

All of the seniors who were present on the day that their school was visited spent about thirty minutes filling out a questionnaire which closely paralleled the student interview schedule except for necessary changes due to the written format. At the end of the questionnaire, the students were asked to write on a tear-off sheet at the back their own names and

---

Riley, Jr., and Mary E. Moore, "Adolescent Values and the Reisman Typology," in Seymour Lipset and Leo Lowenthal (eds.), *Culture and Social Character* (New York: Free Press, 1961; H. H. Remmers and D. H. Radler, *The American Teenager* (New York: Bobbs-Merrill, 1962); and Denise B. Kandel and Gerald S. Lesser, *Youth in Two Worlds* (San Francisco: Jossey-Bass, 1972), Chapters 9-10.

[6]For a full description of the methodology, data transformation and management, and detailed results of the sociometric data, see Suzanne Koprince Sebert, "The Influence of Friends on the Political Attitudes of High School Seniors." (unpublished Ph.D. thesis, University of Michigan, 1974).

[7]Financial and human limitations prevented our utilizing the other schools. Since the questionnaires from these 13 schools were received from the field first, they were the ones for which the sociometric data were processed.

the names of those five[8] members of the senior class of their own sex[9] with whom they "went around most often."

Having all of the seniors provide questionnaires which included the names of their best friends offered the opportunity to reconstruct the friendship patterns of the class members and to trace political attitudes among the friendship groups. At various points we refer to this part of the research as a "sociometric study." In fact, only in part is this nomenclature accurate. For while the methods by which the data were collected resemble those of a traditional sociometric study in most respects,[10] the uses to which the data were later put and the procedures for the analysis are unique. In contrast to classic sociometric research, with its emphasis on the nature of friendship patterns per se, our primary concern is with the impact of friends on the individual's social and political values.

For each senior an individual set of sociometric relationships was constructed with the senior at the center and friends as the other members. Three slightly different friendship groups were defined for each student. The first consisted simply of those fellow students the senior had named as friends. The second looked at the collective group of students who had named the senior as a friend of theirs. The third group defined for each student consisted of those individuals who had chosen and had been chosen by the student as a friend—the traditional sociometric measure of a reciprocated friendship—in an attempt to locate close, mutually perceived friendships.[11] As discussed in more detail below, the friendship

[8]Although five names were specifically asked for in this question, the mean number received was somewhat less (4.02). Other studies which have simply asked for a list of friends with no limits specified usually yield an average of from three to five volunteered choices.

[9]The decision to limit the students to friends of their own sex was based on the assumption that among high school students same-sex friendships are still the most stable and influential. Some literature challenges this assumption. See, e.g., Calvin W. Gordon, *The Social System of the High School* (Glencoe: Free Press, 1957).

[10]Those who have worked extensively in the field propose six requirements as criteria for good sociometric measurement:

    (1) The limits of the group should be known to the subjects.
    (2) The subjects should be permitted an unlimited number of choices or rejections.
    (3) The subjects should be asked to indicate the individuals they choose or reject in terms of specific criteria.
    (4) Results of the sociometric questions should be used to restructure the group.
    (5) The subjects should be permitted to make their choices and rejections privately.
    (6) The questions should be gauged to the level of understanding of the members of the group.

Although criteria two and four are not strictly fulfilled in the present study, the basic procedure used here falls within accepted practices. From Gardner Lindzey and Donn Byrne, "Measurement of Social Choice and Interpersonal Attractiveness," in Gardner Lindzey and Elliot Aronson (eds.), *Handbook of Social Psychology*, 2nd ed. (Reading: Addison-Wesley, 1969), Vol. 2, p. 455.

[11]The literature reveals that the word "peer" is employed with a wide variety of meanings, from an age cohort, to members of a socio-economic class, to those individuals in face-to-face interaction, to acquaintances, to friends. In this chapter the word "friend" will ordinarily be used to designate an individual in one of the personal friendship groups. "Peer" will ordinarily be used to mean any larger set of age cohorts.

group treated in our presentation will ordinarily be that of the first definition, that is, those friends named by the student.

Comparisons between students and their friends are based on responses to common items in the self-administered questionnaire. The range of political orientations is restricted by the brief nature of the questionnaire and by our desire to deal primarily with attitudes and value preferences rather than behaviors. Two measures, political trust and political efficacy, are integer-scored indexes built from responses to several questions. Three others—party identification, the hypothetical 1964 presidential vote, and opinion on the eighteen-year-old vote issue—are responses to a single question.[12] In much of the analysis we make interval level assumptions about these measures. Thus the friends' values or scores are represented by the mean scores achieved by the friends on each measure.

Of keen interest to us was the subset of 231 students in the thirteen schools whose parents had been interviewed. The availability of the parent data provided a rare opportunity to make direct tests of the "influence" of parents versus friends. For this analysis we constructed student-friend-parent triads in much the same fashion that we developed student-mother-father and student-teacher-parent triads. The friends' values are again represented by the mean scores of those persons designated by the students as friends. Parent values are taken from the parent interviews, and the student's own values from the self-administered questionnaire data.

AGREEMENT BETWEEN ADOLESCENTS AND THEIR FRIENDS

Before introducing the results of matching student and (mean) friend values, an important methodological problem should be entertained. As with all forms of comparing two or more individuals on the same dimensions, one cannot be sure that positive relationships between students and their friends demonstrate that the friends are actually helping shape the students' own value constellations. Both students and friends may be responding to other, common forces affecting all of them in similar fashion. Indeed, since there is some degree of assortative friend making on the basis of important socio-economic variables, it might well be argued that this is likely. To be sure, the same argument can be made in principle about the student-parent and student-teacher pairs—that any similarity between the partners is more a function of common causal agents pushing both partners to similar stances.

---

[12]The five questions used in developing the political trust measure are reported in Chapter 5, note 14; the three for efficacy include the two in Chapter 5, p. 125, plus the second item in note 6 of that chapter (slightly modified for students); and the party identification question is as reported in Chapter 2, note 9, except that the two probes were not employed.

Yet there is a fundamental difference. The hierarchical properties, the legitimized socialization functions, and—in the case of families—the heavy filial component all make the place of families and teachers quite different than that of friends. The latter are still primarily socializees, at least to a much greater extent than parents and teachers. Thus, whereas there is almost certainly a flow of political learning between parents and teachers on the one hand and the growing child on the other, there may be little flow at all amongst friendship groups, with similarity among friends simply reflecting the influence of home, school, and the instruments of the larger culture.

Because of these considerations, we must be even more careful than usual in imputing socialization forces in the case of friendship groups. As a guard against overinterpreting such results we have introduced into the analysis some of those elements which might be causing spuriously high levels of agreement. For example, when we suspected that social class differences account for the observed political similarity between students and their friends, then we built social class considerations into the analysis.

Another important confounding possibility is that friendship groups are established along explicitly political lines. This seems most unlikely in the American context of secondary schools. And in our study, political criteria were almost never offered as a prerequisite for being in the student's general circle of friends. Since 1965 the salience of political likeness may well have increased, but just how much is not known. Even if political values do constitute a criteria for friendship, this in no way diminishes the role of the friendship group in the political socialization process. The reinforcement and elaboration of the values which originally brought the friends together would be expected to prosper accordingly, and the

TABLE 9.1

AGREEMENT ON POLITICAL VALUES BETWEEN STUDENTS AND THEIR FRIENDS, USING THREE DEFINITIONS OF FRIENDSHIP GROUPS

(Zero-order product moment correlations)

Political Values	Student-Friends Named	Student-Friends Naming	Student and Friends Naming Each Other
1964 presidential vote preference	.34	.24	.32
Political efficacy	.32	.31	.32
18-year-old vote	.30	.28	.25
Political trust	.29	.24	.20
Party identification	.25	.18	.24

evolution of yet more or different additional group-inspired political perspectives would likewise be expected.

Turning now to the data, we first present the simple correlations between students and their friends, using the three different definitions of friendship pairs (Table 9.1). Disregarding for the moment the distinctions among the three, can we make some evaluation of the absolute magnitudes of the correlations? Clearly, they are all positive and all are above a level of triviality. They are not as high as the associations on some other student characteristics, e.g., grade average (.58), extracurricular participation (.49), and father's education (.45). But the latter are relatively "hard," salient indications of social attributes, and are usually key correlates of friendship cliques. These criteria are not totally fulfilled with the political values being used here. If we take into account these shortcomings as well as measurement error, the correlations may be said to reflect at least moderate political similarity between twelfth graders and their friends —however defined.

Despite the overall set of positive relationships, there are some differences according to which definition of friendship is employed. A typical finding in sociometric inquiries is that reciprocated pairs usually resemble each other more than do pairs based on nonreciprocated choices. That typicality does not apply in the instant case. Nowhere is the agreement between reciprocating pairs higher than that for "friends named" or "friends naming" pairs. Only for the political efficacy measure is the reciprocated pair value as high as for either of the other two.

The most probable explanation of this departure from the usual sociometric pattern is that political traits are not a frequent, overarching basis for *intimate* friendships. This is not to say that common political traits do not help adolescents get along with each other or that one's friends may not affect one's political character development. Rather, it is that the criteria for intimacy—defined here in terms of reciprocated selection—will not ordinarily include political qualities. Thus little or no increment is achieved in student-friend congruency by considering only those persons choosing each other.

Further inspection of Table 9.1 shows that the highest levels of agreement occur when the students are matched with those they designate as their best friends (col. 1). This is perhaps not surprising, especially when laid against the results obtained when the pairs are defined by those naming the student (col. 2). To the extent that political traits are embedded in friendship groups it seems probable that the persons named by adolescents would be more like them than would people naming the adolescents. In the first instance the students have control over the selections and presumably apply fairly uniform criteria. In the second instance the persons being named have no direct control over who picks them. As a result, the composition of their "friends" may well have much more heterogeneity than when students name their own friends. Some corroborating evidence along these lines comes from considering social background similarities. Although the differences are not large, students do name people more like them socially than are the people who name the students.

Our subsequent analysis utilizes the friends named as the basic friendship pair. This decision flows from three considerations. First, it is the traditional approach, being well-grounded in theory, technique, and application. Second, it is intuitively appealing because it represents the adolescent's *own* subjective definition of the friendship group. It seems likely that these "subjective" friends are the ones most prized and those with whom interaction most often occurs. Thus we are using the potentially most relevant friends, as seen through the eyes of the individual student. Third, the number of friends named is relatively constant across respondents, most of them having named four or five friends. By way of contrast, the number of times a person was named varied from zero to fourteen, and the range of reciprocal choices went from its minimum of zero to its maximum of five. Not only do we preserve more cases for analysis by employing the "friends named" criterion but we also standardize the size of the close friends circle for each person.

Although the agreement between twelfth graders and their friends is only modest in degree, even that level could be reflecting other factors bringing about political similarity. These might include such things as social status, academic standing, student leadership, or even popularity. If such factors are related to holding divergent political views while at the same time helping to bring students together as friends, then any similarity between the friends could be a function of the factors shared in common rather than anything having to do with the friendship itself. In short, the correlations may be spurious.

To test this possibility, Table 9.2 represents the correlations according to four prominent social characteristics, all of which are linked statistically to two or more of the political values. While some of the patterns embedded within the table are intriguing in their own right, the most significant aspect of the results is the relative persistence of the total sample patterns across the various subgroups. All of the correlations remain positive and usually at a level in the neighborhood of the original, uncontrolled relationships.

These results do not "prove" that students are being affected in a political way by their friends, but they do discredit the argument that the agreement levels are simply artifacts of other properties of the friendship group. If the latter were true across the board, the correlations should diminish severely within each control category. This state is definitely not

TABLE 9.2
STUDENT-FRIEND CONCORDANCE, CONTROLLING BY
FOUR SOCIAL CHARACTERISTICS

	1964 Presidential Vote	Political Efficacy	18-Year Old Vote	Political Trust	Party Identification
Total sample	.34	.32	.30	.29	.25
Father's education					
Elementary	.35	.35	.36	.20	.23
High school	.26	.16	.21	.38	.12
College	.34	.13	.20	.40	.46
Grade average					
B− or lower	.41	.31	.14	.26	.22
B or higher	.28	.32	.42	.34	.32
Officer or comm. chrm. in school					
0	.45	.09	.15	.14	.22
1	.26	.58	.40	.41	.28
2+	.27	.34	.38	.33	.28
Times named as friend by others					
0–4	.31	.33	.21	.28	.36
5+	.40	.29	.40	.31	.11

reached. Alternatively, if friendship groups are more important within certain strata than others, then the correlations should be consistently higher in those strata. There are, in fact, hints of such patterns as, e.g., the higher correlations for B or higher students versus those for B− or lower students in four out of five possibilities. But even these variations are not of the magnitude to suggest that only in certain social categories do the bonds of friendship have political overtones.

On balance we must reject the explanation that hidden, third causes operate to bring about student-friend political similarity. It would seem, rather, that 1) friendships are made with some (probably implicit) political similarities involved in the attraction; or that 2) after friendships are formed, the political values of the parties are brought into modest alignment; or that 3) some combination of these two processes is operative. Experimental evidence indicates that pre-existing similarities in values are more crucial in establishing social choices than are the choices in establishing or changing the values.[13] Unfortunately, none of the experimental evidence deals with adolescents and politics. Even if causal flow is in the direction indicated by the experimental evidence, there is every

[13]See Lindzey and Byrne, "Measurement of Social Choice and Interpersonal Attractiveness," pp. 506–07.

reason to believe that the pre-existing value similarity is enhanced and reinforced by close social contacts.

As just noted, there is no consistent trend whereby one subgroup of friendship pairs is much more alike than another subgroup. There is one major, important exception to that generalization, however. Female pairs are visibly more politically alike than are male pairs, as Figure 9.1 conclusively demonstrates. This ties in with the oft-reported greater affiliative needs and interpersonal foci of female adolescents, their development of intense dyadic relationships, and their lower emphasis on autonomy. The picture is also of a piece with findings from our own analysis that girls agree more with their best friends than do boys about future educational plans.

Just as significantly, these differences by sex form a nice addition to a recurrent theme of this volume. Females seem to be more sensitive, in general, to the values of people immediately surrounding them. We saw that girls tended to be more like their parents, especially when their parents were like-minded. Girls also gravitate more toward their mothers than boys toward their fathers (or mothers) when the parents are in political disagreement. Elsewhere we show that wives are more susceptible to the partisan influence of their husbands than vice versa.[14] Here we see that girls are much more like their same-sex friends than are boys; inferentially they are more affected by them.

Again this would not appear to be an artifact of third causes. For example, boys are actually more like their friends when it comes to grade average and participation in extracurricular activities; and boys and girls equally resemble their friends in terms of family social class. Higher female concordance is not, therefore, a function of greater background similarity. Rather, the psycho-cultural conditioning of girls seems to lead to a greater stress on harmony and like-mindedness with one's intimates. While boys are, if anything, more loyal to a group or gang in general, girls use close friendships more for mutual self-explorations and intimate exchanges. Admittedly, it is not clear whether girls (compared with boys) more often consciously select more congruent pairings or whether the greater harmony comes after the pairings. But as we argued above, the friendship ties—especially for females—would help sustain pre-existing congruences.

Another way of viewing these sex-related differences is to say that at any given time a male adolescent is surrounded by more political dissimilarity than is the female. He exists in a field of forces containing more disparate signals. Thus the political rites of passage may well be more difficult for him than for a girl, surrounded as she is by more sympathetic

---

[14]Paul A. Beck and M. Kent Jennings, "Parents as 'Middlepersons' in Political Socialization," *Journal of Politics* (forthcoming).

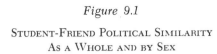

Figure 9.1

STUDENT-FRIEND POLITICAL SIMILARITY
AS A WHOLE AND BY SEX

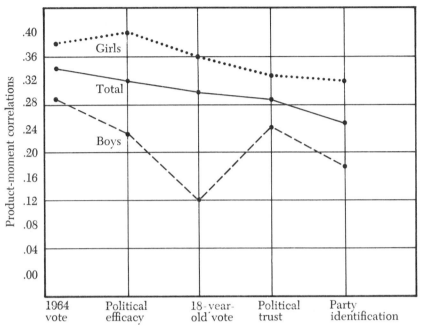

elements. Adding to the difficulty for boys are the special political obligations attached to being male, such as serving in the military. With the
recent surge of the women's liberation movement, however, the rites of
passage may well become more difficult for young females. For many of
them there will be conflict between rather long-standing cultural norms
on the one hand, and the pressures of liberationists on the other. If our
data serve as a reliable quide, it will be the immediate circle of friends
and families which will guide the resolution of these conflicts.

STUDENTS, FRIENDS, AND PARENTS

Having sketched in the nature of student-friend parallelism on matters
political, we now move to the intriguing question of how parents fit into
the scene. Two conflicting models are available here. On the one hand, it
is argued that as adolescents become immersed in the peer group they
come increasingly under its sway. If the values characterizing the friendship group are at odds with those of the parents, it follows that adolescents will resemble their friends more than their parents. Notice that this
hypothesis does not require a gap between the generations. Instead, it

merely requires differences between the adolescents' circle of friends and their parents. Naturally, the likelihood of intense peer pressure is greater when there are dramatic, cohort-wide differences between the adolescent and adult subcultures. Peers versus parents in a deadly struggle for the soul of the adolescent is, of course, a caricature. Even the most vigorous proponents of the subculture thesis grant that certain areas of life are much more subject to the press of the friendship group's values than are others.

The counter-model stresses the unique place of the family in the inculcation of political values, accompanied by the relatively low salience of politics in the everyday lives of most adolescents. To the extent that the students' political values mirror those of surrounding agents it is argued that these agents will be the parents—due in large part to bonds of affection, loyalty, and protracted exposure. Furthermore, it has never been demonstrated that politics looms large in pre-adolescent and adolescent friendship networks. Again, the portrait of the family as all-important is a caricature, as our data have amply demonstrated.

The materials at hand offer at least a start in resolving the contrasting expectations. It will be recalled that interviews were held with the parents of from 15-20 students in each of the schools. Those interviews from the subset of 13 schools included in the sociometric analysis were integrated with the other materials.[15] Our first step will be to match the student-friend against student-parent pairs in those schools. Then, by merging the two sets of pairs, we can analyze the combinations resulting in student-friend-parent triples.

Comparing the two sets of pairs yields support for both predictions, that posing more agreement with friends versus that posing greater agreement with parents (Figure 9.2).[16] Especially in the domain of party identification and to a lesser extent in presidential preference the similarity between students and their parents is impressively higher than that between students and friends. We see once more the strong pull of the parental partisan tradition on offspring, a pull which is seemingly unique. Had we restricted our inquiry to partisan orientations we would have concluded that parents are much more influential than friends.

Once the area of partisanship is vacated the position of parents and friends alters appreciably. There is essentially no difference in the two correlations with respect to trust in the national political system. And

[15]When both parents were interviewed, each parent was given half weight in the analysis, in the same fashion as outlined in Chapter 1.

[16]The exact correlations for student-friend pairs presented in Figures 9.2 and 9.3 will depart slightly from those given earlier because only those pairs which have a parent attached to them are used for calculations in Figures 9.2 and 9.3. Given the nearly identical correlations between the total set of student-friend pairs and this subset, it appears that the subset represents rather well the total set of student-friend pairs.

progressing to political efficacy and the eighteen-year-old vote issue the advantage now shifts, with students being more like their friends than their elders. Any generalizations about the presumed impact of the friendship group must take into account specific types of political values.

How might we distinguish the arena of partisanship from that of the other values under review? The unique aspects of partisanship have been cited frequently. Salience, concreteness, reinforcement, and application are hallmarks of partisan orientations on the American scene. One of the first things children learn about the political nature of their parents is the partisan leaning and candidate preferences. Nor is partisanship something with which the educational system is likely to tamper in any severe way; similarly, other primary groups seldom try to drive a wedge between the partisan connections of children and their progenitors. Like religion, partisanship has an aura of sacredness.

Figure 9.2

CONCORDANCE ON POLITICAL VALUES BETWEEN
STUDENTS AND FRIENDS AND STUDENTS AND PARENTS

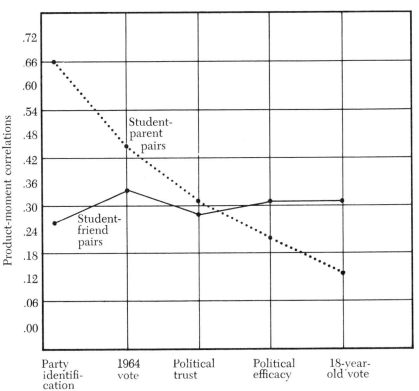

Not so with the other three orientations. They are more amorphous, less salient as political topics, less easily identified, ostensibly less stable, and their applications not so easily detected. Furthermore, they do not have the sacrosanct and private quality of partisan values. Given these marked differences the developing child is more susceptible to the influence of models, including friends. Political efficacy and the suffrage issue illustrate this contrast most aptly. Efficacy develops in part as a function of interacting with others; as the child matures these interactions are increasingly with others and the need for approval and like-mindedness accelerates.

The suffrage issue requires, in part, a different explanation. Here we have an age-specific issue. Even though it was argued in Chapter 3 that the issue was not a dramatic one for adolescents in 1965, it seems fair to assume that its age-specific application made it more vulnerable to peer effects than would many other issues. This is one issue where a group interest might be defined for adolescents, regardless of whether they and their friends were pro or con the issue. In this connection it is instructive that the frequency of political discussions with friends is directly related to issue-agreement with friends. The relevant product-moment correlations are .24, .29, and .37 as conversation frequency rises from almost never up to several times a month. There is no denying that the presumed influence of friends may have been indirect as well as direct. As a result of more political conversations the students and their friends may have converged simply because they were learning more about each other—hence adolescents in general—without the issue of a lower voting age ever having come up. Regardless of the mechanism, however, friends apparently have more impact than parents.

The suffrage issue, with its age-specific wrinkle, comes as close to any measure we have in approaching a topic which might be peculiar to the adolescent subculture. Matters of taste in clothing, entertainment, food, and life style in general are notorious for their teenage idiosyncracies and innovations. Certainly we would expect to find relatively greater pressures from friends in those areas, transient though some of them might be. While the voting age issue did not evoke an adolescent-adult split at the macro level, it is the one topic under study which touched the students directly. Just as friends would be more instrumental in matters of adolescent styles and fashion, so too they might well be in adolescent-specific politics. Recent movements in the politicization of high school youth offer at least superficial evidence in support of this reasoning. When the political issues involve local school issues or national issues of direct youth concern—such as the draft or the Vietnam war—the prominence of friendship groups as reference groups seems to rise.

Examining the student-friend and student-parent dyads separately does not answer the question about the independent and combined effects of friends and parents. To accomplish this we must utilize the triadic combinations. The independent effects of friends can be determined with partial correlations, holding constant the contribution of parents; the effects of parents are determined in like manner, holding constant the contribution of friends. Multiple correlations permit estimates of the total contribution to student values derived from the effects of friends plus parents.

Figure 9.3 presents the relevant simple (zero-order), first-order partial, and multiple correlations. Each partial correlation is lower than its

Figure 9.3

THE IMPACT OF PARENTS AND FRIENDS
ON STUDENT POLITICAL VALUES[a]

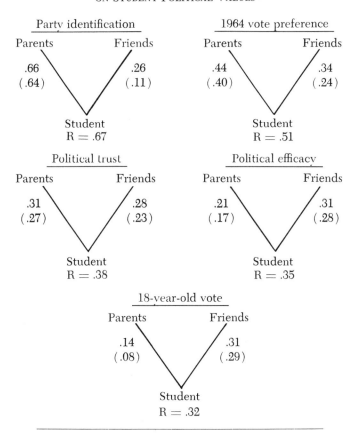

[a] Entries without parentheses are zero-order product-moment correlations; those enclosed in parentheses are first-order partials controlling for the values of friends in the case of parent-student correlations and of parents in the case of friends-student correlations.

companion simple correlation, indicating at least some degree of artificiality in each zero-order relationship. What is much more impressive, however, is the staying power of each simple correlation, especially when it was relatively strong at the outset. Illustratively, in the two partisan measures the originally strong position of the family is only marginally affected by introducing the partisan orientations of the friends. Similarly, the relatively strong position of friends with respect to political efficacy and the suffrage issue is but barely reduced when the parents' views are brought into play. Finally, on political trust the original relationship for each dyad was about the same and of modest strength; the partial correlations remain nearly as high for each dyad.

Comparing the multiple correlations (R) with either the simple or partial correlations reveals the additional explanatory power achieved by considering both parents and friends. If only parents had been included in the analysis the R for party identification would have been but little affected, but all four of the other R's would have been noticeably lower. Similarly, using only the friends would have scarcely touched the R on the eighteen-year-old vote question and to only a small degree that on political efficacy. The remaining R's would have been dramatically lower.

Taken together, the partial and multiple correlations tend to sustain the original juxtapositioning of family and friends. The areas in which parents emerged as strongest in the bivariate analysis continue to do so. Those characterized by stronger friend "influence" also continue unabated. These findings strengthen our earlier rendering. Both parents and friends ostensibly contribute to the adolescents' political value structure, but the strength of that contribution varies enormously by areas. And in no instance does the impact of the friendship group approximate that which the family achieves in the domain of partisanship.

At this point we digress for a moment to introduce yet a third potential source of influence on the adolescent. Each school may be said to have a climate of opinion with respect to the various political values being dealt with here. This climate would be represented by the total configuration of student preferences or opinions, not just those of one's friends. It has been argued—and some evidence is supportive—that it is the value climate or context which exerts the key influence on the individual. On the other hand, sophisticated work in the area of educational and occupational aspirations points toward the friendship group rather than the overall climate as being the more determinative.

We can make a brief test of the contrasting hypotheses. The value climate may be estimated by taking the responses of all members of the senior classes who filled out the self-administered questionnaire. These responses can then be scored to produce mean scores for each senior class. These scores then become a third independent variable, taking their place alongside those of the student's friends and parents. Employing correlational techniques we can then see if the overall value climate contributes to the student's scores on the political measurements. Regardless of whether we consider the simple, partial, or multiple correlations the contribution of the overall climate is miniscule. We are not appreciably better off for knowing the value climate.

While a more intensive analysis would be necessary to establish firmly the point, our present judgment is that the influence of the peer culture comes almost exclusively via close friendship ties. What is important for adolescents is to have at least a few like-minded peers whom they can trust and who accept them. True, the overall climate structure may facilitate or undercut the impact of the friendship group, depending upon their joint similarity. Nevertheless, when we speak of how the adolescents' political values are shaped and reinforced by peers, it is the immediate circle of friends which is doing the shaping and reinforcing.

Returning now to the basic set of student-friend-parent triples we can gain yet more insight into the way in which adolescents come to gravitate toward and away from each of these socializations agents. In treating the student-mother-father and student-teacher-parent triples we found that students were more likely to converge toward a given agent (or model) when that agent looked like another agent in the students' fields of contacts. That is, the more homogeneous the models in the adolescent's environment, the more likely will they resemble any given model. On the other hand, the more any given agent was dissimilar to other agents the less likely were the students to resemble that agent. What is more, we were able to see toward which agent the students inclined when these agents were in conflict.

Utilizing the student-friend-parent triads we can ascertain if these principles of homogeneity and heterogeneity of models apply here also. Percentage comparisons will be used in the presentation, but the same conclusions would emerge using correlational techniques. First, let us see how homogeneity operates. Table 9.3 gives, in the first two rows, the overall agreement between students and friends and students and parents, respectively. Row three contains the percentage agreement for that subset of students whose parents and friends agreed with each other (i.e., are homogeneous). Visual inspection leaves no doubt that homogeneity induces higher concordance with both friends and parents. Obviously the gain varies a good bit, from a low of four percent to a high of 24 percent. Nevertheless, the overall image is impressive, showing as it does the strong marginal effects of model homogeneity.

So far the results accord with previous findings for other sets of triples. Consistency among socializers yields more predictable outcomes among socializees. Does the same apply in reverse when the socializers are

TABLE 9.3

AGREEMENT BETWEEN STUDENTS AND THEIR FRIENDS AND PARENTS—OVERALL
AND UNDER CONDITIONS OF HOMOGENEITY AND HETEROGENEITY

	Party Identification	1964 Presidential Vote	Political Trust	Political Efficacy	18-Year-Old Vote
Overall agreement with					
Friends	52%	78%	62%	72%	66%
Parents	72	83	66	57	55
	(240)	(230)	(237)	(239)	(238)
Agreement when friends and parents are homogeneous	76	93	72	77	69
	(151)	(164)	(178)	(126)	(142)
When friends and parents are heterogeneous, agreement with					
Friends	12[a]	42	46	65	62
Parents	64	58	54	35	38
	(89)	(66)	(109)	(113)	(96)

[a]This pair of figures will, unlike the others in these two rows, equal less than 100 percent. This is because party identification was not treated as a dichotomous variable, whereas the others were.

inconsistent? Rows four and five in Table 9.3 supply an affirmative answer. Now the triads are restricted to the subset where friends and parents disagree with each other, thus forming a heterogeneous field for the twelfth graders. By matching these percentages against either the corresponding overall or homogeneous figures it is possible to observe the deleterious effects of heterogeneity. Percentages are well below the overall and homogeneous ones—particularly the latter, of course, where the range is from seven percent to 64 percent.

Inferentially, these attritions in percentage agreement mean that the influence of both parents and intimates is lessened under conditions of inconsistent models. We say inferentially because, to reiterate, there is no foolproof fashion in which true influence processes can be demonstrated with these sorts of data. The circumstantial evidence, though, is more than encouraging. Why should there be such a gross disparity between the agreement levels with agents in a state of homogeneity versus those in a state of heterogeneity unless these agents are indeed exerting an impact? It is, to be sure, quite probable that some portion of this impact is spurious. Take, for example, the huge difference in agreement regarding the 1964 presidential candidates. When friends and parents are inconsonant, only 58 percent of the students agree with their parents; when friends and parents are congruent, 93 percent agree. Now is the lower concordance with parents in the first condition due directly to the friends or to experiences shared in common by students and their friends? Common experiences would perhaps include media coverage, class-related school work, and various short-term forces.

It is certainly likely that many adolescents and their close companions would be exposed to common stimuli pushing them in a direction opposed to that of their parents. Yet this argument runs afoul of the fact that many of the parents would also be exposed to many of these same stimuli themselves; and as we know the short-term forces of the 1964 election did result in a net shift toward Lyndon Johnson. A second and more fundamental theoretical point is that these external, common forces are to some degree perceived, absorbed, mediated, and processed within the context of the friendship network. This may occur in very subtle, latent ways, or in much more obvious and manifest ways. To imagine that the friendship group plays a completely passive, neutral role, as reference group or locus of interaction, is to ignore the centrality of the adolescent's primary groups. It seems unlikely, therefore, that the debilitating effect of friends' preferences on student-parent concordance can be attributed solely to external experiences common to all partners in the friendship group.

Aside from demonstrating the general consequences of inconsistent agents, the set of heterogeneous friends and parents also provides the raw materials for assessing the relative impact of friends versus parents. A strong hint of what is to come lies in the partial correlations (above, Figure 9.3). But the percentage approach of Table 9.3 has the virtue of working with the variables in a dichotomous fashion (except for party identification), so that students are faced with conflict between parents and friends.

Not surprisingly, we continue to see the pattern of differentiation by type of value. Parents are the clear "winners" in the partisan areas of party preference and presidential choice, reaffirming once more the preeminent place of the family in partisan affairs. On the other hand, friends are the easy "victors" with respect to political efficacy and the eighteen-year-old vote question. The closest division lies in political trust, with parents having a slight edge. If, as we have argued, the sharpest test of agent influence comes in the "cross-pressured" setting, then it is patent that the influence of friends versus parents will vary with the type of orientation. Assuming that five orientations used here are symptomatic, the variance across orientations may be dramatic.

In sum, the friendship group plays a consequential role in the development of youthful political orientations. Students and their friends are more alike than unalike in political terms. Indeed, students resemble their friends more than their parents in some (nonpartisan) domains. While it is difficult to determine whether this compatibility emerges before or after the friendship, it is clear that the compatibility is not artificially produced by social background similarities. Lending support to the idea of an independent contribution by friends is the fact that when friends and parents agree, the students' concordance with their parents is enhanced; when friends and parents disagree, the students' concordance with their parents is depressed. Thus the late adolescent, in a matrix of family and friends, responds to the influence of each. Of great significance is the fact that the configuration of the matrix—homogeneous versus heterogenous—has predictable consequences. In this respect the patterns uncovered here match those for other matrices in which the students are involved.

The three chapters in this part of the book have demonstrated the variable impact of school-related factors on the political character of late adolescents. The mediating effects of these factors are especially intriguing. As with the chapters dealing specifically with the family, we usually took a rather static approach to our materials while recognizing full well the keen importance of the dynamic side. Indeed, we have made references throughout to the temporal dimensions of political socialization, to the question of change and stability over the life cycle and across generations. It is now time to take a more sustained, comprehensive look at the temporal dimension; that is the task of Part IV.

IV LONGITUDINAL PERSPECTIVES

CHAPTER TEN

Political Development over
the Life Cycle

I N PART II we commented frequently on differences in the aggregate distributions of student and parent orientations. Only by implication, however, did we confront the question of why those differences existed. Here we take up that question directly by focusing on the developmental pattern of political orientations over the life cycle. In particular, we wish to utilize our data as well as other available evidence concerning age and political behavior and attitudes in order to specify the variety of developmental sequences through which political orientations move.

Initial studies of political socialization focused attention on three major aspects of political development.[1] First of all, very little change is said to occur during the four years of high school. Contrary to expectations, the first in the series of University of Chicago studies revealed no major changes during that period with regard to interest in public affairs, political activities, party identification, and a variety of opinions about public officials and the government in general. The kinds of attitudes that were expected to crystallize at about that time were already present among ninth graders, and an active interest in politics had already begun. Similarly, the analysis of civics course effects from our own study (Chapter 7) has been interpreted as showing little change in the high school years.

A complementary aspect of the development of political attitudes is that major changes do occur during the elementary school years. Politically relevant attitudes begin to take shape very early in life, if one judges by the responses of second graders, the youngest age-group tested so far. On some topics stable attitudes are formed quickly, so that aggregate responses change very little after the fifth grade. In other instances learning occurs more slowly, with considerable strides being taken late in the elementary years. In any case, by the time youths enter ninth grade, most of them can respond meaningfully to a variety of political questions, have an intuitive grasp of what is political and nonpolitical, have engaged in some low-level political activity, express preferences for political parties

[1]See especially Fred I. Greenstein, *Children and Politics*, (New Haven: Yale University Press, 1965) and the various reports made by Dennis, Easton, Hess, and Torney of the series of studies begun at the University of Chicago, particularly Robert D. Hess and Judith V. Torney, *The Development of Political Attitudes in Children* (Chicago: Aldine, 1967).

and candidates, and have established what are presumably stable opinions about the nation and political system in which they live.[2]

The third major aspect of political learning is that the attitudes, opinions, and behavior established by the end of elementary school correspond very closely to those of adults. The changes in children's feelings during the elementary school years are away from personalized, highly benevolent images of government toward the more abstract and realistic conceptions held by adults. Detached observation turns into personal involvement at what appear to be adult levels. These conclusions are based on comparisons of youngsters' responses with those given by elementary schoolteachers and by explicit and implicit comparisons with the adult population. The surface similarity of the overall patterns suggests that during the high school years and afterwards only minor changes occur.

Some qualifications to the above conclusions have been generally recognized, of course. On a few specific matters—notably knowledge about the political parties and about governmental forms—it is apparent that much learning occurs during high school or after, although even here the roots are laid late in the elementary school years. Political interest may also vary after the eighth grade, but the evidence here is mixed. It is also regularly noted that some systematic changes do occur during the adult life. However, the extent of, and especially the rate of, these changes are not always clear. Nor has there been any careful delineation of just what things do vary systematically over the life cycle. The most common view seems to be that except for a few matters affecting all age-groups to some degree, such as voting turnout and changes caused by cataclysmic events (e.g., the Depression), changes during adulthood are relatively small and of minor importance.

For the most part, then, the first major socialization studies suggested one characteristic pattern of political learning. This pattern is roughly sketched in Figure 10.1. Political orientations begin early, develop rapidly although with varying speed, and reach stable, nearly adult levels by the end of elementary school.

Recently this extreme view has begun to recede. Easton and Dennis, for example, have suggested that socialization related to allocative, competitive, contentious aspects of politics probably begins in late adolescence, whereas learning of what they call "system" politics begins at a very tender age and is presumably more stable later in life.[3] This distinc-

---

[2]More recent work emphasizes *how* the child begins to define and conceptualize the political world. See especially, R. W. Connell, *The Child's Construction of Politics* (Carlton, Victoria: Melbourne University Press, 1971).

[3]Even "system" views are not unchanging, as the rapid growth of cynicism among college students in the mid 1960s would suggest. Easton and Dennis also note some changes in evaluations of the policeman over the late-teenage and adult life span; David Easton and Jack Dennis, *Children in the Political System* (New York: McGraw-Hill, 1969), Chapters 4 and 14.

Figure 10.1

ASSUMED PATTERN OF DEVELOPMENT OF POLITICAL ATTITUDES AND BEHAVIOR

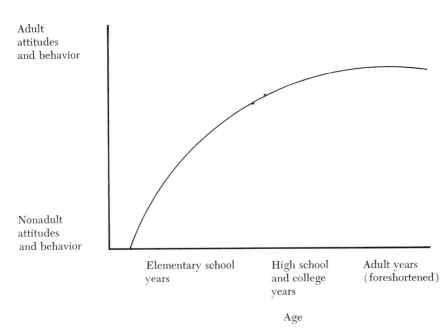

tion is useful, but it leaves open the question of the extent of and pattern of development of political orientations once they have begun to form.[4] It is this question that forms the basis of the present chapter.

Our basic procedure is to compare aggregate responses of students and parents to determine the degree to which the seniors resemble the older population. Differences in the overall responses of the two samples are an indication of the extent to which changes can be expected of the students. Whenever the use of similar questions permits, direct comparisons will also be made between the elementary schoolchildren studied by Greenstein or the Chicago investigators and the high school seniors. Finally, materials will be introduced from the Survey Research Center (SRC) election studies, particularly the 1964 and 1966 cross-section surveys, in order to provide evidence of developmental trends over the adult period.

[4]Some progress has already been made by Easton and Dennis, as suggested, and by a number of recent studies using cohort analysis. See William R. Klecka, "Applying Political Generations to the Study of Political Behavior: A Cohort Analysis," *Public Opinion Quarterly*, 35 (Fall 1971), pp. 358–73, and the references cited therein. See also Richard M. Merelman, *Political Socialization and Educational Climates* (New York: Holt, Rinehart, and Winston, 1971), Chapter 3; and Jack Dennis, "Political Learning in Childhood and Adolescence: A Study of Fifth, Eighth, and Eleventh Graders in Milwaukee, Wisconsin," (Madison: University of Wisconsin Research and Development Center for Cognitive Learning, 1969), Chapter 2.

In a sense, our strategy is predicated on minimal intergenerational change, an assumption which is challengeable. With two possible exceptions, however—perceptions of party differences and cosmopolitanism—we strongly believe that the political orientations considered in this chapter are unlikely candidates for marked generational discontinuities. Were we to include attitudes toward such matters as race, sex, and many contemporary political issues, generational change would certainly be greater. For this reason we have deliberately excluded from the present analysis the policy issues examined in Chapter 3.[5]

As a host of studies have documented, education is strongly related both directly and indirectly to a variety of political orientations. In order to compensate for the fact that the student sample excludes the least-educated segment of the seventeen- to eighteen-year-old population (i.e., dropouts), only parents with at least a high school education will be used in making student-parent comparisons (N = 1,170).

Since all of the seniors by definition have had a high school education, it is appropriate to compare them with parents with at least this much education. To the extent that college has some effect on the development of political attitudes, the comparison is usually conservative. That is, since a larger proportion of the seniors than of their parents will go on to college, the overall effects of college will be greater on the younger generation. We will also control on education when looking at the adult cross-section samples. This is especially important because of the considerable change in the educational distribution between older and younger cohorts.

We shall discuss briefly most of the topics considered in Part II. This will illustrate a variety of developmental patterns which exist. It should also help specify the kinds of attitudes and behavior for which the sequence illustrated in Figure 10.1 is applicable. The topics include political interest, media usage, attitudes and knowledge about the political parties, the salience of politics at different governmental levels, the norms of citizenship behavior, and political trust and efficacy.

POLITICAL INTEREST

One of the surprising conclusions of the Chicago studies is that late adolescence is not a period of rapid growth in political interest and activity. On the contrary, the elementary school years seem to be the time of major development. By the end of the eighth grade, nearly adult levels

[5]Admittedly the matter of life cycle versus generational factors is a difficult problem to attack. Our analysis here should be supplemented by cohort analysis, or ideally, by panel studies. For a lucid presentation of pitfalls and how to overcome them, see Matilda White Riley, "Aging and Cohort Succession: Interpretations and Misinterpretations," *Public Opinion Quarterly*, 37 (Spring 1973), pp. 35–49.

have been reached for "having worn campaign buttons and having passed out campaign literature," "having read about candidates," and "having talked with parents and friends about candidates and political problems."[6] Some question does remain, however, about expressed political interest (see below) and various kinds of activities.[7] In the first two sections we will discuss political interest and one form of political activity—use of the mass media for political news.

The developmental pattern for political interest is unclear. The Chicago inquiry, using a direct question, found that political interest dropped significantly during the elementary school years. However, as the investigators point out, the relatively high interest among the youngest children may really represent interest in the personal figure of the President. In addition, more active expressions of interest, such as discussing politics, rise dramatically at the same time. No major change in the level of interest was found during the high school years.[8] In contrast to this last finding, a Remmers' survey of high school students reported that the proportion following a presidential campaign "hardly at all" dropped from about a third of the ninth graders to a fifth of the seniors.[9] Whether this measure is comparable to overall interest, plus the methodological problem imposed by dropouts, are factors making direct comparisons with the Chicago study risky.

Our own data contain suggestive evidence that political interest rises during high school. Students were asked whether they had taken courses during the past three years that required them to pay attention to current events, public affairs, and politics. All but six percent of them replied affirmatively. Forced attention, naturally, does not guarantee increased interest. But when asked, slightly over half of the total sample replied that such a course did increase their political interest by "a great deal," while another 34 percent said that there was "some" increased interest. If the students' own reports are reliable, there is considerable increment in political interest during the high school years.

Comparison of the seniors and parents indicates that a moderate increase in political interest can certainly be expected as the students move into the adult electorate. On the basis of a sample of parents with at least a high school education, the reported levels of interest are given in Table 10.1. The figures suggest that there will continually be a small group of uninvolved individuals for whom neither high school teaching nor adult citizenship responsibilities stimulates political interest. For many others,

[6]Hess and Torney, *Development of Political Attitudes*, pp. 10, 71, 88.

[7]For these activities there were unusually large differences between eighth-graders and their teachers. These differences, however, may be due to abnormally high interest among teachers rather than subsequent change on the part of the students. See *ibid.*, pp. 70–72.

[8]*Ibid.*, pp. 68–70, 79.

[9]Herbert Hyman, *Political Socialization*, (Glencoe: Free Press, 1959), p. 53.

TABLE 10.1
INTEREST IN PUBLIC AFFAIRS OF STUDENTS AND PARENTS

	Low	Medium	High	Total	
Students	16%	42	41	99%	(2062)
Parents (education ≥ 12 grades)	13%	29	58	100%	(1112)

adult life will occasion a moderate shift from a casual to a more regular sensitivity.

Post-high school changes in political interest are evidently greatest near the beginning of the adult life span. This is shown by data from the SRC 1966 election study, where the question about following public affairs was also employed. We have displayed levels of interest (in terms of a mean value) by age in Figure 10.2. Because there are wide differences in interest levels between education groups, and because younger cohorts have relatively much more education, we also employ a four-way education control.[10] Partly because of small N's, it is difficult to judge the amount of change among the very youngest adults. It is evident, however, that political interest continues to climb well into the adult period. Moreover, the amount of the increase seems to be quite substantial. At middle age, for example, people of a given educational level are at least as interested as younger, but better-educated citizens.

Interestingly, the reported level of interest among the high school seniors is well above that of all young adults. Such a comparison must be taken somewhat lightly, since high interest to a high school senior may mean something quite different than what it means to an adult. Nevertheless, there is some suggestive evidence from the adult cross-section survey that helps explain the low political interest among young adults and is at least consistent with the notion of a decline between high school and early adulthood.

If we array political interest figures not by age but by life cycle, we find that political interest is relatively low in the first group. This category includes young to middle-aged adults, married or unmarried, who have no children. Political interest is held down in this group by the personal preoccupations of many of these adults, especially the younger ones who are concerned about finding a spouse and a suitable job. Even so, political interest seems to drop at the next stage of the life cycle. Here respondents are of any age but they have a child not over 4½ years old. Inevita-

[10]Glenn has shown just how important it is to control on education when making comparisons among age-groups. If no control is used, observed trends may be due to rising education levels rather than life cycle effects. See Norval D. Glenn, "Aging, Disengagement, and Opinionation," *Public Opinion Quarterly*, 33 (Spring 1969), pp. 17–33.

Figure 10.2

MEAN POLITICAL INTEREST AMONG ADULTS,
BY AGE AND EDUCATION[a]

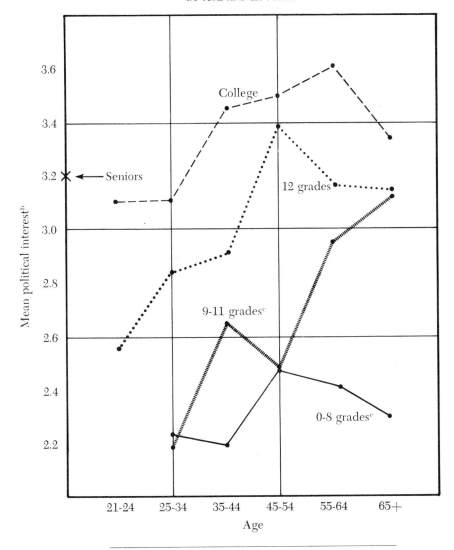

[a] Data are from the SRC 1966 election study.
[b] The responses were scored hardly at all, 1; now and
then, 2; some of the time, 3; most of the time, 4.
[c] Points are eliminated when there are fewer than 15 cases.

bly, it seems, the presence of a young child absorbs some of the time and energy that might otherwise be devoted to politics or other extrafamilial concerns. Since many young people fall into this category, it depresses the aggregate levels observed among new adults. Moreover, it may well be that the factors we have cited—launching a career, finding a spouse, and raising a young child—actually lower the amount of interest from the level it reached at the end of high school.

Be that as it may, it is clear that the middle stages of the life cycle, like the middle age-groups in general, witness a substantial growth in political interest. From the evidence in Figure 10.2, it would appear that the degree of interest may also change after the middle years of adulthood, declining from the maximum interest reached at that time. However, the data are not altogether clear on this point. Additionally, in a careful recent analysis of a variety of types of poll data, it was concluded that no dropoff in interest or even knowledge of contemporary political figures occurred among the older cohorts.[11] At this point, then, it appears that changes in interest among older people are probably small or nonexistent.

To summarize, the pattern of development of political interest seems to include fluctuations over much of the life span. Expressions of absolute interest apparently decline somewhat during the elementary years, although the willingness and ability to convert this interest into reading, discussion, and so on, tend to climb. During high school, interest probably increases, perhaps a great deal. After high school, interest may drop off for a while, but it rises sharply well into the adult years, and is maintained at least until retirement age.

Mass Media Usage

For mass media usage and overt political activity, we find one sense in which development is virtually completed by the beginning of high school. By this time similar proportions of students and adults have paid *some* attention to politics, have read about a candidate and discussed political problems at some time or other, and have taken part in some political campaign activity. Strictly speaking, once these proportions of "ever" having engaged in certain activities are reached they can never decline.[12] In this sense, development has reached a stable plateau.

This development is neatly documented by the grade school studies. Aside from a minimal involvement, however, there can be wide variations in the frequency of activity. With regard to political discussions, for example, high proportions of the high school seniors say they discuss poli-

[11]*Ibid.*, pp. 17–33. As Glenn points out, the problem of assessing life cycle changes is not easy. In general his own analysis is excellent. If we had to pick one fault it would be that his age-groups are quite large, 21–39, 40–59, and 60+.

[12]Note that the questions asked about "things you have (ever) done." Hess and Torney, *Development of Political Attitudes in Children*, pp. 71, 88.

tics with their friends and parents, 80 and 86 percent, respectively. But we also noted that of this group, about 60 percent held such discussions only a few times a month or even less. Unfortunately, there are no comparable data from eighth graders and high school seniors about the frequency of political activities. It seems unlikely that eighth graders would be as active as seniors in discussing politics or in media usage when frequency is the criterion. Detailed studies of media usage among elementary and high school students support the view that twelfth graders are more attuned to public affairs and politics than younger children, both in the form and content of their media usage.[13]

With greater assurance we can say that at least one type of activity, regular usage of the mass media for political news, rises substantially after high school. A comparison of seniors and their parents shows that parents pay more attention to each of the four media (Table 10.2). However, there are important differences among the media. Somewhat surprisingly, there is a large discrepancy between students and parents in the case of television. Although students watch a good deal of television, they pay

TABLE 10.2

MASS MEDIA USAGE IN REGARD TO PUBLIC AFFAIRS AND POLITICS AMONG STUDENTS AND PARENTS

Medium	Frequency of Use					
	Almost Daily	2-3 Times a Week	3-4 Times a Month	Not at All[a]	Total	
Television						
Students	38%	31	16	15	100%	(2058)
Parents[b]	64%	18	9	8	99%	(1097)
Newspapers						
Students	46%	32	6	16	100%	(2057)
Parents	76%	14	2	8	100%	(1111)
Radio						
Students	43%	15	6	35	99%	(2054)
Parents	51%	11	4	34	100%	(1110)
		Read regularly	Read but not regularly	Do not read		
Magazines						
Students		56%	10	34	100%	(2056)
Parents		66%	5	29	100%	(1111)

[a]Includes a small number of respondents who said "a few times a year."
[b]Includes only parents with at least 12 grades of education.

[13]See Wilbur Schramm, Jack Lyle, and Edwin B. Parker, *Television in the Lives of Our Children* (Stanford: Stanford University Press, 1961), especially Chapter 3.

attention to its news broadcasts much less regularly than parents. Daily attention to the newspapers is also much less frequent among the students, while the differences in the use of radio and magazine news are smaller but in the same direction. As with political interest, there are rather similar proportions of nonusers among students and parents. For the most part, increased media usage in adulthood means shifting from irregular to regular use.

Data about media usage during adult life are found in the 1964 SRC cross-section survey. A useful summarization of the results is made by computing the mean number of media (including radio, television, newspapers, and magazines) used by each set of respondents to gather at least some political information about the election campaigns. These mean values provide the graphic display of age trends in Figure 10.3. The different heights of the curves show, as expected, that overall media usage rises with increasing education. However, the most striking thing about the graph is not the heights of the curves, but that the developmental *patterns* are different. There is an increasing arc among the three lower levels of education, but the college educated seem to have reached their peak attention levels early. The decline from then on is slow and erratic, but the early level is never quite regained.[14] Among the three lower levels of education one finds the sharply increased attention that is suggested by the student-parent comparisons; significantly, the rate of increase appears to rise as education level declines. The figures for all three groups climb quite steadily to the middle to later adult period. It appears quite unlikely that a reversal sets in with old age.[15]

In summary, by the end of elementary school most children have made at least intermittent use of the mass media. While in this sense a plateau has been reached, regular usage becomes more widespread during the high school years, because of class assignments if for no other reason. The process continues after high school, so that for most of the population regular media usage continues to climb well into the adult years. For the growing segment who have reached college, however, a prominent counter trend exists, with a slow decline following an early peak in mass media usage.

PARTY IDENTIFICATION

At least within the United States, party identification is thought to be a prime example of an attitude which develops at a very early age and

---

[14]This same pattern was found in 1960. See Philip E. Converse, "Nonvoting Among Young Adults in the United States," in William J. Crotty, Donald M. Freeman, and Donald S. Gatlin (eds.), *Political Parties and Political Behavior* 2nd ed., (Boston: Allyn and Bacon, 1971).

[15]Unfortunately, we cannot directly compare responses of students and adults since the election study questions deal specifically with the campaigns.

Figure 10.3

MEAN NUMBER OF MEDIA USED BY ADULTS,
BY AGE AND EDUCATION[a]

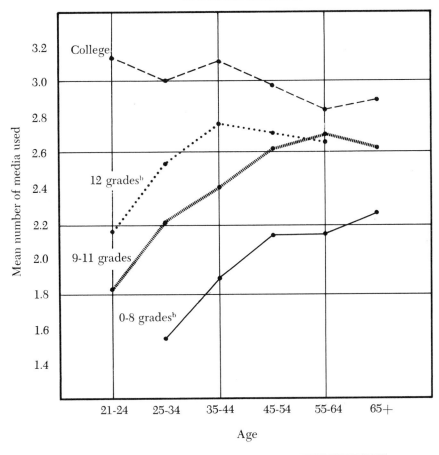

[a] Data are from the SRC 1964 election study.
[b] See footnote c, Figure 10.2.

remains relatively stable thereafter. Even before children learn much in the way of political information or develop coherent attitudes on particular political issues, they acquire a feeling of partisanship. By the fourth grade, as Greenstein points out, the frequency of partisan attachments is about as high as among young adults.[16] Similarly, in their high school

[16]Greenstein, *Children and Politics*, pp. 71–73. Actually, however, Greenstein may underestimate change in later years. Comparison with Hess and Torney's figures suggests that the high rate of partisanship among Greenstein's sample may be partially due to the strongly partisan nature of New Haven. See Hess and Torney, *Development of Political Attitudes in Children*, p. 90.

pilot study, Hess and Easton discovered no significant changes in the partisan attitudes of ninth through twelfth graders.[17] Many studies of adults further emphasize the stability of party identification and its relationship to political behavior.

In one sense it is true that party identification develops during the elementary school years and, barring major changes in the party system,[18] remains relatively constant from then on. We are speaking here of those for whom political party has no meaning. Fifty-eight percent of the second graders in the Chicago study did not know what the terms "Republican" and "Democrat" stood for or had not yet decided which, if either, party to favor. By eighth grade only 15 percent of the students gave this response.[19] While this is somewhat larger than the apolitical stratum in the adult population, it represents a much closer approximation of that stratum than the proportion of "don't know" and "undecided" respondents among the second graders. And most available evidence shows that a constant low rate of apolitical responses is found throughout the late adolescent and adult periods.[20]

If we now turn our attention to the relative proportion of partisans and Independents, the pattern of development changes in a significant way. Combining the Chicago study findings, our own results, and figures from three SRC surveys gives us a good idea of this development during a period of relatively stable partisan loyalties. There is, first of all, a rapid increase in the proportion of Independents over the elementary school years. Of the children who have made any decision, there is an increase from about a fifth of the second graders to over a third of the eighth graders who say that they will sometimes support one party and sometimes the other party.[21] Our own data show that about the same proportion of high school seniors (36 percent) as eighth graders (37 percent) claim an Independent position. It would appear that a maximum is reached sometime during the adolescent years.

The data from the adult period show an uneven long-term decline in the proportion of Independents until only about 15-20 percent of the population 75 and over claims to take a neutral position between the

[17]Reported in Hess and Torney, Development of Political Attitudes in Children, p. 9. The lack of change is confirmed by Jerrald Bachman and Elizabeth Van Duinen, Youth Look at National Problems (Ann Arbor: Institute for Social Research, University of Michigan 1971), p. 32.

[18]We comment below on current developments.

[19]Hess and Torney, Development of Political Attitudes in Children, p. 90.

[20]Bachman and Van Duinen, Youth Look at National Problems, p. 33, found a much larger proportion of apolitical responses. That the question wording they used can make so much difference is no doubt a sign of the fragility of young people's partisanship.

[21]Hess and Torney, Development of Political Attitudes in Children, p. 90. "Don't know" was one of the alternatives listed on the questionnaire.

parties (Figure 10.4).[22] Of course, the rate of change is much slower in the adult years than in the elementary period. The growth in the proportion of Independents over a five-or six-year period of youth is matched by the decline over a thirty- to thirty-five-year period after high school. Nonetheless, over the entire life span the proportion of Independents drops as low as and even below the level found in the early elementary grades.

It is not our task to explain fully why this pattern of development exists, but a few comments are in order. The early growth of Independents suggests the influence of the school and of the teachers in particular. Attempts to keep "partisan bickering" out of the classroom as well as direct inculcation of the norm that one should vote for the man and not the party probably counteract the partisan cues which many children receive at home. If it is true that many elementary teachers are themselves Independents, this may heighten their impact.[23] The same process may continue into the high school years. While data from our study suggest that high school teachers are no more frequently Independent than the adult population as a whole, more than half still say that they teach their students to vote "according to the man." It is also possible that part of the increase in Independents is due to a weakening of parental influence when students encounter opposing attitudes and arguments. This is most likely to affect older students, who discuss politics more frequently.

After high school graduation, a number of factors are no doubt at work encouraging and strengthening individual partisanship. Acquaintance with party activists, awareness of the personal implications of political decisions, and involvement in political crises stimulate party ties. There also appears to be a general strengthening of group ties the longer one identifies with a group. A spark of partisan feeling may result, after a period of time, in a strong party supporter.[24]

Given the pattern of development that we have observed, it is understandable that other investigators have uncovered no apparent trend in

[22]The relationship between education and party identification has certainly been changing since 1966, with the more educated becoming increasingly more Independent. This is clear in both SRC and Gallup data. For this reason we have controlled on education even though the criss-crossing of the curves is indicative of the lack of a strong relationship in 1964 and 1966. (Combining all education levels into one curve yields a strong monotonic decline in the proportion of Independents.) It may be that as we undergo stress in the party system, the relationship between age and partisanship is also changing. However, this is not at all apparent in the 1968 data, so that all three years were combined.

[23]Hess and Torney report that 55 percent of the teachers in their sample schools vote "sometimes Democrat, sometimes Republican" (p. 90). A smaller proportion would probably claim to be Independents if the SRC party identification question were used.

[24]See also Philip E. Converse, "Of Time and Partisan Stability," *Comparative Political Studies*, 2 (July 1969), pp. 139–71.

Figure 10.4

PROPORTION OF INDEPENDENTS AMONG ADULTS,
BY AGE AND EDUCATION[a]

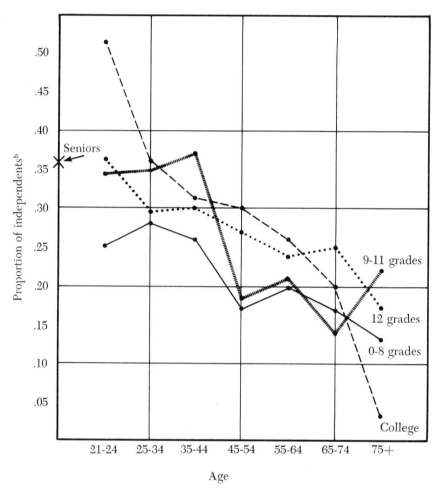

Age

---

[a] The data are combined from the SRC 1964, 1966, and 1968 election studies.

[b] Includes all Independents whether or not they lean toward a party.

party identification during the high school years. What they captured was a crucial turning point which capped about ten years of growth in the proportion of the population claiming independence of either major party. While in a narrow sense it is true that little (linear) change takes place in high school, in a broader sense these years represent an extremely significant juncture in the development of partisan orientations. More generally, this line of development represents one kind of departure from the pattern which posits a permanent crystallization of attitudes and behavior by the early teens. A rapid period of growth during the school years is followed by a slower but equally large decline extending over the remainder of the life cycle.

This description of party identification is most applicable during periods of relative constancy in the party system. Contemporary currents in our own country make us aware that it is not likely to be an accurate representation when the party system is itself undergoing change. Similarly, the pattern in Figure 10.4 is unlikely to be matched in new electorates or in countries in which changes in governmental forms (such as suspension of democracy or establishment of new nations) make the traditional parties irrelevant. It is equally true, however, that under such conditions the pattern in Figure 10.1 is not appropriate. In fact, it may be that partisanship is most fully developed among the younger cohorts, with the greatest amount of independence or resistance to new loyalties found among the older portions of the electorate.[25] Our point, then, is not that Figure 10.4 is characteristic of all times and places. Rather, it is that an adequate representation of the development of partisanship over the life cycle will certainly contain the possibility of considerable adult as well as pre-adult change. And in lengthy periods of political and partisan stability, the most likely pattern is the curvilinear trend of growth and decay in the number of Independents.

PERCEPTIONS OF POLITICAL PARTY DIFFERENCES

Both the New Haven and the national inquiries indicate that knowledge of differences between the political parties develops rather late —certainly after most children have established either a party identity or a feeling of independence. Not until the last years of grade school is there a flickering awareness of party differences, and then only among a small portion of the students. On the basis of our own data, we can add here that there is a major acquisition of such knowledge during the high school years, but adult levels are not reached and some learning still occurs in the post-high school period.

[25]This idea is expressed in Converse's model by his "resistance" phenomenon, "representing the declining ease of learning as a function of the absolute age at which the individual commences his experience within the system." *Ibid.*, p. 148.

Greenstein observed that only six percent of the New Haven eighth graders managed to cite party differences that were ideological in nature (mostly references to liberalism or conservatism) or referred to socio-economic groups that benefit more from one party than the other.[26] Dennis reports the same figure for eighth graders in Milwaukee, and finds that it grows to 16 percent among eleventh graders.[27] By the end of the twelfth grade, according to our sample, some 16 percent of the students noted a broad ideological difference between the parties. An additional 10 percent cited differential group benefits. Comparison of the seniors with their parents shows that the former have very nearly achieved adult level responses. Of the parents with at least a high school education, 18 percent observed an ideological difference between the parties and 12 percent mentioned group benefits.[28] Altogether, 26 percent of the seniors and 30 percent of the parents cited party differences mentioned by only about one out of twenty eighth graders.

Another direct comparison between the seniors and their parents is provided by the series of questions with which we estimated the level of recognition and understanding of the liberal-conservative dimension. As indicated in Chapter 4, respondents were classified into the five categories developed earlier by Converse. At one extreme (stratum 1) were those who showed no apparent recognition of the terms, while those at the upper end (stratum 5) showed a fairly broad understanding of the concepts.

The seniors and their parents were distributed among these categories as indicated in Table 10.3. It is apparent, first of all, that the students are not yet as knowledgeable as their parents. We must assume that post-high school learning helps account for the distribution of adult responses. At the same time, it seems almost certain that the seniors are far more like their parents than are eighth graders. The level of recognition and understanding of party differences rises significantly during the high school years.

[26]Greenstein, *Children and Politics*, p. 68. Even among the upper status group, only six percent gave these responses. This makes it unlikely that the difference between the eighth graders and the high school seniors (noted below in the text) is due to the dropout problem. Hess and Torney, *Development of Political Attitudes in Children*, p. 81, report higher proportions of eighth graders who identify the Republicans with "helping the rich" and Democrats with "helping the unemployed," when presented with these choices; but the relative proportions of "right" and "wrong" answers as well as the wording and the forced-choice nature of the questions suggest the reasons for these more "ideological" results than were found in New Haven.

[27]Dennis, "Political Learning in Childhood and Adolescence," pp. 17–18.

[28]The question referred to here, which was also used by Dennis, was "Do you think there are any important differences in what the Republicans and Democrats stand for?" (If yes) "What are they?" This is a close approximation to the question used by Greenstein. The measure of ideological sophistication to which Greenstein refers (*Children and Politics*, pp. 68–69), was based on different, more probing questions.

TABLE 10.3

RECOGNITION AND UNDERSTANDING OF PARTY DIFFERENCES AMONG
STUDENTS AND PARENTS

	Recognition and Understanding						
	None 1	2	3	4	Broad 5	Total	
Students	37%	16	13	10	24	100%	(2026)
Parents (education ≥ 12 grades)	25%	12	7	31	24	99%	(1093)

Adult cross-section data for both measures of party differences support the conclusion that there is a significant amount of learning after completion of high school. In fact, comparison of the seniors with adults having at least a high school education suggests a stronger contrast than that between students and parents. For example, on the first measure, 36 percent of these adults in 1966 cited an ideological or group benefits difference, which is 10 percent more than among the seniors. Similarly, on the continuum of recognition and understanding, contrast the following adult figures with those in Table 10.3: 15 percent, 6 percent, 13 percent, 32 percent, and 34 percent in strata 1–5, respectively. There clearly seems to be a further development in sophisticated perceptions of the parties in the adult period.

Just when adult changes come about is difficult to tell since generational factors may play a part, at least in altering the meaning if not the aggregate distribution of responses. For both measures the response pattern by age (controlling for education) does seem to indicate a curvilinear trend, with the highest proportions of "knowledgeable" responses reached in the middle adult years. Although this pattern is not completely uniform,[29] what we can conclude is that there are no obvious generational discontinuities that would account for the differences between student and parent or student and adult cross-section responses. Thus, while the timing is unclear (and may depend as much on external events as on age-related phenomena), we must conclude that some, possibly substantial, adult learning takes place.

Overall the evidence suggests that the development of knowledge about differences between the parties differs from the pattern shown in Figure 10.1 in that rapid learning takes place during the high school years rather than the elementary school years. A significant but smaller amount of learning takes place after high school graduation.

[29] The greatest deviation is in the very sophisticated responses of the youngest college-educated respondents—some of whom may still be in college.

THE SALIENCE MAP OF PUBLIC AFFAIRS

The studies of elementary children have revealed the extent to which the child is socialized into the political community via national symbols. These symbols, for the very young child, tend to be historical objects and people, whereas for the older child they are more likely to be such things as voting and representative institutions.[30] There is also persuasive evidence that the Presidency, past and present, is a key initial connection between the child's world and the larger political world. It is evident, however, that the child's perspectives change. For example, an overwhelming majority of eighth graders assign the world peace-keeping role to the United Nations, whereas the young child sees the United States in that role.[31] Even though the child thus comes to see the nation as part of the larger community of nations, it is important to note that this itself represents an extrapolation and extension of the national political community rather than more restricted communities.

If this trend continues throughout the high school years, it seems likely that larger political systems would be more salient than smaller units for our high school seniors. The focus of formal civic education on the national political structure and history as well as the high visibility of national and international affairs encourage a salience map favoring the larger, more cosmopolitan arenas of politics and public affairs. While we do not possess comparable measures to those used in the elementary school studies, the surrogates at hand suggest that activities and institutions associated with the larger policy domains continue to capture most of the pre-adult's political attention.

In the first column of Table 10.4 we give the distribution of student scores on the cosmopolitanism scale. As these figures demonstrate, the high school seniors are decidedly more drawn toward the cosmopolitan end of the continuum. It is doubtful that the secondary school years witness any particular shift away from the larger sphere of politics. If anything, there is probably some upsurge of awareness of and interest in the international sphere. Such an increment could result in part from the heavier concentration in the secondary than in the elementary grades of curriculum materials on the world scene.

Arraying the parents' scores along the same dimension reveals again a salience map slanted more toward larger geopolitical domains than toward smaller ones. At the same time it is perfectly obvious that the parents are less cosmopolitan than are their offspring. There are a number of reasons why this configuration could emerge. Unlike some of our previous measures, this one may be more vulnerable to a true generational discontinuity. The experience of the high school seniors—all of whom

[30]Easton and Dennis, *Children in the Political System*, Chapter 6.
[31]Hess and Torney, *Development of Political Attitudes in Children*, p. 31.

TABLE 10.4
COSMOPOLITANISM OF STUDENTS AND PARENTS

Cosmopolitanism		Students	Parents[a]
Least	1	3%	8%
	2	3	6
	3	5	9
	4	17	24
	5	18	18
	6	33	26
Most	7	21	9
Total		100%	100%
		(1837)[b]	(945)

[a]Only parents with at least twelve grades of education.
[b]N's exclude respondents who did not discriminate among all the levels of public affairs and those not following public affairs at all.

have grown up in the "cold war" world—may be such as to have fostered greater concern with larger domains of politics. Whatever the cause, it would not alter the fact that we have here another instance where the contours of a rather important set of orientations are different between pre-adult and adult samples.

An equally if not more plausible case can be made that orientations to changing domains of the political system parallel stages of the life cycle. "Confrontation with the world of *real politik*, new orbits of educational, social, and occupational endeavors, attachments to specific locales, tangible and intangible investments associated with and contingent upon the conditions in certain geopolitical domains, and simply the business of everyday living may all work to . . . result in a net movement toward less, rather than more cosmopolitanism."[32] Thus the investment of a precious political resource, namely, time and energy, is differentially allocated in response to changing circumstances in the individual's life space.

Assuming this explanation has some validity, is it possible to spot the age at which the salience map begins to acquire a different topography? Fortunately, data from the 1966 SRC election study can perform this very function. Utilizing the same questions and constructing a similar cosmopolitanism scale, and then controlling for age and education, makes quite clear the staging effect at work. As Figure 10.5 shows, there appears to be a sharp decline in cosmopolitanism in the immediate post-high school period. Young adults with a high school education are already much less nationally and internationally oriented than the seniors. And

[32]M. Kent Jennings, "Pre-Adult Orientations to Multiple Systems of Government," *Midwest Journal of Political Science*, 9 (August 1967), pp. 291–317, at p. 312.

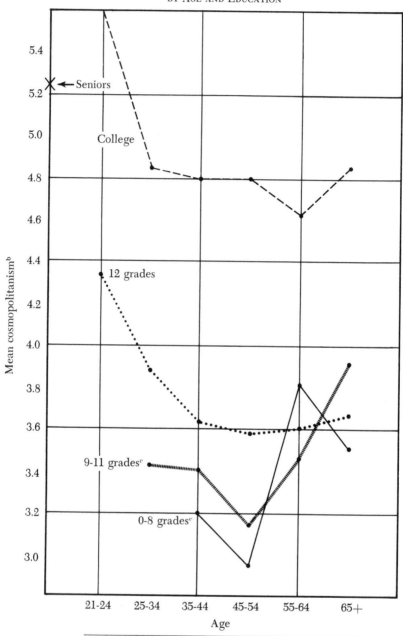

Figure 10.5

MEAN COSMOPOLITANISM AMONG ADULTS,
BY AGE AND EDUCATION[a]

Mean cosmopolitanism[b]

Seniors

College

12 grades

9-11 grades[c]

0-8 grades[c]

21-24   25-34   35-44   45-54   55-64   65+

Age

[a] Data are taken from the SRC 1966 election study.
[b] The scale values were scored least cosmopolitan, 1, to most cosmopolitan, 7.
[c] See footnote c, Figure 10.2.

adults in the second age category are even more localist.[33] Moreover, unlike the case of political interest, this reorientation of geopolitical orientations does not seem to be stemmed by the presence of very young children. Those in the second stage of the life cycle index are more locally oriented than those in the first stage. After young adulthood the reorientation process slows down, although the minimum point is not reached until well in the adult years. What happens in the late adult period is once again unclear, particularly in the face of possible generational effects.

Thus we observe a marked shift in political viewpoints for at least a decade after the high school years. Orientations then shift more slowly, but continue to change well into the adult life span. The chief importance of larger arenas wanes, and is replaced by different priorities. Such reorientations are unlikely to be restricted to geopolitical units. For example, issue-arenas and political functions cutting across governmental units also seem likely to be in flux. Some of these reorderings of perspectives undoubtedly occur primarily during the first decade after high school, but this is by no means the only change period. To the extent that life cycle rather than generational dynamics are at work, the changes we have observed in the salience map of public affairs imply the additional learning of new political roles across the life span.

THE GOOD CITIZEN

As the Almond-Verba five-nation study illustrates, the individual's conception of the citizen role varies widely across political cultures and within strata of particular cultures. These conceptions are, moreover, closely linked to the ways in which political systems function.[34] In the American context, these role constructions begin early, but great changes occur during the elementary school years in the child's conception of the good citizen. During the early period this notion is extremely diffuse and includes much in the way of social, neighborly, and religious behavior in addition to, or instead of, the more political activity normally associated with the concept of sterling citizenship. Over the span of the elementary grades, however, this ambiguity gives way to a more crisply defined and restricted characterization. By the eighth grade the child's prescriptions lie chiefly in the realm of the political, with a general interest in public affairs, participation in the electoral process, and obedience to the laws —in that order—constituting the bulk of the good citizen's attributes.[35]

[33]The surge of localism among the college-educated undoubtedly reflects the fact that many in the youngest group have not yet settled into a community.

[34]Gabriel Almond and Sidney Verba, *The Civic Culture* (Princeton: Princeton University Press, 1963).

[35]Hess and Torney, *Development of Political Attitudes in Children*, p. 39. The schoolchildren were asked: "If the President came to your town to give prizes to the two grown-ups who were the best citizens, which grown-ups would he choose?" The options included a picture and an accompanying caption.

To what extent does this highly politicized role description persist throughout the high school years and into later life? Analogous materials from the present study demonstrate that it carries on at least through secondary school. Respondents answered an open-ended question (in contrast to the fixed-alternative format of the Chicago inquiry) asking them to describe what makes a good citizen in the United States. The responses tended to fall into clusters similar to those used in the elementary school study.

Substantively, the orientation of the twelfth graders is also toward a role conceptualization heavily laden with political content. There are two basic types of such conceptualizations. One is represented by a syndrome of responses indicating passivity, obedience, and loyalty (the second category in Table 10.5).[36] In effect these are equivalent to the grade school child's selection of obedience to the laws as the mark of citizen virtue. The other "political" cluster is considerably more active and participatory in nature. It includes references to voting, paying attention to public affairs, and other forms of political participation (the first category in Table 10.5). These responses parallel the younger child's preference for electoral participation and general interest in the way the country is being run as hallmarks. From these clearly political descriptions there is a marked drop to other attributes more often associated with a good person in general than a good citizen in particular.

TABLE 10.5

CHARACTERISTICS OF THE GOOD CITIZEN, AS DESCRIBED BY
STUDENTS AND PARENTS

Characteristic	Seniors	Parents[a]
Active, participative political orientations	39%[b]	25%
Loyalty, passive political orientation	31	28
Community activism and concern[c]	10	10
Good interpersonal relationships and proper social behavior	9	16
Moral, ethical, religious attributes	7	13
Other personal properties	4	7
Total	100%	99%
	(2040)	(1113)

[a]Includes only parents with at least twelve grades of education.

[b]Percentages are based on first responses to the question.

[c]This category is comprised of both political and nonpolitical references focusing on the local community.

[36]Research dealing with socialization and the legal system is one of the more exciting recent departures. Much of this is under the heading of moral development. See, e.g., June L. Tapp and Lawrence Kohlberg, "Developing Sense of Law and Legal Justice," *Journal of Social Issues*, 27 (No. 2, 1971), pp. 65–92.

That the norms applied by the twelfth graders are not necessarily fixed is suggested by the good citizen descriptions supplied by their parents. The political content of the parents' characterizations continues to overshadow the nonpolitical, but attrition has set in. For one thing the active component of the political role is less prominent. In addition, how a person behaves toward other people, his deportment in the areas of morals, ethics, religion, and various other personal characteristics now constitute more important elements. The good citizen's role stretches beyond the polity to include other transactions and postures. Comparisons with parents of lesser education produce far more striking student-parent differences in definition (not shown).

Though no comparable data are available for a cross-section of adults, Dennis's data from Milwaukee generally support our conclusions. His findings show an increase between fifth and eighth grade and between eighth and eleventh grade in the proportion citing a politically active response; he also finds a sharp decrease in parental responses of this type. Similarly, responses invoking a wider construction of good citizenry drop between fifth and eighth grades (as political responses become more frequent), followed by increases from eighth to eleventh grade, and *especially* from there to adulthood (as the broader conceptions again become more dominant).[37]

The differences between younger children, adolescents, and their parents probably stem from two sources. In the first place, as a glance at traditional curriculum materials will confirm, social studies instruction in junior and senior high schools strongly emphasizes the active, political aspects of citizenship. Helping other people, being trustworthy, going to church, or working hard are not a conscious part of the attempt to mold good citizens during these years, although such goals are prominent in the earlier grades and are, of course, part of the subtle process of inculcating children of all ages with the Protestant ethic. What we obtain from students is most likely a faithful reproduction of classroom rhetoric about citizenship behavior. While it may be rhetoric, there is little reason to believe it departs in any significant way from the "true" beliefs of the students.

A second foundation for the discontinuity is the age and experience difference on the parental side. Further removed from the days of overt instruction and undoubtedly less idealistic about the citizen's role in the polity, the parents in essence have expanded the good citizen's repertory to embrace more of the nonpolitical and have also deemphasized the

[37]Dennis, "Political Learning in Childhood and Adolescence," pp. 20–21. There is one difference between Dennis's and our own data. He gets a lower proportion of "loyalty" responses, especially among eleventh graders. This may be due to the difference in questions, with his question asking "what should an adult *do* to deserve such an award?" (as best citizen).

relative importance of active over passive political roles. Since the conduct of everyday life usually does not involve explicit political acts such as voting, and for many people involves only the most cursory efforts to absorb and interpret political information, there is perhaps a substitution process at work whereby activities that most people *do* engage in become attributes of the good citizen. Ordinarily people do have to relate to each other; they do have to exhibit some modicum of personal integrity and morality; they do try to show that they work hard; and that they are good family people. By characterizing the good citizen in terms more closely approximating their own behavior, dissonance reduction may be accomplished.

Thus, to the extent that the various samples and measures are tapping the same phenomenon, a curious trend exists. The young child starts out by equating the good person with the good citizen. In the later elementary and high school years the good citizen has a distinctive, vigorous political aspect, yet later still there is a reversion to a more variegated conception. The conclusion is that even for such a central dimension as the norms of citizenship behavior the form is not completely set by the time the child finishes grade school or high school, and that there is actually a reversal of the trend observed among pre-adults.

POLITICAL TRUST

Trust in the government and belief in the benevolence of political leaders characterize young children's views of the political system. All laws are fair, the government rarely makes mistakes, and the President is responsive to the needs of individual citizens. Feelings such as these change rapidly during the elementary school years. Older children's viewpoints are more realistic, acknowledge a greater amount of unfairness, reveal less heroic pictures of governmental leaders, and show an awareness of the distinction between roles and the persons who fill them.[38]

TABLE 10.6
POLITICAL TRUST OF STUDENTS AND PARENTS

	Least Trust 1	2	3	4	5	Most Trust 6	Total	
Students	5%	3	13	37	25	17	100%	(2053)
Parents (education ≥ 12 grades)	22%	10	20	29	11	8	100%	(1094)

[38]Hess and Torney, *Development of Political Attitudes in Children*, Chapter 3; Greenstein, *Children and Politics*, Chapter 3. As noted in Chapter 5, absolute levels of trust among children may have declined during the sixties, but relatively speaking they were still highly trusting.

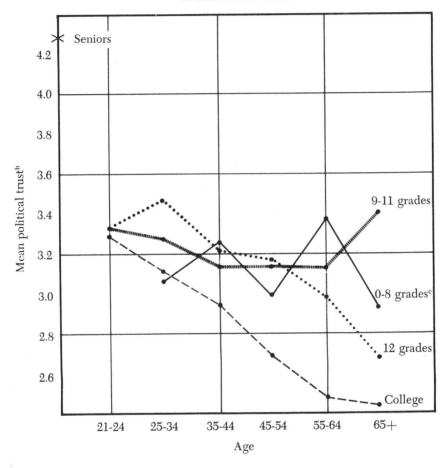

Figure 10.6

MEAN POLITICAL TRUST FOR ADULTS,
BY AGE AND EDUCATION[a]

[a] Data are from the SRC 1964 election study.
[b] The scale values were scored least trust, 1, to most trust, 6.
[c] See footnote c, Figure 10.2.

There is no expectation of a reversal of this trend. There remains, however, the important question of when individuals shift from this "realistic" view to the even less favorable or more cynical attitude which characterizes the adult population. Recent studies have made it reasonably certain that distrust begins to emerge strongly between eighth and twelfth grades (see Chapter 5). However, it is also clear that if cynicism does begin to surface during the high school years, the seniors are still left with a relatively trusting image of the government when compared with their parents (Table 10.6).[39] Clearly a further decrease in political trust can be expected after the students leave high school.

The magnitude of this decrease can be seen by comparison of the student data with a parallel trust scale derived for participants in the 1964 election study. Mean scores for students and adults are provided in Figure 10.6. They show a substantial gap between the seniors and the youngest adults—in fact as large a gap as appears over the entire adult period for any education group. Among the adults the loss of trust apparently depends on their level of education. Very obvious decrements appear in the curves for the two better-educated groups, but the slope tapers off and then becomes very erratic among those with less education. This pattern is especially interesting since there is no statistical relationship between education and trust in the sample as a whole.

The decay of political trust thus represents still another pattern of development of political orientations. Major changes occur during the elementary years and continue on into adult life. Although the process is continuous, we might think of one plateau, realism, having been reached during the late elementary school years with a second stage, cynicism, taking root at about that time.

Just as the shape of political trust shifts after maturity is attained, it also appears that some shifting occurs with respect to various attitude-objects in the political realm. These objects could be particular governmental units, institutions, processes, or actors in the political system. To illustrate the point, we will draw upon the two questions asking students and parents in which level of government—national, state, or local—they had the most faith and confidence, and in which they had the least. Among both generations the national government is most often invested with the greatest amount of trust, and it is also least often viewed as undeserving of trust.

At the same time it is equally apparent that the bias in favor of the national government is considerably greater in the student sample (Table 10.7). Our supposition that a post-adolescent shift occurs in the objects of trust as well as in the general level of trust, receives some confirmation. Most of the difference in outlooks is made up by how the two generations view national and local government, inasmuch as they rate state governments in a similar fashion.

Figures for the adult period are available in the 1968 SRC election study. In order to present the data succinctly, while capturing variations in mentions of all three levels, we have given the response of local government a 1, state government a 2, and national government a 3. Averaging the responses for age-groups thus gives us a single number, in which higher figures represent relatively more confidence in the higher levels of

[39]Bachman and Van Duinen, pp. 25–31.

TABLE 10.7

FAITH AND CONFIDENCE IN THE THREE LEVELS OF
AMERICAN GOVERNMENT

Level of Government	Most Faith		Least Faith	
	Students	Parents[a]	Students	Parents
Local	6%	24%	71%	53%
State	12	11	20	26
National	82	64	9	21
Total	100%	99%	100%	100%
	(1987)[b]	(947)	(1807)	(819)

[a]Includes only those parents with at least twelve grades of education.

[b]N's exclude all those respondents not making a choice among the three levels, such as those saying there is no level in which they had least or most trust, and those giving a combination of levels in their answers.

government. The results, presented in Figure 10.7, show no particular pattern of change over the adult years. While fluctuations do occur (partly due to random variations, given the relatively small number of individuals at each point), the general picture is one of a more or less constant attitude toward the three layers of government. What is also apparent, however, is the strikingly higher average response of the high school seniors. Their responses show relatively more confidence in the national government than even the youngest, college-educated adults in 1968. Thus, the post-adolescent change in objects of trust takes the character of a step-function. A shift to a new plateau occurs in the few years after high school, and this level is maintained throughout the remainder of the life cycle.

We will not try to account in detail for this sudden change, but two lines of explanation come to mind immediately. One is that the thrust of education in the schools emphasizes very heavily the role of the federal government in both domestic and international affairs. Furthermore, what direct and vicarious participation children and adolescents are likely to have in adult level political activities most often involves national issues and election campaigns. By contrast, adults are often caught up in parochial matters and, as we saw above, they are more likely than children to devote their energy to local questions which affect them directly. Greater local attention would not necessarily lead to more trust in local government, and a diminution in trust in national government, but that in fact seems to be an outcome. It is also probable that adults begin to feel a certain sense of distance and estrangement from a remote and immovable national government.

In any event, high school seniors seem destined to undergo some alteration in the trust bestowed upon different parts of the political sys-

Figure 10.7

MEAN RATING OF FAITH AND CONFIDENCE
IN THREE LEVELS OF GOVERNMENT AMONG ADULTS,
BY AGE AND EDUCATION[a]

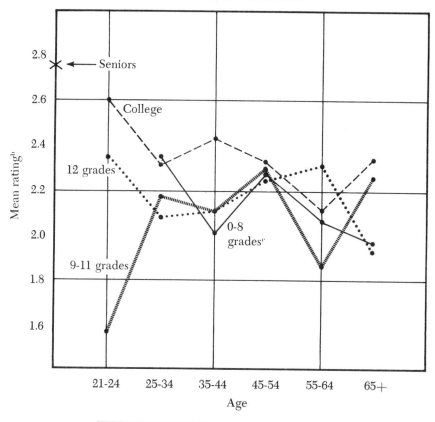

---

[a] Data are from the SRC 1968 election study.
[b] The responses were scored local government, 1; state government, 2; national government, 3.
[c] See footnote c, Figure 10.2.

tem. Unlike some of the developmental patterns noted previously, changes in the placement of trust and confidence most likely occur almost entirely in the post-adolescent period. Different governmental levels are, of course, only one set of attitude-objects which may undergo a reevaluation as the person goes through the life cycle.

POLITICAL EFFICACY

The development of political efficacy over the elementary and high school years seems to follow the classic pattern of Figure 10.1. Beginning early in the elementary grades, children are increasingly able to express an opinion other than "don't know," in response to efficacy questions, and they show a rising sense of effectiveness. Easton and Dennis found that three-quarters of the third graders in their sample were able to respond sufficiently often to be scored on their efficacy index. By eighth grade this proportion had grown steadily to the point that 95 percent of the students could be scored. This figure obviously will remain at a constantly high level throughout the rest of the life cycle. An equally impressive growth occurs in the degree of efficacy expressed. On an index with a range of 1–16, mean scores rose monotonically from 8.0 in third grade to 11.6 in eighth grade.[40]

There is less evidence for the high school period, but what is available suggests little or no further change during these years. Hess and Torney report that the pilot study of high school students called for "opinions about who in the country has easy access to governmental officials, and who is most likely to have influence upon governmental policy."[41] Apparently these were among the items showing little trend over the high school years. Dennis's study in Milwaukee also includes two measures of efficacy, one tapping access to officials and the other recording perceived governmental responsiveness. In both cases there is an increase in scores between the fifth and eighth grades, but one shows a smaller increase and the other a minor reversal of scores between eighth and eleventh graders.[42]

Comparison of seniors and their parents in our own data suggests that levels of efficacy after high school are also less variant than most of the other orientations we have considered. The comparison must be limited

TABLE 10.8
POLITICAL EFFICACY OF STUDENTS AND PARENTS

	Disagree	Depends	Agree	Total	
Voting only way to have a say					
Students	67%	0	33	100%	(2060)
Parents (education ≥ 12 grades)	64%	0	36	100%	(1112)
Government too complicated to understand					
Students	41%	0	59	100%	(2052)
Parents (education ≥ 12 grades)	36%	1	63	100%	(1110)

[40]David Easton and Jack Dennis, "The Child's Acquisition of Regime Norms: Political Efficacy," *American Political Science Review*, 61 (March 1967), pp. 25–38, at p. 33.
[41]Hess and Torney, *Development of Political Attitudes in Children*, p. 9.
[42]Dennis, "Political Learning in Childhood and Adolescence," p. 27.

to the two efficacy questions asked of both samples. The figures presented in Table 10.8 show that in both cases nearly identical proportions of students and parents gave an efficacious response. While not sufficient proof in itself, this similarity of responses is what we would expect if the life cycle development were that sketched in our original figure.

Fortunately we have data from both the 1964 and 1966 SRC surveys that help us examine the adult period. In each year an index was constructed based on the same four efficacy items that were used in the

Figure 10.8

MEAN POLITICAL EFFICACY AMONG ADULTS,
BY AGE AND EDUCATION[a]

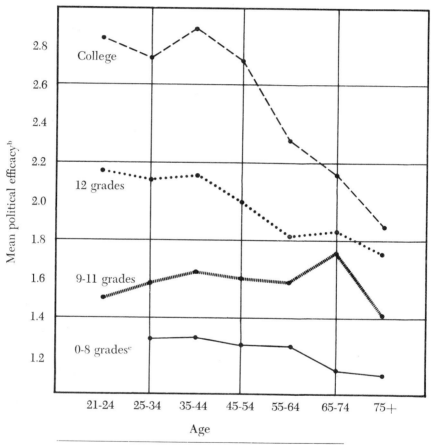

[a] The data are combined from the SRC 1964 and 1966 election studies.

[b] The index values were scored least efficacious, 1, to most efficacious, 4.

[c] See footnote c, Figure 10.2.

parent interview. The results for the two years are combined and presented in Figure 10.8.[43] Although the curves are somewhat different for the two lowest and two highest education categories, they all show a fairly steady level of efficacy through the 35–44-year-old group. That is, while there is some variation, the movement is relatively small and is sometimes in one direction and sometimes in the other.

Beyond age 45 or so (the precise age may be an artifact of our cutting points) efficacy begins to fall off. However, the curves for the two lower education groups taper off more slowly and irregularly. It is as if efficacy were already so low in these groups that further declines are unlikely. In contrast, the dropoff in the higher education brackets is sharper and more continuous, especially so among those who have attended college. To return for a moment to the student-parent comparison, we might recall that the parents are heavily concentrated in the 35–55-year-old age span. While a decline in efficacy is observable in the latter half of this range, it is not sufficient to depress the parents' scores by a large amount. If there are no changes in the period just after high school, we would thus expect parents to be just a little less efficacious than their seniors. This indeed was the case.

Combined with the elementary school findings, these data suggest yet another pattern of development to add to those we have already seen. Feelings of political efficacy rise rapidly and continuously in the elementary grades. They level off about the time of high school and remain at a fairly constant level into the middle adult years. A decline in efficacy then sets in, although it is most noticeable among the better-educated respondents. It is significant, then, that we not only find important changes in the adult life span, but the developmental pattern itself varies, as we found previously for media consumption and political trust.[44]

CONCLUSION

In commenting on the need for socialization after childhood, Brim says:

The socialization that an individual receives in childhood cannot be fully adequate as preparation for the tasks demanded of him in later

[43]The index score is basically the number of items on which the respondent gave the efficacious response (with appropriate variations where some missing data occurred). The range of the scores is thus 0–4. In 1966 the format of the items was changed so that the responses ranged from agree strongly to disagree strongly. These responses were dichotomized before counting the efficacious answers, with the "depends" category scored agree or disagree in the same way as the majority responded. The similarity of the indexes is verified by the closeness of the overall means (1.91 in 1964 and 1.90 in 1966) as well as the similar scores among education categories.

[44]It has also been shown that these trends are subject to secular modifications and, moreover, that the presumed underlying dimension to the four standard items tapping efficacy is now suspect. See Philip E. Converse, "Change in the American Electorate," in Angus Cambell and Philip E. Converse (eds.), *The Human Meaning of Social Change* (New York: Russell Sage Foundation, 1972), Chapter 8.

years. As individuals mature, they move through a sequence of statuses corresponding to different stages in the life cycle. Even though some of the expectations of society are relatively stable through the life cycle, many others change from one age to the next. We know that society demands that the individual meet these changed expectations, and demands that he alter his personality and behavior to make room in his life for newly significant persons such as his family members, his teachers, his employers, and his colleagues at work.[45]

For our purposes, the key question is whether such statements fit the case of political socialization. Are there properties associated with political socialization—but not found in other areas of socialization—which make political learning *sui generis*? A question of this magnitude cannot be quickly answered, nor is there sufficient research yet available to answer it satisfactorily. Nevertheless, we are prepared to venture the conclusion that political socialization is not particularly distinctive from other types, since it appears that critical changes and developments do occur over the entire life cycle.

The basis for the conclusion lies mainly in the kinds of trend lines presented and discussed in this chapter. We began with a developmental model which posited rapid and enormous socialization in the elementary school years and then leveled off with relatively little change over the rest of the life cycle. This is the model which can result from a casual, generalized interpretation of the research on young children. Our task was to compare this implied learning sequence with what we believed to be other appropriate data. We compared late adolescents with their parents and, where possible, made further comparisons with various age-education groupings in the adult public and with pre-high school children.

Our analysis shows that the hypothesized pattern is by no means an accurate description of the development of a variety of political orientations. In the first place, some changes do occur in the high school years. These may be largely in areas associated with cognitive capacities, as the data on the perceived differences between the political parties suggest. Additional research by Adelson and others supports the idea that considerable development of political conceptualization takes place during high school.[46] There is also strong presumptive evidence that the frequency of

[45]Orville G. Brim, Jr. and Stanton Wheeler, *Socialization After Childhood: Two Essays* (New York: Wiley, 1966), p. 18.

[46]Joseph Adelson and Robert P. O'Neil, "The Growth of Political Ideas in Adolescence: The Sense of Community," *Journal of Personality and Social Psychology*, 4 (September 1966), pp. 295–306; Joseph Adelson, "Individual Rights and the Public Good," *Comparative Political Studies*, 3 (July 1970), pp. 226–42; Judith Gallatin and Joseph Adelson, "Legal Guarantees of Individual Freedom" *Journal of Social Issues*, 27 (No. 2, 1971), p. 93–108; Tapp and Kohlberg, "Developing Sense of Law and Justice;" and National Assessment of Educational Progress, Report 6, "Citizenship: Group Results for Sex, Region, and Size of Community," (Washington: U.S. Government Printing Office, July 1971), Appendix C.

politically related activities rises during the secondary school years. Moreover, the decay of political trust indicates that change is not limited entirely to cognitive capabilities.

Because the data are more truly comparable, we feel more secure in drawing conclusions about change from the twelfth grade on through the life span. We observed sizeable alterations in political interest and activities, in the conceptualization of political parties and attachment to them, in the differential salience of political systems, in the relative emphasis on various citizenship norms, and in overall political trust and objects of political trust.

Much, but by no means all, of the modification and reorientation appears to occur in the first decade or so of adult life. In fact, we were impressed by the extent to which changes continued into the 45-54-year-old age bracket. The movement from the social role of protected juvenile in the nuclear family to the role of a single adult, a spouse, parent of young children, parent of older youth, and later adulthood are some reasons for these changes. Another obvious factor is that one's political role shifts dramatically. There is a movement from a restricted status of token legal rights and few political responsibilities into a status carrying the normal expectations of adult citizenship. In practice these expectations also change for some period of adulthood as young adults settle into new communities and into different life styles. The discontinuities in the life span and the confrontation with the realities of the political world change roles, beliefs, and behaviors from those experienced previously.

We have argued that the political development curve assumes a variety of shapes, depending upon the particular dimensions involved, and often on the education of those under consideration. The picture of rapid development to a permanent plateau may still be appropriate for some orientations. What we have shown here are the necessary alterations of that pattern as it applies to a wide variety of domains and circumstances.

CHAPTER ELEVEN

Re-Creation and Change of
the Political Culture

How faithfully does the younger generation reproduce the pattern of political orientations found in the older generation? Conversely, how great is the change in political attitudes and behavior from one generation to the next? These are deceptively simple questions, and ones that deserve our full attention in this chapter. In a sense, of course, much of Part II was devoted to this topic. There we examined in detail the transmission of certain political attitudes between parents and their children. Had we found a high degree of parent-child correspondence, our opening questions would already have received a clear answer. But the message conveyed by our analysis was that there is only a modest resemblance between parents and their high school-aged children, both in the total sample and within most control groups. This leaves an ambiguous response to the questions above, for we demonstrated in numerous instances that a low correlation at the individual level does not necessarily imply aggregate dissimilarity.[1] Closer examination of the opening questions reveals that there are at least two interrelated ways of looking at this matter of re-creation and change. These two approaches form the backbone of the present chapter.

In the first place, the simple distribution of adult and student responses could differ sharply. For both of the samples this possibility was examined for a number of orientations in Part II, and there is no need to review the results here. What we have not yet thoroughly explored is the possibility of aggregate discrepancies within the broad panoply of socio-political groups defined at the individual level and at the level of geo-political units such as community, state, and region. There are sufficient indications of consistent discrepancies in portions of the population so as to warrant a careful investigation of the most important of these groups.

What we are in a sense doing in this first phase is pointing out the location and size of the so-called generation gap. We must be careful,

[1]It should be reiterated that we are primarily concerned with recreation of nonconsensual components of the political culture. Where there is consensus among the older generation, as on questions of whether premeditated murder is right, whether political assassinations are a good thing, whether a winning candidate should be allowed to take office, whether laws are necessary, re-creation is nearly always assured by the unanimity with which the child is confronted. He virtually never hears contradictory remarks from parents, schools, or other socialization agents. But this perforce does not explain instances in which there is a lack of consensus.

however, about just what sorts of inferences we draw. First of all, we do not mean that all the differences are due to political "generations" as that term is usually defined. As we showed in the last chapter, many of the differences between parents and students are related to life cycle changes. Second, it is clear that many students and parents do not recognize cleavages even when their existence is determined by independent measurement of the two generations. Only about a third of the seniors cited any "major disagreement" between themselves and their parents, with a similar number of parents noting some bone of contention. And most of these disagreements were about nonpolitical topics. We also saw in regard to partisanship that parents often failed to perceive the students' feelings. Finally, we argued in this connection that a considerable divergence of political opinion is allowed without resulting in intergenerational clashes.

With these caveats in mind, we must interpret student-parent differences with considerable caution. Nevertheless, it is important to search out where and to what degree divergent orientations exist. In some cases these differences will point to true generational conflict. Whether due to normal life cycle developments, to students outdistancing their parents' education, or to actual shifts in societal norms, large gulfs between student and parent views are sometimes indicative of a polarization of attitudes which pits the older and younger generations against each other. Here, as we mentioned, the emphasis will be on finding segments of the population in which generational differences are extensive and/or especially large. Hopefully these findings will give us some insight into the general conditions under which generational conflicts occur as well as some hint of actual cleavages that appeared late in the 1960s. Parent-student differences can also instruct us about where the greatest changes are occurring in political views. It will become patently clear that some parts of the population are changing rapidly while in other parts attitudes are undergoing little alteration. These results are not at all apparent from observing the gross student and parent distributions.

The first major point in this chapter, then, is to sort out portions of the population in which students and parents have divergent political orientations. The second major point is closely related to this. If parts of the population are undergoing differential rates of change, the possibility is raised that relationships between independent variables and student orientations and between independent variables and parent orientations are very different. Thus, for example, region may be a good predictor of attitudes of the parents, but may make little difference among the students. In some cases the direction of the relationship may even change. Among parents, for example, non-Southerners may have more of some attribute while at the student level the advantage shifts to Southerners.

Just how and why such changes come about constitute the second major focus of this chapter.

A caveat is in order with respect to this goal also. Some of the variations in relationships that we will observe are due to the nature of the student sample. Since by design all students have the same amount of education, less-educated persons of the same age—who certainly differ with respect to some political views—are excluded. Similarly, the effects of college education have not yet been able to influence the students. These facts become especially important when we compare groups in which educational attainment varies widely—e.g., blacks versus whites. Note, moreover, that the parent sample is not so restricted. Thus a difference between, say, blacks and whites at the adult level, if due largely to education, would not necessarily show up among the students even if racial differences existed in the entire seventeen- to eighteen-year-old cohort.

There is, nonetheless, good reason to examine these relationships.[2] In a few cases it turns out that students, despite their educational homogeneity, show as much as or more variation than the parents. This appears to happen where student views as a whole are shifting away from parental ideas, with the change occurring faster in some parts of the population than in others. Even when altered relationships are due to the nature of the student sample, however, there are implications which should be considered. If one thinks of potential social interaction among the students, for example, the fact that they are highly similar may be outweighed by the differences among their parents. That is, students or groups of students who share the same interests or who have similar attitudes may find that their parents are quite different from one another, and this no doubt tends to restrict rates of interaction. Differences at the parental level thereby impinge on student behavior even though these relationships are erased among their children. In this way parents contribute to the maintenance or re-creation of social and political divisions within the population even as the common education of the students pulls them together.[3]

It should be made clear that the two kinds of comparisons to be considered in this chapter are interdependent and are in fact the same data looked at from two different perspectives. Our primary mode of presentation makes this clear. A hypothetical example follows:

[2]For one thing, the homogeneity of the student sample is less of a problem with some variables than with others. With race as a control, for example, less-educated seventeen-to-eighteen-year-olds would contribute very disproportionately to the nonwhite group, but with region as the control, the less-educated part of the cohort would fall less heavily into one group.

[3]In passing we might note that this is another subtle influence of parents that is not picked up by the correlation of specific parent and student attributes.

	South	Non-South	South advantage
Student	1.8	1.7	−.1
Parent	2.0	2.5	+.5
Student advantage	+.2	+.8	

In this example the entries are mean scores on a political variable for each of the four categories created by the cross-tabulation of generation and region. Sometimes percentages will be used instead, especially for dichotomous variables. In any event, our initial concern is whether the parent-student differences are themselves different for Southern and non-Southern residents. Comparisons are facilitated by use of the "student advantage" row. The plus and minus signs are rather arbitrary. We use a plus sign when students have more of the quality being discussed, whether this happens to be indicated by a higher or lower number. Even this is arbitrary, however, since we could say, for example, that students have more cosmopolitanism or less localism. In practice the text and tables should make clear just what the numbers mean.

Our second point of comparison is whether Southern and non-Southern students differ in approximately the same way as parents. Here the comparison is aided by looking at the "South advantage." (We could just as well use a "non-South advantage.") In the example above, these summary numbers show us that among parents, Southerners score higher on the measure in question while the advantage is reversed among the students. This would suggest a possibly significant change in regional contrasts in the upcoming generation.

The interdependence of these two comparisons should be intuitively clear from the way the "advantages" are calculated and presented. One way of expressing this is that if any entry in the (four-fold) table is changed, it necessarily alters both the row and column "advantages." Because of this, significant differences will appear in both the student advantage and the column advantage or in neither. But the varying interpretation and meaning of the two comparisons compel us to pay attention to both.

The example provided above is followed precisely in the sections on race and sex. With region a slight variation is necessary. Since there are four regions used, we could have, for example, a "South advantage," or a "Northeast advantage." In lieu of this we include the extreme difference between regions as the single most meaningful intragenerational comparison. When relative education is the control, no intragenerational comparison is appropriate, as explained below. However, the intergenerational comparisons are sufficiently exciting to warrant our close attention.

In the case of each "independent" variable, an analysis has been made of the orientations discussed in Part II. While all orientations have been examined intensively, only those which involve substantial differences and which make theoretical sense are reported in detail. In the conclusion we draw together the results in a discussion of the theoretical and practical meaning of the recreation and change that we have observed.

RACE

Consideration of the racial factor is an appropriate way to begin our analysis of recreation and change in the political culture. For obvious reasons we expect to find greater change—or less faithful re-creation—in the black population. However, this hypothesis must be tempered by a consideration of the life cycle position of the students. In a number of cases, students as a whole are "below" parental levels at this point in their lives, although we fully expect them to reach comparable levels as they get older. For such an orientation, greater change among blacks might mean that currently, as students, they are very similar to parents (rather than below them as most students are). We must be careful, then, not always to equate the current parent-student differences with changes expected between generations. This point is relevant as we turn to the first substantive topic.

We begin with general expressions of political interest and with usage of the mass media. If the civil rights movement has meant anything in terms of blacks' participation in conventional political activities, the impact should be apparent here. We have previously seen that students as a whole are less attentive to politics than their parents, especially when education is controlled (Chapter 10). But presumably this gap will be smaller or even reversed among blacks. Young blacks, including high school students, are much more likely to be swept up by current ideas and activities than are older persons. Thus the generation gap observed among whites should be less visible or reversed among blacks, where the students more quickly achieve the low parental levels of interest and participation. This prediction carries with it a corollary proposition. If parent-student differences are lower for blacks, the racial differences will almost certainly be smaller for the younger generation. Still, we should expect to find a residuum of prior socialization and cultural patterns, with the politicization of black students trailing somewhat behind that of their white counterparts.

The results clearly and consistently support these theoretical expectations. The evidence is presented in Table 11.1 in the form of mean

TABLE 11.1

POLITICAL INTEREST AND MEDIA USAGE, BY GENERATION AND RACE

		Race[a]		White Advantage
	Generation	White	Black	
Interest in	Student	3.22	3.17	+.05
public affairs	Parent	3.25	2.91	+.34
1 (Low)—4(High)	Student advantage	−.03	+.26	
Read newspaper	Student	2.05	2.16	+.11
1 (Almost daily)—	Parent	1.81	2.54	+.73
5 (Don't read)	Student advantage	−.24	+.38	
Watch TV news	Student	2.23	1.76	−.47
1 (Almost daily)—	Parent	1.73	1.74	+.01
5 (Don't watch)	Student advantage	−.50	−.02	
Read magazines	Student	1.77	1.80	+.03
1 (Regularly)—	Parent	1.85	2.21	+.36
3 (Don't read)	Student advantage	+.08	+.41	

[a]Average N's, from left to right: for students, 1852, 207; for parents, 1720, 199. Means (or percentages) for the total student and parent population are virtually identical to those given in the section on relative education below. Where totals are not provided there, they will be provided in footnotes.

figures.[4] Note first the generational differences. For three of the four items, white students are "lower" than their parents. Among blacks this pattern is reversed in two instances and reduced to almost nothing in the other case. On the fourth item, white students are slightly more active than their parents, but the black students considerably outdistance the previous generation. The racial differences predicted for the two generations can also be seen. For interest in public affairs, newspaper, and magazine reading, a fairly large gap between black and white parents is very nearly erased at the student level, although a residual difference

[4]Not having precise, uniform scores (like prices) sometimes makes it difficult to interpret means and to know just how meaningful are differences between means. Though it does not overcome this problem entirely, the fact that the distributions for many of the measures presented in this chapter were given (for the whole sample) in Part II makes it easier to interpret and understand the means and differences between them. In addition, the tables always give the range of the scores as a reminder. To be sure that the differences we cite as especially large actually represent substantial differences between the populations in question, we have observed the underling distributions as well. However, only the means are presented.

still exists. Television viewing is the only one of these areas in which the two sets of parents were on a par; as one would expect with this initial condition, the white advantage actually becomes a large deficit in the student sample.

An obvious implication of these results is that race will gradually decline as a significant variable in the explanation of spectator aspects of political behavior. In the adult generation one can usually count on race as one among a number of independent variables which help account for individual attitudes and behavior. But, as those who were students in and beyond the sixties enter into and gradually dominate the electorate, differences typically observed among adults will be watered down toward the nonexistent relationships noted among the students.[5] On occasion, of course, something of the opposite nature can happen. When adult blacks and whites are highly similar, race may become a *more* significant explanatory variable in the next generation. An example might be television viewing, wherein the racial difference among students is larger than among parents. We say this might be an example because white students may catch up to blacks in television viewing as they get older. If this were the case, race would remain a poor discriminator of television viewers and nonviewers at the adult level.

These findings are meaningful by themselves, as we argued in the introduction. Nevertheless, we should reiterate that they are partly a function of educational characteristics of the samples and subsamples. Thus the slim differences between blacks and whites in the student sample certainly underestimate the racial differences in the entire cohort of high school-aged youth. Still, it is interesting and meaningful that among blacks who achieve educational parity with whites, they very nearly achieve parity on several types of conventional political activity. They do this despite the absence of socialization in the home which is comparable to that of whites, despite the likelihood of less supportive peer groups, and in the face of the likely differences in the quality of their education. It is hazardous to generalize from the students to all blacks, but the results do suggest that increased education will very quickly transform the political outlook of the black minority of the population.

Having said this, it is important, in order to understand further and interpret the observed differences, to reexamine the evidence after imposing an education control. While such a procedure will not change the results shown above, it may indicate that the greater relative politicization of black students over their parents compared to white students over their parents can be attributed to the greater intergenerational educa-

[5]Of course such a prediction assumes that the relationships observed in each sample will remain unchanged.

tional disparity in the black population.[6] Alternatively, we may find that black students are relatively more politicized compared to parents regardless of their educational background and accomplishments.

To answer these questions, we utilized the five-category relative education measure to be described in the section below. Basically the measure categorizes student-parent pairs into those in which the student is much less educated through much more educated than the parent. For political interest and each media question, comparisons across generations were repeated but with the education control imposed. This results in 20 comparisons of relative advantage scores for whites versus blacks. In 18 of these, the difference is in the same direction, and usually of a comparable magnitude, as the scores observed in Table 11.1 above. And one of the two deviant cases occurred when the number of cases was very small. Thus the evidence seems overwhelming that the greater relative politicization of black students compared to their parents is not due solely to increasing education, for it is observed even when the students will not achieve the education level of the parents.[7]

Differences in the re-creation of parental configurations do not occur solely on activity measures. We noted earlier (Chapters 5 and 10) both racial and age differences in conceptions of the good citizen. Combining these comparisons here yields the following percentages mentioning an active orientation:

	White	Black	White Advantage	Total
Student	58%	32	+26%	56%
Parent	45	36	+ 9	44
Student advantage	+13%	−4		+12%
	(ave: 1075)	(104)		(1179)

[6]The relative education distributions for blacks and whites are as follows:

	St<<P	St<P	St=P	St>P	St>>P	Total
White	9%	18	30	30	12	99% (1724)
Black	6%	17	15	38	23	99% (197)

[7]It should be made clear here that what is maintained with the education control is the relative generational advantage for blacks *compared with whites*. The actual advantage for blacks (or whites) may change value and/or direction from the overall score. E.g., for political interest the extreme cases (eliminating St<<P because of a small number of cases) are:

		White	Black			White	Black
St<P	ST	1.82	1.98	St>>P	St	1.58	1.58
	P	1.70	1.97		P	1.85	2.05
		−.12	.01			+.27	+.47

In both cases blacks are relatively more interested compared to their parents than are whites, even though the direction of student-parent differences goes in opposite directions in the two instances.

The differences are not large, but significantly, while white students had a more active orientation than their parents, the opposite was true of blacks. Thus, rather than closing the modest gap observable among the parents, the student generation reveals a greater divergence in racial views. Moreover, this pattern persists when relative education is controlled.

The conflict between this finding and the previous one is self-evident and strongly suggests an uneven development in the political attitudes and behavior of blacks. The younger generation of blacks are patently more active than their parents, and yet their attitudes have not changed to reflect this. In this case, of course, the lag may be due to the failure of what is taught to keep pace with what is actually taking place. One of the long-term effects of the protest of the sixties will be to bring these two components together. In the meantime, this rupture between attitude and action will contribute to the uneasiness of youthful blacks as well as whites.

A third area in which race figures prominently in inter- and intragenerational comparisons is that of political efficacy and trust. Given the upsurge of civil rights activities by blacks in the decade of the sixties, it has been widely speculated that the political efficacy of black youth is outpacing that of the older generation, and what is crucial here, outpacing parental levels by a greater margin than among whites. Precisely because they have often gone outside conventional, traditional modes of political participation to achieve their goals, young blacks might be relatively more willing to subscribe to the notion that voting (for example) is not the only way in which they can have a say about governmental outcomes. At the same time, however, black youth—at least in the mid 1960s—still suffered a tremendous disadvantage *vis à vis* whites in terms of the resources which they could bring to bear on their problems and in terms of their self-image as equals in a society largely dominated by whites. While we noted earlier that this disadvantage was less among blacks who finished high school, we would still expect this group to feel less efficacious in an absolute sense than their white counterparts.

Much of the same reasoning applies to feelings of trust about governmental activities and motives. Young blacks may be more trusting than their parents because of life cycle effects, but they should be more like cynical adults than white youths are. Within generations, blacks of the younger group ought to be relatively less trusting of governmental affairs.

Evidence with regard to both efficacy and trust is presented in Table 11.2. In the first part is the percentage of efficacious responses to each of the items asked of both student and parent samples. Mean political trust scores are used in the second part of the table. Each of our annunciated propositions is borne out. In the first place, the black students on the

TABLE 11.2
POLITICAL EFFICACY AND TRUST, BY GENERATION AND RACE

		Race[a]		White Advantage
	Generation	White	Black	
Voting only way to have a say (% disagree)	Student	69	40	+29
	Parent	54	17	+37
	Student advantage	+15	+23	
Government too complicated to understand (% disagree)	Student	42	35	+ 7
	Parent	30	16	+14
	Student advantage	+12	+19	
Political trust 1 (Low)—6 (High)	Student	4.26	4.06	+.20
	Parent	3.22	3.80	−.58
	Student advantage	+1.04	+.26	

[a]Average N's, from left to right: for students, 1848, 207; for parents, 1707, 197. For political trust the total sample means are 4.25 and 3.31.

whole feel more efficacious than their parents. While this is true of whites also, the relationship is weaker. Second, the black students feel less efficacious than their white peers, although the difference is slim for the item referring to the complicated nature of the governmental process. Importantly, however, if the white advantage among parents is aligned with that same advantage among students, it is apparent that the cross-race gap is narrowing. Indeed, it has nearly evaporated with respect to the second item.

With respect to trust, both student generations are more trusting than their elders, but the difference is much less for blacks. Concomitant with this is a noteworthy alteration in cross-race comparisons. In the older generation blacks are actually less cynical than whites, while in the student group the blacks have not only caught up with but surpassed the whites' level of distrust. It is interesting that it is among young blacks —who, partly because of governmental actions, have a far greater chance than their parents of being integrated into and accepted by the white majority—that civil rights activities of the sixties seem to have led toward cynicism rather than faith and trust. It appears to be the case that the civil rights movement has made blacks more aware than ever of the inequalities and injustices in society and that this has particularly affected young blacks. The result is a reversal in the relative levels of trust between racial groups.

Considering race and relative education simultaneously illustrates two important aspects of the racial comparisons. First, the greater edge of black students over their parents compared with white students over their parents *tends* to persist at each level of relative education. Thus, the overall racial difference is not simply an artifact of exceptional differences in one category, although the pattern for the two efficacy items varies considerably. Except for the handful of cases in one extreme category, the greater intergenerational shift among blacks is a common phenomenon.

A second point is that the orderly ascending lines for both efficacy and trust acquire some irregularities when blacks only are considered. Although part of the reason may be a vastly diminished number of cases with which to work, another explanation has to do with the disparate educational and class levels of blacks and whites. The upwardly mobile black student starts from a lower parental base than does a comparable white. It has also been argued, and it seems undeniable, that blacks and whites with the same amount of formal education have not really had the same kind of educational experiences. Therefore, upward mobility, stationary, and downward mobility signify rather different things for black and white students. These different properties are reflected in the data on efficacy and trust. Statistically speaking, race has an interactive effect on the connection between relative education and relative efficacy and trust. Without more cases it is difficult to explore the precise dimensions of this interaction. What can be concluded is that the kind of processes reflected in the dominant white culture are not necessarily true of the black culture.

Turning our view toward other political orientations, we find several cases of constant differences between and within generations. Political knowledge, cosmopolitanism, and faith and confidence in various levels of government are good examples. Using mean scores, black and white students differ from their parents by almost identical scores. Correspondingly, racial differences are the same among both older and younger respondents. Interestingly, partisanship is another case in point. While parents differ significantly from students (fewer Independents), the comparison is not materially altered by the introduction of a control for race. Similarly, blacks differ sharply from whites (more Democrats), but the gap is nearly identical in the two generations. There is a moderate change in the relationship between race and candidate preference in 1964, but the interpretation of this is muddied by ceiling effects (every black parent said he or she voted for Johnson) and by the uncertain meaning of student candidate choices.

There is only one aspect having to do with the political parties on which there are noticeable contrasts. This case takes on added meaning because it is at the same time a kind of political resource—namely, recognition and understanding of ideological differences between the parties. The differences here remind us of those observed for political interest, media usage, and efficacy, as the following figures show:

		White	Black	White Advantage
Recognition and under- standing of parties 1 (None)-5(Broad)	Student	2.68	2.56	+.12
	Parent	2.89	2.33	+.56
	Student advantage	−.21	+.23	
		(ave:1758)	(200)	

The mean values for parents and students are not too divergent, but they vary in opposite directions for blacks and whites. Whereas whites have yet to achieve the level of their parents, black students have already surpassed theirs. One obvious effect of this is to reduce greatly the gap in understanding which characterizes the older sample. As with other political resources, black high school graduates have nearly, but not quite, been able to eliminate this particular handicap which was so pronounced a feature of the parent generation.

A control on relative education is particularly important here since formal schooling is so strongly related to awareness of party differences. When our relative measure is imposed, the generational and racial contrasts remain basically similar to those for the entire sample. Therefore, the pattern observed above cannot be traced solely to educational achievements among the different parts of the population. Blacks' understanding of the meaning of party labels, like their level of other political resources, compares favorably with whites' when equality of education is achieved.

We round out the evidence concerning re-creation of the political culture vis-à-vis racial groups by noting that black-white comparisons for the four public policy questions show highly similar patterns. Though the sizes of the student-parent and black-white differences are variable, the results yield no contrasts across generations or races. There is, however, one issue on which possibly meaningful differences occur. This is the question calling for an interpretation of the Bible. Forty-five percent of the white students replied that it is "God's word," indicating a slightly less fundamentalist view than parents, of whom 52 percent responded in this fashion. The comparable figures for blacks, 58 percent versus 75 percent, show a greater generational contrast. Concurrently, of course, the racial differences is reduced from 23 percent to 13 percent. Although we cannot generalize on the basis of one item, it is informative that there is at least one nonpolitical example in which change parallels that found for a number of political variables, with greater intergenerational change among blacks reducing the distance between blacks and whites of the younger generation.

Reflecting on the results of this section, we emphasize the relevance of our findings to the study of political change as well as stability. Here, in fact, two significant types of changes were observed. First, we located a source of intergenerational contrasts and potential conflicts. Throughout, when changes occurred, they suggested less faithful re-creation of adult attitudes in the black population. We say "suggested" because the results sustained our observation that currently, as high school seniors, the parent-student differences are often smaller among blacks than among whites. Nonetheless, the direction of future change is unmistakable. The new generation of blacks is very much more politicized than the preceding one, in conventional political ideas and activities as well as in the more publicized ways. Nor is this change solely due to rising educational achievements, for the results were preserved even as this factor was controlled.

The second change occurred in the racial contrast in the adult and student samples. While there are still some examples of strong racial differences in the younger population (e.g., partisanship), it was often the case that black seniors were almost on a par with whites. As we noted earlier, this means that race will lose its significance as a convenient explanatory variable for certain orientations—especially political resources and skills.[8] For two reasons, however, this will be a gradual process. Since we have dealt here only with high school graduates, the racial differences for the entire cohort are probably underestimated. But as the percentage of blacks finishing high school creeps upward, racial differences attributable to the current educational disadvantage will be reduced.[9] Closing the education gap is, of course, a long-term process, so that we will not immediately see large effects on these grounds. The second reason for expecting a gradual decline in the explanatory power of race is simply that the younger generation replaces the older one only slowly rather than in quantum fashion. Because of the nature of this change, then, it will not easily be detected except in the long run. The important point here, however, is that the study of socialization patterns has led us to predict such a change as well as the timing of this change.

One further point remains to be made about the data in this section. The differences in parent-student similarities strongly imply that sociali-

[8]There are many matters concerning race on which black and white youths are widely separated, perhaps more so than in the older generation because of faster change among blacks than whites. Therefore we specifically delineate political skills and resources.

[9]This line of thinking is supported and extended by a recent study which has perhaps the best data base yet utilized for black-white comparisons. See Anthony M. Orum and Roberta S. Cohen, "The Development of Political Orientations among Black and White Children," *American Sociological Review*, 38 (February 1973), pp. 62–74.

zation patterns differ for the current generation of blacks and whites. Specifically, they suggest that the contribution of the family is less significant in the black population. Among whites we observed what is probably the typical pattern of adolescents being less politicized, more efficacious, more trusting than their parents.[10] Black students did not follow this pattern, but not evidently because of family pressures.[11] Instead school, peers, and the events in the wider world have molded them to a greater degree than their white counterparts.

What we are observing here is probably a general pattern of influence which accompanies a changing element in the population. Extrafamilial sources exert a greater pull on these people than on more stable parts of society. This kind of pattern has been noted frequently in the context of developing nations, where modernizing forces compete with the more traditional influence of the family. Our work here indicates that this is a general feature of a changing society by no means limited to developing nations. We have added, in addition, an awareness of the twin effects of this process—namely, that it acts as a stimulant for *inter*generational conflict and change and a depressant for *intra*generational differences. Interestingly, what may be a stabilizing factor in the long run—the lessening of racial differences—has an upsetting effect in the short run for both individual families and for society as a whole.

RELATIVE EDUCATION

As with so many other aspects of socialization, education is an important factor in the re-creation of the political culture. Our concern here, however, is not with education per se, but with the relative education of students and parents. This measure is utilized because it is appropriate for two explanatory purposes. First, while educational achievements are rising throughout the population, and while the students are (currently) homogeneous with respect to absolute education, the relative increase is greater for some types of individuals than for others. To the extent that increased education alters political orientations, variations in the relative increase will be one determinant of where and to what degree re-creation of the political culture takes place.

Second, use of a relative education measure may help explain some earlier, puzzling results. A frequent observation in Part II was that students defected from parental views in more than one direction. For example, many students were more efficacious than were their parents, but

---

[10]Typical, that is, for the overall student population. Obviously there are important group differences.

[11]The lower politicization of black parents suggests that, other things being equal, their children would show an exaggerated adolescent disinterest rather than being relatively more interested.

also a substantial minority were less efficacious than were their parents. This two-way movement meant that the student-parent correlation was reduced without necessarily changing the aggregate distribution very much. Such a state of affairs may be partly attributable to relative education levels of parents and offspring. That is, students who were more educated than their parents may have deviated from parental views primarily in one direction; but balancing this movement was a flow in the opposite direction among students who had yet failed to attain their parents' education levels. To put it another way, if upward mobility were complete, students would most likely differ from parents almost exclusively in one direction. As it is, the presence of upward and downward educational mobility contributes to the re-creation of the aggregate political outlook of the older generation in the younger one. Testing the validity of this notion constitutes a major purpose of this section.

To create the relative education measure, students and parents were apportioned into five categories which express the relative educational advantage of students over their parents. Students' plans for higher education were used as a surrogate for their actual attainment, since, of course, that could not be determined at the time of the study.[12] As a precaution against overestimates of their future schooling, the subjective certainty attached to the students' educational plans was employed in gradating the students. Parents' education is here defined as that possessed by the head of the household. Because of the secular rise in educational attainment between the parental and student generations, it proved both advisable and necessary to deflate the students' expectations and, conversely, to inflate the accomplishments of their parents. We took all these factors into account when allocating respondents into five categories, running from high parental advantage to high student advantage. The distribution of the sample can be seen in the following table:

St<<P	St<P	St=P	St>P	St>>P	Total	
9%	18	29	31	13	100%	(1921)

As expected (and partly due to the sample design), there are more cases in which students will outstrip their parents' education than the reverse. However, the presence of numerous cases in which students are classified as "lower" than their parents suggests that the students' estimates are not overinflated. Although the end states of the students' education had not yet been reached, and thus the final relative education placement not actually established, we will speak as though these final states had been reached.

[12] The fact that students have not yet had all the education ascribed to them means that the effects of students being more educated than their parents will be muted, assuming college actually affects student views. In this sense our comparison is conservative.

Our first substantive concern is with overall political interest and with attention given to politics in newspapers, television, and magazines. Mean scores have been calculated for each of these items and student advantage scores have been determined. The results, as shown in Table 11.3, are monotonic only for political interest.[13] However, taken together they suggest a major step between students whose education is less than or equal to their parents and those students who have done better than the parental levels.

The range of "advantage" scores by which students trail behind or surpass parental levels is impressive. Moreover, note that for three of the measures, student-parent differences go in both directions. Students with relatively higher education are more interested and more attentive to the printed media than their parents even at this stage of the life cycle, while the remaining students fall slightly to far behind their parents. Here, then, is a case in which educational factors clearly work to reduce the correlation between parent and student behavior. The aggregate distributions are also affected by the educational factor. Were it not for the rising educational levels, parent-student aggregate differences would be even greater than they are (except for magazine reading). Thus the substantial numbers of students who overtake their parents' formal schooling do both things noted above—lower the parent-student correlation but increase the aggregate similarity of the two generations.

The results for the political efficacy items are equally impressive as those for interest and media usage. Table 11.4 presents the results for each of the two efficacy statements common to both samples. Quite clearly relative education has a good deal to do with relative feelings of efficacy. In contrast to the interest and media items, however, students differ from parents in only one direction (with the exception of St<<P for the second question). Here it is the rising educational levels that make the aggregate student-parent contrast as great as it is, rather than making the two generations similar. As before, the differential levels of student advantage contribute to a reduction in the student-parent correlation.

A second contrast is apparent in the two sets of data so far presented. In the case of interest and media, generational differences occurred among families at both extremes. Though the direction of the differences changed, in something of a step-function fashion as noted, students did differ from parents at every level of relative education. On the two efficacy items, on the other hand, substantial differences occurred primarily among students who were more educated than their parents. If differences between parents and students were to occur as a result of differential levels of efficacy, only this latter group would be affected. Similarly,

[13]As mentioned we have not calculated "relative education advantages" or "extreme differences" comparable to the "South advantage" given in the example in the introduction. The meaning of such scores with a *relative* student-parent measure would be questionable.

TABLE 11.3

POLITICAL INTEREST AND MEDIA USAGE, BY RELATIVE EDUCATION
AND GENERATION

	Generation	Relative Education[a]					
		St<<P	St<P	St=P	St>P	St>>P	Total
Interest in	Student	3.04	3.16	3.33	3.12	3.42	3.22
public affairs	Parent	3.25	3.27	3.43	3.01	3.12	3.21
1 (Low)—4 (High)	Student advantage	−.21	−.11	−.10	+.11	+.30	+.01
Read newspaper	Student	2.01	2.17	1.96	2.10	2.23	2.05
1 (Almost daily)—	Parent	1.79	1.74	1.52	2.18	2.24	1.88
5 (Don't read)	Student advantage	−.22	−.43	−.44	+.08	+.01	−.17
Watch TV news	Student	2.31	2.17	2.35	2.08	2.02	2.18
1 (Almost daily)—	Parent	1.50	1.68	1.85	1.67	1.84	1.73
5 (Don't watch)	Student advantage	−.81	−.49	−.50	−.41	−.18	−.45
Read magazines	Student	1.90	1.83	1.68	1.81	1.72	1.77
1 (Regularly)—	Parent	1.84	1.83	1.65	2.06	2.06	1.88
3 (Don't read)	Student advantage	−.06	0	−.03	+.25	+.34	+.11

[a]Average N's, from left to right: 169, 336, 555, 597, 258, 1915. In the case of relative education, N's are virtually identical for students and parents because missing education data for either forced the deletion of the pair.

TABLE 11.4

POLITICAL EFFICACY, BY RELATIVE EDUCATION AND GENERATION

	Generation	Relative Education[a]					
		St<<P	St<P	St=P	St>P	St>>P	Total
Voting only way	Student	61	67	74	61	66	66
to have a say	Parent	59	60	59	43	30	50
(% disagree)	Student advantage	+2	+7	+15	+18	+36	+16
Government too	Student	32	39	46	40	42	41
complicated to	Parent	36	31	39	21	20	29
understand (% disagree)	Student advantage	−4	+8	+7	+19	+22	+12

[a]Average N's, from left to right: 170, 338, 554, 592, 257, 1980.

to the extent that change rather than re-creation characterizes the newer generation, it is found almost exclusively in those elements of the population where relative education has been on the upswing.

These contrasts in the extent of re-creation of and deviation from parental levels are interesting. Nonetheless, the most significant aspect of what has been presented is that the meaning of each case seems consistent. In both instances, generational differences with political overtones are most likely to occur in families with rising educational levels. Students in these families, on the average, are more interested in and attentive to politics than their parents, and they think they can do more about it. It is likely, then, that they contribute more than their share to political contrasts and conflict between generations. The relatively less educated students, on the other hand, are "appropriately" (so the parents might think) less involved with political ideas and feel no more effective than their parents.

At the same time, the students who surpass their parents' education levels are the source of much of the dynamic element in political life, and may contain more than their share of political leaders. Conversely, students who are not more educated than their parents are peaceful at the cost of little political dynamism. As we turn briefly to other political orientations, we will keep these perspectives in mind, and see whether later findings support the interpretation given here.

Political knowledge provides yet another instance in which relative education is related to the nature of student-parent differences. The following figures show mean scores on the political knowledge scales:[14]

		St<<P	St<P	St=P	St>P	St>>P	Total
Political	Student	.63	.65	.73	.62	.72	.67
knowledge	Parent	.76	.75	.78	.68	.68	.73
0(Low)-	Student						
1(High)	advantage	−.13	−.10	−.05	−.06	+.04	−.06
		(170)	(338)	(556)	(596)	(258)	(1918)

It is apparent that students who have not equalled their parents' education levels have also failed to attain their parents' level of knowledge about politics. In contrast, those with equal or greater relative education have more nearly equivalent levels of knowledge.

Several orientations we mention only in passing, simply to indicate that relative education does not always have the effect and the kind of explanatory role that it does for efficacy, interest, media usage, and knowledge. Two primary examples are political trust and cosmopolitanism. For these variables relative education makes no difference at all—students are more trusting and more cosmopolitan at all levels. This means, of course,

[14]Since the political knowledge scale ran from 1–7 for students and 1–6 for parents, the scores have been standardized by dividing the raw means by 7 for students and 6 for parents.

that relative amounts of schooling cannot account for the low student-parent correlations found for these orientations as well as others. Nor does it suggest that any types of families, based on educational factors, are prone to politically relevant change.

It is not until we turn to partisan factors that we again find significant differences based on educational achievements. Here we uncover one of only two pieces of evidence that contradict the interpretation pointing to greater differences where student relative education is highest. For party identification itself, the differences are not inconsistent. On candidate preferences, however, students who are less educated than their parents differ from them the most. The following percentages show the excess Democratic preferences, running from students much less to those much more educated than their parents: 13%, 8, 6, 5, 1. The fact that these differences are not aggravated by comparable partisan affiliations suggests that their effect on the interpretation above will be minimal.[15]

The remaining partisan indicator—recognition and understanding of party differences—reveals very nearly the pattern established earlier, as shown by the following figures:

		St<<P	St<P	St=P	St>P	St>>P	Total
Recognition and	Student	2.28	2.55	3.03	2.52	2.68	2.66
understanding	Parent	2.86	2.86	3.27	2.58	2.44	2.84
of parties	Student						
1(None)-5(Broad)	advantage	−.58	−.31	−.24	−.06	+.24	−.18
		(163)	(328)	(548)	(591)	(255)	(1886)

Here only students who are much more educated than their parents are more attuned to conventional ideas about the parties. Students with somewhat higher education are about equal in understanding to parents, while the remaining students are considerably less aware of party labels and meanings than are their parents. These results are consistent with, but add another element to, the interpretation above. We now see that students who out-do their parents in relative terms not only have greater interest in and confidence about politics, along with at least as much general political knowledge, but they seem to know as much as or more about partisan politics than their parents. This can only add to the potential for conflict and change stemming from this type of family.

The final orientations that we consider here are opinions on policy questions. On the two issues of racial integration and school prayers we

[15]While these differences do not fit the pattern set by the others, they do make theoretical sense. What we know about education and partisanship tells us that upwardly mobile students should be relatively more Republican. That the Republican preferences among students are uniformly less than among parents can be attributed to factors affecting the entire student population.

find constant differences between parents and students when relative education is controlled; students are more in favor of federal integration efforts and less favorable toward school prayers in all groups. Note that this partially contradicts the interpretation given above. In these two issue-areas, students at all relative education levels show nearly equal degrees of change from parental feelings. Still, it is only partially contradictory because there are constant differences rather than a reversal of the usual pattern above. This example, then, has the virtue of pointing out that in all types of families there are some reasons for noncongruence over political ideas. By and large, however, those in which students have relatively more education than their parents are the most likely to be the source of change.

The civil liberties issues provide a further illustration of this latter tendency. Although the pattern is not perfect, it appears that the greatest divergence of student opinion from parental views is found among the relatively more educated youth. On the matter of allowing speeches against churches and religion the students are more "libertarian" by the following percentages, from lowest to highest relative education: 8%, 7, 10, 20, 23. On whether a Communist should be allowed to take office, the percentages in the same order are: −8%, 0, 15, 11, 10.

Before summarizing this material on recreation and change, we take note of the Biblical question we have so frequently used. It turns out that students at all levels of relative education have a less fundamentalist view than their parents. But the margin of differences is barely perceptible at one end of the continuum, and is significantly larger at the other end. On the basis of mean scores grounded in the four response categories, the "student advantage" is −.01, −.06, −.03, −.12, and −.14, where the order is from least to most relative education. Thus there is at least one other sensitve issue-area in which student-parent differences are likely to be greatest when the student has surpassed the parent's education level. Given the importance of religion to many people, the potential conflict arising from these differences could be explosive if it actually surfaced. While important in its own right, then, the religious question would have political consequences to the extent that religious fundamentalism is related to questions of civil liberties and other political issues.

The evidence presented to this point rather consistently supports the interpretation put forth above that students' traits diverge most sharply from parents' in families in which the younger generation receives (or expects to receive) relatively more education than the older one. From a very broad perspective, the importance of this lies in the realization that as in the previous section, socialization data have been used to speak directly to the issue of political change as well as stability. Very often the charge is levelled that research in the field of socialization is biased toward political stability, or worse yet, that it is inherently incapable of contributing to our understanding of political change. Often this claim of bias is justified. But we think that the present material demolishes the second charge, not by rhetoric, but by demonstration of just what we can learn about political change from socialization data. Specifically, we have identified a segment of the population in which change is especially likely to take place. In these families the students were more politicized than their parents even at their present stage in the life cycle. And from what we saw in Chapter 10 about age-related developments, we can predict even greater parent-student differences as the seniors move into the adult world. This finding is all the more important because it involves a very simple and general kind of measurement which is applicable to nearly everyone in modern times. The fact that we have been able to speak of change based on such a measure suggests the suitability of our methods in most contexts. And the correspondence between our results and theoretical expectations based on general educational effects supports the contention that our conclusions are equally widely applicable.

As should be the case, our findings also suggest the locus of re-creation of the political culture. While this is less surprising of socialization findings, it is important that our results are not biased in the direction of change either. It should be noted that students with relatively less education than their parents were by no means identical to their parents, even in the aggregate. In fact, the differences observed in these families were often greater than those in families at the other end of the relative education spectrum. But the direction of the differences was such that they were not likely to generate conflict or change. Instead, as these students matured, their developing attitudes and feelings would more closely approximate those of their parents. In this way the recreation of the political culture is accomplished.

SEX

If the re-creation of the existing political culture were perfect, male dominance in the political world would continue unchecked. Obviously no such thing has happened. But the later 1960s onward may be particularly significant in this regard because of the speed with which role changes occurred. The unisex look in fashions, the official end to sex discrimination in employment, as well as more spectacular events, may have signaled the beginning of a new era in male-female role definitions. Here we raise the question of whether this turnabout of affairs was visible in the political orientations of the student generation, circa 1965.

For the political resources covering interest in public affairs and media usage, girls are always more like mothers than boys are like fathers (Table

11.5).[16] This is true even though the intergenerational change is some-times "up" (more magazine reading) for both boys and girls, sometimes "down" (less newspaper reading and television viewing) for both, and sometimes moving in opposite directions (interest in public affairs). Com-parisons across sexes reveal that boys and girls differ little, regardless of whether mothers and fathers are alike. In the first two cases in Table 11.5, a large male advantage is almost eliminated in the youth sample. In the remaining cases, males and females of both generations are quite similar, although girls do have a perceptible edge over boys in television viewing.

TABLE 11.5

POLITICAL INTEREST AND MEDIA USAGE, BY GENERATION AND SEX

	Generation	Male	Female	Male Advantage
		Sex[a]		
Interest in public affairs 1 (Low)—4 (High)	Student	3.25	3.18	+.07
	Parent	3.46	3.03	+.43
	Student advantage	−.21	+.15	
Read newspaper 1 (Almost daily)— 5 (Don't read)	Student	2.05	2.08	+.03
	Parent	1.73	2.01	+.28
	Student advantage	−.32	−.07	
Watch TV news 1 (Almost daily)— 5 (Don't watch)	Student	2.26	2.13	−.13
	Parent	1.73	1.72	−.01
	Student advantage	−.53	−.41	
Read magazines 1 (Regularly)— 3 (Don't read)	Student	1.77	1.79	+.02
	Parent	1.91	1.86	−.05
	Student advantage	+.14	+.07	

[a]Average N's, from left to right: for students, 1061, 998; for parents, 828, 1092.

Scanning all of the other political orientations leads to a singular con-clusion: there are few sex differences among the parents, but those that do exist are considerably muffled in the younger generation.[17] In most instances the former is true. Even among the parents, males and females

[16]In the tables in this section both students and parents are divided by sex since our primary interest is in the male-female contrast in the two generations. This means, of course, that male students are compared with fathers and female students with mothers. If so desired, we can compare them with all parents by using the total sample means.

[17]The only ambiguous case is for political knowledge, where the comparison is somewhat complicated by the different scale ranges for students and parents. But both the distribu-tions given in Chapter 8 and the (standardized) mean scores suggest a small reduction in male-female differences in the younger generation.

are very similar with respect to political efficacy, trust, faith and
confidence in multiple governmental levels, partisanship, and opinions
on policy questions. In these cases parental patterns are faithfully re-
created.

TABLE 11.6

COSMOPOLITANISM AND RECOGNITION AND UNDERSTANDING,
BY GENERATION AND SEX

		Sex[a]		
	Generation	Male	Female	Male Advantage
Cosmopolitanism	Student	5.32	5.17	+.15
1 (Least)—7 (Most)	Parent	4.65	4.18	+.47
	Student advantage	+.67	+.99	
Recognition and	Student	2.80	2.54	+.26
understanding of	Parent	3.11	2.62	+.49
parties	Student advantage	−.31	−.08	
1 (None)—5 (Broad)				

[a]Average N's, from left to right: for students, 993, 939; for parents, 748, 968. For cosmopolitanism the total sample means are 5.24 and 4.39.

Two areas in which husbands and wives differ sharply are cosmopolitanism and recognition and understanding of the political parties.
As shown in Table 11.6, husbands are more oriented toward the outside
world while women pay more attention to local matters. Of course this
corresponds to common notions about the interests and outlooks of
mothers and is strongly supported by other evidence.[18] Yet among the
student population girls were only slightly behind boys in their cosmopolitan interests. This occurs, as the results show, because girls diverge from mothers' orientations more sharply than boys differ from
fathers'. The intergenerational aspect is important because it shows that
daughters are not always more similar to mothers in the aggregate, and
still the end result is a reduction in male-female differences. On the
recognition and understanding of party differences, some sex differences
remain in the younger respondents. The split, however, is only about half
that found among the parents. Once again daughters differ from mothers
less than boys diverge from fathers. A similar pattern was found with
respect to the related topic of factual information, as reported in
Chapter 4.

[18]Elsewhere we note that fathers usually have a net advantage over mothers on measures
of politicization. But this advantage is eliminated for participation in community activities
and reversed for local school involvement. See M. Kent Jennings and Richard G. Niemi,
"The Division of Political Labor Between Mothers and Fathers," American Political Science
Review, 65 (March 1971), pp. 69–82.

These findings are in accord with our theoretical expectations that sex differences are declining in the new generation. Before embracing this conclusion, however, we need to consider the factor of education. By design the boys and girls currently have the same level of education, whereas this is not true of the parents. If fathers ordinarily achieved a higher degree of education than the mothers, this might largely account for the results we found. We controlled for this factor by using the sub-sample of students, mothers, and fathers. We essentially duplicated Tables 11.5 and 11.6 except that only mothers and fathers with equal education were utilized.[19] This comparison corroborates in every instance the results shown in those tables. The exact figures vary, of course. However, the direction of the intergenerational change is never reversed, and the direction and magnitude of change in the male advantage scores are basically undisturbed. Hence, incorporating an educational control does nothing to invalidate the conclusion of declining sex differences.[20]

These changes in political orientations among males and females reveal a pattern in the re-creation and change of the political culture not unlike that for race. Whereas race often provided a convenient point of differentiation in the older generation, it is much less likely to do so in the younger one. In the case of sex, however, the results are even more consistent than for racial contrasts. Except for political knowledge measures (recognition and understanding of party differences and factual information), the male advantage in the student population remained at or was reduced to a small amount. Moreover, there is another reason to believe that the diminution of sex differences may be faster than in the case of race. We pointed out in the latter case that education of blacks in the entire youthful cohort will lag behind that of whites for some time, with the effect of maintaining a gap between the races in many kinds of political orientations. Women, however, already achieve about the same average education as men. Thus there is less reason not to generalize our findings to the entire cohort of the 1965 seniors.

A decline in sex differences in political attributes would signal several changes in sex roles relevant to socialization. Elsewhere we found that in the parent generation wives had to have some advantage relative to their husbands, such as greater education, before they achieved parity in polit-

[19]This procedure was deemed more appropriate than using the relative education measure because our major interest is in the contrast between males and females within each generation. Use of the relative education control would not assure equality of education among the mothers and fathers—the condition found among the students which we are trying to match.

[20]It is possible, of course, that sex differences are muted at the high school level but will appear later on in the life cycle. While more evidence on this matter is desirable, an analysis of cosmopolitanism by age using the 1966 SRC cross-section of adults shows no tendency for sex differences to increase with age.

ical resources and behavior.[21] In the next generation, this encumbrance on wives may well be removed. We have also pointed out that evidence from our study supports the view of considerable socialization of wives by their husbands after marriage.[22] While a stark reversal of this pattern is unlikely, greater equality of influence may occur. Curiously, the mother's role in the socialization of children, presently at least equal to the father's role, might not expand further. The fact that mothers are increasingly away from the home may signal a renewal of the father's impact or of the influence of nonfamily agents. It would indeed be ironic if the greater politicization, freedom, and general liberation of women resulted in a reduction of their influence on the political orientations of the growing child.

From the more general perspective of socialization theory, the importance of these conclusions is that the canvass of male and female political orientations not only helps uncover present change (i.e., between parents and students), but suggests directions of future changes as well. This indicates in yet another way that the study of political socialization should be as potent for determining political change as stability.

REGION

The nationalization of political ideas and movements is a common theme of contemporary writings. And indeed there is much support for this idea.[23] At the same time regional variations are known to be persistent, and empirical evidence has been used to question whether the theme of homogenization of society is not a bit premature.[24] Moreover, other kinds of sectionalism (such as the Northern and Southern split in California[25]) and renewed emphasis on older cleavages (as embodied in the "Southern strategy" associated with President Nixon) have suggested the vitality of regional differences. Regions are thus important because they contain important political units, units which perform functions of

[21]Jennings and Niemi, "Division of Political Labor."

[22]Paul A. Beck and M. Kent Jennings, "Parents as 'Middlepersons' in Political Socialization" *Journal of Politics* (forthcoming).

[23]A particularly compelling piece is Donald E. Stokes, "Parties and the Nationalization of Electoral Forces," in William Nisbet Chambers and Walter Dean Burnham (eds.), *The American Party Systems* (New York: Oxford University Press, 1967), pp. 182–202.

[24]See, among others, Norval D. Glenn and J. L. Simmons, "Are Regional Cultural Differences Diminishing?" *Public Opinion Quarterly*, 31 (Summer 1967), pp. 176–93; M. Kent Jennings and Harmon Ziegler, "Political Expressivism among High School Teachers: the Intersection of Community and Occupational Values," in Roberta S. Sigel (ed.), *Learning about Politics* (New York: Random House, 1970), pp. 434–53; and Ira Sharkansky, *Regionalism in American Politics* (Indianapolis: Bobbs-Merrill, 1970).

[25]See Raymond E. Wolfinger and Fred I. Greenstein, "Comparing Political Regions: The Case of California," *American Political Science Review*, 63 (March 1969), pp. 74–85, and the references cited therein.

their own and which also constitute building blocks in the national political system. For these reasons it is especially appropriate to consider the re-creation and change of regional contrasts as they appear in the parent and student samples.

Our present treatment of regional differences can be parsimonious because we have discussed several major features in previous chapters. These findings will only be referred to here in order to put them in the context of the present discussion. The first such material was introduced in connection with partisanship. We pointed out there that the defection rate among Southern parent-student pairs was very similar to that for the population as a whole, and yet the aggregate movement among identifiers was toward the Republicans in the South and toward the Democrats elsewhere. The increase in proportion Democratic was also noted for the Northeast and the Midwest. The point to be emphasized here is that these partisan shifts had the effect of reducing interregional variations in party loyalties. Taking just the identifiers, there was a 22 percent difference between the most and least Democratic regions among the parents. At the student level this difference dropped to 12 percent, with the Southern and Northeastern students moving from opposite directions toward the figure for the whole country. We shall have to ask whether this pattern of weakening regionalism persists for other orientations.[26]

An immediate answer is provided by the second major regional contrast discussed previously. In Chapter 3 we took up the issue of school prayers in some detail. There we observed sizeable differences in the proportions willing to approve of school prayers—differences which were striking even when religious identification and attitude toward the Bible were controlled. More to the present point, we noted that intergenerational movement ranged from a mere three percent in the South to 22 percent in the West. This meant that the largest regional differences, already 29 percent among the parents, rose to 48 percent at the student level. Regional differences could hardly be said to be in universal decline.

What about the remaining orientations? Is there a dominant theme to the changes that take place? Unfortunately, if one desires simple interpretations, the changes are not all that straightforward. What we will do here is to present several results briefly, emphasizing a few major patterns rather than trying to account for all of the fluctuations that occur. Then we will try to sort out the meaning of what we have found.

The evidence on political interest and media usage shows some of the consistent changes that occurred as well as some of the complexity of changes in regional patterns (Table 11.7). On three of these measures the West stands out as the most distinctive. Overall political interest, for

[26]There was little variation in the parent-student difference in percentage of Independents, and the extreme regions were seven percent apart in both generations.

TABLE 11.7
POLITICAL INTEREST AND MEDIA USAGE, BY GENERATION AND REGION

		Region[a]				Extreme Difference
	Generation	Northeast	Midwest	South	West	
Interest in	Student	3.16	3.42	3.28	3.16	.12
public affairs	Parent	3.17	3.20	3.21	3.30	.13
1 (Low)—4 (High)	Student advantage	−.01	+.04	+.07	−.14	
Read newspaper	Student	2.17	1.94	2.08	2.11	.23
1 (Almost daily)—	Parent	1.90	1.90	1.96	1.74	.22
5 (Don't read)	Student advantage	−.27	−.04	−.12	−.37	
Watch TV news	Student	2.47	2.17	1.90	2.33	.57
1 (Almost daily)—	Parent	1.77	1.72	1.62	1.89	.27
5 (Don't watch)	Student advantage	−.70	−.45	−.28	−.44	
Read magazines	Student	1.79	1.72	1.83	1.78	.11
1 (Regularly)—	Parent	1.90	1.83	1.98	1.81	.17
3 (Don't read)	Student advantage	+.11	+.11	+.15	+.03	

[a]Average N's, from left to right: for students, 511, 632, 566, 348; for parents, 461, 583, 545, 328.

example, rose slightly in the Midwest and South and moved imperceptibly in the Northeast. But in the West, students lagged behind their parents' levels of interest. Newspaper readership was less regular among students in all regions, but the largest drop was in the West. Students in this area were barely ahead of their parents in magazine usage, but this was the smallest gain in any of the regions. Only television viewing mars the perfect pattern.

The effect of these changes was to make the West more like the other regions of the country. Note that for political interest, newspaper, and magazine usage, Western parents were the most politicized, i.e., had the lowest numerical scores. In the student generation, on the other hand, the West was between the other regions on all three of these indicators. On the fourth measure, parents in the West made the least use of television news and programs about politics. The moderate generational change meant that the students fell between the other regions on this measure also.

In other respects regional shifts were less systematic. For example, the order of the regions is not consistent across generations or variables. Differences are in many cases small, so that sampling variability alone could change the ordering observed. It is clear, however, that the changes in the West notwithstanding, regional differences are not uniformly reduced in the student generation. If one looks at the extreme differences between regions, there are only slight changes on three of the measures. Television viewing is the only one to show substantial change, virtually doubling the mean differences, from .27 to .57.

There is an interesting parallel to the foregoing results in the areas of political efficacy and trust. First of all, one region again stands out as distinctive in the amount and direction of intergenerational change. In this case it is the Midwest, which shows a greater increase in aggregate levels of efficacious responses than any of the other regions and a greater jump in political trust than all but the West (to which it is very similar). The details are given in Table 11.8. Note in the figures at the right, the second parallel with the interest and media results. The extreme differences are by and large the same in the two generations. But the one noticeable change, though not really very large, heightens the mean differences. Thus regional variations in efficacy are not diminishing and, if anything, they are becoming greater in the realm of political trust.

The final set of items to which we call attention are political knowledge, cosmopolitanism, and faith and confidence in multiple levels of government. Unlike the previous cases, one region, the Northeast, is at the extreme for both generations on all three measures (Table 11.9). On the latter two, however, the distinctiveness of this region falls off in the

TABLE 11.8
POLITICAL EFFICACY AND TRUST, BY GENERATION AND REGION

		Region[a]				Extreme Difference
	Generation	Northeast	Midwest	South	West	
Voting the only way to have a say (% disagree)	Student	64%	71	58	73	15
	Parent	53	50	43	59	16
	Student advantage	+11	+21	+15	+14	
Government too complicated to understand (% disagree)	Student	44	45	36	38	9
	Parent	33	26	28	28	7
	Student advantage	+11	+19	+8	+10	
Political trust 1 (Low)—6 (High)	Student	4.20	4.40	4.06	4.37	.34
	Parent	3.47	3.31	3.22	3.22	.25
	Student advantage	+.73	+1.09	+.84	+1.15	

[a]Average N's, from left to right: for students, 509, 631, 563, 348; for parents, 461, 581, 545, 328.

TABLE 11.9

POLITICAL KNOWLEDGE, COSMOPOLITANISM, FAITH AND CONFIDENCE,
BY GENERATION AND REGION

		Region[a]				Extreme Difference
	Generation	Northeast	Midwest	South	West	
Political knowledge 0 (Low)—1 (High)	Student	.73	.67	.62	.67	.11
	Parent	.77	.72	.71	.74	.06
	Student advantage	−.04	−.05	−.09	−.07	
Cosmopolitanism 1 (Low)—7 (High)	Student	5.44	5.29	4.92	5.38	.52
	Parent	4.63	4.31	4.22	4.51	.32
	Student advantage	+.81	+.98	+.70	+.87	
Faith and confidence in government 1 (Local)—3 (Nat'l.)	Student	2.79	2.77	2.73	2.71	.08
	Parent	2.47	2.27	2.35	2.35	.20
	Student advantage	+.32	+.50	+.38	+.36	

[a]Average N's, from left to right: for students, 485, 605, 539, 334; for parents, 403, 524, 473, 294. For faith and confidence the total sample means are 2.75 and 2.35.

student population. The Western students are almost as cosmopolitan as those in the Northeast, while Midwestern students show nearly the same tendency toward confidence in the national government.

Parent-student differences in geo-political orientations are particularly large in the Midwest. The younger generation in this region seems to have shed much of the isolationism which characterized previous generations. The South-non-South difference is exaggerated on cosmopolitanism in the student sample. However, the narrow difference in faith and confidence should keep us from putting too much weight on this divergence. Extreme differences show both previous patterns of narrowing and widening regional contrasts.

Summarizing our findings about re-creation and change of regional cultural differences is not so easy as with relative education, race, and sex. While changes were observed that were consistent throughout a set of related measures, such as the declining politicization in the West, no single region showed a marked tendency in one direction or the other across all orientations. Nor was the order of the regions either stable or changed in a meaningful manner throughout the various attitudes and behaviors. Two salient points emerge, however.

First, the evidence is at least as strongly suggestive of the persistence of regional differences as of their decline. In fact, nine separate measures showed more than minimal changes in the extreme differences among regions. Just under half of these—faith and confidence in levels of government, party identification, recognition and understanding of party differences, reading magazines—revealed declining regional variation. The others—trust, political knowledge, cosmopolitanism, attitudes on school prayers, and television viewing—indicated increasing divergence among areas of the country. The remaining items showed no movement one way or the other; both homogeneity and heterogeneity of regions was maintained. In the sense, then, that regional differences are found equally often in parent and student generations, re-creation of the political culture was taking place. It ought to be clear, however, that this is re-creation of diversity and implies that areal differences are being maintained rather than succumbing to a homogenization of the entire youth generation. As Easton and Dennis point out, re-creation or "replication" need not create cultural uniformity. Instead, as in the present example of regional differences, it may be the very means by which cultural diversity persists.[27]

While re-creation of differences is thus an important part of our results, we cannot overlook the changes that occurred. We already noted the rise and decline in magnitude of regional variations for a half-dozen indicators. Moreover, we noted throughout the shifting order of the regions and the changes in which regions were most extreme. Numerous changes in regional outlooks thus underlie the re-creation of cultural diversity.

CONCLUSION

Studies of elementary schoolchildren have explained the maintenance of political systems largely by virtue of children's benign attitudes toward authority. There is no doubt considerable truth in this view, although it is slightly tarnished by the development of cynicism and radicalism among youth in the mid–sixties. In what other way might we explain the persistence of political systems as a whole and of the attitudes, characteristics, opinions, and behavior of their individual members, particularly in cases in which there is a lack of consensus? Of course, parent-student transmission plays a part in maintaining system support, but there is obviously too much dissimilarity for this to be the sole explanation.

One aspect of system maintenance, to which we have been particularly attentive in the last chapter and in this one, is that children are unlike their parents to a certain extent due to life cycle effects. We have shown that later in their lives the students will most likely develop closer parallels with the present parental mode. Thus one reason for aggregate and

[27]See David Easton and Jack Dennis, *Children in the Political System* (New York: McGraw-Hill, 1969), Chapter 2, especially pp. 39–40.

intrafamily dissimilarity at this stage of the students' lives, but similarity later on, is the way in which and the extent to which attitudes change over the lifetime of individuals.

Another factor asserted itself with abundant clarity in this chapter. This is the role played by the relative educational attainments of the two generations. The contrasting movements of those less educated and those more educated than their parents provide a simple yet highly reasonable explanation of the persistence of aggregate similarity in the face of low to moderate individual parent-student agreement.

The persistence of regional cleavages suggests another factor in the maintenance of existing political cultures. As we pointed out earlier, re-creation of existing patterns includes the continuation of existing differences and cleavages. Interestingly, then, parent-student agreement in these instances works to preserve existing differences, regardless of whether these differences promote the stability of the system as a whole.

Despite the maintenance of differences just mentioned, there were instances in which change resulted in greater homogeneity of the upcoming generation. Such was the case with race and sex. Whereas blacks and whites and males and females differed sharply among the parents, they were considerably more similar among students. This points to a change in patterns within society; the changes of this sort may well help society as a whole maintain itself. In earlier times this sort of change was "Americanization" of foreign immigrants. Now it is homogenization of elements in which the parents as well as children belong to the society.

Another obvious factor in the persistence of the culture is the slow turnover between generations. New cohorts enter the population slowly, so that in any short period of time most of the adult population is the same as in the previous time. And if a change in the new cohort is not staggeringly large, its impact will probably be barely perceptible for the short run.

Change is also a crucial feature in the socialization of a new generation. Thus it is important that our findings shed light on this as well as on stability. On this matter there is little doubt of the contribution made by forces uncovered in this chapter. The changes observed when relative education was controlled suggest why movement is afoot at all. In families where students achieve more than their parents' education, pressure is exerted by the differing perspective that develop with rising education. Note that this need not be only "higher" education (i.e., college), but relatively greater education than the parents, at whatever level that may be. Even at this stage of the life cycle student views often contrasted with parental orientations.

Changes in racial, sex, and regional contrasts provide insight into substantive alterations to appear in future political contexts. Our discussion also suggests something of the timing of these changes. With race and relative education, they also shed light on variations in socialization patterns and intrafamily agreement. In particular, we suggested that change in the black population was probably due more to nonfamily sources than to pressures emanating from parents. It is probably a fact that when large-scale social changes take place, the roles of peers, media, and social pressure are more determinative than in quiescent times. We also pointed out that change and intrafamily differences go hand in hand. The greatest tendency for change comes from families in which children diverge in a consistent fashion from parental viewpoints. Thus intrafamily disagreement is likely to accompany periods of change and is to be found precisely among those elements of the population that are changing most.

By our emphasis on both recreation and change, we have tried to preserve the interest of socialization studies in explaining the maintenance of existing societies and cultural patterns while at the same time giving life and substance to the statement that socialization studies need not have a bias towards stability and homogeneity. By so doing, we hope that our inquiry properly reveals the seeds of both stability and change within the existing political culture.

V · CONCLUSION

CHAPTER TWELVE

Political Learning in
Perspective

MUCH OF OUR discussion has concerned, in one way or another, the sources of the late adolescent's political character. In particular the role of the family and the school came under scrutiny. Surveying this vast array of findings, we are left with something of a paradox. No single source stands out as obviously dominant across all political orientations; indeed it sometimes seems as though *no* source has contributed to the formation of the adolescent's political make-up. The similarity between students and their parents was often modest and even in the best of circumstances less than half of the variance in student scores could be attributed to the parental scores on the same orientation. Similarly the effects of the secondary school—curriculum, teachers, extracurricular affairs, and friendship groups—proved to be of uneven quality. Most disturbing from a policy standpoint were the feeble consequences of formal instruction.

To what, then, can we attribute the state at which the late adolescent has arrived? Is it a matter of historical accident, of inertia, or of autonomy? More generally, to what can we attribute political change and continuity among individuals and, at a further remove, in political systems? Are these simply matters of historical accident, of inertia, or of autonomy? Is the place of home and school of secondary or even tertiary importance? Our answers to these questions are in two parts: 1) We, as well as others who have previously interpreted our results, have tended to overdraw the weakness of family and school as transmitters and cue sources; 2) Re–creation and change are indeed partly due to accident, inertia, and autonomy, and this ought to be recognized and emphasized.

THE BALANCE REDRESSED: THE IMPACT OF HOME AND SCHOOL

Compared with the extravagant claims sometimes made, our emphasis has been on the side of minimizing the role of the family. In the context of past and current socialization research this emphasis was deemed justifiable. The focus on the family to the exclusion of other socialization agents in early reviews of the literature is usually regarded as exaggerated. It has, however, been extraordinarily difficult to document the precise place of other socialization sources so that by default, as much by persuasive arguments or empirical evidence, the family continues to be regarded by many as the chief agent of political socialization. While some have unequivocally singled out the elementary school as the most determinative instrument of socialization in the United States, their conclusions have been widely criticized on the grounds that empirical demonstration was lacking.[1]

In addition it is well-known that almost the only empirical evidence heretofore available regarding family influence dealt with partisanship and general interest in politics. The former is now known to be a deviant case. Moreover, the evidence on partisanship was often handled in such a way as to inflate the effects of parental traditions. Instances in which the parents disagreed with each other were often treated as some sort of aberrant situation, and conclusions were often drawn on the basis of families with like-minded parents. As for general sensitivity to politics, the evidence was almost universally based on retrospective judgments of adults about phenomena occurring during their childhoods. On the basis of our own data, these judgments are often marked by severe error

Into this context marched our parade of low to moderate correlations between student and parent attitudes and behaviors. At such variance with prior thought was this cross-current of evidence, that it could not help but be the basis of many of our conclusions. Nor did the results flowing from an examination of the high school's impact provide a compensatory balance, for such impact operated unevenly and at the margins of political development most of the time.

At the same time we are aware that our conclusions stand in danger of being caricatured. For this reason we begin by recapitulating several points made earlier and by introducing some additional perspectives on family and school influence. These will help set in place a more balanced picture of the total impact from home and school.

First, there is a strictly methodological point. The various measures of association used throughout our analysis are customarily lowered by the presence of measurement error. As in most socialization research, many of the dimensions we used are comprised of "soft" variables. They are neither as reliable nor as valid as they should be. While we cannot estimate just how much measurement error this "softness" introduces, it is certain that the presence of such error not only lowers the parent-student correlations from their true values but also distorts the probable effects of the school.

Second, it should be reiterated that the impact of family and school with respect to consensual values and behaviors passes by largely unde-

---

[1]The major statement supporting the overwhelming importance of the elementary school is Robert D. Hess and Judith V. Torney, *The Development of Political Attitudes in Children* (Chicago: Aldine, 1967). Two reviews which question the empirical basis of their statement are David O. Sears, in *Harvard Educational Review*, 38 (Summer, 1968), pp. 571–77; and Richard G. Niemi, *Contemporary Psychology*, 14 (No. 9, 1969), pp. 497–98.

tected in our work. Longitudinal, experimental, and observational studies are needed to see exactly how families and schools go about instilling these consensual norms. Thus our finding that both parent and teacher descriptions of the model citizen bore little definite relationship to the adolescent's own descriptions should not be taken to mean that families and schools do not shape in fundamental ways the conceptions of good citizenship. This shaping seems to occur by establishing various acceptable alternatives and several nonacceptable ones. The specific direction taken by the child within the several acceptable alternatives will vary according to a host of personality and life space properties. But the critical point here is that both home and school have helped establish the parameters.

Because we were dealing with late adolescents we were unable to establish the origins and development of these parameters. More generally, we did not consider the nascent forms of political membership enunciated by Easton and Dennis: politicization, personalization, idealization (or hostilization), and institutionalization.[2] These pre-adolescent attainments would seem inevitably to be guided in direct and indirect fashion by home and school as well as the mass media. To the extent that they are neglected in our undertaking, the place of the family and the educational system in the political learning process is correspondingly understated.

If there is one uncontested and unequivocal result from our work it is that the articulation between socializer and socializee varies markedly according to the orientation being considered. Such variation is most transparent in the case of students and their parents, where the correlations linking generations go from around .05 to .60. This span alone demonstrates that blanket, all-encompassing statements about *the* political socialization process are ill-founded. Adding other information about the family, the educational system, and the larger environment only confirms the assertion that the sources of political learning vary by domain.

Fluctuation by domain leads to a third point in redressing the balance concerning home and school effects. Both sources have ranges of influence, and the upper and intermediate regions should not be forgotten while pondering the lower ones. Two dimensions supply a pattern to the range of relationships. First is that of concreteness and specificity versus abstractness and diffuseness. By concreteness we mean objects and referents which can in some sense be physically described and manipulated. Everything we know about learning behavior says that the more concrete the items the easier the learning process ordinarily is. Conse-

[2]David Easton and Jack Dennis, *Children in the Political System* (New York: McGraw-Hill, 1969), pp. 387–93.

quently, when dealing with political orientations we should expect children to copy and adopt the concrete orientations of their parents more readily than the abstract ones.

A second dimension is prolonged saliency and visibility versus short-term saliency and obscurity. It is obvious that some political objects have much more sustained currency than do others. Even some important matters are not highly or consistently visible to the mass public. Observational and other modes of learning are probably maximized when the objects are salient to both the teacher and the taught.

These two criteria of concreteness and saliency go a long way toward explicating the fluctuation by domain and especially the range of agreement between parent and child. At the apex of intergenerational transmission success are partisanship matters, specifically party identification and its companion, candidate preference. Here the criteria for successful transmission are most fully met in that parties and their candidates are very specific attitude-objects which continually impinge upon perceptual screens. Assuming parental valence, the conditions for parent-to-child carryover are very favorable.

The range of intermediate correspondence between parent and offspring consists primarily of attitude-objects and political issues. All involve relatively concrete, specific matters, e.g., school issues and evaluations of minority groups. They also reflect schisms of one sort or another which have persisted for some time. But they fail to achieve the permanence or salience of partisanship. Independent evidence of this is the well-known attitudinal instabilities on what are presumably major political issues. Similarly, issues or even groups seldom attain the concreteness of a specific presidential candidate.

The lowest range of correspondence consists of two types of orientations. On the one hand are behavioral and cognitive traits such as media behavior and conceptual sophistication about politics. The weak articulation in this case stems from the fact that pre-adults ordinarily have had little opportunity or incentive to participate in politics. Since there is a lack of participation experience, the formative years for such behavior, as well as for cognitive features derivative of participation, are pushed back to a time when nonfamily forces exercise greater control on youths' development.

The second cluster of orientations in the lower range comprises more abstract, ambiguous, and diffuse objects. Here we find political trust, efficacy, interest, cosmopolitanism, idealized versions of the good citizen, imputed attributes of American society, and relatively obscure issues. While some of these matters are concrete and some have had prolonged visibility, virtually all lack both the specificity and durability of partisanship, group orientations and many issues. Most are also rather global orientations to the political world, embracing several separate dimensions.

We now believe that parental cues in these global areas are likely to be poorly communicated in one sense but rather successfully so in another. Originally we reasoned that while many particular traits and attitudes might not be reproduced, more general, global value structures would be transmitted, because the child would acquire the general sense of most parental dispositions. Such thinking was consistent with the research findings on younger children, demonstrating that basic postures toward political life develop rather early and that the home, along with the school, was a prominent source of these postures. As argued above, we believe that children do acquire a minimal set of basic commitments to the political system and a realization of their political membership. These comprise extremely broad foundations for later growth and permutations. Upon the generous confines of these foundations arise widely diverse value structures. Consequently, parental dispositions are often a feeble guide as to what the twelfth grader's *precise* global perspectives will be within the larger parameters.

Of parallel significance to the type of orientation in comprehending the passing on of political values and behaviors is the configuration of agents acting on the pre-adult. One of the most imposing and singular threads of continuity in our findings is the differential impact of congruent versus noncongruent agents. Here is a fourth consideration which, on balance, elevates the place of family and school in the scheme of political learning. Its significance is achieved by highlighting circumstances in which the level of value transmission is relatively high.

With regard to virtually every orientation studied we found student segments with profiles distinctly more similar than average to those of their parents. What set these students off from others was like-mindedness in *both* parents. Although based on a smaller number of orientations, student-parent and student-teacher agreement was also higher when the students' parents and teachers were consistent. Significantly, the same pattern holds for parent and friend combinations.

These results are in full accord with observational learning theory's postulate that model consistency is a vital element in reproducing a given value or behavior. In the measure that agent effectiveness is gauged by reproduction fidelity, homogeneity with other agents vastly improves the effectiveness. The practical implication is worth citing: if society or a given institution therein desires purposely to mold its young citizens, the establishment of congruity across agents is a prime facilitator. Theoretically the crucial point is that family and school influence is prominent for selected portions of students, and is of even greater potential prominence. Underscoring these implications is the situation to which we now turn, that of conflict among sources of learning.

Heterogeneity and inconsistency is the reverse side of the homogeneity and consistency principle, and when two agents are at odds with each other the likelihood that the student will agree with either is much lower than if the two agents are in accord (or if their juxtaposition is unknown). We regularly observed this among the student-mother-father triads. The manipulation of student-teacher-parent and student-friend-parent triads was more limited but lent added strength to the generality of the principle.

At first blush one is inclined to surmise that the reduced statistical relationships in the instance of inconsistent models denote reduced learning relationships as well. Paradoxically, however, the lower values provide presumptive evidence that *both* agents are having an impact. Part of the reasoning here stems from the fact that the relationships are usually lowered for both agents and not just one. Within the family, for example, if only one parent were customarily more determinative, the reflection of that parent would be highly positive and the reflection of the other would be negative. Such was obviously not the case. Even when a number of controls were introduced, the same pattern of lower associations with each parent was maintained. Instead of simply signifying the absence of any parental influence the pattern strongly intimates that each has some impact; but this impact is often combined with that from the other parent to produce a unique pattern within the child. Adding to the strength of the argument is the fact that the same sorts of relationships obtain when teachers and peers are brought into play.

Adolescents with incongruent models do not necessarily adopt a position somewhere between those exhibited by the models. We were not able to state with assurance why these students sometimes converged more toward one model, at other times toward another, and at still other times occupied a position betwixt the two. The closest we came to a thorough accounting of these probabilities was in the intensive look at families where mothers and fathers had partisan differences. There it became quite clear that affective ties, levels of politicization, and same-sex links all helped push the adolescent in one direction or another. Although such results were less clear-cut in other domains, our hypothesis is that these kinds of dimensions qualify the resolution of agent conflict when the orientations are especially salient to the adolescent. In any event our contention remains the same, *viz.*, the lower agent-learner similarity in heterogeneous settings points toward influence paths reaching out from all the involved agents.

Congruency and incongruency of socialization agents exert an influence beyond the specified confines of family, friends, and teachers. When these agents act in accord with larger opinion and behavioral structures a bonus effect is achieved. Thus fewer defections from homogeneous parents occurred when the parental views were matched by dominant national trends. Similarly, student defections from parental stands on controversial issues were fewer when the parents agreed with specific regional trends. Our assumption is that the further specification of congruent forces would lead to still greater certainty about the shape and direction of youthful orientations.

Again the other side of the coin is that in a complex society the thrust of all forces is not necessarily in the same direction; nor do the homogeneous vectors fall equally on all segments of the population. If developing children move in a field of inconsistent models and if they reflect some fraction of all such forces, they may well wind up looking like no particular model in one sense, yet like all of them in another. This may be a major clue to the irony of high aggregate similarities in the face of modest pairwise similarities.[3] It also helps explain the emergence of new ways of political thought and action as a means of resolving the conflicting cues.

A fifth point to be made in reevaluating the role of family and school is that certain circumstances over and above the nature of the orientations and the operation of the congruity principle enhance their impact. These are of two main types, those deriving from roles in the social structure and those representing supportive behavioral and attitudinal configurations.

While we expressed an *a priori* preference for other approaches, we freely acknowledged the utility and sometimes necessity of looking at the pre-adults' social location as a key to understanding their political growth. Sex, race, and various indicators of current and anticipated educational achievement proved especially rewarding in our analysis. Certainly our understanding of generational change, peer influence, curriculum effects, and intrafamilial socialization would have been far shallower had we not employed social role variables.

One of the most obvious social differentiators, sex, merited particular attention because of its central location in much socialization theory and because it did, in fact, illuminate the gross results of our study. Customarily we found negligible differences between boys and girls, especially when compared with fathers and mothers. Yet there emerged persistent instances of sex-linked findings, especially in relations with the socializing environment. Easily the most significant sex-linked result is that girls in

[3]A similar point has also been made by R. W. Connell "Political Socialization in the American Family: The Evidence Re-examined," *Public Opinion Quarterly*, 36 (Fall 1972), pp. 323–33.

general reflect the image of immediately surrounding agents to a far greater degree than do boys. They seem to have somewhat less autonomy, carrying on less synthesizing and reprocessing than boys. Thus girls tended to agree with their parents more, especially so when the parents provided consistent models. Girls also agreed more with their friends in school.[4] Finally, even though the pattern is not unanimous, mothers were more likely to see their orientations reflected in their children than were fathers, a result most easily observed when mothers and fathers disagreed with each other.

Curiously, then, despite the fact that male-female differences were usually trivial on the major dimensions examined, there emerged quite visible vestiges of sex-typing and the definite imprint of sex-related roles. Perhaps the most prominent feature inhering in these results is the major role played by females in passing on the political culture. If one could imagine a world inhabited only by grandmothers, mothers, daughters, and girlfriends, the prospects for political continuity would be greater than they now are. One is tempted to say that among primary groups the bearers of the political culture are more often female than male. Again, however, the principal theoretical point should not be missed—*viz.*, that reproduction of agent orientations occurs more faithfully in meaningful population segments.

Attitudinal and behavioral *configurations* also impinge on the likelihood of "successful" performance by the agents of learning, and indicate greater influence than is suggested by the statistics showing the level of congruency on discrete measures. Our most detailed evidence on this count comes from data on the family. Illustratively, in the analysis of opinions on school integration and school prayers the introduction of companion parental opinions permitted a more elaborate specification of parental opinion structures which was clearly reflected in the opinions of the students. Similarly, knowing parental voting habits permitted us to identify which students were more likely to deviate from parental partisanship and which were less likely to do so. A complementary finding with respect to partisan-related matters is that parent-student similarity rose in more highly politicized families.

The point in all these instances is not simply that we were able to identify another factor contributing to the formation of the student's political make-up. Rather, it was that a related, supporting *parental* attitude or behavior was the additional factor. In general, this suggests that parent-to-student transmission flows would be judged as being heavier if we

---

[4]Working with multigeneration data, we have also demonstrated that wives are more likely to switch to their husbands' party preferences than vice versa. See Paul Allen Beck and M. Kent Jennings, "Parents as 'Middlepersons' in Political Socialization," *Journal of Politics* (forthcoming).

were able to flesh out more fully the various political stances held by parents.

A sixth aspect of home and school influence is that these agents condition student development in a number of indirect ways that may escape our attention, especially if we focus only on the similarity between the major orientations of agent and student. One of the most striking examples of this occurred in the area of media behavior. We found (in analysis not included here) that students were two and a half to five times as likely to read a given magazine if their parents also read the magazine. Certainly the effect is even greater for newspaper readership and may well hold for television viewing as well and, in general, for many other types of written and verbal communications to which the growing child is exposed. The nature of these effects lies not just in the direct effect of parents serving as the model for imitation, but also in the indirect effects whereby parents partially determine the particular political cues with which their children will come in contact. Similar processes occur in the schools, so that the quantity and quality of political stimuli to which the students are exposed lies largely in the hands of teachers and administrators. Inadvertently, the schools also give their charges some experience in handling "allocative" politics, as the material presented elsewhere on student and parental grievances illustrates.[5]

The seventh and final point to be made in restoring the place of family and school has to do with their independent strength vis-à-vis each other. Let us take up the family first. Although the impact of parents on their offspring varied enormously across the range of political orientations, residues of that impact almost always remained when other relevant characteristics in the schools and the larger environment were controlled statistically. This preservation was manifested in several ways. When considering the possible contribution of the civics curriculum through a multivariate analysis, the effects of family, as measured by education and level of politicization, were largely undiluted by curriculum effects. Much the same held true when we dealt with the social studies teachers, although there were some important exceptions. Similarly, a multivariate aggregate analysis, while showing that a modest amount of the family's impact is jointly shared with school properties, nevertheless demonstrated a genuine unique impact of the family on student political development.[6] Finally, parents continued to make a positive, though quite varying dent on their offspring even when the values of student friendship groups were introduced.

[5]M, Kent Jennings, "Parental Grievances and School Politics," *Public Opinion Quarterly*, 32 (Fall 1968), pp. 363–78.
[6]This is reported in M. Kent Jennings, "An Aggregate Analysis of Home and School Effects on Political Socialization" (unpublished paper, 1973).

When we turn our attention to the school, the picture is somewhat less uniform. In large part this is because it has been very difficult to pinpoint exactly which properties of the school are crucial in the socialization processs. As a result the effects of the secondary school are underexaggerated. If we think about this carefully we can see that assessing parental influence is not dramatically different. Parental influence as measured by the simple correlation between the student's score and that of a single parent was often not very high, particularly given our initial expectations. However, we have spent some time arguing that the true extent of family influence must take into account a variety of other factors. The same seems to hold for the school. Taking any single dimension of school life, its reverberations on adolescent political orientations are customarily modest. When these dimensions are combined, however, they suggest that the school has significant though not overwhelming importance. This is the chief message, with respect to interschool variance, of the aggregate analysis. Though each of the isolated variables played a minor role when taken alone, together they accounted for about as much interschool variance as did family background characteristics.[7]

School influence stood out in several other ways. The civics curriculum, while seemingly redundant for the majority of students, contributes significantly to the development of political ideas in a significant subpopulation. Again, even though teachers had but a modest impact across a range of political orientations, on those where they did have an impact it was far from negligible. That students in cross-pressured situations do not invariably swing toward the parental side indicates pull from the teachers' direction. And the typically high agreement between students and parents when the teachers and parents are homogeneous may be due in large part to the underscoring of parental perspectives supplied by those teachers.

The more informal, nonacademic side of school life also survives as a contributor in the socialization process, especially with respect to political values. Students gravitated toward the opinions of their friends more so than toward those of their social studies teachers. What is more, the friendship group as an agent of socialization fared quite well when compared with the family.

In sum, the high school's influence, while not as strong across the board as that of the family's, has independent strength in a number of areas. To which it should be added that an assessment of the school in its role as developer of political cognitions, skills, and information was scarcely undertaken here. Any full rendering of the school as an agent of political learning would have to consider these aspects in some detail.

[7] Ibid.

The foregoing summary does not permit us to pin a precise number representing the total influence of the family versus the school versus other agents of socialization. Nor should this be our goal, since it is unlikely to further our understanding of the processes and consequences of socialization. What we can conclude, however, is that both family and school have a significant enough impact on pre-adult political development that each must be examined in rather meticulous detail regardless of whether our goal is to explicate the origins of youthful political character or to present modes by which the development of that character might be altered.

We can also conclude that it is very unlikely that the outcomes of the political learning process can be substantially bent by piecemeal alterations in the pre-adult's home and school environment. Not that young people's political character is invariant across time, as attested to by the startling contrast between the college student generation of the 1950s and 1960s. But this relatively rapid change, as we will argue below, was due primarily to forces outside the family and secondary school. To achieve a dramatic change in pre-adult orientations by manipulating family and school characteristics would require massive adjustments rather than the marginal adjustments usually made. Similarly, to understand the making of the pre-adult's political character on the basis of family and school properties requires not just the most obvious of these properties but a wide range of seemingly major and minor features.

INERTIA, HAPPENSTANCE, AND SELF-DEVELOPMENT

Having restored the balance, we reiterate an earlier point: taking into account all family and school factors by no means accounts in full for the political dispositions of eighteen-year-olds. There is much in their political profiles that cannot be explained by direct appeal to the principal agents of learning. Nor is it likely that later-life developments will make such appeal that much more rewarding across a range of orientations.

Several reasons lie behind this state of affairs. First, there is the sheer pluralism of socialization forces, not all of which have the same direction and focus. Except perhaps for consensual values, this multidirectionality of forces seems to characterize most advanced societies. Rather than being a product of a monolithic set of conditioners, the growing child in a complex society is more often the product of variegated, multihued conditioners. Not only does this make it more difficult in an analytic sense to pinpoint how the various agents affect political developments; it also makes it more likely, as noted below, that the child will evolve unique solutions which do not directly reflect any particular sources.

A second reason is that much of what passes for political socialization—especially in the home—is low-key and haphazard. While socialization in this mode may occasionally be as effective as that in the conscious, direct, and systematic mode, it tends to create a vacuum to be filled, if at all, by other sources or at later times. This is partly because the cues will be more ad hoc in nature, perhaps contradictory in direction, and infrequently reinforced. The most explicit demonstration of the casual approach came in the case of partisanship, wherein we observed that a substantial number of parents were unaware of or incorrectly apprised of their children's preferences. We argued that this was strong evidence of a *laissez faire* approach because of the nature of partisanship and because the question attempted to induce an answer from the parents even if they were relatively uncertain. Only because of the extreme salience, concreteness, and recurring nature of partisan expression do many children come to take on their parents' preferences. The *laissez faire* approach in other areas bereft of these qualities must surely impede the successful passing over of orientations from parent to child. In addition we saw that very few parents felt that they and their children disagreed about any major political or social issues.[8] But direct comparisons often revealed wide gulfs between individual parents and their offspring. Again, this points toward a low-key, haphazard socialization process.

Various pieces of evidence from the adolescent's perspective also suggest weak overt attempts at socialization. In the one comparison of perceived versus actual parental values outside the realm of partisanship and voting—political interest—students were nearly unaware of the correct location of their parents.[9] Another indication rests in the relative uniformity of parent-student agreement across all manner of family affect relationships, implying that there were scarcely any students consciously trying to mimic their parents while others were deliberately trying to rebel against them. Finally students, like parents, regularly denied any conflicts along socio-political dimensions. The lack of perceptual accuracy and the paucity of either overconformity or rebellion underscore the casual, sometimes completely absent efforts of parents to mold their children politically. Thus considerable slack is introduced into the process of learning.

A third reason why adolescents derive their political character only in part from home and school lies in the direct and vicarious experiencing of political events. Sometimes these experiences are dramatic and leave a visible imprint on those undergoing them and particularly vulnerable to

---

[8]M. Kent Jennings and Richard G. Niemi, "The Transmission of Political Values from Parent to Child," *American Political Science Review*, 62 (March 1968), pp. 169–84.

[9]Richard G. Niemi, *How Family Members Perceive Each Other* (New Haven: Yale University Press, 1974), Chapter 3.

their effects. The great Depression, World War II, and more recently the massive protest movements are major examples. A specific, but striking example of events shaping opinion lay in the spectacular increase from 1965 to 1969 in youth support for the eighteen-year-old vote. Another example was the growing political cynicism evident during the late 1960s, especially noticeable among the young. In both of these examples the attitudes of the young were partially dependent on their direct and indirect experiencing of external events, quite apart from cue-giving within the family and school.

A fourth, and perhaps major, reason why sole reliance on specific agents is insufficient rests in the importance of the self as an independent and mediating influence in the socialization process. We stressed in the introduction that even in the very earliest stages of political life the child is not simply a reflecting glass which mirrors the image of others. Rather, the child's own needs and drives, mental and physical endowments, and evolving cognitive structure vitally influence the way in which political stimuli are initially interpreted and absorbed and later on are sought out and used.

A number of explicit inferences along these lines were applied to various of our substantive findings. Illustratively, we saw the importance of the role played by the student's perceptions of parental political traits. What the parents are really like and what the students perceive them to be are not always the same thing. And the differential perception makes a telling difference in student-parent similarity. A second example consisted of the effects of student policy preferences on probable defection from parental partisan identification. Clearly, the adolescent was "putting two and two together" to arrive at a solution which resulted in a "rational" deviation from parental practice. Similarly, we argued that the norm of projected participation is one of a number of political traits that draws on the individual's own experiences and internal synthesizing as much as or more than on a wholesale passing over from parent to child. In much the same vein, the level of political cosmopolitanism owes as much or more to the adolescent's own construction of the political map as it does to what school and home have stressed.[10]

Although we have no direct evidence on this point, virtually all learning theories posit that as children age, the more extensively they rely on

[10]Perhaps the major exception to this generalization is identification with a particular nation or other relevant unit such as a tribe. Intense ethnic rivalry in developed states and the problems of adjusting group loyalties in new nations carved out of colonial areas—to say nothing of enduring *national* loyalties in established systems—attest to the exception. Nevertheless, the hostile repudiation of the United States' political system by thousands of young people, to the point of emigration and political violence on the one hand and utter despair on the other, demonstrates that even these primordial inclinations can be turned around in relatively short order.

internal processing to adapt and work over the materials received from the external environment. By the same token, the more active they become in determining exactly what phenomena will be sought out and ingested. It is quite probable, then, that much of the lacking articulation between high school seniors and their socializing agents stems from the mediating and active role of the political self.

One of the reasons the political self can be so important is that many political orientations are not firmly set until well into adulthood; and even then noticeable changes can occur. This means that attitudinal and behavioral transformations readily occur in response to alterations in one's life space, the experiencing of political events, and work-related learning as well as from the more conventional sources of home and school. Some of the illustrations given previously indicate that even pre-adult movements are not solely due to the more conventional sources. But it is particularly likely that alterations during the early adult years are traceable to nonfamily and nonschool sources.

Despite the foregoing, children tend to develop in the direction of the preceding generation, as witnessed by the frequent aggregate similarity between their political profiles. When strong intergenerational differences were observed, we often had justification for believing that the younger generation would converge toward the older one as it matured. Still, even in our own data—gathered before the stormy years of the last half of the decade—there are signs of discontinuity. More recent evidence suggests even greater gaps between the generations, or at least a slower rate of change among older versus younger cohorts.

Our characterization of the socialization process suggests the relative ease with which these discontinuities can develop. Because of some conflict amongst socialization agents even in "quiet" times, because parents in particular do not systematically try to mold the political character of their children, because political events are experienced, and because one's political learning proceeds apace with maturational and life space changes, only a moderate intrusion is required to deflect young people from the main paths laid down by family and school. Oftentimes the forces are random in nature, so that divergent developments at the individual level cancel out one another. Thus it is possible to achieve high aggregate similarity between the generations in the face of low to moderate similarity between particular pairs of socializers and socializees. At certain points in time and with respect to certain orientations, however, the currents move in one main direction and become distinctively observable in the aggregate.

These dual features—that the younger generation resembles aggregate features of the older one and that only moderate energy is required to alter the expected line of development—illustrate inertia, happenstance, and self-direction. There is always some tendency for the upcoming generation to be like the preceding one. This is the passing on of orientations by family, school, and other institutions of the extant culture. It is particularly effective during the early years, when children are seldom willfully or even unwittingly different from parents and teachers, except in age-appropriate ways. Not that they necessarily look just like their own parents, but they resemble parents as a whole. In the absence of forces deflecting them in one direction or another the inertia of this early period sustains them through the turbulence and growth of adolescence and they go on as adults to develop into a fair resemblance of the older generation.

But sometimes, and especially for subpopulations, highly significant events occur prior to or with the advent of political maturity. Such events may be as cataclysmic and manifestly political as a depression, world war, or large-scale defiance of the government; or they may be politically relevant and slower moving such as the introduction of a new communication medium, new modes of transportation, or the growth of counterculture life styles. Under the press of such circumstances young people in particular can be deflected out of the channels in which their previous development has been rooted. Alterations in the maintenance and sanction structures of society can also work their will more easily on the upcoming generations, thereby modifying the attitudes and behaviors emanating from socialization per se.

Young people are especially vulnerable to the impact of external events and structural changes because their prior socialization has not been monolithic, severe, or complete. In a very real sense their political identities, as with their psycho-social identities, are still being forged. Malleable as they are, they can be bent and transformed in a remarkably short period of time.[11] If they deviate from the previous generation at this critical, identity-forming period of their lives, they may later partly revert back to the pattern of the older generation, but the resemblance between the two will never be as close as it would otherwise have been.[11]

It should be obvious that what we are proposing is analogous in a certain respect to concepts which have been applied in other domains. Specifically, the concepts of immunization and resistance are applicable here as well as in the narrower ranges of electoral behavior and partisan attitudes. Immunization comes about through defensive exposure to foreign elements. In the case of medical vaccinations the body is aided in developing defenses against the foreign agents introduced, thereby acquiring temporary or longer-lasting immunity against the disease carriers

---

[11]None of this should be taken to mean that early socialization—even of allocative politics, to use the Easton and Dennis term—is unimportant. It raises the probability that as adults the individuals will sustain the politics of the preceding generation. But it only increases the probability; it does not guarantee continuity.

themselves. Similarly, one's ability to stave off new or divergent political elements comes about in part from the successful experience of having fought off and rejected foreign elements in the past. Thus the partisan voter, for example, by rejecting other parties most of the time, comes to develop an immunity against future appeals of other parties. Simultaneously, resistance is also increased by the sheer dint of repetitive performance of the same behavior, thereby inducing habitual patterns of behavior. Such habitual patterns help maintain a state of equilibrium, lower the costs involved in making political judgments and performing political acts, and help avoid or reduce cognitive dissonance.

Now if we apply these concepts to political socialization it is quite apparent that immunization and resistance have had far less chance to flower in the child than in the adult. Indeed, for many specific types of behavior and sets of skills the pre-adult has no direct opportunities at all, and even anticipatory socialization may be unavailable or unheeded. Although the education system in particular tries to immunize the child at a very general level against various "nondemocratic" system norms, the individual does not undergo much in the way of reality testing until at least the adolescent stage. To which it may be added that socialization involving allocative functions, for which the family seems more responsible, may also be relatively uncrystallized because of the lack of implementation before adulthood.

As we have suggested, there are certain initial socialization vectors propelling children along developmental lines which will make them a near resemblance of the preceding generation. Since the path is not yet deeply etched and the resistance mechanisms not fully developed, however, deflections from this path may readily occur. Many times these are minor deflections and offset one another in the aggregate, thereby preserving intergenerational continuity but some intrafamilial discontinuity. If the forces are strong enough in one direction, the unfolding character of an entire generation, or units thereof, will be transformed in a similar way. These common "communities of experience" will lead to what is truly called generational change.[12]

In the nature of things the family and schools are unlikely candidates as major *sources* of change in the political culture, at least in the American case. Usually what modest political teaching the family does in the area

[12]Many of the questions and speculations raised in this chapter and throughout the book concerning the dynamics of socialization call out for longitudinal data. In early 1973 we were able to secure a second round of information from over 75% of the original samples of parents and students. The resulting set of 1965–1973 panel data will constitute the basis for an attack on some of the dynamic problems of socialization. An initial report of our findings at the aggregate level is found in M. Kent Jennings and Richard G. Niemi, "Continuity and Change in Political Orientations: A Longitudinal Study of Two Generations" (paper delivered at the annual meeting of the American Political Science Association, New Orleans, September 1973).

of system norms is positively supported by, and seldom contradicted by, other primary agents. In fact one reason the United States elementary and secondary schools so often look bland is that they are generally not proponents of change. They do not, by and large, seek to alter the developmental path of politics along which the children are bound, but rather support the movement thereon by supplying appropriate tools such as literacy and by reinforcing widespread values of the political order. If youngsters stray from the usual path or if they come from segments of the society which for some reason do not share in the widely recognized trends, then the school may exert a push for change, but typically in the direction of shared norms. Such an accounting is suggestive of why the civics curriculum seemed to have more effect on black than white students.

Not that all socialization agents will push children in a direction consistent with the orientations of their own parents, who may themselves be inconsistent. In most such cases, however, the deviation is still well within the bounds of widely accepted cultural norms. Consequently, it is to rather unpredictable events and circumstances outside these traditional sources that we must usually look for an explanation of changing socialization outcomes. Thus the college generations of the fifties and sixties bear a different imprint not so much as a function of any gross changes in family and school socialization processes, but much more as a result of how these students were reacting to and working over the raw materials of their political worlds. But to make the circle complete, it is the nature of family and school socialization—with its built-in inefficiencies and slack—which makes possible the profound impact of these external events and circumstances.

Study Design and Execution

THE DESCRIPTION below is most easily followed by frequent reference to the following summary table:

Interviews with *high school seniors*	1,669
Interviews with *parents* of interviewed seniors	1,992
Interviews with most relevant *social studies teachers*	317
Interviews with *principals*	96
TOTAL number of interviews	4,074
Questionnaires on *school characteristics* for school officials	97
Mass-administered questionnaires for *all seniors* in 79% of sample schools	20,833

SAMPLING PROCEDURES

The *students* selected for this study are a probability sample of second semester seniors in public and private high schools of conterminous United States in the spring of 1965. To meet the study requirement that seniors would have been enrolled in classes taught by the social studies teachers of grades 10-12 in the sample schools, new schools opening after September 1963, were excluded from the study population. In order to provide efficient use of field resources, schools with senior classes of less than nine members were also exluded. The procedure was to select a sample of seniors within the schools, and then a sample of mothers, fathers, or both parents of the seniors in the sample. Principals were thus automatically selected; social studies teachers were designated somewhat differently, as described below.

Selection of Schools

The probability sample of schools progressed through several stages. In the first stage an area probability sample of Standard Metropolitan Statistical Areas (SMSA's) and of the remaining United States counties was selected with probabilities proportional to total population of the SMSA's and counties. Thus the 12 largest metropolitan areas, 32 other SMSA's and 30 non-SMSA's were designated as sample areas. These 74 primary sampling units (psu's) are those selected for the Survey Research Center's national sample of dwellings.

A subselection of central cities and of suburban areas was made from the 12 largest metropolitan areas. In the remaining sample psu's, a sub-

337

selection of counties was made in those cases where the psu contained more than one county. In all cases probabilities of selection were in proportion to population, and controls were maintained by geographical region, SMSA classification of the psu's, and enrollments in public and in private secondary schools.

The sampling frame of schools for each psu (county, city, or suburban area) was compiled from school lists obtained through an anonymous national organization and several published lists of schools. Estimates of senior class enrollments were calculated on the basis of these sources.

After these steps the actual selection of schools was based on a probability proportionate to the size of the senior class. From the sampling frame 98 schools were selected at the rate of one school for each estimated 26,000 seniors. Of the 98 sample schools, 12 were unable to cooperate. Because of initial refusals, an additional thirteen schools were selected. Each substitute school matched the original selection, insofar as possible, with respect to geographic location, type of psu, expected number of seniors, type of school system (public or nonpublic), and curriculum (general or technical). Altogether 97 of the 111 schools (87 percent) were included in the study.

In securing the school's cooperation, we decided to start with the school principal. The main advantage to contacting only the principal initially was that cooperation was often gained quite early without inviting an extended round of negotiations with the school system bureaucracy. Approximately two-thirds of the principals contacted felt free to act unilaterally or with immediate informal clearance from the superintendent or school board personnel.[1]

Although there were 73 immediate decisions (72 acceptances plus one refusal), further contacts were necessary with the remaining 38 schools. In all but four instances the principals stated they would have to refer the matter to higher authorities. Approximately one-third of these referrals were pro forma in the sense that the principals felt they should cover themselves by a formal authorization from a superior. The balance, however, appeared to be instances where the principal truly could not make the decision or preferred not to. Of the 38 schools where further negotiations ensued, 34 percent eventually refused permission.

Three types of stipulations were made by a number of cooperating schools. One concerned the circumstances under which the students were to be interviewed. Ordinarily school officials proved quite flexible and cooperative. However, in two schools it was necessary for interviewing to be done outside the school. Another condition imposed by four

[1]Further details on the strategies and problems involved are found in M. Kent Jennings and Lawrence E. Fox, "The Conduct of Socio-Political Research in Schools: Strategies and Problems of Access," *The School Review*, 76 (December 1968), pp. 428–44.

accepting schools (and two others which eventually declined) was that parental permission would have to be obtained for each student interviewee. We developed a short permission form and supplied copies to these schools. In practice, this procedure resulted in only two student interviews being lost. A final contingency was that certain questions be deleted from the interview schedule. Fortunately, the reservations involved only three schools and only a few questions; not surprisingly, the objectionable questions had to do with family matters, religion, or politics.

In considering the disposition of the study request, the schools' reactions can be divided into three categories: (1) immediate acceptances; (2) delayed acceptances; and (3) refusals. Of the 111 contacted some 72 accepted immediately, 25 accepted after a delay, and 14 refused.

There are three easily obtained and relevant indicators of the way in which schools responded. As Table A.1 reveals, the Northeastern and the Western schools proved the most recalcitrant. Immediate acceptances were lowest there and delayed acceptances and refusals highest. Northeastern schools as a class were much more sensitive to the supposed infringement of personal and minority rights posed by the interview schedule. The study request had its most cordial reception in the Midwest states, probably due to the high visibility of the University of Michigan throughout the Midwest and to the presence of the very active and research-minded North Central Association.

As the figures in Table A.1 also show, there is a positive relationship between size of community and refusals and a negative one between size and immediate acceptances. This is due in part to the hierarchical arrangements of school systems in the larger cities. Typically, requests to conduct studies are referred to specialized personnel in the superintendent's office. Such mechanisms were clearly operative in the case of the delayed acceptances and to some extent in the case of refusals. A second source of difficulty encountered as community size increases —one which is particularly noticeable in the very large communities—is the schools' sensitivity to community publics. In at least a few large cities (e.g., Chicago and New York) this sensitivity has been formalized in rules and guidelines for evaluating study proposals. Such rules make it quite difficult to gain access to these school systems.

Much of the foregoing argument can be applied to another demographic classification used to characterize the communities: 1) those located in the central cities and the surrounding suburbs of the twelve largest standard metropolitan statistical areas (SMSA's) of the United States; 2) those located in the central cities and the surrounding area which form the smaller SMSA's; and 3) those towns and surrounding areas which are non-SMSA's. Again we see (Table A.1) the importance of ur-

TABLE A.1
RESPONSE OF SCHOOLS TO STUDY REQUEST,
BY THREE CHARACTERISTICS

	Immediate Acceptance	Delayed Acceptance	Refusal	Total	
Total	65%	22	13	100%	(111)
Region					
Midwest	87%	6	6	99%	(31)
South	62%	25	12	99%	(32)
West	55%	30	15	100%	(20)
Northeast	50%	32	18	100%	(28)
Population					
0–4,000	79%	17	3	99%	(29)
4,001–30,000	75%	17	8	100%	(24)
30,001–100,000	69%	19	11	99%	(26)
100,001+	41%	34	25	100%	(32)
SMSA					
Non-SMSA areas	84%	14	3	101%	(37)
Smaller SMSA areas	60%	21	19	100%	(43)
Twelve largest SMSA areas	48%	36	16	100%	(31)

banness and size as they are related to the schools' posture toward the study. Schools located in areas without a central city were most receptive, schools in the largest metropolitan areas were least friendly, and those in the smaller central-city locale occupied a middle position.

Since all of the foregoing factors would almost certainly have biased the sample (even though the school's refusal to cooperate reflects no bias directly due to the students), the decision was made to substitute schools for those which initially refused. The alternative to replacement was simply to acknowledge a certain refusal rate with its possible resulting biases. Because of the careful matching procedure that was used in selecting the replacements, we feel that the substitution procedure was wisest, and resulted in a highly representative sample of seniors. Of course it is still possible that factors prompting school refusal might have been reflected in relevant student characteristics in those schools. Since it is impossible to obtain the latter information, substituting on the basis of several important, known properties of the school is the best way to alleviate the potential bias.

Selection of Students and Parents

To satisfy the requirements for an eventual sample of approximately 1,700 students, 18 seniors were to be selected from each sample school.

When permission to enter a sample school was granted, the total number of seniors was obtained. Because the original estimates of senior class sizes were unavoidably imprecise (no recent lists covered all senior classes), the number of selected seniors varied from 15 to 21 per school, to correct for the original estimates. In the analysis a system of weights further corrects for inequalities in selection probabilities.[2] Individual students were selected by taking a systematic random sample from an up-to-date class list provided by the school.

As sampling instructions were prepared for the probability selection of seniors from each sample school, a probability sample of parents was also designated. Within each school, interviewers were instructed to interview the fathers of one-third of the seniors, the mothers of one-third, and both parents of the remaining one-third of the seniors. Each student would then be represented by at least one parent and one-third (ideally) by two. The specific designation of mother, father, or both parent interviews was predetermined; interviewers were permitted no personal choice in the selection. However, in the interest of obtaining family level information in those cases where the designated parent was deceased or otherwise absent from home (e.g., divorced or overseas) during the entire study period, an interview was attempted with the other parent or parent surrogate. In practice well under 10 percent of the interviews assumed this provisional form.

The Teacher Sample

Our teacher sample was designed to select teachers on the basis of the number of sample students whom they had taught. This type of sampling procedure was chosen in view of our desire to "link up" as many students as possible with their social studies teachers. Unfortunately, turning this rough characterization of our sampling procedure into operational form proved rather difficult.

Initially we considered one major criterion, that of achieving the maximum possible coverage of students. That is, as nearly as possible we wanted every sample student to have been taught by at least one of the selected teachers. It soon became apparent that this criterion alone was insufficient. In the first place, it was virtually impossible to select a teacher for every student; for example, a few students were in special programs for the retarded and did not take any social studies courses.

[2]Assuming a self-weighting sample, a sampling fraction was calculated for each school. If the application of this fraction to the number of seniors yielded a sample of 15 to 21 students, no adjustment was made. If the expectation was less than 15, the sampling fraction was increased to raise the expectation to a minimum of 15; if the expectation was more than 21, the sampling rate was decreased to keep the maximum expectation at 21. The final weight assigned to each senior is the reciprocal of his/her probability of selection over all stages of the sampling.

More important, to "cover" every student would have required some very unreasonable choices (assuming that we must keep the sample size within reasonable limits). Frequently a teacher had taught only one sample student and the student had had no other social studies teachers. To cover this student would have necessitated interviewing that teacher while perhaps ignoring a teacher of seven or eight sample students all of whom were covered by another teacher.

Obviously some decision had to be made about the relative value of various levels of depth and breadth of coverage. This was done by means of a simple weighting scheme.[3] The first task was to list the teachers within a school and record for which social studies courses, if any, each teacher had taught each sample student. In practice we worked from the student interviews, recording the courses taken and teachers' names. The result of this operation was a list such as the one in Table A.2. (The example is from a small school; most lists were much longer.) The scores on the right side of the lists will be explained below.[4]

In a number of small schools there was an "obvious" selection since there was only one main social studies teacher (although another one or two teachers might have taught a few sample students each). It seemed unreasonable to choose a second teacher in these schools, but a definite cutoff point was needed. We decided that in order to be chosen, a second teacher had to have taught at least three students. This figure was chosen to be consistent with the cutoff point used in selecting additional teachers by our weighting scheme (see below).

In the remaining schools we decided to select two automatically teachers from each school. Except in the smallest of schools a single teacher could not be expected to characterize the social studies teachers as a group. More important, one selection could hardly give us coverage in depth. Nor would it give us even a slight indication of the variety of teachers in a school. In addition, at least two teachers were usually

---

[3]Some consideration was also given to two other factors. First we wanted to be sure that the sample included teachers of a variety of social studies courses and that the distribution of subjects taught was reasonable in terms of the distribution of social studies courses taken by the seniors. If possible it was also desirable to have teachers of a variety of subjects within each school. Secondly we hoped to have some teachers who had taught sample students in their sophomore year, some in their junior year, and some in their final year. In the end these criteria were not taken into account in any explicit manner in our selection procedure. We checked the distribution of courses and grades taught while determining our tentative sampling procedure. The distributions seemed reasonable in light of the distribution of courses offered by all the high schools and by each school individually so that no alterations were made on this basis.

[4]Since we asked students about the social studies courses they had taken throughout the three years of high school, we had names of a number of teachers who were no longer teaching at the school in question. Before carrying out the initial selections, these absent teachers were eliminated. In a few rare cases mentioned below in the text, they were later added.

TABLE A.2
EXAMPLE OF TEACHER SELECTION SCHEME

	Students																Score
	1	2	3	4	5	6	7	8	9	10	11	12	13	14	15	16	
Teacher A																	
U.S. History	x[a]			x		x	x		x			x	x[b]	x	x[b]		Automatically selected
World History		x				x	x					x					
Teacher B																	
U.S. History			x		x			x		x			x[b]		x[b]	x	Automatically selected
Teacher C																	
American Government			x	x				x			x		x	x			13
Teacher D																	
Sociology				x								x	x				
Economics				x		x						x	x	x			9

[a] x's indicate which students, if any, a teacher had taught for each of the courses listed under his name.

[b] This illustrates "Team Teaching." Teachers A and B taught one class of U.S. History together.

needed to cover a large percentage of the sample students even a single time. Thus two teachers was considered a minimum sample for each school. Those automatically selected were in each case the two top teachers in terms of the number of sample students whom they had taught.[5]

With the exception of the "one social studies teacher" schools explained above, two teachers were readily chosen. Additional teachers, if any, were chosen in the following manner. Each teacher (besides the first two) was given a score determined as follows. A score of four was given if a teacher had taught a student who had not had either of the top two teachers; a score of two was given if the student had had one of the top two; a score of one was given if the student had had both of the top two teachers. This simple weighting scheme, which is by no means the only one which could have been used, was intended to solve the difficulties mentioned above. By giving a weight of four for students not covered by the first two teachers, we gave most emphasis to coverage of a wide number of sample student. The score of two for students covered by one of the first two teachers gives credit for achieving depth coverage of our sample students, while a score of one for students covered by both of the top teachers gives some, but less, credit for providing even further depth of coverage.

This method of weighting teachers is illustrated by the scores for Teachers C and D in the illustrative example given above (Table A.2). It should be noted that no teacher who had less than three of the sample students could be selected. A teacher with three of the students could be selected only if none of these students had either of the two top teachers. If a teacher had taught as many as twelve sample students, he would necessarily be selected since we would receive a score of at least twelve (which turned out to be our cutoff point). In case of ties for the second position, scores were calculated using each of the tied teachers as the second teacher. The highest score was used as the teacher's score. We felt, of course, that teachers should not be excluded simply because of the order in which we recorded the teachers' names.

By raising or lowering the cutoff point for choosing teachers, we could adjust the sample size to the desired level. It turned out that selecting teachers with a score of 12 or more yielded a sample of 318 teachers, which was close to the desired size. Judging by our criterion of the number of students covered, this appeared to be a good sample. That is, in a large majority of the schools, over 90 percent of the students had one of the chosen teachers. Of the schools in which fewer than 90 percent of the students were covered, six of them had teachers who would have been selected if they had still been teaching in the sample school. In

[5]If there was a tie for the second choice, all (usually two) tied teachers were chosen.

these six cases an effort was made to interview the departed teachers if they were relatively accessible to our interviewing staff (for example, if they were teaching at another school in the same city). Three of these teachers were available, bringing the total number of selected teachers to 321 of whom 317 were subsequently interviewed. The table below shows the percentage of sample students covered within each school:

Precentage of students within the school who had been taught by at least one selected teacher	Number of Schools
≥90%	81 (84%)
85–89	4 (4%)
80–84	5 (5%)
75–79	1 (1%)
70–74	3 (3%)
≤69	3 (3%)
	97 (100%)

Note, finally, that the teacher sample is not a representative sample of social studies teachers in U.S. high schools or even in the high schools in our sample. It is best described as representing those social studies teachers bearing the heaviest load of social studies teaching during grades 10-12 for a national sample of twelfth graders.

Weighting of Cases

As noted, the unavoidably imprecise estimates of senior class sizes made it necessary to employ a system of weights at the analysis stage. The weights are clustered about the mean of about 1.2, but the range is from 0.4 to 2.4. Of course, any analysis or reanalysis of the data should employ weighted N's in order to make the sample a representative one. For this reason, weighted N's are cited in the text. As a reference we give the unweighted and weighted N's for each sample and combination of samples in Table A.3.

The weighted N for parents and for student-parent pairs is lower than the unweighted N because of half-weighting of mothers and fathers when both parents were interviewed. That is, there were 1,132 cases in which one parent was interviewed and 430 cases in which both parents were interviewed. This means that there were 1,132 + 860 = 1,992 parents in all; but when the mother and father are each given half weight, this number reduces to 1,132 + 430 = 1,562. Then when the weights to correct for the imprecise sampling frame are assigned to these cases (average weight approximately 1.2), the weighted N is arrived at—1,927. This procedure of half-weighting mothers and fathers utilizes more cases and thereby reduces sampling error when compared with the alternative procedure of randomly selecting one or the other parent.

TABLE A.3
UNWEIGHTED AND WEIGHTED N'S

Sample or Combination of Samples	Unweighted N	Weighted N
Students	1669	2063
Parents	1992	1927
Mothers only	1106	1362
Fathers only	886	1096
Student-parent pairs	1992	1927
Husband-wife pairs	430	531
Student-mother-father triads	430	531
Teachers	317	385
Student-parent-teacher triples	1483	1778
Student-peer pairs	2080	2080[a]
Student-peer-parent triples	294	231[b]
Principals	96	118

[a]These N's are not adjusted since they are not a random subset of the larger data set.
[b]These N's are adjusted to take care of the fact that *both* parents of 63 students were interviewed; in the analysis each of these parents is weighted at one-half.

The weighted N for mothers plus the weighted N for fathers exceeds the weighted N for them combined because when sex is controlled it is not necessary to use the half-weighting. This is because the sample of each sex represents a random sample of two-thirds (before mortality) of the parents of that sex.

COLLECTING THE DATA

All instruments utilized in the study were thoroughly pre-tested. For the student interview schedule this meant an initial pre-test among 15-20 randomly selected seniors in each of three schools and a revised second pre-test among a like number in two additional schools. Parents of students in two of the first pre-test schools were interviewed using the initial parent interview schedule. Social studies teachers in all five schools were interviewed in a pre-test. Because of the similarities between much of the teacher and principal instruments, it was thought unnecessary to pre-test the principal interview. The student self-administered questionnaire was completed by varying numbers of students in the five pre-test schools (over 200 altogether).

In preparing the instruments, identically worded questions were used extensively among the samples so that data on the various interconnected pairs and triples would be comparable. Special care was also exercised to include, where such inclusion was congruent with the basic aims of the study, questions which replicated those used in previous studies at the

Survey Research Center (particularly the 1964 election study survey) and elsewhere.

The study entered the field in April 1965. All personal interviews were conducted by Survey Research Center field interviewers. The circumstances of the student interviews included complete privacy. With the exception of two schools all interviews were conducted in the school and on school time. The students were informed that they had been selected by chance to participate in the study. It was made quite explicit that the interview did not involve a test of any kind and that the student's responses would in no way be passed on to the school. Complete anonymity was stressed. Some students were interviewed during their study hours, gym classes, or free periods. Others were excused from regular courses. The interviews averaged slightly over an hour in length. Depending upon the number of interviewers working in the school (one or two) the student interviews were usually completed in from one to two weeks. With occasional exceptions, school officials and the students were extremely cooperative. Prior screening of the instruments by school officials, a general air of voluntary cooperation, plus the assurances given to the students helped produce a response rate of 99 percent.

Interviews with the parents followed those with the students. A letter was sent to the designated parent or parents, informing them about the study and the fact that their offspring had been interviewed. Subsequently, the interviewer (often the same one who had interviewed the student) contacted the parent and arranged for the interview. The student was not present during the parental interview. Similarly, in those cases where both mother and father were interviewed, the spouse was requested—if present—to leave the room during the interview. Although there were possibilities of contamination between the time of the student and the parent interviews, we detected few signs of this. This is due in large part to the length of the interview and the great range and variety of questions, and to the fact that at least two or three weeks intervened between the time of the student and parent interviews.

The overall response rate among parents was 93 percent. The one-third "mother only," one-third "father only," and one-third "both mother and father" designations (see sampling section) were, of course, not realized in practice. Primarily because there are more single-parent households headed by mothers than fathers, the 1,992 parent interviews consist of 1,106 mothers and 886 fathers, with 430 mother-father pairs enveloped in the totals. We have at least one parent interview for all but six percent of the seniors.

Interviews with the social studies teachers and the school principals ordinarily occurred near the end of the study. The teachers were informed as to how they had been selected and the general purposes of the study. Interviews were conducted either at the school or in the respondent's home. By this stage the teachers were expressing keen interest in the study and its outcomes. Refusals were virtually nonexistent among these two samples, the response rate being 99 percent in each case. Thus our attempt to maximize student-teacher pairs succeeded.

After the students had been interviewed we broached to the school officials the idea of the paper-pencil, self-administered questionnaires which would be completed by all members of the senior class. This was an optional phase of the study, designed to tap class-wide political orientations and peer-group relationships. Surprisingly, perhaps, 79 percent of the schools assented. Again, the exact circumstances for the administration of the questionnaire varied somewhat from school to school, but in most cases all students were assembled en masse. Our interviewers aided in the administration. Most questionnaires were completed in less than 30 minutes. Because of absences, official school trips, and so forth, every senior in the school did not complete the questionnaire, but the norm was in the 80-95 percent range.

A final aspect of the data collection involved information about some properties of the school itself. A "School Characteristics Form" completed by the principal or a principal's aide in all of the schools provides invaluable information about the physical, social, and academic characteristics of the school. These forms were self-administered, but they underwent extensive double-checking and backtracking after they were received by the study staff. Social, economic, and political information about the communities and states in which the schools are located was also collected from standard references sources and from scholars who have compiled similar data.

All of the data referred to above were coded by the Survey Research Center coding staff, keypunched, verified, and transferred to magnetic tape. Thorough checks were made for "wild punches" and "consistency errors." All errors detected were corrected by reference to the original interviews. The major segments of the study are now available through the Inter-University Consortium for Political Research, University of Michigan.

Library of Congress Cataloging in Publication Data

Jennings, M   Kent.
   The political character of adolescence.

   Includes bibliographical references.
   1. Youth—United States. 2. Youth—Political
activity—United States. 3. Political socialization.
I. Niemi, Richard G., joint author.   II. Title.
HQ796.J45   301.5'92   73-16779
ISBN 0-691-09362-8